Chopin in Britain

In 1848, the penultimate year of his life, Chopin visited England and Scotland at the instigation of his aristocratic Scots pupil, Jane Stirling. In the autumn of that year, he returned to Paris. The following autumn he was dead. Despite the fascination the composer continues to hold for scholars, this brief but important period, and his previous visit to London in 1837, remain little known. In this richly illustrated study, Peter Willis draws on extensive original documentary evidence, as well as cultural artefacts, to tell the story of these two visits and to place them into aristocratic and artistic life in mid-nineteenth-century England and Scotland. In addition to filling a significant hole in our knowledge of the composer's life, the book adds to our understanding of a number of important figures, including Jane Stirling and the painter Ary Scheffer. The social and artistic milieux of London, Manchester, Glasgow and Edinburgh are brought to vivid life.

Peter Willis was an architect and Reader in the History of Architecture at Newcastle University. He completed a PhD in Music at Durham University in 2010. His publications include Charles Bridgeman and the Landscape Garden, New Architecture in Scotland, and Chopin in Manchester.

Chopin in Britain

Peter Willis

LONDON AND NEW YORK

First published 2018
by Routledge
2 Park Square, Milton Park, Abingdon, Oxon OX14 4RN

and by Routledge
711 Third Avenue, New York, NY 10017

Routledge is an imprint of the Taylor & Francis Group, an informa business

© 2018 Peter Willis

The right of Peter Willis to be identified as author of this work has been asserted by him in accordance with sections 77 and 78 of the Copyright, Designs and Patents Act 1988.

All rights reserved. No part of this book may be reprinted or reproduced or utilised in any form or by any electronic, mechanical, or other means, now known or hereafter invented, including photocopying and recording, or in any information storage or retrieval system, without permission in writing from the publishers.

Trademark notice: Product or corporate names may be trademarks or registered trademarks, and are used only for identification and explanation without intent to infringe.

British Library Cataloguing-in-Publication Data
A catalogue record for this book is available from the British Library

Library of Congress Cataloging-in-Publication Data
A catalog record for this book has been requested.

ISBN: 978-1-4724-5127-9 (hbk)
ISBN: 978-1-315-57182-9 (ebk)

Typeset in Times New Roman
by Apex CoVantage, LLC

Bach musicological font developed by © Yo Tomita

Every effort has been made to contact copyright-holders. Please advise the publisher of any errors or omissions, and these will be corrected in subsequent editions.

Printed in the United Kingdom
by Henry Ling Limited

FREDERICK CHOPIN (1810–49)
Stanisław Stattler, based on portrait by Ary Scheffer, circa 1847 (destroyed)
Print from the 'Corpus Imaginum' of the Photographic Society
Private collection

Other books by Peter Willis

(Editor) *Furor hortensis: essays on the history of the English landscape garden in memory of H.F. Clark* (Edinburgh: Elysium Press, 1974)
New architecture in Scotland (London: Lund Humphries, 1974)
(Editor, with John Dixon Hunt) *The genius of the place: the English landscape garden, 1620–1820* (London: Paul Elek, 1975). Second edition (Cambridge, MA, and London: MIT Press, 1988)
Charles Bridgeman and the English landscape garden. Studies in Architecture, volume XVII (London: A. Zwemmer, 1977). Second edition, reprinted with supplementary plates and a catalogue of additional documents, drawings and attributions (Newcastle upon Tyne: Elysium Press, 2002)
Dom Paul Bellot: architect and monk, and the publication of 'Propos d'un bâtisseur du Bon Dieu', 1949 (Newcastle upon Tyne: Elysium Press, 1996)
Chopin in Manchester (Newcastle upon Tyne: Elysium Press, 2011)

For Jenny, Magnus, Gemma, Imogen, and Erin
and my parents Robert Willis (1902–1967)
and Mary Ormston Willis (1903–1983) in devotion

Contents

List of figures	xi
List of colour plates	xxi
Preface	xxv
Acknowledgements	xxviii
Introduction: Paris 1830s: prologue	1
1 London: summer 1837	17
2 Paris 1840s: interlude	37
3 London 1848: Chopin in London	58
4 London 1848: recitals	91
5 Edinburgh	128
6 Scottish Country Seats	147
7 Manchester: concert in Gentlemen's Concert Hall, Monday 28 August 1848	175
8 Glasgow: concert in Merchants' Hall, Wednesday 27 September 1848	195
9 Edinburgh: concert in Hopetoun Rooms, Wednesday 4 October 1848	206

x Contents

10 London: concert in Guildhall, Thursday 16 November 1848   215

Conclusion: Paris 1849: Epilogue   226

Bibliography   241
Index   271

Figures

Cover	Chopin. Bronze head by Józef Markiewicz, presented by the Frederick Chopin Society of Warsaw to the citizens of Edinburgh, Friday 28 February 1975. Usher Hall, Edinburgh. Photograph: Paul Zanre, 2014	
Frontispiece	Frederick Chopin (1810–49). Stanisław Stattler, based on portrait by Ary Scheffer, circa 1847 (destroyed). Print from the 'Corpus Imaginum' of the Photographic Society. Private collection	v
P.1	British Isles. Sidney Hall, A New General Atlas [1849], plate V. National Library of Scotland, Edinburgh	xxvi
I.1	Prince Adam Jerzy Czartoryski (1770–1861). Engraving by Andrew Duncan, after Louis Rubio, 1831. Private collection	3
I.2	Harriet Grote (née Lewin) (1792–1878). Lithograph by Charles George Lewis, printed by Jérémie Graf, after Charles Landseer (circa 1840). Copyright National Portrait Gallery, London	6
I.3	'Italian Opera House, Paris' (Salle Ventadour), home of the Théâtre-Italien, 1841–76. Engraving of auditorium by Charles Mottram, after Eugène Lami, from Jules Janin, *Summer and winter in Paris* (1844). Private collection	7
I.4	Camille Pleyel (1788–1855). Print by Boileau. Cité de la Musique, Paris	8
I.5	Christian Friedrich Samuel Hahnemann (1755–1843). Engraving by L. Beyer, after J. Schöppe, senior, 1831. Mary Evans Picture Library/Interfoto/Sammlung Rauch	12
1.1	Chopin. Bronze medal, by Jean François Antoine Bovy, 1837. Mary Evans Picture Library/SZ Photo/Scherl	17
1.2	Quay at Dover, Kent, showing Wright's Hotel in the centre. Drawn by George Sidney Shepherd, engraved by Thomas Garner, circa 1830. Private collection	19
1.3	Part of the West Side of Regent Street, London. Drawn by Thomas H. Shepherd, engraved by W. Watkins, 1828. Private collection	20

xii *Figures*

1.4	Lord Dudley Coutts Stuart (1803–54). Engraved portrait. *Illustrated London News*, 1843, left of page 325. Mary Evans Picture Library	21
1.5	Julian Fontana (1810–69). Bronze medal by Władysław Oleszcyński, 1837. Bibliothèque Polonaise de Paris. Akg-images/De Agostini Picture Library/G. Dagli Orti	22
1.6	The King's Theatre, Haymarket, London (from 1837, Her Majesty's Theatre). Engraved view, showing exterior remodelling by John Nash and G.S. Repton, 1816–18, from Dugdale, *England and Wales delineated* (circa 1848). Private collection	25
1.7	James Shudi Broadwood (1772–1851). Anonymous watercolour portrait (detail), circa 1820. Broadwood Trust, from Wainwright, *Broadwood by appointment* (1982), between pp. 184 and 185. Broadwood Trust, Surrey History Centre, Woking	27
1.8	Detail of contract of 20 July 1837, signed by Chopin and Pleyel, with Wessel & Co, then of Frith Street, Soho Square, for the publication of the Twelve Études or Studies (Op.25), 'conjointly in France & Germany'. Sotheby's sale catalogue, London, 5 December 2003, lot 57 (p. 56)	30
1.9	Twelve études or Studies (Op.25). Title page to Wessel & Co, ed., London, [October 1837], from CFEO online (www.cfeo.org.uk)	31
1.10	Chopin, Trois Nocturnes (Op.9, book 2), 'Les murmures de la Seine'. Title page to Wessel & Co, ed., London, [1833], from Platzman, Chicago catalogue 1, p. 48. University of Chicago Library	32
2.1	George Sand (1804–76). Engraved portrait by August Weger, from a photograph. Private collection	38
2.2	Maison de George Sand, Nohant. Entrance front. Copyright, Centre des monuments nationaux/Monum, Editions du patrimoine, Paris, 2002	39
2.3	Hôtel Lambert, 'Ball des Fürsten Czartoryski im Hotel Lambert zu Paris', *Illustrirte Zeitung*, vol.6, no.151, Leipzig, 23 May 1846, p. 340. Akg-images	41
2.4	Princess Marcelina Czartoryska (née Radziwill) (1817–94). Lithograph by Auguste Sandoz, 1850. Mirska and Hordyński, *Chopin na obczyźnie* (1965), p. 113	42
2.5	Henry Fothergill Chorley (1808–72). Portrait in pencil and chalk by Alfred, Count D'Orsay, 1841. Copyright National Portrait Gallery, London	43
2.6	Jane Wilhelmina Stirling (1804–59), with Lady Frances Anne [Fanny] Bruce (1831–94), daughter of the 7th Earl of Elgin. Lithograph by Achille Devéria, circa 1842, from Ganche,	

	Frédéric Chopin: sa vie et ses oeuvres, 1810–1849, 3rd ed. (1913), opposite p. 418. Private collection	45
2.7	Thomas Dyke Acland Tellefsen (1823–74). Portrait from Tellefsen, *Thomas Tellefsens familiebreve* (1923), frontispiece (circa 1860). Private collection	50
3.1	Admiralty Pier, Dover, showing the Lord Warden Hotel. Engraving published by Rock and Co, London, 1869. Private collection	61
3.2	Pavilion Hotel, Folkestone. Published by W. Tiffen, engraved by J. Newman, circa 1850. Private collection	62
3.3	Wojciech Grzymała (1793–1871). Photograph by Etienne Carjat. Bibliothèque Polonaise, Paris. Akg-images/DeAgostini Picture Library/G. Dagli Orti	63
3.4	Piccadilly, London, and adjacent streets, from Jackson, John Tallis's London street views, 1838–1840 (2002 reprint), part 14, p. 68. Private collection	64
3.5	Bentinck Street, London. Pencil sketch by Thomas Colman Dibdin, circa 1850 (detail). London Metropolitan Archives	65
3.6	Wigmore Street, Welbeck Street, and Bentinck Street, London, from Jackson, *John Tallis's London street views, 1838–1840* (2002 reprint), part 50, p. 141. Private collection	66
3.7	Henry Fowler Broadwood (1811–93). Undated portrait, by unknown photographer. Broadwood Trust. Surrey History Centre, Woking, Surrey	71
3.8	Alfred James Hipkins (1826–1903). Undated portrait, by unknown photographer. Broadwood Trust, from Wainwright, *Broadwood by appointment* (1982), p. 217. Private collection	73
3.9	James William Davison (1813–85). Pencil sketch by G.D. Davison, from a daguerreotype, circa 1857, from Davison, *From Mendelssohn to Wagner* (1912), frontispiece. British Library, London	75
3.10	Charles Hallé (1819–95). Frontispiece (1890) from Hallé and Hallé, *Life and Letters of Sir Charles Hallé* (1896). Private collection	76
3.11	Theatre Royal, Covent Garden, London. Engraving of exterior from Dugdale, *England and Wales delineated* (circa 1848). Private collection	78
3.12	Italian Opera House, London. Engraving of exterior from Dugdale, *England and Wales delineated* (circa 1848). Private collection	79
3.13	Premises of Cramer, Beale & Co, No. 201 Regent Street, at the corner of Conduit Street, London, from *Grand panorama of London, Regent Street to Westminster Abbey*, by Leighton and Sanderson, 1849 (1966 reprint). Private collection	82

xiv *Figures*

4.1	24 Cheyne Row, London. Detail from *A Chelsea interior*, by Robert Scott Tait, 1857. National Trust Picture Library/ Michael Boys	92
4.2	Harriet Elizabeth Georgina Leveson-Gower, Duchess of Sutherland (1806–68). Portrait by Winterhalter, 1849. Private Collection. Scottish National Portrait Gallery, Edinburgh	95
4.3	Stafford (now Lancaster) House, St James's, London. Watercolour of west front, by Thomas Hosmer Shepherd, circa 1845, showing additional storey of 1833–8. Museum of London	96
4.4	Sir Julius Benedict (1804–85). Portrait from the *Illustrated London News*, 13 June 1885, p. 607. Private collection	97
4.5	Adelaide Kemble (Mrs Sartoris) (1814–79). Albumen print by Camille Silvy, 1860. Copyright National Portrait Gallery, London	99
4.6	Publicity for Chopin's *matinée musicale* at Mrs Sartoris' house, from Tomaszewski and Weber, *Diary in images* (1990), p. 238, and Mirska and Hordyński, *Chopin na obczyżnie* (1965), p. 286	101
4.7	Programme for Chopin's *matinée musicale* at Mrs Sartoris' house, from Mirska and Hordyński, *Chopin na obczyżnie* (1965), p. 286	103
4.8	Wilhelm Kuhe (1823–1912). Photograph by Richard Bentley & Son, 1896. Frontispiece to Kuhe, *My musical recollections* (1896). Private collection	105
4.9	Giovanni Matteo Mario, Cavaliere de Candia (1810–83). Undated portrait lithograph by Cäcilie Brandt. Private collection	106
4.10	*Un Secret: paroles de Alfred de Musset, musique de G. Alary*, p. 1 of score. London: Chappell, [n.d.]. Private collection	107
4.11	Title page of *No.13 of The Album Mario, containing all the most popular French songs, sung by Signor Mario*, edited by J. Benedict. London: Chappell, [n.d.]. Private collection	108
4.12	St James's Square, London. Photograph of exterior of No. 2 (left) and No. 1 (right), circa 1934–8. Copyright The Canada Life Insurance Company, from *Survey of London: the Parish of St James*, *Westminster*, part 1 (1960), plate 164a	110
4.13	St James's Square, London. Photograph of No. 2, after direct hit by bombing, 14 October 1940, from Forrest, *St James's Square* (2001), p. 145	111
4.14	Programme for Chopin's *matinée musicale* at the Earl of Falmouth's house, Friday 7 July 1848. Mirska and Hordyński, *Chopin na obczyżnie* (1965), p. 288	112
4.15	Marguerite, Countess of Blessington (1789–1849). Mezzotint by William Giller, published by J. McCormick, after Edmund Thomas Parris, 1835. Copyright National Portrait Gallery, London	113

4.16	Gore House, Kensington, elevation towards Kensington Gore. Watercolour by Thomas Hosmer Shepherd, circa 1840s. Kensington Central Library	114
4.17	'Women in politics. Lady Blessington's Salon at Gore House, Kensington', circa 1840s. Print from drawing by 'Johnson'. Westminster City Archives	115
4.18	John Muir Wood (1805–92). Photograph by Muir Wood of himself holding a photographic printing frame. Scottish National Photography Collection. Scottish National Portrait Gallery, Edinburgh	117
4.19	London & Birmingham Railway Terminus, Euston Square, London. Drawn by Thomas Hosmer Shepherd, engraved by H. Bond, circa 1848. Private collection	119
5.1	Edinburgh, New Town. The Royal Institution (now the Royal Scottish Academy) seen from Hanover Street, looking beyond it to the Mound and the Old Town. Drawn by Thomas Hosmer Shepherd, engraved by S. Lacy, from *Modern Athens* (1829/31). Private collection	129
5.2	Edinburgh. Princes Street, the Scott Monument, and the Royal Institution (now the Royal Scottish Academy). Albumen print by William Donaldson Clark, circa 1858. Scottish National Photography Collection. Scottish National Portrait Gallery, Edinburgh	130
5.3	Edinburgh. The Scott Monument, newly completed, April 1845. Photograph by David Octavius Hill and Robert Adamson. Scottish National Photography Collection. Scottish National Portrait Gallery, Edinburgh	131
5.4	John Stirling, of Kippendavie (1742–1816) and his youngest daughter, Jane Wilhelmina Stirling (1804–59), by Sir Henry Raeburn, circa 1810–14. Collection of the National Trust for Scotland. Scottish National Portrait Gallery, Edinburgh	132
5.5	Jane Stirling (left), with Mrs Katherine Erskine, of Linlathen. Photograph, provided by Mme Ganche, from Bone, *Jane Wilhelmina Stirling* (1960), opposite p. 89. Private collection	133
5.6	Jane Stirling (centre), with Mrs Katherine Erskine, of Linlathen (right), and their niece Mrs William Houston (née Marion Douglas Russell, of Woodside). Portrait by Ary Scheffer, 1844. Private collection. Scottish National Portrait Gallery, Edinburgh	134
5.7	Jane Stirling (?). Photograph of lost drawing attributed to Ary Scheffer, ?1844. Location unknown. Image recorded in reference section, Scottish National Portrait Gallery, Edinburgh	135
5.8	Chopin, title page of Deux Nocturnes (Op.55), dedicated to 'Mademoiselle J W Stirling'. Leipzig: Breitkopf & Härtel, 1844 (German first edition). Platzman, *Chicago catalogue* 1, p. 178. University of Chicago Library	136

xvi *Figures*

5.9	John Harden (1772–1847). Pen and ink drawing of his wife Jessy at the piano in No. 28 Queen Street, Edinburgh, with her sons and a female relative, 1805. National Library of Scotland, Edinburgh, MS 8866, II.33b	137
5.10	Edinburgh, New Town. Detail of plan, drawn and engraved by John Rapkin, with illustrations drawn and engraved by H. Winkles, with additional indication of places connected with Chopin's visit to Edinburgh in 1848. Published by John Tallis & Co, London and New York, [1851] (2003 facsimile). Private collection	138
5.11	Edinburgh, New Town. East side of St Andrew Square, showing the Douglas Hotel (directly behind coach). Engraving by Thomas Hosmer Shepherd and J. Johnstone, from *Modern Athens* (1829/31). Private collection	140
5.12	Chopin. Recto of autograph letter in Polish of 3 November 1848 sent by Chopin from No. 4 St James's Place, London, to 'Dr Lishinski' at No. 10 Warriston Crescent, Edinburgh, asking him to forward an enclosed note to Jane Stirling at Barnton. Special Collections, Edinburgh University Library, Dc.2/82/1	141
5.13	Barnton House, Edinburgh. View from Small, *Castles and mansions of the Lothians* (1883). Mitchell Library, Glasgow	142
6.1	Map of Scotland, engraved by Sidney Hall (London, 1852–4). Private collection	148
6.2	Detail of Map of Scotland, engraved by Sidney Hall, showing location of country seats related to Chopin's visit in 1848. Private collection	149
6.3	Calder House, Midlothian. View of entrance front from across the River Almond (detail), by William Wilson, circa 1820s. Private collection. Scottish National Portrait Gallery, Edinburgh	150
6.4	Calder House, Midlothian. View of house and the Kirk of Calder (detail), by William Wilson, circa 1820s. Private collection. Scottish National Portrait Gallery, Edinburgh	150
6.5	James Sandilands, 10th Baron Torphichen (1770–1862). Portrait by Ary Scheffer, 1849. Private collection. Scottish National Portrait Gallery, Edinburgh	151
6.6	Letter from Chopin to unidentified female pupil, Calder House, 12 August 1848, recto. National Archives of Scotland (Edinburgh), Ogilvy of Inverquharity Papers, GD 205/47/11/1	152
6.7	Leather cover for the copy of the first page of the lost MS of a Waltz in B major, entitled 'F. CHOPIN/VALSE IN SI MAJEUR/(POUR MADAME ERSKINE) / 12 OCTOBRE 1848'. TiFC (Warsaw), F 1791	153
6.8	Copy of the first page of the lost MS of a Waltz in B major, inscribed by Chopin 'pour Madame Erskine', and dated 12	

	October 1848, when he was staying at Calder House. TiFC (Warsaw), F 1530	154
6.9	Sir William Stirling Maxwell, 9th Bt (1818–78). Stipple engraving by William Holl, Junior, 1856 or later, after chalk drawing by George Richmond. Copyright National Portrait Gallery, London	155
6.10	Keir House, Perthshire. Drawing by David Hamilton of the south elevation (1829), showing the drawing room extension to the left. Copyright Historic Environment Scotland (HES), Edinburgh	156
6.11	Keir House, Perthshire. 'Keir – 1837', from Fraser, *Stirlings of Keir* (1858), showing to the left the three-bay extensions to the house by David Hamilton, from 1829. National Library of Scotland, Edinburgh	157
6.12	Marie de Rozières (1805–65). Drawing by George Sand. Musée Carnavalet, Paris. Mirska and Hordyński, *Chopin na obczyźnie* (1965), p. 216	158
6.13	Johnstone Castle, Johnstone, Renfrewshire. Engraving by William H. Lizars, from Ramsay, *Views in Renfrewshire* (1839). Mitchell Library, Glasgow	159
6.14	Johnstone Castle, Johnstone, Renfrewshire. Photograph by Thomas Annan, from Millar, *Castles and manors of Renfrewshire and Buteshire* (1889). Thomas Annan Collection, Glasgow City Libraries	160
6.15	Johnstone Castle, Renfrewshire. Remains, 2008. Photograph: Peter Willis, 2008	161
6.16	Milliken House, Renfrewshire. Engraving by William H. Lizars from Ramsay, *Views in Renfrewshire* (1839). Mitchell Library, Glasgow	162
6.17	Milliken House, Renfrewshire. Photograph by Annan, from *The old country houses of the old Glasgow gentry*, 2nd edition (1878). Mitchell Library, Glasgow	163
6.18	Wishaw House, Lanarkshire. Engraving from Neale, *Views of noblemen's and gentlemen's seats in Scotland* (circa 1830). Private collection	163
6.19	Kippenross House, Perthshire, birthplace of Jane Stirling in 1804, now extensively altered. Photograph: Peter Willis, 2008	164
6.20	Gargunnock House, Stirlingshire. Pencil drawing by W.F. Lyon, 1870. Copyright Historic Environment Scotland (HES), Edinburgh	165
6.21	Hamilton Palace, Lanarkshire. Engraving by Joseph Swan, from a painting by John Fleming, from Swan, *Select views on the River Clyde* (1830). Private collection	165
6.22	Susan Euphemia (née Beckford), Duchess of Hamilton (1786–1859). Portrait by Willes Maddox, circa 1845. Private	

xviii   *Figures*

	Collection, Scotland. Scottish National Portrait Gallery, Edinburgh	166
6.23	Sir John Archibald Murray (?1778–1859), Scottish judge, Lord Advocate, and Lord of Session. Portrait by Sir John Watson Gordon, 1856. Scottish National Portrait Gallery, Edinburgh	168
7.1	View of Manchester. Engraving by C. Reiss, Hildburghausen [1842]. Private collection	176
7.2	Crumpsall House, Lancashire. Detail from Ordnance Survey, 1847–8. Manchester City Libraries	177
7.3	Glyn Garth Anglesey. View from the Menai Straits, from Thomas Catherall, *Views in north Wales* (Chester and Bangor, circa 1850). Courtesy Thomas Wright	177
7.4	Salis Schwabe (1800–53). Bust by William Bally, circa 1853. Old Grammar School, Middleton, Manchester. Courtesy Middleton Civic Association. Photograph: Alan Seabright, 2003	178
7.5	Chopin. Autograph of song 'Wiosna', with Polish words by Witwicki, inscribed 'souvenir de Crumpsal House à Mademoiselle Fanny Erskine', and dated 1 September 1848. Fitzwilliam Museum, Cambridge [from Harasowski, *The skein of legends around Chopin* (1967), plate 89]	179
7.6	Gentlemen's Concert Hall, between Peter Street and Mosley Street, Manchester, with St Peter's Church to the right. Ground-floor plan, from Ordnance Survey, 1849–51. Manchester City Libraries	181
7.7	Gentlemen's Concert Hall, Peter Street, Manchester, with portico of St Peter's Church on left. Engraving by John Fothergill, 1832. Manchester City Libraries	181
7.8	Gentlemen's Concert Hall, Peter Street, Manchester. Interior from William Arthur Shaw, *Manchester old and new . . .* (London: Cassell [1896]), vol.3, p. 36. Manchester City Libraries	182
7.9	Programme for Dress Concert, Gentlemen's Concert Hall, Peter Street, Manchester, Monday 28 August 1848, from Brookshaw, *Concerning Chopin in Manchester* (1951), between pp. 22 and 23. Manchester City Libraries	184
7.10	Notice of substitutions by Chopin in the programme of the Manchester concert, from Brookshaw, *Concerning Chopin in Manchester* (1951), between pp. 22 and 23. Manchester City Libraries	185
7.11	George Alexander Osborne (1806–93). Undated lithograph by Charles Motte, from drawing by Achille Devéria. Royal College of Music, London	188

7.12	Revd Alexander John (Sandy) Scott (1805–66). Portrait from Hair, *Regent Square* (1898), opposite p. 86. Private collection	190
8.1	Glasgow, the Merchant City. County Buildings, Wilson Street, by Robert Carrick, 1852, showing the Merchants' Hall, Hutcheson Street, to the left. Mitchell Library, Glasgow	196
8.2	Merchants' Hall, Hutcheson Street, Glasgow. Undated lithograph by Maclure and Macdonald, from *View of the Merchants House of Glasgow* (1866), p. 443. Mitchell Library, Glasgow	197
8.3	Advertisement for Chopin's *matinée musicale* in the Merchants' Hall, Glasgow, on Wednesday 27 September 1848, from Bone, *Jane Wilhelmina Stirling* (1960), plate opposite p. 76. Private collection	198
8.4	James Hedderwick (1814–97). Photograph by Dawsons from Hedderwick, *Backward glances, or some personal recollections* (1891), frontispiece. Private collection	201
9.1	Ordnance Survey plan of Edinburgh (1849–53). Detail showing the Hopetoun Rooms and the British Hotel, Queen Street, and Queen Street Gardens (top right). National Library of Scotland, Edinburgh	207
9.2	British Hotel, Queen Street, Edinburgh, which contained the Hopetoun Rooms, designed by Thomas Hamilton, circa 1825. The top storey was added in 1873 by MacGibbon and Ross, from Skinner, *A family unbroken* (1994), p. 34	208
9.3	Hopetoun Rooms, Queen Street, Edinburgh. Section by Mairi Anna Birkland, from Rock, *Thomas Hamilton* (1984), p. 13	208
9.4	Hopetoun Rooms, Queen Street, Edinburgh. Sketch plan from C.R. Cockerell's diary, entry for Monday 17 March 1828, Series 7.9. CoC/10/3. Royal Institute of British Architects/ British Architectural Library, London	209
9.5	Hopetoun Rooms, Queen Street, Edinburgh. Photograph of lantern, during demolition, 1967. Copyright Historic Environment Scotland (HES), Edinburgh	209
9.6	Advertisement for Chopin's *soirée musicale* in the Hopetoun Rooms, Edinburgh, on Wednesday 4 October 1848, from *The Scotsman*, 4 October 1848. Edinburgh City Library	210
10.1	Guildhall, London, entrance. Drawn by Thomas Hosmer Shepherd, engraved by Robert Acon, 1828. Private collection	218
10.2	Court of Common Council, Guildhall, presentation of a petition. Drawn by Thomas Hosmer Shepherd, engraved by Henry Melville, [1842]. Private collection	219
10.3	Chopin. Plaster bust by Jarosław Giercarz Alfer, 1978. Presented by Her Royal Highness Princess Alice, Duchess of Gloucester, 1979. Royal Academy of Music, London	220

xx *Figures*

10.4	Folkestone, Kent. Drawn by George Shepherd, engraved by S. Lacey, 1829. Private collection	222
11.1	Thomas Erskine of Linlathen (1788–1870), attributed to Charles Baillod. Scottish National Portrait Gallery, Edinburgh	230
11.2	Kirk of Calder, Mid Calder. Plaque to Stirling family. Photograph courtesy of Robert Ross, 2014	231
11.3	Dunblane Cathedral, Perthshire. Exterior from the south-west. Drawn by Thomas Allom, engraved by W. Radclyffe, circa 1840. Private collection	232
11.4	Dunblane Cathedral, Perthshire. North aisle of nave (the 'Keir' or 'Stirling' aisle) with Stirling and other memorials along the north wall. Photograph: Peter Willis, 2008	233
11.5	Dunblane Cathedral, Perthshire. North aisle of nave. Brass memorial erected by Patrick Stirling, of Kippendavie, in 1892, to members of the House of Stirling, of Kippendavie, from 1595 to 1859, 'interred in this aisle', which may include Jane Stirling (died 1859). Photograph: Peter Willis, 2008	234

Colour plates

1 Ary Scheffer (1795–1873). Self-portrait, 1838. Rijksmuseum,
  Amsterdam. Akg-images/Quint & Lox   P-1
2 Landing at Dover from the steam packet. Painting attributed to
  Michael William Sharp, circa 1826. Copyright National Maritime
  Museum, Greenwich, London   P-2
3 Sablonière Hôtel, Leicester Square, London. Watercolour by
  Charles John Smith, circa 1830. London Metropolitan Archives   P-3
4 Bryanston Square, London. Entrance doorway to No. 46 on west
  side. James T. Parkinson, architect, circa 1811. Photograph: Peter
  Willis, 2003   P-4
5 Pauline Viardot (1821–1910). Portrait by Carl Timoleon von
  Neff, circa 1842. Akg-images/RIA Nowosti   P-5
6 Hôtel Lambert, Île St-Louis, Paris. External view from across the
  Seine. Photograph from website *www.insecula.com* (2006)   P-6
7 Érard Grand Pianoforte No. 713 (London, 1843), purchased by
  Jane Stirling in 1843, and perhaps at Keir when Chopin stayed
  there in 1848. Cobbe Collection, Hatchlands, Surrey. Photograph:
  Salvatore Arancio   P-6
8 Poster for the South Eastern Railway Company, circa 1845,
  advertising cross-Channel services between London and France,
  via Folkestone and Dover. National Railway Museum, York   P-7
9 Pleyel Grand Pianoforte No. 13,819 (Paris, circa 1848), brought
  from Paris to London by Chopin, April 1848. Cobbe Collection,
  Hatchlands, Surrey. Photograph: Salvatore Arancio   P-7
10 Broadwood Grand Pianoforte No. 17,047 (London, 1847),
  played by Chopin in 1848 in London recitals. Royal Academy
  of Music, London, on Permanent Loan to the Cobbe Collection,
  Hatchlands, Surrey. Photograph: Salvatore Arancio   P-8
11 No. 99 Eaton Place, London. Exterior, showing plaque
  commemorating Chopin's recital there on Friday 23 June 1848.
  Photograph: Peter Willis, 2008   P-9
12 No. 99 Eaton Place, London. Detail of plaque commemorating
  Chopin's recital there on Friday 23 June 1848. Photograph:
  Peter Willis, 2008   P-9

xxii *Colour plates*

13 Jemima Blackburn (née Wedderburn). *A rehearsal*. Watercolour, 1844, showing music-making, under Ella's direction, at the home of her uncle, Sir George Clerk, with the Earl of Falmouth fourth from right, playing the violin or viola. Copyright National Portrait Gallery, London — P-10

14 Alfred, Count D'Orsay (1801–52). Portrait by Sir George Hayter, 1839. Copyright National Portrait Gallery, London — P-11

15 No. 35 St Andrew Square, Edinburgh (formerly the Douglas Hotel). Exterior facing St Andrew Square. Photograph: Paul Zanre, 2007 — P-12

16 No. 35 St Andrew Square, Edinburgh (formerly the Douglas Hotel). Imperial staircase leading off entrance hall. Photograph: Paul Zanre, 2007 — P-13

17 No. 10 Warriston Crescent, Edinburgh, with plaque on right commemorating Chopin's stay in 1848. Courtesy of Miss Jane Kellett. Photograph: Peter Willis, 1998. The plaque reads: — P-14

FRYDERYK CHOPIN
1810–1849 POLISH COMPOSER
STAYED HERE ON THE OCCASION
OF HIS CONCERT IN EDINBURGH
ON THE 4TH OCTOBER 1848
TO COMMEMORATE THE HUNDREDTH
ANNIVERSARY OF THIS EVENT THIS PLAQUE
WAS PLACED BY THE POLISH COMMUNITY
AND THEIR SCOTTISH FRIENDS IN 1948

18 Keir House, Perthshire. Entrance, designed by David Hamilton (1820), resited in 1969. Photograph: Peter Willis, 2008 — P-15

19 Pleyel Grand Pianoforte No. 1,318 (Paris, circa 1827), mahogany, owned by Sarah, Duchess of Hamilton, now at Lennoxlove, East Lothian, and formerly at Hamilton Palace, where it may have been played by Chopin in 1848. Courtesy the Duke of Hamilton — P-15

20 Strachur House, Argyll. Central block, from west-south-west, with entrance porch added after Chopin's time. Copyright Historic Environment Scotland (HES), Edinburgh — P-16

21 Strachur House, Argyll. Entrance hall and staircase. Copyright Historic Environment Scotland (HES), Edinburgh — P-16

22 Julie Schwabe (1819–96). Portrait by Ary Scheffer, before 1858. Copyright Roehampton University Library and Special Collections — P-17

23 Johanna Maria (Jenny) Lind (1820–87), and Marietta Alboni, Countess Pepoli (née Maria Anna Marzia) (1824–94). Hand-coloured, half-plate daguerrotype, 1848, by William Edward Kilburn. Copyright National Portrait Gallery, London — P-18

24	Chopin. Plaster death mask, based on original by Auguste Clésinger, Paris, 1849. Gift of Miss Susan Fisher Scott to the Royal Manchester College of Music, 1910. Royal Northern College of Music, Manchester. Photograph: Michael Pollard, 2008	P-19
25	Chopin. Plaster left hand, based on original by Auguste Clésinger, Paris, 1849. Gift of Miss Susan Fisher Scott to the Royal Manchester College of Music, 1910. Royal Northern College of Music, Manchester. Photograph: Michael Pollard, 2008	P-20
26	Chopin. Detail of bronze statue by Ludwika Nitschowa. Gift of the Frederick Chopin Society of Poland, to the Royal Northern College of Music, Manchester, 1973. Royal Northern College of Music, Manchester. Photograph: Michael Pollard, 2010	P-21
27	Chopin. Bronze statue by Ludwika Nitschowa. Gift of the Frederick Chopin Society of Poland, to the Royal Northern College of Music, Manchester, 1973. Royal Northern College of Music, Manchester. Photograph: Michael Pollard, 2010	P-22
28	Chopin. Bronze statue by Robert Sobociński, Deansgate, Manchester, unveiled 2011. Photograph: Michael Pollard, 2014	P-22
29	Chopin. Bronze head by Józef Markiewicz, presented by the Frederick Chopin Society of Warsaw, to the citizens of Edinburgh, Friday 28 February 1975. Usher Hall, Edinburgh. Photograph: Paul Zanre, 2014	P-23
30	Chopin. Setting of bronze head by Józef Markiewicz, Usher Hall, Edinburgh. Photograph: Paul Zanre, 2014	P-24
31	Exterior of No. 4 St James's Place, London, showing plaque commemorating Chopin's stay there before his Guildhall concert on 16 November 1848. Photograph: Peter Willis, 2008	P-25
32	Exterior of No. 4 St James's Place, London. Photograph: Peter Willis, 2008	P-25
33	Detail of plaque at No. 4 St James's Place. Photograph: Peter Willis, 2008	P-26
34	Pleyel Grand Pianoforte No. 13,716 (Paris, 1848), inscribed 'Frederic Chopin 15 Novembre 1848', of rosewood inlaid with veins of copper. Collegium Maius (Cracow), MUJ 6887: 1945. Akg-images/De Agostini Picture Library/A. Dagli Orti	P-26
35	Sir James Clark, 1st Bt (1788–1870), Physician in Ordinary to Queen Victoria, by Hope James Stewart, 1849. Scottish National Portrait Gallery, Edinburgh	P-27
36	Chopin's grave, and monument by Auguste Clésinger, 1849 (detail). Cemetery of Père Lachaise, Paris. Akg-images/De Agostini Picture Library/G. Dagli Orti Permissions for the reproduction of illustrations in Chopin in Britain have been obtained and are listed on p. xxiv	P-28

Akg-images
Alexander Atwater
British Library, London
British Museum, London
Broadwood Trust, Surrey History Centre, Woking
Cobbe Collection, Hatchlands, Surrey
Edinburgh City Libraries
Edinburgh University Library
Fitzwilliam Museum, Cambridge
Glasgow City Libraries
The Duke of Hamilton
Historic Environment Scotland (HES), Edinburgh
Kensington Central Library
London Metropolitan Archives
Manchester City Libraries
Mary Evans Picture Library
Middleton Civic Association
Mitchell Library, Glasgow
Museum of London
National Archives of Scotland, Edinburgh
National Library of Scotland, Edinburgh
National Maritime Museum, Greenwich
National Portrait Gallery, London
National Railway Museum, York
National Trust Picture Library
Roehampton University Library and Special Collections
Royal Academy of Music, London
Royal College of Music, London
Royal Institute of British Architects/British Architectural Library, London
Royal Northern College of Music, Manchester
Scottish National Portrait Gallery, Edinburgh
Towarzytwo imienia Fryderyka Chopina (TiFC), Warsaw
University of Chicago Library
Usher Hall, Edinburgh
Westminster City Archives
Thomas Wright

Preface

Although Chopin's life and music have been written about extensively, little attention has been given to his two periods in England and Scotland (see Figure P.1). These are the subject of Chopin in Britain. Chopin's first visit to London in 1837, with Camille Pleyel, lasted a mere eleven days and came shortly after he had met George Sand; the second, in 1848, to London, Edinburgh, Manchester, and Glasgow, and country houses in Scotland, spanned some seven months and was sponsored by his aristocratic Scots pupil, Jane Stirling, whom he had taught in Paris. Dogged by debilitating illness, Chopin returned to Paris that October. The next autumn he was dead.

Primary evidence of Chopin's visits to Britain comes from his letters, and from Dr Édouard Ganche's collection, formerly at Lyons, now divided between the Biblioteka Jagiellońska and the Collegium Maius, Cracow, the Frederick Chopin Society (TiFC), Warsaw, and the Bibliothèque nationale, Paris (Département de la Musique); remnants of Miss Stirling's own collection, partly scattered, lost, or destroyed, are also in Cracow, Warsaw, and Paris. The holdings of the Frederick Chopin Society in Warsaw are indispensable, too. Other unpublished sources are widely spread; a key source is the second edition of Smialek and Trochimczyk, Frédéric Chopin: a research and information guide (2015). Newspapers and other periodicals (notably in the writings of Henry Fothergill Chorley in the Athenaeum, and J.W. Davison in the Musical World and The Times) provide contemporary observations on Chopin's comings and goings. Electronic sites continue to expand, and scholarly research on Chopin is virtually impossible without access to the web. Among invaluable online sources used are the Dictionary of Scottish architects (DSA), Oxford DNB online, Grove music online, scotlandspeople.gov.uk, the Chicago Chopin online catalog (maintained by the University of Chicago), and the online material of the Frederick Chopin Society in Warsaw. On a practical level, the writing of Chopin in Britain has depended upon work in libraries and archives in England, Scotland, France, and Poland, and on the purchase of books, prints, and manuscript letters. Beyond these, there lies the invisible university of other scholars in a variety of fields, whose contribution has been indispensible.

At the end of the day, the Chopin who emerges from Chopin in Britain is a tragic figure, as he struggled against his desperate illness. Yet, his persistence to pursue his musical life, in the face of innumerable difficulties and disappointments,

Figure P.1 British Isles. Sidney Hall, A New General Atlas [1849], plate V. National Library of Scotland, Edinburgh

[Annotation: 1 Paris 2 Newhaven 3 Calais 4 Dover 5 Folkestone 6 London 7 Birmingham 8 Carlisle 9 Edinburgh 10 Glasgow]

gives him a fragile nobility. With hindsight, there is a sense of inevitability about Chopin's last year in London, Scotland, and Paris, leading up to his death; his subsequent resurrection sees him as a figure of almost divine gifts. All told, it is a fascinating, revealing, and poignant story.

Most biographies of Chopin refer only briefly to his visits to Britain; there is no significant separate study of his visit in 1837, and none of his period in London in 1848, although his visit to Scotland is covered in Iwo and Pamela Załuski's *The Scottish autumn of Frederick Chopin* (1993). Chopin in Britain aims to fill this gap, and brings together a wide range of material, some of it published for the first time, to illuminate the cultural context of Chopin's visits to England and Scotland. No musician is an island, and a consideration of the social, architectural, and personal background to Chopin's life is essential to our study of him. For this, no apology or further explanation should be needed.

Acknowledgements

Chopin in Britain began its life as a PhD dissertation submitted to the Department of Music at the University of Durham in 2009, written with the generous academic support and encouragement of Jeremy Dibble. The thesis, in three volumes, and entitled 'Chopin in Britain: Chopin's visits to England and Scotland in 1837 and 1848; people, places, and activities', can be seen online at etheses.dur.ac.uk/1386/, and contains material which it has not been possible to include in this book. A version of Chapter 7 was previously published as Chopin in Manchester (Newcastle upon Tyne: Elysium Press, 2011).

For their kindness and help on various matters, I should like to thank, in particular:

John Alban, James C. Albisetti, John H.G. Archer, R.K. Aspin, William G. Atwood, Walther Bach, Eleanor Bailie, Paul Banks, Michael Barfoot, Nicolas Bell, George Biddlecombe, Almut Boehme, Iain Gordon Brown, Connie Byrom, John Byrom, Stuart Campbell, Sheila E. Cannell, Aleksandra Capiewska, Rose Cholmondeley, Tristram Clarke, Anne-Marie Clarkson, Alec Cobbe, Paul Collen, Anne Crowther, Jacqui Dale, Oliver Davies, Craig Drummond, Kenneth Dunn, Cyril Ehrlich, Jean-Jacques Eigeldinger, Juliusz J. Englert, Leo Ewals, Andrew Fairbairn, the Earl of Falmouth, Robert Ferguson, Rosemary Firmin, Jamie Flett, Duncan Forbes, Cathy Fowler, Alison M. Gardiner, Morris Garratt, Joanna Gasiorowska, Maggie Gibb, Imogen Gibbon, Halina Goldberg, Sissel Guttormsen, Kenneth Hamilton, Rima Handley, Joyce Harasowska, Paul Harding, Clare Hartwell, Vigdis Head, Sylwia Heinrich, Yvonne Hillyard, Sheila Hingley, James Hogg, Susan Horner, Peter Horton, Roy Howat, Una Hunt, Richard Hunter, Alan Jackson, Zadisław Jagodiński, Emma Jarvis, Douglas Johnson, Rosemary Johnson, Glen F. Jones, Marita Albán Juárez, Jeffrey Kallberg, Jane Kellett, Michael Kennedy, Alison Kenney, Susanna Kerr, Richard Kitson, Thalia Knight, Andrzej Laska, Alastair Laurence, Bernard Leary, Anna Lęgowska-Radosz, Alison Lindsay, Cathy Lowne, Mona Kedslie Macleod, Hilary Macartney, Hugh Macdonald, George P. MacKenzie, Simon Maguire, Wojciech M. Marchwica, Catherine Massip, Alastair H.B. Masson, Grażyna Michniewicz, Agnieszka Mietelska-Cieperska, Iain Milne, Roy Milne, Lyn Morgan, Edward Morris, Eleanor Morris, Ian Mowat, Jean-Michel Nectoux, J. Philip Newell, Roger Norris, Janusz Nowak, Sir Francis Ogilvy, Bt, Ian O'Riordan, Keith G. Orrell, Richard Ovenden, Ursula Phillips,

George W. Platzman, Elizabeth M. Rainey, John Rink, David Robinson, Alison Rosie, Jim Samson, Robert Simonson, Murray Simpson, Zbigniew Skowron, John Smith, Janet Snowman, Sir James Stirling, of Garden, Patrick and Susan Stirling-Aird, E. Street, Renata Suchowiejko, Artur Szklener, David J. Taylor, Lord and Lady Torphichen, Francis Treuherz, J. Rigbie Turner, Jeremy Upton, David M. Walker, Judith Walton, Stanisław Waltoś, Elizabeth Wells, Peter Weston, Morley Whitehead, Paul Muir Wood, Susan Wood, Tom Woolley, Anna Wright, William Wright, Hanna Wróblewska-Straus, and Janet Zmroczek.

At Ashgate Publishing, and later Routledge, I am grateful to Heidi Bishop, Emma Gallon, Laura Macy, and Annie Vaughan for their contribution to the book and for seeing it through the press. Nicole Lee compiled the index. My friend Ian Chilvers provided editorial advice throughout the final stages of preparation. Technical help came from John Cullingworth at the Apple Store in Newcastle upon Tyne. To the medical staff at the Freeman Hospital, Newcastle, I owe the benefits of the National Health Service.

Finally, and most importantly, my family, Jenny, Magnus, Gemma, Imogen and Erin, provided support at all times, and in all weathers. This book is devotedly dedicated to them, and to the memory of my parents.

Peter Willis
2016

Every effort has been made to contact copyright-holders. Please advise the publisher of any errors or omissions, and these will be corrected in subsequent editions.

Introduction
Paris 1830s: Prologue

In 1831, following the Polish revolution the previous year, Chopin arrived in Paris from Poland. He had travelled via Vienna, and was never to return to the land of his birth. Paris was to be his home for the rest of his life. Politically, this meant living in the city between two revolutions: those of July 1830 (the July Monarchy), establishing Louis-Philippe as King of France, and of February 1848, leading to the Second Republic under Napoléon III. Indeed it was the second of these which, in part, precipitated his visit of some seven months to England and Scotland in 1848.

This visit, and to a lesser extent the two weeks he spent in London in 1837, have to be seen in the context of his Parisian life, both the years leading up to 1848 and the eleven months following his return to Paris in November 1848, which ended with his death the next October. His spells in Britain were directly related to, and dependent upon, specific features of his life in Paris: his connection with members of the Polish community-in-exile, notably at the Hôtel Lambert; his piano lessons given to pupils from the British aristocracy; his friendship with leading pianists and other musicians, and his joint concerts with them; his love of opera, and familiarity with operatic composers and with celebrated singers such as Alboni, Mario, and Viardot, who performed at the Paris Opéra and the Théâtre-Italien; his preference for giving *matinées musicales* in domestic settings rather than public concerts; his closeness to Camille Pleyel and his firm of piano manufacturers; his links to the painter Ary Scheffer and patrons of the arts, some British; and his declining health and interest in homeopathy, shared with others in his circle. All these factors came into play when Chopin ventured across the English Channel.

That said, Chopin's visits to England and Scotland were significant in another way, in that so far as we know he composed little, if anything, when in Britain. By 1848, his summers of composition at Nohant, the country estate of George Sand, were over, as was his close relationship with her.[1]

Culturally, the Paris which greeted Chopin, under Louis-Philippe, was a centre of intellectual ferment, and the musical capital of Europe. Instrumental virtuosos flocked there, and played regularly in public halls, their triumphs being recorded in the widely read newspapers. Added to this were the splendours of the Opéra, and the rapid growth in music publishing and the manufacture of musical instruments.[2] All of which took place against the backdrop of great urban change.[3]

2 Paris 1830s: prologue

Between 1815 and 1848 the population of Paris grew from 700,000 to nearly one million. In the 1820s onwards, led by architects, bankers, and financial speculators, new districts of the city were built: the quartier La Fayette, centred on the rue St Vincent-de-Paul, where the church of that name was later erected; the quartiers François 1er and St-Georges, surrounding the church of Notre Dame de Lorette; the quartier Beaujon, close to the Champs Élysées; and the quartier de l'Europe, on the site of the old Tivoli Gardens.

Building carried out under the July Monarchy was even more extensive. Led by the Comte de Rambuteau, Louis-Philippe's Prefect of the Seine from 1833 to 1848, a vast programme of major works was undertaken. A hundred new streets were completed, and the boulevards between the place de la Bastille and the place de la Concorde were levelled and widened. Pavements, gas lighting, and newly planted trees were given prominence; so were fountains, which increased in the city from a mere 146 in 1830 to more than two thousand in 1848. Rambuteau continued the policy of erecting prestigious buildings, including the Arc de Triomphe (1836), the church of the Madeleine (1842), and the Palais du Quai d'Orsay. He also enlarged the Hôtel de Ville, and developed the Champs Élysées and the place de la Concorde. Of major impact, too, was the building of the railways, which led to the construction of the Gare St-Lazare (1842), the first Gare du Nord (1845), followed by the Gare de l'Est and the Gare de Lyon; by 1848, all that remained to be done was to link all the stations. The scene was set for the *grands projets* of Baron Haussmann during the Second Empire.[4]

Throughout his time in Paris, Chopin lived within striking distance of the Comédie Française, the Opéra, the Opéra-Comique, and the Théâtre-Italien. His first apartment, in 1831–2, was at No. 27 boulevard Poissonnière, a handsome tree-lined street stretching between the boulevard Montmartre to the west and boulevard de Bonne Nouvelle to the east. Thereafter he moved to various other addresses, for a short time each: to No. 4 cité Bergère (1832–3), to No. 5 (1833–6) then No. 38 (1836–9) rue de la Chaussée d'Antin, to No. 5 rue Tronchet (1839–41), and to No. 16 rue Pigalle (1841–2). Eventually, for the nigh on seven years from August 1842 to May 1849, he settled near George Sand at No. 9 place d'Orléans (now square d'Orléans).[5] The summer and autumn of 1849 found him, first, at No. 74 rue de Chaillot, and then at No. 12 place Vendôme, where he died.[6]

When he arrived in Paris, Chopin linked up with the Polish community in the city, led by the Czartroyski family. Prince Adam Jerzy Czartoryski, Polish general and statesman, president of the Polish provisional government (1830) and the national government (1831), had been forced to take refuge in France with his family in 1831 after Russia crushed the Polish state (see Figure I.1). He became the figurehead of Poland in exile. Prince Adam, and his wife Princess Anna, then led an international campaign to restore Polish sovereignty. The Czartoryskis, apart from entertaining at a level befitting their social standing, used opportunities for enrichment through the Paris bourse to fund the Prince's political activities.[7] Under their aegis, the Czartoryskis ensured that French and Polish musicians, Chopin included, joined up for convivial evenings.[8]

Chopin assisted in the fund-raising activities of the Czartoryskis, attended many of their soirées, and played occasionally at the concerts they arranged for

Figure I.1 Prince Adam Jerzy Czartoryski (1770–1861). Engraving by Andrew Duncan, after Louis Rubio, 1831. Private collection

Poles in exile. Polish musicians, arriving in Paris, inevitably gravitated towards Chopin.[9] Among Chopin's other Parisian friends from Warsaw days were Julian Fontana, pianist and composer, fellow student at the Warsaw Lyceum and at the Conservatory, who moved to Paris in 1832; Wojciech Grzymała, critic and man of letters; and Jan Matuszyński, physician and fellow student at the Warsaw Lyceum, whose wedding Chopin attended as a witness on 21 December 1836.[10] Polish literary figures of a 'messianic' orientation whom Chopin knew included Julian Niemcewicz, Juliusz Słowacki, and the poet Adam Mickiewicz, who was prominent in the Polish Literary Society in Paris.[11] Chopin was elected a member of the Society in 1833, but his relationship with it seems to have been ambivalent.[12]

As Halina Goldberg has emphasized, Chopin

> remained profoundly committed to his Polishness and to his country's pursuit of independence; he was intimately associated with Polish poets, political

4 *Paris 1830s: prologue*

activists, historians, and heroes of the uprising in the Polish émigré circles; and the enthusiasts of messianic philosophy were among his closest friends. Many of his non-Polish friends (George Sand, Marie d'Agoult, Franz Liszt, among others) were also concerned with politics, often pursuing French branches of messianism, and were sympathetic to the Polish plight.[13]

Mazurkas and polonaises in particular served such 'nationalist purposes'. It is a complex issue. But, some would say, 'to hear Chopin, it appears, is in some sense to "hear Poland".'[14] Indeed, as the *Musical Times* expressed it, Chopin was to Poland, as Dvorák was to Bohemia, and Grieg to Norway: they were all 'patriots in music, embodiments of the musical instincts of their people'.[15]

Chopin's other Polish friends in Paris included the painters Leon Kapliński and Teofil Kwiatowski, and two writers whose poems were used in Chopin's seventeen songs published posthumously in 1857 as Op.74 – Count Zygmunt Krasiński and Stefan Witwicki.[16] Whereas Krasiński's words were employed only for song No. 9 ('Melodya'), poems by Witwicki were used for no fewer than ten settings.[17] Chopin and Witwicki had known each other in Warsaw, and the Pole was one of those friends who had encouraged Chopin to compose a Polish national opera.[18] For his part, Mickiewicz provided settings for Chopin ballades, though not for his original songs.[19]

The Polish artistic community in Paris is brought together in the work of the Dutch-born painter Ary Scheffer (see Plate 1). Yet, although one of the most admired portraits of Chopin is Scheffer's of circa 1847, now in the Dordrecht Museum (Frontispiece),[20] the composer's relationship with him remains largely unremarked.[21] Scheffer spent virtually all his career in Paris, where he had many friends among musicians and Polish émigrés, and became a French citizen in 1850.[22] Since 1822 Scheffer had been giving drawing lessons to the children of Louis-Philippe, Duc d'Orléans. When the Duc came to power during the Revolution of 1830, the artist found himself in an 'influential position'.[23] The high point of Scheffer's career coincided with the period of the July Monarchy (1830–48). He painted portraits of the royal family, and other notables, but his greatest successes during this period were his paintings of literary and religious themes, such as *Francesco da Rimini* (1835) and *St Augustine and St Monica* (1845). The latter work, immensely popular in his lifetime, often strikes the contemporary eye as sentimental and mawkish.

In 1933, Léopold Wellisz published his book entitled *Les amis romantiques: Ary Scheffer et ses amis polonais*, which included twenty-five reproductions of paintings by Scheffer. The volume deals specifically with Chopin's friend Zygmunt Krasiński, described by Gabriel Sarrazin in Wellisz's book as 'Le poète anonyme de la Pologne'. Krasiński – who, with Mickiewicz and Słowacki, formed Poland's triad of 'messianic' poets – was known chiefly for the tragedies *Nieboska komedja* (1835) and *Irydion* (1836), and the poems *Przedświt* (1843) and *Psalmy przyszłości* (1845). Apart from portraits of Krasiński himself (1850), his wife the Countess (1845), and his mistress the Countess Delfina Potocka, Scheffer painted other Poles such as Prince Adam Jerzy Czartoryski, and musicians such as Gounod, Rossini, and Pauline Viardot, Chopin's student Camille Dubois, and Franz Liszt.[24] His British subjects included Dickens, Mrs Julie Schwabe, and Lord Torphichen, brother-in-law of Jane Stirling, who was to be a driving force behind Chopin's visit to Britain in 1848, and who, with her sister Mrs Katherine Erskine, was a periodic visitor to Paris. Miss Stirling herself was the subject of several portraits, and Scheffer used her as a model in religious paintings, notably his *Christus consolator* (1837).[25] One of his two, if not three, portraits of Chopin may have been commissioned by her, and conceivably hung after the composer's death at Calder House, Lord Torphichen's country seat near Edinburgh. In 1857, at the time of Manchester's 'Exhibition of Art Treasures', Scheffer stayed for three weeks with Mrs Schwabe at Crumpsall House, and later in the year visited her Welsh home, Glyn Garth, Anglesey.[26]

Ary Scheffer and Ingres were among the painters whom Charles Hallé met when he arrived in Paris in 1836 from Darmstadt. Hallé records in his *Autobiography* that Ingres, with whom he played Mozart violin sonatas, was 'passionately fond of music – a passion shared by nearly all the great painters with whom I have come into contact – while among poets and literary men the devotees to music seem to form an exception'. Of Ary Scheffer, he remarks,

> the noble painter whose fame was at its zenith in the forties, was never happier than when listening to music; hence his friendship with Chopin, Liszt, and a select number of musicians amongst whom I was happy to hold a place. To play to him in his studio, whilst he was engaged upon one of his great canvases, was one of my greatest delights. The well-known picture of 'Christ tempted by Satan' (Liszt sitting as a model for Satan) was commenced and finished with the accompaniment of my music.[27]

Scheffer's studio, or atelier, was part of his house in No. 16 rue Chaptal, later known as L'Hôtel Scheffer-Renan, now La Musée de la Vie romantique, which contains fascinating souvenirs of George Sand, including a Scheffer portrait of her. To Hallé, his life in Paris was

> of uninterrupted intellectual enjoyment, which will be easily understood . . . when I enumerate a few of the names of distinguished men, in the most various walks of life, whom I could call personal friends: Ary Scheffer, Lamartine, Salvandy, Ledru Rollin, Alexandre Dumas père, Ingres, Meyerbeer, Halévy, Delacroix, Louis Blanc, Guizot, 'Maître' Marie, not to forget Berlioz, Heller, Heine, Ernst, Jules Janin, Liszt, Chopin, and a host of others equally remarkable.

The effect was intoxicating. 'Paris was then in reality what Wagner wished to make Bayreuth, the centre of civilisation', Hallé wrote, 'and such a galaxy of celebrities as it contained has, I believe, never been assembled again.'[28]

Also a friend of Scheffer, and of Chopin, was Mrs Harriet Grote, wife of George Grote, the banker, historian, and radical politician, and author of a twelve-volume

6 *Paris 1830s: prologue*

History of Greece (1846–56) (see Figure I.2). Chopin met Mrs Grote in Paris at the house of Carlotte Marliani, wife of the Spanish consul, and a friend of George Sand.[29] Evidence of Mrs Grote's close friendship with Scheffer can be seen from her biography of the painter, *Memoir of the life of Ary Scheffer* (1860). Lady Eastlake, in her book *Mrs Grote: a sketch*, quotes Mrs Grote's verdict on Scheffer: 'His spotless integrity, his great gifts, his inflexible political principles, and withal his sadly sombre existence, combine to shed over the history of Ary Scheffer a mingled effect of admiration and pity.'[30] To this should be added the place of music in his life. Mrs Grote, in her *Memoir*, says that Scheffer 'was keenly sensible to the charm of good instrumental music, especially when given in the "atelier", as it was by some of the best musicians in Paris'. Mrs Grote had 'seen Scheffer yield himself up to the fascinations of sound with a sort of dreamy enjoyment, such as is rarely attained by persons who have not cultivated musical knowledge'. Pauline Viardot and her husband, Louis Viardot, were among Scheffer's circle, 'and since,

Figure I.2 Harriet Grote (née Lewin) (1792–1878). Lithograph by Charles George Lewis, printed by Jérémie Graf, after Charles Landseer (circa 1840).
Copyright National Portrait Gallery, London

along with Madame Viardot's vocal power was united a talent for pianoforte playing of a superior kind, Scheffer had often the pleasure of listening to her tasteful execution of the best compositions for that instrument'.[31]

For Chopin, part of the intoxication felt by Hallé came from the opera. In Warsaw, in Vienna, and now in Paris he found himself in a city with a lively operatic life, centred around the Opéra (the Académie Royale de la Musique) in the rue Le Péletier, and the Italian Opera House, otherwise the Salle Ventadour, home of the Théâtre-Italien (see Figure I.3).[32] In Paris, 'where Rossini and Auber reigned supreme, singers like Malibran, Pasta, Grisi, Cinti-Damoreau, Rubini, Lablache and Nourrit raised the standard of the performances to a level to which no other city could aspire'.[33] Vincenzo Bellini, too, had gained prominence, notably with his operas *Norma* (1831), *La sonnambula* (1831), *Beatrice di Tenda* (1833) – all of which featured the Italian soprano Giuditta Pasta – and *I puritani* (1835), and a warm friendship existed between him and Chopin. 'They had much in common, both as men and musicians, but to speak of Chopin's "indebtedness" to Bellini is to ignore historical fact', wrote Arthur Hedley. 'It is not difficult to show that the very elements in his style that Chopin is supposed to owe to the Italian – the luscious thirds and sixths, the curve of his melody and the *fioriture* – were already

Figure I.3 'Italian Opera House, Paris' (Salle Ventadour), home of the Théâtre-Italien, 1841–76. Engraving of auditorium by Charles Mottram, after Eugène Lami, from Jules Janin, *Summer and winter in Paris* (1844). Private collection

being exploited by Chopin long before he had heard a note of Bellini's music, or even his name.'[34]

Once in Paris, Chopin was overwhelmed by the splendour of the productions at the Théâtre-Italien, and at Le Péletier, where so-called 'Grand Opera' form had already been established. Chopin eulogized Meyerbeer's *Robert le diable*, a work which seems to have resonated with him for a time; the Italian tenor Giovanni Mario made his debut in the title role at the Opéra in 1838.[35] Chopin attended the opera at every opportunity, and his letters to Warsaw from these early Paris months are replete with commentaries on productions and on individual singers. Understandably, Chopin's experiences at the opera influenced the refined and sophisticated melodic style of his piano music, and in all probability encouraged his thoughts about composing an opera himself.[36]

One of Chopin's immediate aims on reaching Paris was to give concerts, and in doing so a key role was played by Camille Pleyel (see Figure I.4).[37] Chopin's connection with the Pleyel family was close. His friend Camille Pleyel was a

Figure I.4 Camille Pleyel (1788–1855). Print by Boileau. Cité de la Musique, Paris

pianist, publisher, and piano manufacturer, business associate of his father, Ignace Pleyel, and husband of the pianist Marie Moke.[38] Chopin's first concert in Paris, on 26 February 1832, took place in 'Les Salons de MM. Pleyel et Cie' at No. 9 rue Cadet. This 'Grand Concert', writes Jean-Jacques Eigeldinger,

> played a decisive role in his career, establishing his reputation as a composer and performer, securing contacts with publishers, opening the doors of the most influential salons, and bringing work as a teacher, mainly among the aristocracy. Before his withdrawal from the concert platform in 1835, Chopin was already singled out in the Parisian press as the representative par excellence of the salon in its most noble sense.'[39]

When receiving lessons in his rooms in the place d'Orléans, Chopin's pupils 'invariably played a grand piano while the master taught or accompanied them on a small upright ("cottage piano")'. Both instruments were made by Pleyel.[40] Chopin, wrote Lenz, 'would never give a lesson on any other instrument; one had to have a Pleyel!'[41] Eigeldinger explains that

> from the time of the début concert, a more or less exclusive verbal contract was drawn up between Pleyel and Chopin: the former would lend his instruments and salons to the latter, who would promote them to his pupils because of their distinctive qualities and his own strong preferences.[42]

Later, Pleyel moved to the rue de Rochechouart, and here the Salons Pleyel held its inaugural concert in December 1839.[43]

Paris was a magnet for virtuoso pianists at a time when Frédéric Kalkbrenner, who was closely involved with the Pleyel firm, 'reigned over the world of Parisian pianists and pedagogues'.[44] Chopin declined to have lessons with Kalkbrenner, though he dedicated his Piano Concerto in E minor (Op.11) to him, and Chopin was one of six pianists (Chopin, Hiller, Kalkbrenner, Osborne, Sowiński, Stamaty) who performed Kalkbrenner's Grande polonaise in 1832.[45] Other pianists in Paris, among many, included George Osborne, who lived there from 1826 to 1843, and was one of the four pianists who accompanied Chopin on 26 February 1832 in a performance of his F minor piano concerto (Op.21).[46] Also in Paris in the 1830s and 1840s were Hallé (1836–48), Liszt (1823–35), Moscheles (1839), Johann Peter Pixis (1823–40), Tellefsen (1842–74), Thalberg, and Charles-Valentin Alkan.[47] Alkan met Chopin in 1832 at the Pole's first Parisian concert. Soon, Alkan 'came under the spell of Chopin, whose close friendship he enjoyed and whose music he much admired. He was friendly too with George Sand and others of their circle.'[48]

Although Chopin's connections with the Czartoryskis, and other Polish families, played their part in his establishment in Paris, Jolanta Pekacz has stressed that

> it seems more likely that it was the salons of the cosmopolitan aristocracy, such as that of the Austrian ambassador, Count Antoine Apponyi, and those of the rich Parisian bourgeoisie, such as the bankers James de Rothschild

and Auguste Léo, that decided Chopin's fate at the end of 1832. At that time, Baroness de Rothschild became one of Chopin's first pupils; we also see him in the presence of the banker Léo, as documented by his wife, and at the New Year's concert given in the Austrian Embassy by Count and Countess Apponyi, together with Rossini, Kalkbrenner, and Liszt.

It seems probable, too, that Prince Walenty Radziwiłł's connections with Parisian bankers and freemasons meant more to Chopin than the influence of the Polish aristocracy.[49]

Chopin, in his performances in Paris, was drawing on his experience elsewhere, notably in Poland. As Halina Goldberg has demonstrated, before Chopin left Warsaw, he had played frequently in homes and salons in the city.[50] His 'elegant presence and astounding performances were highly sought after', Goldberg continues. 'At times Chopin complained that he was so busy socially that he could not find time for composition.'[51] In 1829, Andrzej Edward Koźmian, reporting on his attendance at the famous Parisian salon of Countess Apponyi ('la divine Thérèse'), remarked that the salons of Warsaw and Paris did not differ much.[52] Small wonder, then, that Chopin fitted so easily into the musical life of the French capital.

Among Chopin's other friends in Paris was Édouard Herbault, who worked in the Pleyel factory in Paris, and was Chopin's piano tuner.[53] Writing from Paris to Fontana, then in New York, on 4 April 1848, Chopin commended Herbault to him:

> Welcome this dear friend Herbault as if he were my father or elder brother, and hence a better man than I. He was the first acquaintance I made in Paris when I arrived from Poland. I conjure you by the memory of our schooldays to be as cordial as possible towards him, for he deserves it. He is in every way a worthy, enlightened and good fellow, and he will love you in spite of your bald head.[54]

In Herbault, Chopin had a link with the Pleyel firm similar to that provided later by A. J. Hipkins with the Broadwoods in London.[55]

James Schudi Broadwood, then head of the piano manfacturers John Broadwood and Sons, may well have met Chopin during the 1830s in Paris, where Broadwood and Pleyel were at one in opposing the rival firm of Érard.[56] Other Englishmen whom Chopin encountered in Paris during the 1830s included Henry Fothergill Chorley, music critic of the *Athenaeum* from 1833 to 1868, and author of *Thirty years' musical recollections* (1862);[57] from Henry Hewlett's account, it seems likely that Chopin and Chorley first met on one of the writer's visits to France in 1836, 1837, or 1839 (the year Chorley met Mendelssohn, when the composer was conducting his *St Paul* in Brunswick).[58] Chorley began working for the *Athenaeum* full time in January 1836, later succeeding John Ella as the magazine's music critic. Many reviews in the *Athenaeum* remain unattributed, but 'it is certain that Chorley wrote most reviews from 1835 on. And it was because of Chorley's reviews that by the end of the 1830s the *Athenaeum* earned a reputation as a musical authority unusual for a general-interest publication.'[59] In Chorley, Chopin had a critical ally and supporter.

Finally, Chopin's years in Paris have to be viewed in the context of his failing health.[60] As explained by William Atwood, the physician and Chopin scholar, 'during Chopin's first few weeks in Paris, the twenty-one-year-old youth enjoyed unusually good health and gadded about the city with frenetic energy. The only illness that afflicted him then was one he aptly diagnosed as "consumption of the wallet".'[61] Despite his father's repeated warnings to look after his finances and health, 'his advice generally went unheeded. The temptations of the opera, concert hall, and theatre, not to mention the innumerable soirées to which the elegant newcomer was invited, kept him on an exhausting social treadmill that soon aggravated the consumption of that of his wallet and that of his lungs.'[62] Although 'the most commonly accepted interpretation of Chopin's illness is that it was caused by tuberculosis', there is considerable doubt about this, and Chopin's medical history is complex.[63] One of his most trusted physicians in Paris was Dr Jean Jacques Molin, a homeopath, who also treated George Sand. 'Although the doctor's cough medicine (gum water with sugar and opium) made him sleepy', Dr Atwood writes, 'Chopin preferred it to the harsh laxatives, leeches, blood-letting, and blistering applications prescribed by most allopaths of the time. Dr Molin, Chopin claimed, had the "secret of getting me back on my feet again". During the severe winter of 1847, he even credited Molin with saving his life and refused to leave for England in 1848 without the doctor's consent.'[64]

The 'founding father of homeopathy' was Samuel Hahnemann (see Figure I.5). Homeopathy (from the Greek words *homois*, meaning 'like', and *patheia*, meaning 'suffering') claimed that the success of all medical therapy was based on 'the law of similars'. This means that

> any given illness could best be cured by those drugs that created symptoms similar to the disease itself. This was directly opposite to the ideas of most allopaths (physicians practising the conventional medicine of the day) who chose remedies designed to oppose rather than mimic the disease under treatment. Furthermore, Hahnemann emphasized that the therapeutic dose of the curative agent must be very small, in fact almost infinitesimal.[65]

After a varied early career, Hahnemann ended up in Paris in 1835, and he and his second wife, Melanie (née the Marquise d'Hervilly) established a clinic at No. 1 rue de Milan, which became popular among an upper-class clientele.[66]

Patients of the Hahnemanns included musicians and British aristocrats, such as Lady Belfast, Luigi Cherubini, Lindsay Coutts, Lord and Lady Elgin (he of the Elgin Marbles), the Erskine family, the Countess of Hopetoun, Frédéric Kalkbrenner and his family, Lady Kinnair, the Duchess of Melford, Nicolò Paganini, Baron de Rothschild, Marion Russell (a niece of Jane Stirling), Henri Scheffer, and Jane Stirling and the Stirling family.[67] Although committed to homeopathy, Chopin was never a patient of the Hahnemanns; however, Dr Henry V. Malan, the British doctor who treated Chopin in London in 1848, spent some eighteen months with

12 *Paris 1830s: prologue*

Figure I.5 Christian Friedrich Samuel Hahnemann (1755–1843). Engraving by L. Beyer, after J. Schöppe, senior, 1831. Mary Evans Picture Library/Interfoto/Sammlung Rauch

Samuel Hahnemann in Paris in 1841 and 1842.[68] Back in Paris, after his sojourn in Britain, it was to homeopaths that Chopin turned in his distress. He relied on their ministrations until the end of his life.[69]

Notes

1 For an analysis of biographies of Chopin, see Harasowski, *The skein of legends around Chopin, passim*. Harasowski, in his chapter 'An early destroyer of legends' (pp. 93–105), gives high praise to Frederick Niecks' two-volume biography, *Frederick*

Chopin as man and musician, first published in 1888, and often cited in *Chopin in Britain*. Broad biographical issues are considered in Pekacz, 'The nation's property: Chopin's biography as a cultural discourse', pp. 43–68; Samson, 'Myth and reality: a biographical introduction', pp. 1–8; and Skowron, 'Creating a legend or reporting the facts', pp. 9–22. For Chopin sources, see Smialek and Trochimczyk, *Frédéric Chopin: a research and information guide* and Michałowski, *Bibliografia Chopinowska*, updated in subsequent issues of the journal *Rocznik Chopinowska*.

2 See Locke, 'Paris: centre of intellectual ferment', p. 44. Further coverage of music is in Bloom, *Music in Paris in the eighteen-thirties, passim*.

3 For architectural background, see Atwood, *Parisian worlds*, especially 'Paris à la Galignani', pp. 1–40.

4 This and the previous paragraph draw on the entry 'Paris, §II, 5(ii): Urban development: Restoration and the July Monarchy, 1815–1848', in *Grove art online*.

5 For Chopin's Paris apartments, see Atwood, *Parisian worlds*, pp. 1–40, and the list on p. 415; Delapierre and Chlunke, *Chopin à Paris, passim*; and Simeone, *Paris: a musical gazetteer*, especially pp. 46–8. A map of Paris, showing the situation of Chopin's apartments, is in Pistone, *Sur les traces de Frédéric Chopin*, p. 11. The locations of Parisian theatres and concert halls, and of the apartments of Berlioz, Marie d'Agoult, Delacroix, Liszt, Charlotte Marliani, and others, can be seen in the map of Paris reproduced in Burger, *Chopin*, pp. 84–5.

6 George Sand lived at No. 5 place d'Orléans from 1842. See Simeone, *Paris: a musical gazetteer*, p. 47. Here, and elsewhere, Simeone valuably specifies the Parisian arrondissements.

7 See Zamoyski, 'Paris', pp. 91–2; and Zamoyski, *Chopin: prince of the romantics*, p. 91.

8 For Poles in Paris, see Atwood, *Parisian worlds, passim*; Kramer, *Threshold of a new world*, pp. 182–3; Pekacz, 'Deconstructing a "national composer": Chopin and Polish exiles in Paris, 1831–1849', pp. 161–72; and Zamoyski, *Chopin: prince of the romantics*, particularly pp. 79–95. See also the table, 'Prominent foreign intellectuals in France between 1830 and 1848', in Kramer, *Threshold of a new world*, Appendix I, p. 235. Portraits of Chopin's Parisian friends can be found in, e.g., Burger, *Chopin*, pp. 89–93.

9 In this context, see Suchowiejko, 'Les pianistes polonais dans la presse musicale parisienne dans l'époque de Chopin', pp. 184–92.

10 For this paragraph see Samson, *Chopin*, p. 134.

11 See the chapter 'Mickiewicz in Paris: exile and the new nationalism', in Kramer, *Threshold of a new world*, pp. 176–228.

12 Samson, *Chopin*, p. 134.

13 Goldberg, '"Remembering that tale of grief": the prophetic voice of Chopin's music', p. 91.

14 Kallberg, 'Hearing Poland: Chopin and nationalism' pp. 222, 223. This article concentrates on Chopin's mazurkas, as does Milewski's 'Chopin's mazurkas and the myth of the folk', pp. 113–35. See also Trochimczyk, 'Chopin and the "Polish race": on national ideologies and the Polish reception', pp. 278–313, and the chapter 'The spirit of Poland', in Samson, *The Music of Chopin*, pp. 100–19.

15 From 'Edvard Grieg', *Musical Times*, February 1888, pp. 73–6, quoted by Carley, *Edvard Grieg in England*, p. 3.

16 For Witwicki, see Rambeau, 'Chopin et son poète, Stefan Witwicki', pp. 107–26.

17 See the tabulation of songs in Brown, *Chopin: an index of Chopin's works in chronological order*, p. 203, and in the entry on Chopin, by Michałowski and Samson, in *Grove music online*. Detailed descriptions are in Kobylańska, *Frédéric Chopin: thematisch-bibliographisches Werkverzeichnis*, pp. 181–208.

18 Samson, *Chopin*, p. 310.

19 For settings of Chopin ballades to words by Mickiewicz, see Witten, 'Ballads and ballades', pp. 33–7. For Chopin's connections with Mickiewicz, Witwicki, Krasiński,

14   *Paris 1830s: prologue*

and Słowacki, see the articles listed in Smialek and Trochimczyk, *Frédéric Chopin: a research and information guide*. For a wider context, see Goldberg, 'Chopin in literary salons and Warsaw's romantic awakening', pp. 53–64. A biographical context is provided by Koropeckyj, *Adam Mickiewicz: the life of a romantic, passim*.

20 For the Chopin portrait, see Ewals, *Ary Scheffer (1795–1858): gevierd romanticus*, pp. 267–9, and Ewals, *Ary Scheffer (1795–1858)*, p. 82. A second portrait of Chopin by Scheffer, formerly owned by Chopin's sister Justyna Izabela Barcińska, was lost in 1863 when the palace of the Zamoyskis in Warsaw was destroyed by fire. See Wróblewska-Straus, 'Jane Wilhelmina Stirling's letters to Ludwika Jędrzejewicz', p. 61, n.4.

21 Chopin biographers say little about Scheffer. Although referred to seven times in the index to Niecks, *Chopin*, 'Scheffer' does not appear in the indexes of either Hedley, *Chopin*, or Samson, *Chopin*, and has only one index entry in Zamoyski, *Chopin: prince of romantics*. The index of names in Eigeldinger, *Chopin vu par ses élèves*, lists only a passing reference to Scheffer, in a footnote (p. 188, n.183). The index to Atwood, *Parisian worlds*, has just two entries under 'Scheffer'.

22 See Rigby, *Hallé*, pp. 55–6.

23 See Leo Ewals's article on Scheffer in *Grove art online*.

24 For Scheffer's portraits of musicians, see Davison, 'The musician in iconography from the 1830s and 1840s: the formation of new visual types', especially p. 158, and plate 5. See also Ruhlmann, 'Chopin – Franchomme', pp. 83–5. For comparison between portraits of Chopin and Liszt, including those by Scheffer, see Gétreau, 'Romantic pianists in Paris: musical images and musical literature', pp. 188–202.

Ary Scheffer's younger brother, Henri Scheffer, was also a painter, and his sitters may have included Prince Adam Jerzy Czartoryski, Samuel Hahnemann, and 'Jane Stirling and two other women'. He was a patient of the Hahnemanns. See Handley, *A homeopathic love story*, p. 112.

25 See Niecks, *Chopin*, vol.2, p. 291, quoting Thomas Erskine, of Linlathen. For Jane Stirling and Scheffer's portraits of Chopin, see Wróblewska-Straus, 'Jane Wilhelmina Stirling's letters to Ludwika Jędrzejewicz', p. 61, n.4.

26 Grote, *Memoir of the life of Ary Scheffer*, pp. 115–19. For the Manchester exhibition, see Hunt and Whitfield, *Art treasures in Manchester: 150 years on, passim*.

For Scheffer's portrait of Chopin, commissioned by Jane Stirling, see Wróblewska-Straus, 'Jane Wilhelmina Stirling's letters to Ludwika Jędrzejewicz', p. 61, n.4. It was later owned by Édouard Ganche, and is reproduced in Ganche, *Dans le souvenir de Frédéric Chopin*, facing p. 54. On pp. 101–49, Ganche has a section (dedicated to 'Mme Anne D. Houstoun') entitled 'Jane Stirling et sa correspondance'.

27 See [Hallé], *Autobiography*, pp. 97–8. The quotation is from the chapter entitled 'Paris, 1838–48'. This is puzzling, as it seems that the Liszt painting was not completed until 1854. See Ewals, *Ary Scheffer (1795–1858): gevierd romanticus*, pp. 296–300.

28 [Hallé], *Autobiography*, pp. 96–7, and Rigby, *Hallé*, pp. 55–6. For Hallé's key statement of his impressions of Chopin, see Hallé and Hallé, *Life and letters of Sir Charles Hallé*, pp. 31–3. Hallé's period in Paris from 1836 to 1848 is considered in Beale, *Charles Hallé: a musical life*, pp. 26–38.

29 See Hedley, *Chopin correspondence*, p. 334. Chopin to his family in Warsaw [10–19 August 1848]. This letter is also quoted in Bone, *Jane Wilhelmina Stirling*, pp. 68–9.

30 Eastlake, *Mrs Grote: a sketch*, p. 98.

31 Grote, *Memoir of the life of Ary Scheffer*, pp. 91–2, and pp. 119–20 in reprint of 2nd edition of 1860. For Mrs Gaskell's visits to Scheffer's studio, see Gérin, *Elizabeth Gaskell*, p. 157.

32 For the context of the Théâtre-Italien and the Opéra, see Johnson, *Listening in Paris: a cultural history*, pp. 182–96, 239–56. Details of the repertoire at the Théâtre-Italien appear in Gossett, 'Music at the Théâtre-Italien', in Bloom, *Music in Paris in the eighteen-thirties*, pp. 327–64.

Paris 1830s: prologue 15

33 Hedley, *Chopin*, p. 44.
34 Hedley, *Chopin*, p. 58. Bellini, a Sicilian, was honoured on 8 May 2007 with the opening to the public of Vincenzo Bellini Catania – Fontanarossa Airport.
35 For Mario's debut see Pistone, *Nineteenth-century Italian opera from Rossini to Puccini*, p. 221.
36 Eigeldinger has shown the range of singers at the Théâtre-Italien, and at the Opéra, who most impressed Chopin, in Eigeldinger, *Chopin vu par ses élèves*, pp. 150–1.
37 For Camille Pleyel, see Eigeldinger, *Chopin et Pleyel*, *passim*, and Eigeldinger's articles 'Chopin and Pleyel', *passim*, and 'Chopin et la manufacture Pleyel', *passim*.
38 For Marie Moke, see *Grove Music online*.
39 Eigeldinger, *Chopin et Pleyel*, p. 389.
40 Eigeldinger, *Chopin et Pleyel*, p. 392.
41 Lenz, *The great piano virtuosos of our time*, p. 56. For background to these remarks, see the commentary by Jean-Jacques Eigeldinger in Lenz, *Les grands virtuoses du piano*, *passim*.
42 Eigeldinger, 'Chopin et la manufacture Pleyel', p. 91.
43 For the Parisian context of the Salons Pleyel, see the entry on the Pleyels, and 'salle de concert', in Fauquet, *Dictionnaire de la musique en France au XIXe siècle*, pp. 980–2, 1113–14.
44 Eigeldinger, *Chopin: pianist and teacher*, p. 95.
45 See Pistone, 'Pianistes et concerts parisiens au temps de Frédéric Chopin', p. 48.
46 See the entry on Osborne by R.H. Legge, revised by Rosemary Firmin, in *Grove music online*.
47 See the pianists considered by Pistone, 'Pianistes et concerts parisiens au temps de Frédéric Chopin', notably the tabulation on pp. 48–50.
48 See the entry on Alkan by Hugh Macdonald in *Grove music online*. For Alkan's relationship with Chopin, see, particularly, Eddie, *Charles Valentin Alkan*, pp. 6–11. See also 'salon', in Fauquet, *Dictionnaire de la musique en France au XIXe siècle*, pp. 1115–16, and the essays in Bloom, *Music in Paris in the eighteen-thirties*. For Chopin, see Janet Ritterman, 'Piano music and the public concert, 1800–1850', pp. 11–31.
49 Pekacz, 'Deconstructing a "national composer": Chopin and Polish exiles in Paris, 1831–1849', p. 168. See also Pekacz, 'The nation's property: Chopin's biography as a cultural discourse', pp. 43–68. In addition, Pekacz touches on this issue in 'Memory, history and meaning: musical biography and its discontents', pp. 71–3. Pekacz's view that Chopin was apolitical is challenged by Halina Goldberg, ' "Remembering that tale of grief": the prophetic voice of Chopin's music', p. 88, n.19.
50 See, particularly, Goldberg, *Music in Chopin's Warsaw*, notably pp. 147–76, and Goldberg, 'Chopin in literary salons and Warsaw's romantic awakening', *passim*.
51 Goldberg, *Music in Chopin's Warsaw*, pp. 159–60.
52 Quoted by Goldberg, *Music in Chopin's Warsaw*, p. 153, n.12. Chopin later frequented Countess Apponyi's salon, and dedicated his Two Nocturnes (Op.27) to her.
53 For Herbault, see Eigeldinger, *Chopin et Pleyel*, *passim*.
54 Hedley, *Chopin correspondence*, p. 311. This letter also appears in Opieński, *Chopin's letters*, p. 49, where Chopin's friend is called 'Herbaut'.
55 Hipkins' connections with the Broadwoods, and with Chopin and Jane Stirling, are considered in later chapters of *Chopin in Britain*.
56 See Wainwright, *Broadwood by appointment*, pp. 135–6. An undated letter, in French, from Princess Marcelina Czartoryska to Henry Fowler Broadwood, making arrangements for dinner in Paris, is in Surrey History Centre, Woking, Broadwood Album.
57 For Chorley, see Bledsoe, *Chorley*, *passim*, and Bledsoe's articles on Chorley in *Grove music online* and *Oxford DNB online*.
58 Hewlett, *Chorley*, vol.2, pp. 303–4. Chorley presented Mendelssohn with a letter of introduction from Moscheles.
59 Bledsoe, *Chorley*, pp. 45–6.

16   *Paris 1830s: prologue*

60   Speculation about Chopin's health is a veritable industry. Key sources are Neumayr, *Music and medicine*, vol.3, pp. 11–137, and O'Shea, *Music and medicine: medical profiles of great composers*, pp. 140–54. For a more recent Polish study, see Sielużycki, *Chopin: geniusz cierpiący, passim*. Further speculation is in Davies, *Romantic anatomies of performance*, especially, pp. 44–5. On p. 198, n.9, Davies claims that Chopin had thirty-three doctors.

61   Atwood, *Parisian worlds*, p. 331. Atwood then considers the possibility that Chopin may have picked up venereal disease in Paris. In this book, the late William Atwood, MD, formerly a dermatologist who practised in New York City, provides a wide conspectus of Parisian medicine and medical education, notably on pp. 330–55.

62   Atwood, *Parisian worlds*, pp. 331–2. For the context of Chopin and homeopathy in Paris, see Atwood, *Parisian worlds*, pp. 348–55, Handley, *A homeopathic love story*, *passim*, and Handley, *In search of the later Hahnemann, passim*. A study by Bernard Charton of Chopin's health from a homeopathic perspective is in Charton and Barbancey, *Personnes et personnages: profils homéopathiques*, pp. 74–93.

63   O'Shea, *Music and medicine*, p. 149. O'Shea presents the 'diagnostic possibilities' on pp. 149–51, and a table of evidence for and against tuberculosis on p. 152. A specific study is Long, *A history of the therapy of tuberculosis, and the case of Frederic Chopin*, particularly pp. 1–35. John O'Shea makes no mention of Dr Molin, but see Neumeyr, *Music and medicine*, vol.3, pp. 89–90, 105, 124–5. Among more recent articles on Chopin's health are Kuzemko, 'Chopin's illnesses', and Kubba and Young, 'The long suffering of Frederic Chopin', with 'Communications to the editor', pp. 654–6. In medical terminology, 'tuberculosis' and 'consumption' are virtually synonymous.

64   Atwood, *Parisian worlds*, pp. 348–9. Dr Molin, who was born on 13 June 1787, and died on 3 September 1848, treated Chopin from 1843 to 1848. He took his MD at Strasbourg, and was President of the Société de Médecine Homoeopathique on his death. His obituary is in the *British Journal of Homeopathy*, January 1849, pp. 130–1. Steven Crossley kindly obtained a copy of this for me.

65   Atwood, *Parisian worlds*, pp. 347–8.

66   For biographical background to the Hahnemanns, see Waugh (later Hobhouse), *The life of Christian Samuel Hahnemann, founder of homeopathy, passim*, and Haehl, *Samuel Hahnemann: his life and work, passim*. The coloured frontispiece to volume 1 of Haehl's biography has the title 'SAMUEL HAHNEMANN, BY SCHEFFER', but no more details are given. Handley, *A homeopathic love story*, p. 112, says that a portrait of Hahnemann was painted by Ary's brother, Henri Scheffer, 'who also brought his daughter to consult' Hahnemann.

67   For details of patients of the Hahnemanns, see Handley, *A homeopathic love story*, especially pp. 105–16, 246–7, and Handley, *In search of the later Hahnemann*, especially pp. 20–3, 224–6. Bone, *Jane Stirling*, p. 49, draws attention to Jane Stirling
   'bringing a young boy of 12 down from Paisley in 1838 to Paris to be treated by Hahnemann . . . When Hahnemann moved to Paris in 1835, he lived at No 1 rue de Milan. This is particularly interesting remembering the undated letter from Lamennais to Jane, saying he would meet her and Chopin, at their request, at No. 3 rue de Milan.' Could this be a mistake for No. 1 rue de Milan?

68   Handley, *A homeopathic love story*, p. 204. Malan's admiration for Hahnemann is recorded here: '[Hahnemann] usually expounds his teaching with wonderful exactness and great erudition. He maintains throughout that pleasant modesty which was always characteristic of him.'

69   Atwood, *Parisian worlds*, p. 351, observes that had Chopin followed the recommendations of his allopathic physicians, instead of homeopaths, he would have been subject to 'debilitating measures'. See Atwood's further discussion on pp. 351–5.

1 London
Summer 1837

The year 1837 marked a significant stage in Chopin's life. Professionally, he had established himself in Paris as both composer and performer; personally, his friendship with the teenage Maria Wodzińska, whose brothers had stayed with the Chopins in Warsaw, was coming to an end. Moreover, the previous autumn he had been introduced by Liszt to George Sand. Bovy's bronze portrait medallion of 1837, with its idealized profile and flowing locks, encapsulates Chopin's status in Parisian musical life at this moment (see Figure 1.1). Yet all was not well with him.

In Dresden, in 1835, Chopin had taken further his friendship with Maria, and his hopes of hearing from the Wodziński family that they agreed to his marriage to their daughter must have been a constant strain. In 1837, as mid-year approached,

Figure 1.1 Chopin. Bronze medal, by Jean François Antoine Bovy, 1837. Mary Evans Picture Library/SZ Photo/Scherl

and Parisian society evacuated to the country or abroad, Chopin declined several invitations for the summer months, including one from Nohant. Any hopes of seeing Maria and her parents, and extracting a final response from them, were dashed. With such emotional stresses, Chopin must surely have regarded the opportunity to spend two weeks in London as a welcome relief.[1]

Chopin's passport, issued on 7 July 1837 by the French police,[2] describes his physical characteristics: he was 5 ft 7 in (1.70 cm) tall, with fair hair, clear skin, and blue-grey eyes.[3] On 10 July Chopin and Pleyel left Paris for London.[4] In the 1830s, travellers between the two cities still had to make their journeys to and from the Channel ports of Dover and Calais by horse-drawn stagecoach: you could travel within a day between Paris and Calais, or Dover and London, but the roads were poor, and there was always the danger of being robbed by highwaymen. Equally perilous was crossing the English Channel itself. Boats were small, and were tossed about in the waves. Passengers, often seasick, travelled on deck with little shelter. Landing could be difficult, as harbours on both sides of the Channel were shallow and ill protected against storms. Ships frequently had to wait offshore at Dover or Calais until the tide was high enough for them to enter the harbour; alternatively, rather than be delayed, some passengers preferred to pay local boatmen to ferry them to the nearest beach (see Plate 2).[5] Chopin and Pleyel survived this hazardous journey, but not entirely happily. 'I will tell you later', Chopin wrote to Fontana when he reached London, 'what agreeable thoughts and disagreeable sensations the sea gave me, and also the impression made on my nose by this sooty Italian sky.'[6] It is likely that Chopin and Pleyel stayed overnight in Dover, perhaps in Wright's Hotel, or in one of the coaching-inns which preceded the hotels in Dover, Folkestone, and Newhaven built later by railway companies for cross-Channel travellers (see Figure 1.2).[7]

Camille Pleyel had separated from his wife, the pianist Marie Moke, two years previously. His friendship with Chopin was important on several counts. We have seen already that Chopin's first concert in Paris in 1832 had taken place at 'Les Salons de MM. Pleyel et Cie', and that his preferred piano was a Pleyel. For his part, Pleyel had already established connections with the Broadwood firm in Paris, and must have wished to take them further by visiting Broadwoods' in London.[8] London musical life was a draw in itself: Camille Pleyel had already experienced it in 1815, when he performed as a pianist before royalty and at the London Philharmonic Society, and in a two-piano recital with Kalkbrenner. Pleyel also gave piano lessons, examined pianos produced by other manufacturers, and reported back to his father, Ignace Pleyel, on their construction.[9] And he linked up, among piano makers, with Thomas Tomkison, as well as the Broadwoods.[10]

Architecturally, London had just experienced the dramatic changes brought about by the great architects and speculators of the Georgian period: Shepherd's engraved views, in his *Metropolitan improvements* of 1829, demonstrate the character of recent building. Whereas in the City of London, for instance, St Paul's Cathedral still towered over Ludgate Hill and Fleet Street, to the north-west Nash's Regent Street cascaded south to Piccadilly Circus, Waterloo Place, and the

London: summer 1837 19

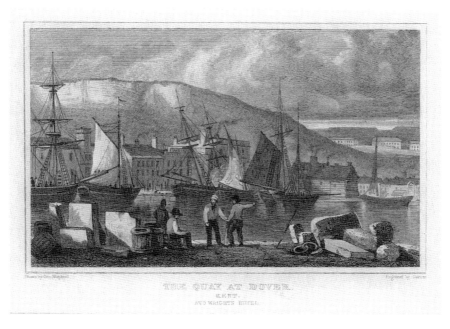

Figure 1.2 Quay at Dover, Kent, showing Wright's Hotel in the centre. Drawn by George Sidney Shepherd, engraved by Thomas Garner, circa 1830. Private collection

Embankment (see Figure 1.3). Here, and in the churches, civic buildings, squares, and terraces which formed part of the great expansion of London, it was urban classicism which held sway, as it did in the centres of Bath and Edinburgh and, later, Newcastle. This was the area north of the Thames in which Chopin was to stay in 1837, safely away from the poverty of much London life elsewhere.

Chopin and Pleyel were in London from 11 to 22 July.[11] Once they arrived, the composer was looked after by a friend from Warsaw, Stanisław Egbert Koźmian, poet and Polish patriot who, with his younger brother Jan (John) Koźmian, had fled Poland after the insurrection of 1831.[12] Jan settled in France, Stanisław in England. (Stanisłaus's translations from English into Polish included works by Shakespeare, and poems by Byron, Cowper, Shelley, Southey, and the Irish writer Thomas Moore. In addition, Stanisłaus translated passages on Poland written by the Scottish poet and journalist Thomas Campbell, and later, in 1862, published in Poznań a two-volume collection of his own essays about England and Poland, entitled *Anglia i Polska*.) Koźmian was Secretary of the Literary Association of the Friends of Poland, founded in London by Campbell in March 1832, and described by a biographer of Campbell as 'one of the proudest monuments of British philanthropy'.[13] Later, the association was led by another acquaintance

Figure 1.3 Part of the West Side of Regent Street, London. Drawn by Thomas H. Shepherd, engraved by W. Watkins, 1828. Private collection

of Chopin, Lord Dudley Coutts Stuart, 'after Campbell, the most constant and devoted friend of the Poles in England' (see Figure 1.4).[14]

The purpose of this association, according to its first prospectus, was 'collecting and diffusing all such information as may tend to interest the public mind in respect to Poland, and also the collecting and distribution of funds for the relief of Polish refugees' forced into exile by the tyranny of Czar Nicholas I of Russia.[15] Through the influence of Coutts Stuart, a Parliamentary grant of £10,000 was twice obtained 'for the relief of Polish political exiles'. Julian Ursya Niemcewicz, Polish patriot and man of letters, provided the initial drive for the foundation of the association, whose first presidents were successively the poet Thomas Campbell, Thomas Wentworth Beaumont, and Lord Dudley Coutts Stuart.[16] The most distinguished Polish supporter of the association was Prince Adam Jerzy Czartoryski, now exiled in Paris. The association's rooms in London were in Sussex Chambers, No. 10 Duke Street, St James's, and there were branches in Warwick, Birmingham, and Aberdeen. It published its own periodical. According to Teresa Ostrowska, most members of the association were Englishmen. 'Among them', she notes, 'were aristocrats, Members of Parliament, men of letters and arts, and industrialists. The Association provided relief to the refugees and furthered the

London: summer 1837   21

Figure 1.4 Lord Dudley Coutts Stuart (1803–54). Engraved portrait. *Illustrated London News*, 1843, left of page 325. Mary Evans Picture Library

Polish cause at the international forum.' As Koźmian observed, it promoted Polish interests among Englishmen, both 'in the most select drawing rooms and at popular gatherings.'[17] Among the 'popular gatherings', held to raise money, was the Annual Grand Dress and Fancy Ball at Guildhall in 1848, at which Chopin played.

On 3 July, a week before Chopin left Paris, his friend Julian Fontana (see Fig. 1.5), who was staying with the composer at No. 38 rue de la Chaussée d'Antin, wrote to Koźmian in London:

> Guess who is going to London on Saturday the 8th of this month? Before I tell you I must urge you to keep it a secret and not to divulge it to anyone. It is Chopin. He will stay in London for a week or ten days at most. He will be sightseeing and will want to see no one. He will be travelling in absolute secrecy and I ask you again to keep this news to yourself. You should have the will to keep a secret for two whole weeks if this letter reaches you early enough. I am writing to you about it only because I talked to him about you and assured him that he would find you an excellent guide, an advisor, and a pleasant companion.

Fontana is in no doubt about Chopin's virtues. 'I am sure you will find him a fine person', he tells Koźmian, 'a man of lofty ideals, equal to any of our own

Figure 1.5 Julian Fontana (1810–69). Bronze medal by Władysław Oleszcyński, 1837. Bibliothèque Polonaise de Paris. Akg-images/De Agostini Picture Library/ G. Dagli Orti

celebrities or of any other European ones. I can assure you that you will not get bored with him.'[18]

Fontana supplemented this recommendation by giving Chopin a letter to present to Koźmian when he arrived in London, addressed to Koźmian at No. 28 Sherrard Street, Golden Square:

> I am writing to you in behalf of Chopin who is about to leave. It's almost as if I were coming too, for we are both packing and getting ready to go – I to the Île-de-France and he to your part of the world. Well, he will hand this letter to you. I am sure you will be glad of the opportunity of getting to know him better . . . I have promised him that he will find in you an agreeable companion

and an excellent adviser in everything concerned with London. I know you will render him every friendly service if you can help him in any way. You have long known how I feel about him – I need say no more.

Chopin, adds Fontana,

> is coming for a short stay – a week or ten days – to get a breath of English air. He does not wish to meet anyone, so I beg you to keep his visit secret, otherwise he will have all the artists after him, together with the leading male violinist or else that female Paganini.

Finally, Fontana asks Koźmian to give Chopin the address of a good hotel in his neighbourhood, should he know of one. 'I'm recommending the Sablonnière [sic] to him', Fontana adds, 'as I can't remember any other names.'[19] And it was there that Chopin and Pleyel may well have stayed (see Plate 3).

The Sablonière Hotel had been in existence since 1788 at Nos 29–31 Leicester Square, not far from the King's Theatre in the Haymarket. In 1816 it was being described as a French establishment where 'a table d'hôte affords the lovers of French cookery and French conversation, an opportunity for gratification at a comparatively moderate charge';[20] on his visit to London in 1848, Chopin reported that Marc Caussidière, a Parisian police-chief, had been thrown out of the hotel with the shouts: 'You are no Frenchman!'[21] As can be seen from C.J. Smith's watercolour of about 1830, the Sablonière consisted of two four-storeyed houses, evidently rendered, each with a front three windows wide. Although situated in a busy part of London, north of the Thames, at the south end of Regent Street, the Sablonière was by no means architecturally pretentious. To judge by its exterior, it was modest rather than luxurious. The hotel was demolished in 1869, and replaced shortly afterwards by new buildings for Archibishop Tenison's School.

Chopin thanked Fontana for recommending him to Stanisław Koźmian, without whom, he said, he would have been 'lost in London'.[22] In a letter to his brother, of July 1837, Koźmian explains how he set about entertaining the composer.[23] 'Chopin has been here for two weeks incognito', Koźmian writes. Chopin, he continues,

> knows no one and does not wish to know any one but me. I spend the whole day with him and sometimes even the whole night, as yesterday. He is here with Pleyel, famous for his pianos and for his wife's adventures. They have come to 'do' London. They are staying at one of the best hotels, they have a carriage, and in a word they are simply looking for the chance to spend money.[24]

Chopin and Koźmian did some sightseeing: one day they went to Windsor, another to Richmond, and another to see the fishquays at London's Blackwall. The list of places visited by the composer also included Hampton Court, Chichester,

Brighton, and Arundel. He was at Arundel during a Parliamentary election campaign, when his friend, Lord Dudley Coutts Stuart, was a Liberal candidate. Sitting on top of a stagecoach, Hedley writes, Chopin witnessed all the excitements of a Dickensian election – not unlike the one at Eatanswill described in *The Pickwick Papers* – joining in the fun 'with gestures and exclamations'.[25] Although Coutts Stuart, who had been Member of Parliament for Arundel since 1832, lost his seat on this occasion to Lord Fitz-Alan, he subsequently returned to the House of Commons, and was MP for Marylebone from 1847 until his death in 1854.[26]

Chopin's own impressions of London are forthright. He tells Fontana to explain to Jan Matuszyński that one can have a good time in London,

> if one stays only a short time and takes care. There are such tremendous things! Huge urinals, but all the same nowhere to have a proper p[ee]! As for the English women, the horses, the palaces, the carriages, the wealth, the splendour, the space, the trees – everything from soap to razors – it's all extraordinary, all uniform, all very proper, all well-washed BUT as black as a gentleman's bottom!

'Let me give you a kiss – on the face', Chopin ends.[27]

Chopin's visit to London coincided with a period during which music flourished in the city. The 'professionalization of music' in London during the 1830s and 1840s was balanced by the social changes which saw the waxing and waning of such organisations as the Philharmonic Society and the Concerts of Ancient Music.[28] Music journals prospered.[29] Chamber music became increasingly popular. Music publishing thrived. Louis Jullien and others promoted 'low-status' concerts.[30] And the Italian opera, at the King's Theatre, enjoyed what Sachs calls 'good times', notably under Pierre François Laporte, who was later joined there by Benjamin Lumley.[31]

Unsurprisingly, visits to the opera featured in Chopin's time in London.[32] 'I often go to the opera', Koźmian told his brother, and Chopin evidently went with him.[33] Koźmian specifically mentions performances by the Italian soprano Giuditta Pasta, one of the operatic stars whom Chopin would have heard in Paris, especially as she was closely associated with Bellini: her creation of the title role in Donizetti's *Anna Bolena* (1830) was followed by that of Amina in Bellini's *La sonnambula* (1831), and the title roles in his *Norma* (1831) and *Beatrice di Tenda* (1833). 'Pasta was marvellous in Medea and Romeo', Koźmian notes, referring to her London performances, 'but I did not see *Hildegonde* [sic] because Chopin refuses to go to hear boring music.'[34] These operas were staged in the King's Theatre in the Haymarket (renamed Her Majesty's later in 1837, on the accession of Queen Victoria), which had been remodelled and given an external arcade by John Nash and G.S. Repton in 1816–18 (see Figure 1.6). Laporte, the manager of the theatre in 1828–31 and 1833–42, employed Michael Costa as conductor, and 'introduced Sontag, Lablache, Rubini, Grisi, Persiani, Viardot and Mario to London audiences, and mounted the London premières of *Le comte Ory*, *Il pirata*, *I puritani*, *La sonnambula*, *Anna Bolena* and *Norma* (the last three with Pasta)'.[35]

London: summer 1837   25

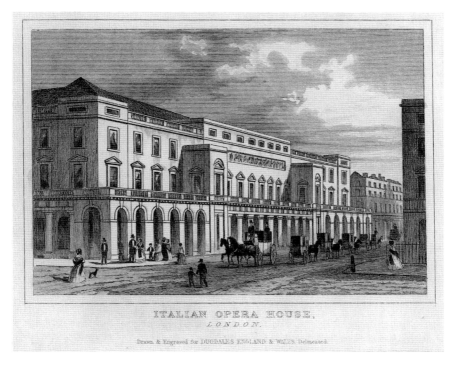

Figure 1.6 The King's Theatre, Haymarket, London (from 1837, Her Majesty's Theatre). Engraved view, showing exterior remodelling by John Nash and G.S. Repton, 1816–18, from Dugdale, *England and Wales delineated* (circa 1848). Private collection

Chopin's musical excursions elsewhere were less successful. In its issue of 8 July 1837 (no.506, p. 509), the *Athenaeum* carried an advertisement for a concert to be given on Wednesday 19 July in the Theatre Royal, Drury Lane, in aid of funds for the erection of a monument to Beethoven in his native city of Bonn. Chopin and Koźmian attended, but Koźmian thought the concert a failure: 'There were very few people, but the performance of his last great symphony was very good.'[36] The German soprano Wilhelmine Schröder-Devrient sang from *Fidelio*, and Moscheles performed a Beethoven piano concerto, noted the *Athenaeum*, 'with more than his usual spirit and finish'.[37] But, according to Koźmian, Chopin found Moscheles' playing 'frightfully baroque'.[38]

Whereas Koźmian took Chopin to the opera, and ensured that he saw the tourist sights, Camille Pleyel played a different role in the composer's first visit to London. Camille had become increasingly involved in the piano-building side of 'Ignace Pleyel et fils aîné', of which his friendship with James Shudi Broadwood was an indication. The intense competition between the firms of Pleyel and

Érard in Paris was reflected in London, where Érard also had a factory and where Broadwood felt threatened by Érard's sales campaign. Thus Pleyel and Broadwood shared common ground in opposition to Érard, and they exchanged pianos for comparison.[39]

The Broadwood family possesses a long lineage in the manufacture of pianos.[40] John Broadwood, born in the Scottish Borders, was apprenticed in 1761 to Burkat Shudi, originally from Switzerland, who had his own harpsichord workshop in London from 1728, and whose royal customers included Frederick, Prince of Wales, and Frederick the Great of Prussia.[41] John Broadwood married Shudi's daughter Barbara in 1769, and took full control of the business on Shudi's death in 1773. In 1796, Manuel de Godoy commissioned a piano for the Queen of Spain, with a case designed by Thomas Sheraton, with Wedgwood medallions. John Broadwood's sons James Shudi Broadwood (see Figure 1.7) and Thomas Broadwood, were made partners in 1795 and 1808, respectively, when the firm became John Broadwood and Sons. Following their father's death in 1812, the brothers expanded production vigorously to meet a burgeoning market. After its early decades of innovation, the firm concentrated mainly on increasing the power, compass, and durability of its pianos, but did not fundamentally change its approach to design, although it did introduce iron bracing to its grands in about 1820. This was devised to improve the tuning stability of the treble, and was further developed by James Shudi Broadwood's elder son Henry Fowler Broadwood (who had joined the partnership in 1836) into the 'iron grand' of 1846.[42] By the 1840s around 2,300 pianos a year were being made at the factory in Horseferry Road, Westminster, and Broadwoods were among the largest employers in London. The firm's showrooms were at No. 33 Great Pulteney Street, Golden Square.

In Paris, Chopin was committed to Pleyel pianos, but in Britain he sided with Broadwoods. Artists' endorsements were, of course, essential to piano manufacturers, and by the nineteenth century most were seeking acclaim by association.[43] For the Broadwoods, Beethoven was a notable supporter. The Broadwoods 'sent an instrument by ship from London to Trieste and then had it carried by horse and wagon 360 miles over the Alps to Vienna for Beethoven's approval'. The piano was a six-octave grand of 1817, and even before it arrived Beethoven had written in gratitude to Thomas Broadwood. 'I shall regard it as an altar upon which I will place the choicest offerings of my mind to the divine Apollo', he wrote. 'As soon as I shall have received your excellent instrument, I will send you the fruits of the inspiration of the first moments I shall spend with it.'[44] After Beethoven's death in 1827, his Broadwood was presented to Liszt, who kept it in Weimar, 'adding to it the silver music-stand presented to him by the people of Vienna'.[45] It is now in the National Museum of Hungary, Budapest.[46] In 1859, Henry Steinway started soliciting testimonials in Europe, and he also sent a piano to Liszt in Weimar; indeed, says Lieberman, Liszt had so many unsolicited pianos in his homes that they 'looked like piano showrooms'.[47]

Among Chopin's contemporaries, Liszt endorsed Érard, although he later changed to Bösendorfer. Érard, as well as adopting an aggressive promotion campaign, made significant technical improvements in its instruments, and, after the

Figure 1.7 James Shudi Broadwood (1772–1851). Anonymous watercolour portrait (detail), circa 1820. Broadwood Trust, from Wainwright, *Broadwood by appointment* (1982), between pp. 184 and 185. Broadwood Trust, Surrey History Centre, Woking

sale of a piano to George IV, was granted a Royal Warrant. Broadwoods, meantime, took the eighteen-year-old William Sterndale Bennett under their wing, and in 1835 gave him a Broadwood grand; the next year, Henry Fowler Broadwood paid for him to go with J.W. Davison to Düsseldorf, where Mendelssohn was to conduct the first performance of his oratorio *St Paul*.[48] The firms of Pleyel and Broadwood shared much, and Chopin's visit to London in 1837 provided an opportunity for them to establish closer contact.

James Shudi Broadwood's home at No. 46 Bryanston Square was part of the Portman Estate in St Marylebone, designed by the architect James Thompson

Parkinson and completed about 1811 (see Plate 4).[49] It was an elegant house, on three floors, with a brick and stucco facade facing the square, and a doorway with columns and classical detail which survives today. 'Pleyel', Niecks observes,

> introduced [Chopin] under the name of M. Fritz to his friend James Broadwood, who invited them to dine at his house in Bryanston Square. The incognito, however, could only be preserved as long as Chopin kept his hands off the piano. When after dinner he sat down to play, the ladies of the family suspected, and, suspicion being aroused, soon extracted a confession of the truth.[50]

As David Wainwright comments: 'The story rings true; it is in character with James Shudi's humour to play such a practical joke.'[51] One assumes that the piano was a Broadwood, but we have no inkling of the pieces Chopin played.

Clearly he made a deep impression on those who heard him. Mendelssohn, who arrived in London from Rotterdam in late August 1837, that is a month after Chopin's return to Paris, wrote to Ferdinand Hiller on 1 September: 'It seems that Chopin came over here quite suddenly a fortnight ago, paid no visits and saw nobody, played very beautifully at Broadwood's one evening, and then took himself off again. They say he is still very ill and miserable.'[52] Similarly, Moscheles refers in his diary to Chopin's visit, and his poor health. 'Chopin', he wrote, 'who passed a few days in London, was the only one of the foreign artists who did not go out, and wished no one to visit him, for the effort of talking told on his consumptive frame. He heard a few concerts and disappeared.'[53]

On 21 July 1837, the *Musical World* was referring to Chopin as 'the celebrated composer', whereas the *Musical Times*, twelve years later, saw him as essentially a pianist.[54] Such ambivalence was not unusual in the press. In 1838, the *Musical World* of 23 February carried an enthusiastic review of 'some of Chopin's nocturnes and a scherzo', which suggests that the author may have been present when Chopin played at the Broadwoods' house.[55] 'During his short visit to the metropolis last season', the commentator observes, 'but few had the high gratification of hearing his extemporaneous performance. Those who experienced this will not readily lose its remembrance.' Then follows a succinct description of Chopin's playing, suggesting that the ambience of the Broadwoods' home would have been ideal for him, not unlike the Parisian salons with which he was familiar:

> He is, perhaps, par éminence, the most delightful of pianists in the drawing-room. The animation of his style is so subdued, its tenderness so refined, its melancholy so gentle, its niceties so studied and systematic, the tout-ensemble so perfect, and evidently the result of an accurate judgment and most finished taste, that when exhibited in the large concert-room, or the thronged saloon, it fails to impress itself on the mass.

Were Chopin 'not the most retiring and unambitious of all living musicians, he would before this time have been celebrated as the inventor of a new style, or school, of pianoforte composition'.[56] Chopin established good relations with the Broadwoods, and played again for the family when he returned to London in 1848.

Chopin took the opportunity when in London in 1837 to call on his English publisher Christian Rudolph Wessel, who at that time had premises at No. 6 Frith Street, Soho Square.[57] Wessel was of German origin, and he and the piano maker William Stodart had founded the firm of Wessel & Stodart in London in 1823. They began as importers of music from abroad, but from 1824 also brought out their own publications. 'By late 1833, if not sooner', Jeffrey Kallberg points out, 'Chopin was firmly entrenched with Wessel.'[58]

In 1837, as he planned his visit to London, writes Kallberg, 'Chopin must have counted on transacting business, for in his luggage he included manuscripts for five works, which he delivered into Wessel's hands when he called on his shop on 20 July.'[59] There were three contracts, all signed by Chopin and witnessed by Pleyel: the first was for Op.25 (see Figure 1.8), the second for Opp.29 and 30, the third for Opp.31 and 32. All contracts are described as for compositions in 'M.S.' Later in 1837 these were published by Wessel: Op.25 as Twelve Études or Studies (see Figure 1.9), Op.29 as Impromptu in A≅ major, Op.30 as Four Mazurkas, Op.31 as Scherzo in B≅ minor, and Op.32 as Two Nocturnes in B major and A≅ major, respectively;[60] typically, Wessel gave these nocturnes the evocative titles of 'Il lamento' and 'La consolazione'. Earlier title pages demonstrate the publisher's similar presentation of Chopin's work: in 1833, for instance, the Three Nocturnes (Op.9, book 2), dedicated to Camille Pleyel's wife, Marie Moke, were entitled 'Les murmures de la Seine' (see Figure 1.10), and in 1836 the Ballade in G minor (Op.23), directed to 'L'amateur pianiste', was called 'La favorite'.

Whereas Chopin may have opposed the use of such imaginative titles, Niecks, for one, in his book *Programme music*, rejects the claim that 'Chopin was a composer of the most absolute of absolute music, that he never thought of anything but the beauty and piquancy of the tonal combinations, and that there is nothing whatever behind these combinations'.[61] Rather, 'subjectivity is the beginning and end of Chopin.' He was, claims Niecks, 'a soul-painter, chiefly and almost solely'. Moreover, 'being a tone-poet, and as such having something to communicate, Chopin must be in one way or another a composer of programme music.' Not, however, in the manner of Liszt, Berlioz, or Schumann. 'Chopin's way was his own supremely individual and original way – the way of the delicate, *passionate âme qui se rend sensible*.'[62]

Unhappy with the publisher's addition of flowery titles to his works, and his sluggishness in sending payment, Chopin in later years avoided dealing with Wessel personally, preferring to use a variety of intermediaries, or to sell the English rights to a French publisher, notably Maurice Schlesinger.[63] Stodart retired in 1838, and Wessel subsequently carried on the business until 1860, with Frederic Stapleton as a partner from 1839 to 1845. In 1840, Wessel's *Complete collection of the compositions of Frederic Chopin*, the first to be issued, was launched; it was to be revised and expanded many times both within and after Chopin's lifetime, and concluded with Chopin's Three Waltzes (Op.64) of 1848.[64] The *Grand*

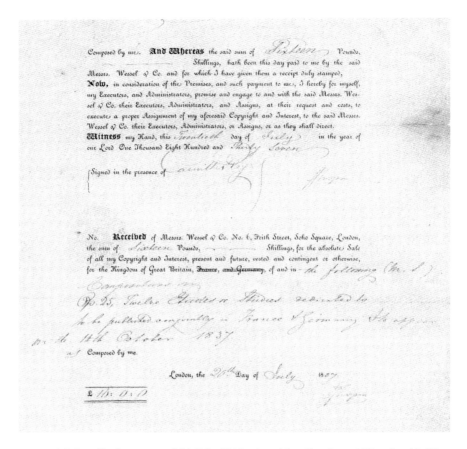

Figure 1.8 Detail of contract of 20 July 1837, signed by Chopin and Pleyel, with Wessel & Co, then of Frith Street, Soho Square, for the publication of the Twelve Études or Studies (Op.25), 'conjointly in France & Germany'. Sotheby's sale catalogue, London, 5 December 2003, lot 57 (p. 56)

architectural panorama of London, Regent Street to Westminster Abbey, published in 1849, shows Cramer, Beale & Co at No. 201 Regent Street, at the corner of Conduit Street, and No. 229 Regent Street, at the corner of Hanover Street, to which Wessel & Co had moved their premises by this time.[65]

On 22 July Chopin and Pleyel set off to return to Paris, one imagines via Dover and Calais.[66] If anything, Chopin must have been more miserable when he left London than on his arrival some two weeks earlier. During his stay, a letter had been forwarded to him from Maria Wodzińska's mother, Teresa, which put paid to any hopes of marriage to her daughter; the text of the letter has not survived, but its effect on Chopin was dramatic. Chopin replied to Mme Wodzińska from

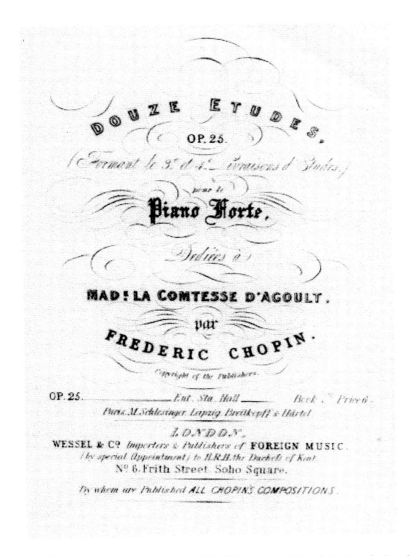

Figure 1.9 Twelve études or Studies (Op.25). Title page to Wessel & Co, ed., London, [October 1837], from CFEO online (www.cfeo.org.uk)

Paris on 14 August, referring to his original plans to return to Paris from London via Germany and Holland, now abandoned. 'The season is far advanced and will doubtless end for me completely in my rooms here', Chopin wrote. 'I hope to receive from you a less gloomy letter than the last one.' Other letters from Mme Wodzińska did indeed follow, but they were not encouraging. Tying up the

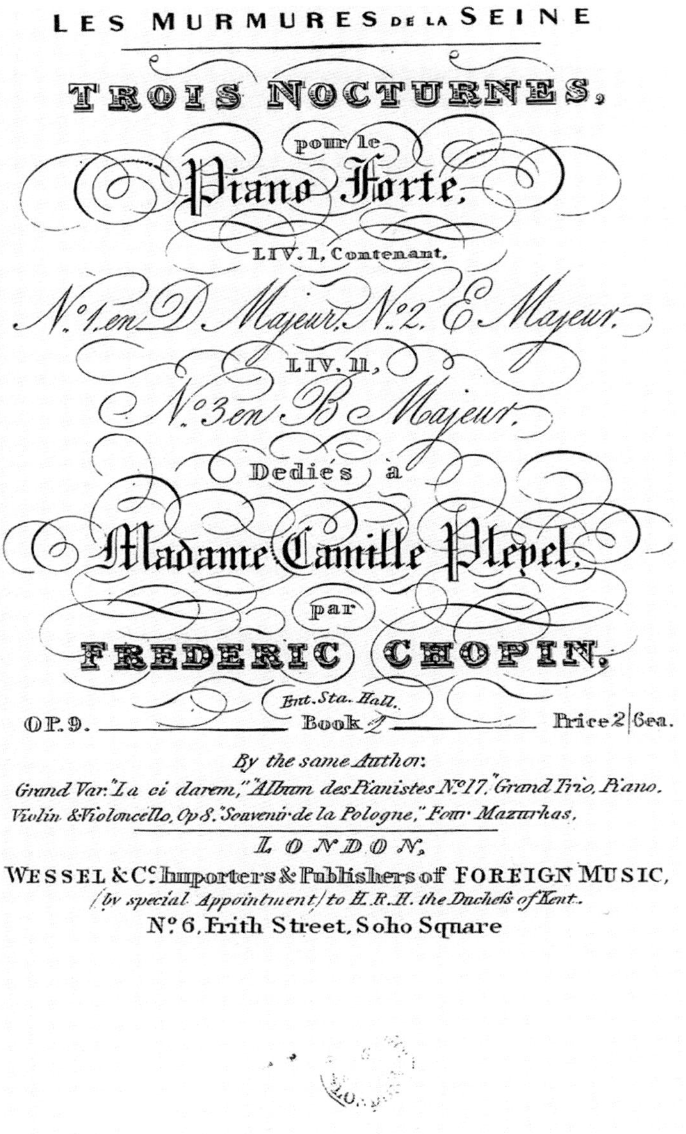

LES MURMURES DE LA SEINE

TROIS NOCTURNES,

pour le

Piano Forte,

LIV. 1, Contenant,

N.° 1 en D Majeur, N.° 2 E Majeur.

LIV. II,

N.° 3 en B Majeur.

Dediés à

Madame Camille Pleyel,

par

FREDERIC CHOPIN.

Ent. Sta. Hall.

OP. 9. — Book 2 — Price 2/6ea.

By the same Author:

Grand Var. "La ci darem," "Album des Pianistes N.° 17," Grand Trio, Piano, Violin & Violoncello, Op 8. "Souvenir de la Pologne," Four Mazurkas,

LONDON,

WESSEL & C.° Importers & Publishers of FOREIGN MUSIC,

(by special Appointment) to H. R. H. the Duchess of Kent.

N.° 6, Frith Street, Soho Square

Nocturnes, Opus 9, Book 2, Wessel (9-W-2)
[91%]

Figure 1.10 Chopin, Trois Nocturnes (Op.9, book 2), 'Les murmures de la Seine'. Title page to Wessel & Co, ed., London, [1833], from Platzman, Chicago catalogue 1, p. 48. University of Chicago Library

Wodzińska letters with ribbon, and adding the poignant inscription 'Moja bieda' ('My sorrow'), along with a flower which Maria had given him in Dresden, Chopin accepted that his friendship with Maria was at an end. They never met again.[67]

Chopin must have found Paris deserted: the Czartoryskis were in Brittany, Liszt and the Countess d'Agoult in Italy. After caring for her dying mother, George Sand had returned to her country estate at Nohant. And it was to be with Sand that Chopin was linked over the next decade – first in their period in Mallorca in 1838–9, and then in successive summers at Nohant. For the moment, Chopin seems to have spent the summer of 1837 immersed in his work, preparing some of his pieces for publication, and composing others – including the *marche funèbre* which would be incorporated into his B♭ minor Sonata. But all was not gloom. Chopin's position as one of Paris's most distinguished artists was already unassailable. He was twenty-seven.

Notes

1. Samson, *Chopin*, p. 134.
2. Samson, *Chopin*, p. 135. See the description in Azoury, *Chopin through his contemporaries*, pp. 105–6.
3. The original passport is in TiFC (Warsaw), M/2642. The English translation here is from Tomaszewski and Weber, *Diary in images*, p. 143.
4. Chopin's visit to London in 1837 is considered in, e.g., Atwood, *Pianist from Warsaw*, pp. 114–15; Belotti, *Chopin, l'uomo*, vol.1, pp. 591–3; Hadden, *Chopin*, pp. 95–6; Hedley, *Chopin*, pp. 66–7; Hoesick, *Chopin*, vol.2, pp. 144–9; Niecks, *Chopin*, vol.1, pp. 311–13; Samson, *Chopin*, pp. 134–5; and Zamoyski, *Chopin: prince of the romantics*, pp. 146–7. Unfortunately, no diary of Chopin for the year 1837 seems to have survived.
5. This paragraph draws on the entries on 'Railways' and 'Channel ferries and ferry ports' on the online sites www.theotherside.co.uk/tm-heritage/background/railways.htm and www.theotherside.co.uk/tm-heritage/background/ferries.htm (2008). See also Bucknall, *Boat trains and channel packets*, passim.
6. Hedley, *Chopin correspondence*, p. 148. Chopin to Fontana [Mid-July 1837].
7. See Carter, *British railway hotels*, pp. 28–9. The Lord Warden Hotel, Dover, for example, did not open until 1853.
8. See Eigeldinger, *Chopin et Pleyel*, passim, particularly pp. 115–16.
9. See Wainwright, *Broadwood by appointment*, pp. 128, 135–6.
10. For Tomkison, see the entry by Margaret Cranmer in *Grove music online*.
11. In TiFC (Warsaw), M/2634, there is a visiting card of Camille Pleyel, with a note in Polish in Chopin's hand, addressed to Stanisław Egbert Koźmian in London. This translates as 'We're expecting you at 5 o'clock / Chopin'. See Wróblewska-Straus, *Chopin: fame resounding far and wide*, item 163.
12. For the brothers Stanisław and Jan Koźmian, see their joint entry in the *Catholic encyclopedia online*, at www.catholic.org/encyclopedia (2008). Confusion has sometimes arisen between Chopin's friend Stanisław Egbert Koźmian (1811–85) and the Stanisław Koźmian (1836–1922) who was a Polish critic, theatre manager, stage director, and creator of the so-called 'Kraków school'.
13. See the article on Campbell by Geoffrey Carnall in *Oxford DNB online*.
14. See the article on Coutts Stuart by Krzysztof Marchlewicz in *Oxford DNB online*. For his Polish links, see Jagodziński, *Anglia wobec sprawy polskiej*, passim.
15. See Biggs, *Literary association of friends of Poland*, passim; Kukiel, *Czartoryski and European unity*, p. 203; and Ostrowska, 'Cultural relations between England and Poland', pp. 293–4.

34   London: summer 1837

16 See Kukiel, *Czartoryski and European unity*, p. 203.
17 Quoted by Ostrowska, 'Cultural relations between England and Poland', p. 293.
18 See Azoury, *Chopin through his contemporaries*, pp. 187–8. Azoury's source is Wróblewska-Straus, 'Nieznany list Juliana Fontany' ['An unknown letter of Julian Fontana'], pp. 34–5.
19 The English translation of this letter is from Hedley, *Chopin correspondence*, p. 148, where it is headed '[London. Mid-July 1837]'. It is not in Sydow, *KFC*, nor in Sydow and Chainaye, *Chopin correspondance*. And who is 'that female Paganini'? She is mentioned also in Fontana's letter to Koźmian of 3 July 1837, quoted in note 18 above.
20 *Survey of London*, vol.34 (1966), p. 502. For the Sablonière Hotel see pp. 502–3, and plates 50a and 50c. The source of the quotation is given as John B. Papworth, *Select views of London* (1816), p. 54.
21 Hedley, *Chopin correspondence*, p. 351. Chopin to Gryzmała, 17–18 [November 1848].
22 Hedley, *Chopin correspondence*, p. 148. Chopin to Fontana [Mid-July 1837].
23 For the Polish text of the letter, see Hoesick, *Chopin*, vol.2, pp. 145–6. English translations, each slightly different, are in Hedley, *Chopin*, pp. 66–7, and Zamoyski, *Chopin*, p. 144.
24 English translation from Hedley, *Chopin*, pp. 66–7.
25 Hedley, *Chopin correspondence*, p. 49. Editorial commentary by Hedley.
26 Coutts Stuart, a Liberal, was returned unopposed in the elections of December 1832 and January 1835. Fitz-Alan was also a Liberal, and in 1837 the votes were split 176 for him and 105 for Coutts Stuart. Fitz-Alan remained MP until he accepted the Chiltern Hundreds in 1851, having become the Earl of Arundel and Surrey on the death of his grandfather in 1842. Details of the Arundel and Marylebone elections are in Dod, *Electoral facts*, pp. 8, 209. John Derry kindly alerted me to this source.
27 Hedley, *Chopin correspondence*, pp. 148–9. Chopin to Fontana [Mid-July 1837]. The Polish text is in Sydow, *Chopin correspondence*, vol.1, p. 306 (letter 217), and a French version is in Sydow and Chainaye, *Chopin correspondance*, vol.2, pp. 224–6 (letter 245).
28 See Weber, *Music and the middle class*, *passim*; and Sachs, 'London: the professionalization of music', *passim*.
29 Sachs, 'London: the professionalization of music', p. 218. See also Ehrlich, *First philharmonic*, pp. 58–9.
30 Sachs, 'London: the professionalization of music', pp. 226–7.
31 Sachs, 'London: the professionalization of music', pp. 220–3.
32 For background to the opera in London in the 1830s and 1840s, see Hall-Witt, *Fashionable acts*, *passim*; Hall-Witt, 'Representing the audience in the age of reform', *passim*; Langley, 'Italian opera and the English press, 1836–1856', *passim*; Nalbach, *The King's Theatre*, *passim*; Parker, *Oxford illustrated history of opera*, index entries under Covent Garden and the King's Theatre; Rosenthal, *Two centuries of opera at Covent Garden*, especially pp. 65–84; and White, *A history of English opera*, notably the listing of London theatres on pp. 260–2. Comprehensive coverage is in *Grove music online*, under London (i), §VI, Musical life: 1800–1945.
33 English translation from Hedley, *Chopin*, p. 67. The first two operas referred to here seem to be Mayr's *Medea in Corinto* (1813), and Bellini's *I Capuleti e i Montecchi* (1830). Pasta was celebrated for singing in both. The third, *Ildegonda*, by Marliani, was first performed in Paris a few months before, in March 1837, with Grisi in the title role. See Forbes, *Mario and Grisi*, pp. 35–6. See also the entry on Marliani by Francesco Bussi in *Grove music online*. Eigeldinger, *Chopin vu par ses élèves*, pp. 150–1, provides a list of singers at the Théâtre-Italien in Paris during Chopin's time.
34 Quoted from the entry on Laporte by Leanne Langley in *Grove music online*.
35 *Athenaeum*, 8 July 1837 (no.306), p. 509.
36 English translation in Zamoyski, *Chopin*, p. 144.
37 *Athenaeum*, 22 July 1837 (no.508), p. 540. The reporter says here that Moscheles played 'the Concerto in F flat'. Presumably this is a misprint, and what is meant is the Piano Concerto, no.5, in E flat (Op.73), the 'Emperor'.

38 English translation in Hedley, *Chopin*, p. 67.
39 Wainwright, *Broadwood by appointment*, p. 136.
40 See John Broadwood and Sons, Limited, Piano Manufacturers, London: Business Records, 1719–1981, Surrey History Centre (Woking), 2185/JB. These were deposited by The Broadwood Trust in 1977, 1984, and 1993, and their cataloguing was made possible by a grant from the Heritage Lottery Fund. My research in the Broadwood archives benefited from the help of Alastair Lawrence, David Robinson, and Robert Simonson. For a history of the firm, see especially Wainwright, *Broadwood by appointment*, *passim*, and the entry on Broadwood by Derek Adlam and Cyril Ehrlich in *Grove music online*. Illustrated accounts are in Burnett, *Company of pianos*, pp. 44–66, and Roudier and di Lenna, *Rifiorir d'antichi suoni*, pp. 108–27.
41 See the entry on John Broadwood by Charles Mould in *Oxford DNB online*.
42 See the entry on Henry Fowler Broadwood by Charles Mould in *Oxford DNB online*; there is, incidentally, no entry for James Shudi Broadwood in *Oxford DNB online*.
43 See Lieberman, *Steinway and sons*, p. 29. It is, writes Richard Lieberman, 'a practice that goes back to Bach, who in the 1740s played and praised Silbermann's improved piano at Potsdam, thereby promoting a sale to Frederick the Great'.
44 Quoted by Lieberman, *Steinway and sons*, p. 29.
45 Wainwright, *Broadwood by appointment*, p. 120.
46 See Wainwright, *Broadwood by appointment*, plate opposite p. 104.
47 Lieberman, *Steinway and sons*, p. 30.
48 Wainwright, *Broadwood by appointment*, pp. 135–7.
49 For Bryanston Square, see Cherry and Pevsner, *London 3: north west*, p. 634; Colvin, *Dictionary*, p. 781; and Weinreb, Hibbert, and Keay, *London encyclopaedia*, p. 107.
    Details of the Broadwoods' occupancy of No. 46 Bryanston Square are given in the rate books, the 1841 census (HO 107/679/4/34), and the 1851 census (HO 107/1489/530), held in the City of Westminster Archives Centre. I am grateful to Alison Kenney, archivist, for her research there on my behalf.
50 Niecks, *Chopin*, vol.1, p. 312. For diminutives of Chopin's Christian name see Harasowski, *Skein of legends around Chopin*, p. 76. Chopin's family referred to him by the sobriquet 'Fritz', as can be seen in the letters in Karłowicz, *Souvenirs*, pp. 52–120. Steen, *Enchantress of nations*, p. 59, notes that Viardot referred to Chopin as 'Mr Fritz, or le bon Fritz, or Chip-chop, or even Chip-chip'.
51 Wainwright, *Broadwood by appointment*, p. 135.
52 Hiller, *Mendelssohn: letters and recollections*, p. 101. According to Todd, *Mendelssohn*, p. 355, during the previous two days Mendelssohn and Klingemann, with whom the composer was staying, had begun 'to draft an outline of Elijah'.
53 Moscheles, *Recent music and musicians*, p. 240; also quoted, slightly differently, in Niecks, *Chopin*, vol.1, p. 312. For Moscheles in London see Hedley, *Chopin*, p. 67, and Samson, *Chopin*, p. 135. See also the entry on Moscheles by Jerome Roche and Henry Roche in *Grove music online*. Chopin's relationship with Moscheles is summarized in Eigeldinger, *Chopin vu par ses élèves*, pp. 191–2.
54 Cooper, *House of Novello*, pp. 139–40. The announcement of the death of 'Chopin the Pianist', in the *Musical Times* (November 1849), is cited by Cooper on p. 136.
55 Niecks, *Chopin*, vol.1, p. 312n, says that this was probably J.W. Davison, who would then have been only twenty-four years old.
56 Quoted in Niecks, *Chopin*, vol.1, p. 312, and Hipkins, *How Chopin played*, p. 3. Niecks, gives the date as 23 February 1838, whereas Hipkins gives 28 February 1838.
    As Hipkins was not born until 1826, he never met Chopin when the composer came to England in 1837, although a description of the visit appears in his daughter Edith J. Hipkins' book, *How Chopin played*, p. 4.
57 For Chopin's critical reputation in England, and the role of Wessel in establishing it, see Rosalba Agresta's doctoral dissertation, 'Présences de Chopin en Angleterre (1833–1860)', and her article 'Chopin in music criticism in nineteenth-century England'. More generally, see Brown, 'Chopin and his English publisher', *passim*, and Kallberg,

36   London: summer 1837

      Chopin at the boundaries, pp. 200–14. Wessel also featured in 'Frédéric Chopin and his publishers', exhibition catalogue, Department of Special Collections, University of Chicago Library, 1998, case 11.

58 Kallberg, *Chopin at the boundaries*, p. 202.
59 Kallberg, *Chopin at the boundaries*, p. 206.
60 Jeffrey Kallberg considers these and related contracts in detail in *Chopin at the boundaries*, especially pp. 206–10. The single-page contract with Wessel for the publication of the Twelve Études or Studies (Op.25), dated 20 July 1837, was sold by Sotheby's (London), 5 December 2003, lot 57. See Figure 1.8.
61 Niecks, *Programme music*, p. 214. Chopin is considered here on pp. 211–17.
62 Niecks, *Programme music*, pp. 216, 217.
63 See Kallberg, *Chopin at the boundaries*, notably pp. 209–10.
64 See Grabowski, 'Wessel's *Complete collection of the compositions of Frederic Chopin*', *passim*.
65 For the premises of Cramer, Beale & Co, see Foreman, *London: a musical gazetteer*, p. 317, and the map on p. 316. The name 'Wessel' does not appear in the index to this book.
66 In *Chopin*, p. 145, Adam Zamoyski suggests that Koźmian accompanied Chopin and Pleyel as far as Brighton in 1837, but the regular cross-channel ferry from Dieppe to Newhaven (for which Brighton was the staging-post) did not start until the mid-1840s. See Bailey and Féron, *Story of the cross-channel ferry service*, *passim*, especially pp. 9–10. See also Carter, *British railway hotels*, p. 29. The London & Paris Hotel, Newhaven, which served Brighton, was not completed until 1847. A 'Jenny Lind' engine of 1847, No. 65 of the London & Brighton Railway, is illustrated in Marshall, *History of the Southern Railway*, vol.1, opposite p. 161.
67 The text of Chopin's letter to Teresa Wodzińska is in Hedley, *Chopin correspondence*, p. 149, with another version in Opieński, *Chopin letters*, pp. 180–1 (letter 86). The episode appears in Samson, *Chopin*, p. 135, Zamoyski, *Chopin*, pp. 145–6, and Zamoyski, *Chopin: prince of the romantics*, pp. 147–8.

2   Paris 1840s
Interlude

The decade between Chopin's first visit to London in 1837 and his second in 1848 saw major changes in his circumstances, as his friendships flowered with musicians, painters, and men of letters. In the intervening years, he gave a few recitals in the Salons Pleyel in the rue de Rochechouart (in 1841, 1842, and 1848) before withdrawing from the concert platform.[1] During these years, Chopin moved home several times.[2] He gave few recitals, but his teaching continued, as did his opera going, his salon life, and his involvement with the Polish community in Paris, now centred on the Hôtel Lambert.[3] Here, the Czartoryskis held court, and its cultural activities were frequented by Polish and French aristocrats alike. Apart from Prince Adam, members of the Czartoryski family active there included his nephew, Prince Aleksander, and his wife, Princess Marcelina Czartoryska, a gifted pianist and favourite pupil of Chopin, who promoted music and organized balls.

One of the most notable changes for Chopin was that he came under the spell of George Sand, whom he first met in 1836 in the Parisian circle of Liszt and Marie d'Agoult (see Figure 2.1). On Chopin's return from London in 1837, his relationship with Sand intensified, and he spent the winter of 1838–9 with her in Mallorca, and subsequent summers at her estate at Nohant, in the Berry. In Mallorca, Chopin and Sand stayed first in the house 'S'on Vent, and then in rooms in the Carthusian monastery in Valldemosa.[4] Eventually, in mid-January 1839, not without angst, Chopin's upright Pleyel piano was delivered from Palma, and he was able to complete his cycle of 24 Preludes (Op.28).[5] 'I am sending you the Preludes', Chopin wrote to Camille Pleyel, on 22 January from Valldemosa. 'I finished them on your cottage piano which arrived in perfect condition in spite of the sea-crossing, the bad weather and the Palma customs.'[6]

Back in Paris, Chopin had already decided to spend the summer at Nohant (see Figure 2.2) and on 1 June he first saw the manor house that was to play such a prominent part in his life for the next eight years. Then, as now, Nohant consists of an eighteenth-century house of two storeys, with a hipped roof and shuttered windows, approached through an entrance court and set in a park and garden; nearby are farm buildings, a church, and houses set around a square. A few miles away is the village of La Châtre.[7]

Here, at Nohant, Chopin wrote some of his finest music. Among his fellow-guests at the house were Sand's children Solange and Maurice, Pauline Viardot

38 *Paris 1840s: interlude*

Figure 2.1 George Sand (1804–76). Engraved portrait by August Weger, from a photograph. Private collection

and her husband Louis, Wojciech Gryzmała, Eugène Delacroix, and Stefan Witwicki.⁸ There is now little at Nohant to mark Chopin's visit there: his piano was disposed of, and his first-floor room altered by Sand and incorporated into her own accommodation. Sand wrote many of her books at Nohant, and furniture among which she received numerous celebrated guests is preserved.⁹ But Chopin's idyll

Figure 2.2 Maison de George Sand, Nohant. Entrance front. Copyright, Centre des monuments nationaux/Monum, Editions du patrimoine, Paris, 2002

was not to last, and a dispute during the summer of 1847 over the marriage of Sand's daughter Solange to the sculptor Auguste Clésinger led to a break between composer and writer. The two were to meet again, briefly, on 4 March 1848, in the passageway outside Charlotte Marliani's Parisian apartment. Subsequently, Chopin continued his correspondence with Solange, wrote to her from London and Scotland, and when in Britain frequently enquired about her welfare. But direct communication with her mother was ended.[10]

Chopin continued to communicate, however, with other friends from Nohant, such as Delacroix and Pauline Viardot – the French mezzo-soprano of Spanish origin, daughter of Manuel Garcia, the elder, and sister of the soprano Maria Malibran (see Plate 5).[11] In addition to being a singer, Viardot was a pianist (a pupil of Liszt and Chopin), composer, and teacher, and ran a prominent salon in the Chaussée d'Antin quarter, which became one of the intellectual and artistic centres of Paris.[12] She had a well-known liaison with Turgenev, and her portrait was painted by Ary Scheffer. George Sand based her novel *Consuelo* on her, and Sand's son Maurice has left us a portrait of Viardot, and a drawing of her being taught by Chopin at Nohant.[13] Chopin and Viardot also performed together in Paris. The programme for Chopin's *Soirée de M. Chopin*, held on 21 February 1842 in the Salons Pleyel, indicates that Chopin played a selection of his own work, Franchomme offered a cello solo of his own composition, and Viardot sang the air

'Felice-Donzella', by Josef Dessauer, a selection from Handel, and her own song 'Le chêne et le roseau', based on words by La Fontaine. Chopin accompanied her at the piano.[14] This last song was among a group of eight which Viardot published in 1843, illustrated with lithographs by Ary Scheffer and Soltau.[15] In London, on Friday 7 July 1848, six years after her concert with Chopin in Paris, Viardot performed with him, and Antonia de Mendi, at the home of the Earl of Falmouth.[16]

Eugène Delacroix was also a frequent companion of Chopin in Paris and at Nohant.[17] The painter met Chopin at a reception on 21 May 1836, after Liszt's piano recital at the Salons Érard on 18 May, having already encountered George Sand in 1834 during a series of portrait sittings.[18] Delacroix, whose double portrait of Chopin and Sand followed in 1838, kept a piano in his studio so that the composer could play it when he visited him.[19] Delacroix's *Journal*, covering the years 1822–63, contains many references to Chopin and his views on art and music.[20] The painter's description of life at Nohant in 1842 sounds idyllic. 'When you are not assembled for dinner or lunch or billiards or for walks', he writes, 'you can go and read in your room or sprawl on your sofa. Every now and then there blows in through your window, opening on to the garden, a breath of the music of Chopin, who is at work in his room, and it mingles with the song of the nightingales and the scent of the roses.' Delacroix's admiration for his Polish friend is strong. 'I have endless conversations with Chopin of whom I am really very fond and who is a man of rare distinction. He is the truest artist I have ever met, one of the very few whom one can admire and value.'[21]

By the start of the 1840s, the Czartoryskis, after renting apartments, and later a *hôtel particulier* in central Paris, felt that they needed to buy a permanent home. In 1843, alerted by Delacroix, Chopin, and his friend Gryzmała, the Czartoryskis acquired a house on the Île St-Louis which was about to be pulled down: this was the Hôtel Lambert, designed in the seventeenth century by the architect Louis Le Vau, with interior decoration by Eustache Le Sueur and Charles Le Brun.[22] Later owned by the Rothschild family, the Hôtel Lambert combined practicality with splendour: it offered the Czartoryskis space to organize their campaign on behalf of the Polish cause, and magnificent rooms for ceremony and entertainment (see Plate 6). The building itself is arranged around a rectangular courtyard, dominated by a grand staircase, approached through two loggias; a vista from the top of the stairs leads through an oval vestibule into the Gallery of Hercules, a long, frescoed chamber with mirrors on one side and French windows (overlooking the garden) on the other. Not inappropriately, it calls to mind the Hall of Mirrors at Versailles.[23] Hardly surprisingly, with the Czartoryskis seen by many in French society as the royal family of Poland, the Hôtel Lambert became a kind of court, frequented by Polish and French aristocrats alike.[24]

Under the aegis of the Hôtel Lambert were established 'a Polish Young Ladies' Institute, a school of young men, a Polish library, the Polish Literary and Historical Society, and even a newspaper, *Wiadomsci Polskie*. Balls and other social events were a prominent feature of its life (see Figure 2.3).[25] Writers and artists who had fled Poland gathered there: apart from Chopin, these included the poets Zygmunt Krasiński, Adam Mickiewicz, and Stefan Witwicki, and the painters

Figure 2.3 Hôtel Lambert, 'Ball des Fürsten Czartoryski im Hotel Lambert zu Paris', *Illustrirte Zeitung*, vol.6, no.151, Leipzig, 23 May 1846, p. 340. Akg-images

Leon Kapliński and Teofil Kwiatowski. Some of these were close friends of the Czartoryskis from Warsaw days. Prominent among the hosts were Adam Czartoryski's nephew, Prince Aleksander Czartoryski, and his wife, Princess Marcelina Czartoryska (see Figure 2.4). Chopin's involvement at the Hôtel Lambert was celebrated by imaginative paintings by Kwiatowski of him performing there. Alas, its future is now threatened.[26]

British aristocrats, responding to the current *anglomanie* in Paris, flocked to the city and joined the cultural milieu.[27] One of the English writers who reported in the London press on Parisian musical life was Henry Fothergill Chorley (see Figure 2.5). We have seen that, as music critic of the *Athenaeum*, Chorley probably met Chopin in Paris in 1836, 1837, or 1839; the editor of the *Athenaeum*, Charles Wentworth Dilke, first employed Chorley in 1833, and prided himself on the magazine's coverage of Continental painting, drama, opera, music festivals, exploration, and scientific developments. Chorley became both music critic and Dilke's right-hand man. Not merely was Chorley a close friend of Mendelssohn and Moscheles, but he 'knew personally most of the great composers and musicians in France and Germany, visited them abroad, and carried on a wide correspondence with them'.[28] One of his most cherished friendships was with Chopin. Hewlett, writing in his *Henry Fothergill Chorley: autobiography, memoir, and letters* (1873), cites an interview between Chorley and Chopin, in which the critic described him as 'pale, thin, and profoundly melancholy'. Chorley was, however, 'gratified by hearing the composer perform a succession of characteristic *morceaux* on the piano'. 'His touch', added Chorley, 'has all the delicacy of a

Figure 2.4 Princess Marcelina Czartoryska (née Radziwill) (1817–94). Lithograph by Auguste Sandoz, 1850. Mirska and Hordyński, *Chopin na obczyźnie* (1965), p. 113

woman's, but is not so fine. *Voilà* a very impalpable distinction! but distinction for all that. No want of fire and passion, no want of neatness, if you regard the whole thing as *veiled music*, and such it is.'[29] Later, in Paris, between 1847 and 1849, notes Hewitt, Chorley 'cultivated his acquaintance with Chopin, of whom, however, he has left no record, beyond merely general expressions of gratification at their intimacy', and a sonnet published after the composer's death.[30] To which may be added Chorley's obituary of Chopin in the *Athenaeum* in 1849, and an article in *Bentley's Miscellany* the following year.[31]

Another of the celebrated salons in Paris was that of the Rothschild family, at No. 19 rue Laffitte, the home of James de Rothschild, Baron de Rothschild, and his wife Betty, the Baroness. This was a magnificent mansion, with luxurious decoration and a collection of paintings by Hals, Hobbema, Murillo, Rembrandt, Rubens, Van Dyck, and Velázquez.[32] 'That the Rothschilds patronized some of the most famous composers and performers of the nineteenth century is well known', writes Niall Ferguson, 'and the most obvious reason for this is that musicians were a prerequisite for a successful soiree or ball.'[33] Indeed, it has been suggested that Chopin's career in Paris was launched by a performance he gave at the Rothschild house in rue Laffitte in 1832.[34] 'He played there again in 1843 alongside his pupil Karl Filtsch', Ferguson continues, 'whose playing James [Rothschild] was reported to "adore".' Other notable performers who played for the Rothschilds

Figure 2.5 Henry Fothergill Chorley (1808–72). Portrait in pencil and chalk by Alfred, Count D'Orsay, 1841.

Copyright National Portrait Gallery, London

included Hallé, Liszt, Mendelssohn, and the violinist Joseph Joachim. Teaching was as significant as performing, and female Rothschilds 'were encouraged from an early age to excel at the keyboard'.[35] Chopin gave lessons to Lionel Nathan de Rothschild's wife, Charlotte, and it seems to at least one of their daughters, Leonora or Evelina. Charlotte Rothschild's *livre d'or*, which contained musical mementoes from her teachers, includes Chopin among its contributors. Chopin dedicated two compositions to Charlotte Rothschild: the Ballade in F minor (Op.52), and the Waltz in C sharp minor (Op.64, no.2).[36] A symbol of Chopin's attachment to the Rothschilds was the presentation to him by one of the family of an embroidered cushion she had made.[37]

Beyond the Rothschilds, the roll-call of Chopin's students in Paris in the 1830s and 1840s is extensive,[38] and contains some of the finest professional pianists of the day, such as Alkan, von Lenz, Mikuli, Tellefsen, and Adolf Gutmann (allegedly Chopin's favourite).[39] Aristocratic women predominated among Chopin's pupils, and often featured in his dedications, including Countess Marie d'Agoult (Twelve Studies, Op.25), Countess Apponi (Two Nocturnes, Op.27), Catherine Maberly (Three Mazurkas, Op.56), Countess Delphine Potocka (Concerto, Op.21, and Waltz, Op.64, no.1), and Princess Marcelina Czartoryska ('Krakowiak' Rondo, Op.14). As Wilhelm von Lenz observed: 'I always went to him long before my hour, and waited. One lady after another came out, each more beautiful than the others.'[40]

Princess Marcelina was one of those Parisian pupils and friends whom Chopin was to meet on his visit to Britain. Apart from Pauline Viardot, Jane Stirling, and her sister, Mrs Katherine Erskine, we may also single out Charles Hallé, the Schwabes, and Auguste and Hermann Léo, cousins of Moscheles, with their links to Manchester, as well as the English pianist Lindsay Sloper and the Irish pianist and composer George Osborne, who reported on Chopin's Manchester concert.[41] Tellefsen was in Britain in 1848 and 1849. Catherine Maberly took lessons from Chopin in London as well as Paris. Other pupils whom Chopin encountered in England or Scotland included the 'daughter of Lady Stanley' and the Countess Emilie de Flahaut (later Lady Shelburne).[42] There was also a 'lady now resident in Bedford', described by Hadden, who was 'a member of a well-known Scottish family, who had the privilege of receiving some lessons from Chopin when he was in Paris in 1846', and who attended his Glasgow concert in 1848. She was, furthermore, a 'distant cousin' of Miss Stirling, to whom she was introduced by Chopin.

In the mid-1840s, Chopin's Scottish aristocratic pupil Jane Wilhelmina Stirling, a member of a prominent Perthshire family, began to take an increasingly prominent role in the composer's life (see Figure 2.6).[43] Her dedication to him was to last until her death in 1859. Although Lindsay Sloper, who lived in Paris from 1841 to 1846, told Niecks that he gave her piano lessons and at her request, introduced her to Chopin, this seems a questionable claim.[44] According to Jean-Jacques Eigeldinger, Jane first took lessons from Chopin in 1843 or 1844, as 'the first mention of Jane Stirling's name from Chopin's pen is dated 3 January 1844, in the form of an autograph dedication on the score of the Nocturnes

Figure 2.6 Jane Wilhelmina Stirling (1804–59), with Lady Frances Anne [Fanny] Bruce (1831–94), daughter of the 7th Earl of Elgin. Lithograph by Achille Devéria, circa 1842, from Ganche, *Frédéric Chopin: sa vie et ses oeuvres, 1810–1849*, 3rd ed. (1913), opposite p. 418. Private collection

op.9.' Moreover, writes Eigeldinger, 'August 1844 was the publication date in Paris of the Nocturnes op.55, dedicated to Jane Stirling, and the Mazurkas op.56, dedicated to her friend Catherine Maberly – also Chopin's pupil. From these dates and facts we may reasonably infer that the composer probably met Miss Stirling around 1843 or, at least, on the 3rd of January 1844.'[45] It was about this time, furthermore, that Jane Stirling, assisted by Jules Benedict, apparently bought the Érard Grand Pianoforte No. 713 (London, 1843), now in the Cobbe Collection at Hatchlands, though we cannot be sure that it was supplied to her in Paris, not London (see Plate 7).[46]

A spinster, Jane Stirling seems to have been a frequent visitor to Paris, with her sister and constant companion, Mrs Katherine Erskine, widow of James Erskine, of Linlathen. Their base seems to have been a house in St Germaine-en-Laye.[47] 'I have known them a long time in Paris', Chopin told his parents in Warsaw, in 1848, 'and they take good care of me.'[48] Chopin was godfather to Albrecht's daughter Thérèse. Jane Stirling and Katherine Erskine, both homeopaths, were among the Scots patients of the Hahnemanns in Paris. Mrs Erskine's family 'was related by marriage to the Pattersons and Stirlings', writes Rima Handley. 'Members of both families called on the Hahnemanns whenever they had problems with their health, and frequently recommended the couple to their friends. As they travelled throughout Europe they carried letters and messages about symptoms and remedies between themselves and the Hahnemanns.'[49]

After Samuel Hahnemann's death in 1843, they continued to receive homeopathic treatment from his widow, Melanie.[50] Samuel's casebooks show how he developed remedies 'to deal with conditions specific, or almost so, to the ailments characteristic of women'.[51] Jane and Katherine had different problems. Hahnemann treated Jane with Sabadilla for her 'dark thoughts', and with Nitri Spiritus Dulci (alcoholised nitric ether), 'desperately seeking to help her', as her condition 'had not been ameliorated by a whole host of soporific remedies including Moschus and Nux Moschata'. For her part, Mrs Erskine, when she first visited the Hahnemanns on 24 August 1836, was forty-five years old, and had suffered from 'female' complaints for fourteen years or so. By 29 September that year, after various prescriptions from Hahnemann, Mrs Erskine reported 'general improvement', and in due course her 'immediate gynaecological problems were cleared up. She continued to return to the Hahnemanns for chronic treatment over the next several years.'[52]

Apart from herself being a student of Chopin, Jane Stirling encouraged others to take lessons from him. J. Cuthbert Hadden, in his biography of Chopin, first published in 1903, quotes from the descriptions of Jane Stirling in the two letters he received from the 'distant cousin' of hers, the 'lady now resident in Bedford'. Her letter of 27 March 1903 gives a valuable description of Chopin as a teacher. 'My first interview with Chopin took place in his rooms in Paris', she recalls:

> Miss Jane Stirling had kindly arranged that my sister and I should go with her. I remember the bright fire in his elegant and comfortable *salon*. It was in this very month of March, 1846. In the centre of the room stood two

pianofortes – one grand, the other upright. Both were Pleyel's, and the tone and touch most beautiful.

After a few moments, Chopin came in from another room and received the ladies 'with the courtesy and ease of a man accustomed to the best society. His personal appearance, his extreme fragility and delicate health have been described again and again, and also the peculiar charm of his manner'. Next, 'Miss Stirling introduced me as her *petite cousine*', the Scottish lady continued, 'who was desirous of the honour of studying with him.' The lessons which followed were a delight, and began with Beethoven's Sonata in A flat (Op.26) before moving on to Chopin's own compositions. 'These I found fascinating in the highest degree, but very difficult. He would sit patiently while I tried to thread my way through mazes of intricate and unaccustomed modulations . . . He spoke very little during the lessons', she continued. 'If I was at a loss to understand a passage, he played it slowly to me. I often wondered at his patience, for it must have been torture to listen to my bungling, but he never uttered an impatient word . . . Once or twice, he was obliged to withdraw to the other end of the room when a frightful fit of coughing came on, but he made signs to me to go on and take no notice.'[53]

Another telling anecdote featuring Jane Stirling in Paris is told by Anne Isabella Thackeray, known as 'Anny', who became Lady Ritchie, elder of the two surviving daughters of William Makepeace Thackeray. It appears in her book *Chapters from some memoirs*, published in 1894. During the 1840s, due to the mental illness of their mother, Anny and her sister Minnie were sent to stay in Paris with their grandparents, Major and Mrs Henry Carmichael-Smyth. One winter, when she was still a young girl, Anny was taken to visit Chopin by Jane Stirling.[54]

In her *Memoirs*, in a chapter entitled 'My musician', Anny remembered 'three Scotch ladies, for whom my grandmother had a great regard, who were not part of our community, but who used to pass through Paris, and always made a certain stay'. Anny was 'very much afraid of them, though interested at the same time as girls are in unknown quantities. They were well connected and had estates and grand relations in the distance, though they seemed to live as simply as we did.'

When it was announced that the 'Scotch ladies' had 'taken an apartment for a few weeks', Anny was sent to see them, with a note of introduction from her grandmother, Mrs Carmichael-Smyth. 'They were tall, thin ladies, two were widows, one was a spinster; of the three the unmarried one [i.e., Jane Stirling] frightened me most', Anny wrote. One of the widows was surely Mrs Katherine Erskine,[55] and the other Jane and Katherine's friend, Mrs Mary Rich, aunt of Fanny Erskine. Jane Stirling indicated that she had to go to see Chopin that morning, and at this point 'a servant came in carrying a large basket with a variety of bottles and viands and napkins.' Not having the 'presence of mind to run away', as she longed to do, Anny in few minutes found herself

> sitting in a little open carriage with the Scotch lady, and the basket on the opposite seat. I thought her, if possible, more terrible than ever – she seemed grave, preoccupied. She had a long nose, a thick brown complexion, greyish

48 *Paris 1840s: interlude*

sandy hair, and was dressed in scanty cloth skirts, grey and sandy too. She spoke to me, I believe, but my heart was in my mouth; I hardly dared listen to what she said.

The carriage stopped at the door of Chopin's house, and Jane 'got out, carefully carrying her heavy basket, and told me to follow, and we began to climb the shiny stairs'. After ringing a bell, the door was almost instantly opened 'by a slight, delicate-looking man with long hair, bright eyes, and a thin, hooked nose'.

When Jane Stirling saw him, reports Anny,

> she hastily put down her basket upon the floor, caught both hands in hers, began to shake them gently, and to scold him in an affectionate reproving way for having come to the door. He laughed, said he had guessed who it was, and motioned her to enter, and I followed at her sign with the basket, – followed into a narrow little room, with no furniture in it whatever but an upright piano against the wall and a few straw chairs standing on the wooden shiny floor.

Chopin beckoned his guests 'with some courtesy' to sit down, and indicated that he was 'pretty well':

> Had he slept? He shook his head. Had he eaten? He shrugged his shoulders and pointed to the piano. He had been composing something – I remember that he spoke in an abrupt, light sort of way – would Miss X. [i.e., Jane Stirling] like to hear it? "She would like to hear it", she answered, "of course, she would dearly like to hear it; but it would tire him to play; it could not be good for him." He smiled again, shook back his long hair, and sat down immediately; and then the music began, and the room filled with continuous sound, he looking over his shoulder now and then to see if we were liking it.

The effect on Jane Stirling, Anny reports, was immediate: Jane 'sat absorbed and listening, and as I looked at her I saw tears in her eyes – great clear tears rolling down her cheeks, while the music poured on and on'. Alas, to her own dismay, Anny could not recall details of the music. When Chopin at last stopped playing, and looked around, Jane 'started up':

> "You mustn't play any more", she said; "no more, no more, it's too beautiful" – and she praised him and thanked him in a tender, motherly, pitying sort of way, and then hurriedly said we must go; but as we took leave she added almost in a whisper with a humble apologising look, – "I have brought you some of that jelly, and my sister sent some of the wine you fancied the other day; pray, pray, try to take a little."

Chopin 'again shook his head at her, seeming more vexed than grateful. "It is very wrong; you shouldn't bring me these things", he said in French. "I won't play to you if you do", – but she put him back softly, and hurriedly closed the door upon him and the offending basket, and hastened away.' As Anny and Jane Stirling left Chopin, and were going downstairs, Jane 'wiped her eyes again'. Anny's response was sympathetic. She had been won over. 'By this time I had got to understand the plain, tall, grim, warm-hearted woman; all my silly terrors were gone. She looked hard at me as we drove away. "Never forget that you have heard Chopin play", she said with emotion, "for soon no one will hear him play any more." ' Looking back, Anny Ritchie 'remembered this little scene with comfort and pleasure', in the knowledge that Chopin 'was not altogether alone in life, and that he had good friends who cared for his genius and tended him to the last'.

In Paris, Chopin had many 'good friends who cared for his genius', some of whom he was later to encounter in Britain. Apart from Jane Stirling and Katherine Erskine, and his fellow-musicians, these included Mrs Harriet Grote, who met Chopin at Mme Marliani's,[56] and Salis and Julie Schwabe, who were to entertain the composer in Manchester. Evidence of the Schwabes' friendship with Chopin in Paris appears in the diary of Fanny Erskine – a distant relative of the Stirlings, and niece of Mrs Mary Rich – part of which covers her two-month stay in Paris, from December 1847 to January 1848.[57] Fanny, then living with her parents in Bonn, was a keen amateur singer, and one of her purposes in visiting Paris was to have lessons with the renowned teacher Manuel García, brother of Maria Malibran and Pauline Viardot. García taught at the Paris Conservatoire from 1847 to 1850, before moving to the Royal Academy of Music, where he was active until 1895. Jeremy Barlow, who first published extracts from Fanny Erskine's diary in 1994, explains that 'interspersed between passages of religious introspection and accounts of sightseeing, shopping and social engagements, are descriptions not only of the thirteen lessons she received from García, but also of four meetings with Chopin.' Furthermore, 'the names of Jane Stirling and her sister Mrs Katherine Erskine appear on almost every page, and there are references to concerts, operas and domestic music-making.'

Fanny had arrived in Paris on Wednesday 1 December 1847, in the company of her widowed aunt, Mrs Mary Rich, and 'the two were received as guests of the Schwabe family, who had rented part of a house on the Champs Élysées.' Later, Chopin dedicated a single-stave transcription of the song 'Wiosna' to Fanny when staying with the Schwabes in 1848 at Crumpsall House, Manchester, where Mary Rich was also a guest.[58] 'The Schwabes emerge from the diary as cultured and musical', writes Jeremy Barlow, 'and together with Mary Rich appear to have had many acquaintances in Parisian artistic and intellectual society.'[59]

At the Schwabes' house, Fanny Erskine also encountered Chopin's Norwegian pupil, Thomas Tellefsen, who had settled in Paris in 1842 (see Figure 2.7). Fanny thought him memorable, 'a wild looking genius, quite devoted to Chopin'. Indeed, she adds,

> I thought him like the pictures of Schiller and he evidently found a likeness to me, for I caught him scrutinizing me once or twice & at last he asked if he

Figure 2.7 Thomas Dyke Acland Tellefsen (1823–74). Portrait from Tellefsen, *Thomas Tellefsens familiebreve* (1923), frontispiece (circa 1860). Private collection

[had] not seen me somewhere before, bolting out of the room looking rather confused and awkward.[60]

When, the following day, Fanny met Jane Stirling and Katherine Erskine, they were, as expected, 'energetic and earnest'. That evening, Tellefsen again visited the Schwabes. He 'enchanted us all', Fanny writes. 'He played principally Chopin, so wild & touching & was delighted with my Jenny Lind songs . . . His music was a great treat.'[61]

Three days after Tellefsen played at the Schwabes', on Monday 6 December 1847, Fanny Erskine met Chopin again when she and Mary Rich dined at Katherine Erskine's house in Paris, one imagines shared with her sister, Jane. The only other guest was Chopin, 'of whom Miss Jane Stirling made much'. His impression on Fanny was unforgettable. 'He is such an interesting looking man but Oh! so suffering, & so much younger than I had expected.' Thoughts of Mendelssohn, who had died that year, made him melancholic. 'He exerted himself to talk at dinner', Fanny wrote, and 'seemed so interested in Mendelssohn & the honors paid to his memory in London but said there was something almost enviable in his fate dying in the midst of his family surrounded by love – & with his wife beside him – & having lived so purely happy a life.' At which point, Chopin 'looked so sad'. Even so, Chopin was 'so happy to see Aunt Mary again, [and] he grew quite *playful* & seemed to forget his suffering'.[62]

After Fanny had sung for Chopin, and he had indicated that he would recommend her to García, he sat down to play Jane Stirling's 'new Érard'.

> Anything so pure & *heavenly*, & delicate I never heard – & *so* mournful; his music is so like himself – & so original in its sadness. The feeling awakened in my heart listening to him was like that inspired by Jenny Lind . . . I was quite sorry to come away but had his exquisite harmonies in my heart for long.[63]

Four days later, on Friday 10 December, Jane Stirling and Katherine Erskine dined with Fanny and her Aunt Mary, Jane bringing a summons from García for Fanny to come for a singing lesson the next day. 'It was very kind of Chopin to manage it all so nicely & quickly for me', Fanny wrote. Fanny then began a course of lessons with García, held twice a week until 22 January 1848, the last entry in the diary.[64]

On Thursday 16 December, six days afterwards, Fanny had her second encounter with Chopin, over an evening meal at Katherine Erskine's. 'He spoke so pleasantly all dinner & seems so *simply true*, with a keen sense of the good & beautiful & full of imagination', Fanny noted. When Salis and Julie Schwabe came, 'he talked more generally & pretty late played – Oh! so exquisitely[.] Such bursts of feeling & passion[.] Such shakes!'[65] Fanny's third meeting with Chopin occurred on Wednesday 12 January 1848, when she picked up 'Miss Stirling & Miss Hall' to take them to Chopin's for a lesson. 'Such a *bijou* of a room & such a lesson I envied it.'[66]

The next day, Thursday 13 January, Fanny went over to Mrs Erskine's to hear Auguste Franchomme accompany Jane Stirling on the cello, and was duly impressed: 'How richly & fully he made it *sing* out!' Later that evening, after dinner, Fanny, with Mary Rich, returned to Katherine Erskine's house for what proved to be Fanny's last meeting with Chopin during her stay in Paris. 'Chopin played for a long time so splendidly & was quite frisky after[,] making rabbits on the wall & shewing off his various accomplishments.'[67] Visitors also included Tellefsen and the portrait painter George Richmond (for whom Fanny sat at least three times), and 'Miss Trotter' – who, Fanny's diary records, had commissioned a sketch of Chopin from Winterhalter, 'as a New Year's Day present for Jane Stirling ('great will be her joy!') for *whatever* it might cost'. As it turned out, 'Miss Trotter' had to pay 800 francs, 'Chopin helping her', although he was 'shocked at the price'.[68] On Saturday 22 January, Fanny received a letter from her mother, Maitland Erskine, summoning her home to Bonn. Her Paris sojourn was over.[69]

Another of the musical salons in Paris was that kept by Auguste and Sophie Léo. It was attended, Jean-Jacques Eigeldinger explains, 'notably by German musicians staying in or passing through Paris: Meyerbeer, Mendelssohn, Hiller, Hallé, Clara Wieck, Heller, and Moscheles, who met Chopin there in October 1839'.[70] 'It is at the Léos that I most enjoy playing', Moscheles wrote.[71] Auguste Léo, a Hamburg banker who was based in Paris from 1817 to 1848, was a cousin of Moscheles, and brother of Hermann Léo, the Manchester industrialist and patron of music who was instrumental in bringing Hallé to that city. Chopin was close to Auguste Léo for his entire stay in Paris, and acted as his financial advisor and intermediary with English and German editors. Although Auguste Léo was a devoted friend of Chopin, and his family was always kind to him,[72] the composer was not beyond referring to Auguste as a 'scoundrel' and 'a Jew!'[73] Léo is mentioned frequently in Chopin's letters (addressed to him in Paris at No. 11 rue Louis-le-Grand) and the composer acknowledges his love of music by dedicating to him his Polonaise in A flat major (Op.53), the *Grande polonaise brillante*. Writing to Léo from Nohant on 8 July 1845, Chopin remarks that he always thinks of him 'when [his] mind is on beautiful music, so you can imagine how often that is, now that we have Mme Viardot with us'.[74]

Auguste Léo's wife, Sophie Augustine Léo (née Dellevie), was born in Hamburg in 1795, and first met Chopin in Paris in 1832.[75] Her memoirs, originally published anonymously in Berlin in 1851 as *Erinnerungen aus Paris (1817–1848)*, cast light on Chopin's life in Paris. Sophie was entranced by him:

> A delicate, graceful, most attractive figure, the man was a mere breath, a spiritual, rather than a corporeal being, and, like his music, harmony itself. His speech, in keeping with his art, was gentle, vibrant, ringing, a concordant blend of the Romance and Slavic inflections inherited from a French father and a Polish mother. He appeared hardly to touch the piano; one might have thought an instrument superfluous.

Yet, despite these gifts,

> Chopin was gracious, modest, and unassuming. He was not a pianist of the modern school, but, in his own way, had created a style of his own, a style that one cannot describe. Whether appearing in the private salon or in the concert hall he stepped quietly and modestly to the piano, was satisfied with whatever seat had been provided, showed at once by his simple dress and natural bearing that all forms of affectation and charlatanry were distasteful to him and, without any sort of introduction, at once began his soulful and heartfelt performance.'[76]

Sophie's sister and her husband, M. et Mme Valentin, were also supporters of music and the fine arts in Paris, as were many others. Charles Hallé remarks that Chopin, despite his 'growing weakness' still used to visit 'principally Count de Perthuis, the banker Auguste Léo, Mallet, and a few other houses'; as Hallé had been introduced to all three, he 'enjoyed the privilege of being invited to their "*réunions intimes*", when Chopin, who avoided large parties, was to be present'.[77] The Léos returned to Germany when the February Revolution broke out in 1848, but were back in France in 1852, living at Versailles.[78]

Private performances for the Schwabes, the Léos, and others, were part of Chopin's daily life in Paris.[79] However, as the year turned, Chopin was persuaded to give another public recital in the Salons Pleyel; the concert, held on 16

February 1848, included the last three movements of Chopin's Sonata in G minor for piano and cello (Op.65), played with Franchomme, to whom it was dedicated, and Mozart's Piano Trio in E major (K 542), performed with Franchomme and the violinist Jean-Delphin Alard. Chopin himself played some of his études, preludes, mazurkas, and waltzes. The tenor Gustave-Hippolyte Roger sang the prayer from *Robert le diable*, and the Spanish mezzo-soprano Antonia di Mendi (cousin of Pauline Viardot and Maria Malibran) also contributed. The *Revue et gazette musicale* reported the event enthusiastically, singling out Chopin for especial praise. 'We won't attempt to describe the infinite nuances of an extraordinary genius who has such powers at his command', wrote the reviewer. 'We will state only that his charm never ceased for an instant to hold his audience completely entranced and that its spell lingered after the concert itself was over.'[80] This was Chopin's last concert in Paris. For, although its success prompted him to consider a sequel, provisionally booked for March, politics intervened before this could take place.

The February Revolution has been called the 'revolution of the intellectuals', involving as it did many leading writers and artists who supported the liberal cause, demand for reform, and need for radical change.[81] The events which led to George Sand's return to Paris, in a fever of excitement, held little appeal for Chopin. Moreover, members of Parisian society who employed musicians such as Chopin had largely fled the capital.[82] The Stirling sisters were returning to London and to their family in Scotland, and Chopin was attracted by the proposal that he join them there. Jane Stirling, born in 1804, the same year as George Sand, may have hoped that she would step into the role recently vacated by her. To Chopin, the appeal of London, to be visited en route to and from Scotland, was considerable, and both in the metropolis and north of the Border he would be welcomed by friends from Paris. Chopin decided to go. On the Wednesday of Holy Week, 19 April, he left for England.

Notes

1 See Eigeldinger, 'Chopin and Pleyel', p. 389.
2 For his addresses in Paris, see Introduction.
3 For background, see Atwood, *Parisian worlds*, *passim*; Locke, 'Paris: centre of intellectual ferment', *passim*; and Weber, *Music and the middle class*, pp. 80–6.
4 See Samson, *Chopin*, pp. 141–7. For Chopin and Sand at Valldemosa, see, for instance, Ripoll, *Chopin's winter in Majorca*, *passim*. The contents of the museum at Valldemosa are described in the writings of Bożena Adamczyk-Schmid, e.g., in 'Katalog Zbiorów Muzeum Fryderyka Chopina', *passim*. Before his death, Arthur Hedley sold most of his extensive Chopin material to Valldemosa; for Adam Harasowski's comments on this collection, see his article 'Arthur Hedley', *passim*.
5 This Pleyel, of circa 1835 (Serial No. 6,668), is described in Clinkscale, *Makers of the piano*, vol.2, p. 295. For illustrations of it, see Burger, *Chopin*, pp. 201–2 (plates 438, 439). A similar instrument, called a 'Pleyel upright pianino', of 1835, is described and illustrated in Colt and Miall, *The early piano*, pp. 108–10.
6 Hedley, *Chopin correspondence*, p. 168. The French and English editions of Chopin's Preludes (Op.28), first published in 1839, were dedicated to Camille Pleyel, and the German edition, of the same year, to J.C. Kessler. See Platzman, *A descriptive catalogue*, pp. 121–6.

54   *Paris 1840s: interlude*

7   For a description of the architecture of Nohant, see Brem, *La maison de George Sand à Nohant*, *passim*.
8   For visitors to Nohant, see Delaigue-Moins, *Chopin chez George Sand*, *passim*, and Delaigue-Moins, *Les hôtes de George Sand à Nohant*, *passim*. For pictorial coverage of Sand and her milieu, see Reid and Tillier, *L'ABCdaire de George Sand*, *passim*. For Sand's views on music, see the entry on her by Louis Bilodeau in Fauquet, *Dictionnaire de la musique en France au XIXe siècle*, p. 1118, and Powell, *While the music lasts*, *passim*.
9   The reconstructed set piece of Sand's dining room of guests-at-table at Nohant has no place for Chopin.
10 Had Chopin not fallen out with George Sand, and spent the summer of 1848 being cosseted at Nohant rather than adrift in Scotland, one wonders at the compositions he might have written.
11 For Viardot, see particularly Eigeldinger, *Chopin vu par ses élèves*, pp. 239–41, and the entry on Viardot by Beatrix Borchard in *Grove music online*. For Viardot and Chopin, see, generally, Berger, 'Histoire d'une amitié Pauline Viardot – Frédéric Chopin', *passim*.
12 For Parisian salons, see Atwood, *Parisian worlds*, pp. 101–36, and Tunley, *Salons, singers and songs*, especially pp. 18–57, Appendix A, and Appendix E (which is an extract from Jules Janin's *The American in Paris* (London, 1843)). Tunley considers Viardot's salon on pp. 47–9.
13 Viardot is here being taught at an upright piano. This drawing, and one of Chopin by Viardot (1844), are illustrated in Eigeldinger, *Chopin vu par ses élèves*, plates 8, 9.
14 See Waddington, *Musical works of Pauline Viardot-Garcia*, pp. 9–10. This concert is discussed in Atwood, *Pianist from Warsaw*, pp. 138–42, and FitzLyon, *Price of genius*, pp. 129–30. The programme for it is reproduced in Tomaszweski and Weber, *Diary in images*, p. 189. Josef Dessauer, the Bohemian composer, was the dedicatee of Chopin's Polonaises in C sharp minor and E flat major (Op.26). He was a friend of George Sand, who nicknamed him '*Maître Favilla*'. For Dessauer, see the article by John Warrack and James Deauville in *Grove music online*.
15 For Viardot's settings, see Cook and Tsou, *Anthology of songs*, pp. ix–x, 32–84. The words here are, variously, in French, German, Italian, and Russian. A selection of Viardot's settings of French and Spanish texts is in Chiti and Paton, *Songs and duets*, pp. 50–92.
16 Viardot's publications are considered again in Chapter 4 of *Chopin in Britain*.
17 For a synopsis of Delacroix's career, see the entry on him in Chilvers, *Oxford dictionary of art and artists*, pp. 171–2.
18 See Azoury, *Chopin through his contemporaries*, pp. 198–9, n.22, which contains a summary of Chopin's friendship with Delacroix.
19 See, for example, Prideaux, *The world of Delacroix*, pp. 145–6. Jean-Jacques Eigeldinger records that Delacroix bought a Pleyel in 1839, and Viardot purchased a Pleyel, on behalf on George Sand, in 1849. See Eigeldinger, 'Chopin et la manufacture Pleyel', p. 106.
20 See Delacroix, *Journal, 1822–1863*, *passim*, and Wright, *Cambridge companion to Delacroix*, p. 2. On p. 191, n.10, Wright cites as her Chopin source Roger Delage's essay, 'Delacroix et la musique', pp. 129–40. See also the essay on Delacroix by J-M Fauquet, in Fauquet, *Dictionnaire de la musique en France au XIXe siècle*, pp. 367–8, and the chapter 'The music of a picture', in Lockspeiser, *Music and painting*, pp. 37–48.
21 Letter from Delacroix of 1842, quoted by Hedley, *Chopin*, pp. 86–7. Hedley does not name the recipient.
22 For the architecture of the Hôtel Lambert, see Bordier, *Louis Le Vau*, pp. 133–68, and Feldmann, 'Maison Lambert', *passim*. The opulence of he interiors can be envisaged

Paris 1840s: interlude 55

from, for example, the two-volume sale catalogue, *Collection du Baron De Redé provenant de l'Hôtel Lambert*, Sotheby's, Paris, 16–17 March 2005, and Servat, 'Guy de Rothschild : le dernier départ', pp. 84–7.

23 See Zamoyski, 'Paris', p. 93. For Prince Adam Czartoryski, including his period at the Hôtel Lambert, see Kukiel, *Czartoryski and European unity, passim*, with references on pp. 227–8 to its purchase by Czartoryski in 1843. In view of this date, it is incorrect to imply, as some authorities do, that Chopin played at the Hôtel Lambert as early as the 1830s.

24 See Atwood, *Parisian worlds*, pp. 52–6.

25 For this paragraph, see Zamoyski, 'Paris', pp. 93–4.

26 In 2009, a proposal to convert the building, 'subject to the demands of a modern luxury residence', was opposed by the Mayor of Paris, and members of the *Association pour la Sauvegarde et Mise en Valeur du Paris Historique*.

27 See Atwood, *Parisian worlds*, pp. 146–50.

28 Marchand, *The Athenaeum*, p. 48.

29 Quoted by Hewlett, *Chorley*, vol.1, pp. 303–5. Chorley believed that, unlike Mendelssohn's, Chopin's sensibility was 'feminine'. See also the Chopin references in Bledsoe, *Chorley*, pp. 141, 144, 145, 324.

30 Hewlett, *Chorley*, vol.2, pp. 94–5. The poem 'Chopin' is on p. 95. A transcript of it is given in Bledsoe, *Chorley*, p. 179.

31 *Athenaeum*, 27 October 1849 (no.1148, p. 1090), and *Bentley's Miscellany*, February 1850 (pp. 185–91), cited in Bledsoe, *Chorley*, pp. 178–9.

32 See the descriptions in Atwood, *Parisian worlds*, pp. 15, 121–3, and Heuberger, *The Rothschilds*, pp. 67–8, 109–10.

33 Ferguson, *World's banker*, p. 363. See here, pp. 363–5, and accompanying documentation, for Chopin's connections with the Rothschilds in Paris. See also Atwood, *Parisian worlds, passim*.

34 Ferguson, *World's banker*, p. 363. Atwood, *Parisian worlds*, p. 45, notes that Chopin had been introduced to the Rothschilds by his friend Prince Walenty Radziwiłł. Steen, *The great composers*, p. 373, also makes connections between Chopin and the Radziwiłłs and Rothschilds.

35 Ferguson, *World's banker*, p. 363.

36 Ferguson, *World's banker*, p. 363. See also the references to the Rothschilds in Holland, 'Chopin's teaching and his students', p. 130. Three letters from Mme Charlotte de Rothschild to Chopin appear in abridged form in Karłowicz, *Souvenirs*, p. 141. For biographical material on Charlotte, see Weintraub, *Charlotte and Lionel, passim*.

Atwood, *Parisian worlds*, pp. 19, 45, 114, 121–3, maintains that Betty de Rothschild was also a pupil of Chopin. However, this seems uncertain. Ferguson states (p. 364) that Chopin gave lessons 'not only to [Lionel] Nathan's daughter Charlotte, but also to her daughter Hannah Matthilde, and to Betty's daughter, another Charlotte'. There is some ambiguity here. The Rothschild Archive, London, has yet to yield its secrets on this and other matters connected with Chopin.

37 See Niecks, *Chopin*, vol.2, p. 135n.

38 See the pupils documented in Eigeldinger, *Chopin vu par ses élèves, passim*, and Jeanne Holland's PhD dissertation, 'Chopin's teaching and his students', supplemented by her articles, 'Chopin the teacher', and 'Chopin's piano method'. See also Bronarski, 'Les élèves de Chopin', *passim*; Jaeger, 'Quelques nouveaux noms d'élèves de Chopin', *passim*; and Methuen-Campbell, *Chopin playing*, pp. 40–4. Details of Chopin's lessons are in his pocket diary for 1848, TiFC (Warsaw), M/378.

39 For fellow-pianists in Paris, see Pistone, 'Pianistes et concerts parisiens au temps de Frédéric Chopin', *passim*; and Lenz, *Great piano virtuosos of our time* (Baker), *passim*. We have two letters from Chopin to Gutmann, sent from London and Calder House, respectively, in 1848, but none to any other pianist.

56   Paris 1840s: interlude

40   Lenz, *Great piano virtuosos of our time* (Baker), p. 50.
41   See Eigeldinger, *Chopin: pianist and teacher*, p. 180, and Eigeldinger, *Chopin vu par ses élèves*, p. 232.
42   Hadden, *Chopin*, pp. 144–8 [147–8]. Letter of 18 March 1903. See also the letter of 27 March 1903, on pp. 185–8, describing a lesson with Chopin. She is the 'Anonymous Scottish lady' quoted in Eigeldinger, *Chopin: pianist and teacher*, p. 161, and Eigeldinger, *Chopin vu par ses élèves*, p. 209. See also the descriptions in Atwood, *Parisian worlds*, pp. 15, 121–3, and Heuberger, *The Rothschilds*, pp. 67–8, 109–10.
43   For the Stirlings generally, see Appendix A of my thesis, 'Chopin in Britain', and the entries for the individual members of the family in the Personalia section there. For a selection of sources of documentation for Jane Stirling and Chopin, see Eigeldinger, *Chopin vu par ses élèves*, pp. 232–3. An invaluable guide to Eigeldinger's research on Chopin is 'Publications de Jean-Jacques Eigeldinger', in Waeber, *La note bleue*, pp. 367–75.
44   Niecks, *Chopin*. vol.2, p. 291. Niecks cautions in a note that '[Sloper's] memory was not of the most trustworthy'.
45   Eigeldinger, *Chopin: pianist and teacher*, p. 180. 'An opinion held by Harasowski', Eigeldinger adds. In French, see Eigeldinger, *Chopin vu par ses élèves*, pp. 232–3.
46   See Cobbe, *Composer instruments*, pp. 51–3.
47   Samson, *Chopin*, p. 253.
48   Hedley, *Chopin correspondence*, p. 336. Chopin to his family in Warsaw, [10–19 August 1848].
49   Handley, *A homeopathic love story*, p. 119.
50   Handley, *In search of the later Hahnemann*, p. 114.
51   Handley, *In search of the later Hahnemann*, pp. 64, 86.
52   Handley, *A homeopathic love story*, p. 121. The gruesome description of her medical history is on pp. 119–21. See also the references to Mrs Erskine in Handley, *A homeopathic love story*, pp. 10, 132, 162, and Handley, *In search of the later Hahnemann* pp. 20, 21, 24, 115, 125, 126, 127. Mrs Erskine, who had married in 1811, had been widowed in 1816, having given birth to four daughters, according to Audrey Bone, but 'each died within four days of birth'. See Bone, *Jane Stirling*, p. 8.
53   Hadden, *Chopin*, pp. 185–7. By 'petite cousine', Jane Stirling presumably meant first cousin once removed, or second cousin.
54   The following text is taken from Ritchie, *Chapters from some memoirs*, pp. 23–8. This volume was initially published in London in 1894 by Macmillan, who brought out a Macmillan's Colonial Library version in London and New York in 1895. It is this edition which is quoted here. The anecdote is recorded in an abbreviated form by Edith Hipkins in *How Chopin played* (pp. 14–15), but she gives no source. The 'Scotch lady' in the incident is identified simply as 'Miss X.', but Edith Hipkins assumes, surely correctly, that this is Jane Stirling. Gérin, *Anne Thackeray Ritchie*, pp. 34–5, where the description of the visit also appears, suggests that it that it took place in 1847, when the Thackeray children were briefly in Paris. For Anny in Paris see Ritchie, *Journals and letters*, pp. 1–10.
55   On 10–19 August 1848, Chopin observed in a letter to his family in Warsaw that Mrs Rich 'is a great friend of both myself and the Stirlings and Erskines'. See Hedley, *Chopin correspondence*, p. 339.
56   Hedley, *Chopin correspondence*, p. 334. Chopin to his family in Warsaw [10–19 August 1848].
57   Barlow, 'Encounters with Chopin', p. 245, for this and the following quotations. Fanny Erskine was Jeremy Barlow's great-great-grandmother. The diary entries are discussed in Samson, *Chopin*, pp. 251–2.
58   For details of versions of 'Wiosna' (published posthumously as Op.74, no.2), see Kobylańska, *RUC*, vol.1, pp. 434–40. See Chapter 5 of *Chopin in Britain*, note 43.

59 Barlow, 'Encounters with Chopin', p. 246.
60 Barlow, 'Encounters with Chopin', p. 246.
61 Barlow, 'Encounters with Chopin', p. 246.
62 Barlow, 'Encounters with Chopin', p. 246. The underlining here and elsewhere is taken from the diary itself.
63 Barlow, 'Encounters with Chopin', pp. 246–7.
64 Barlow, 'Encounters with Chopin', p. 247.
65 Barlow, 'Encounters with Chopin', p. 247. Fanny later refers to Angelica Catalani, the Italian soprano who, on a visit to Warsaw in 1820, gave the ten-year-old Chopin a gold watch with an engraved inscription. The incident is recorded in Niecks, *Chopin*, vol.1, p. 34, and the watch described in Wróblewska-Straus, *Chopin. Fame resounding far and wide*, item 105.
66 Barlow, 'Encounters with Chopin', pp. 247–8. The identity of 'Miss Hall' has not been ascertained. Perhaps she, too, was a pupil of Chopin?
67 Barlow, 'Encounters with Chopin', p. 248.
68 Barlow, 'Encounters with Chopin', p. 247. 'Miss Trotter' may also have been a pupil of Chopin. This refers to one of two pencil portraits of Chopin by Winterhalter, both dated 1847. See Wróblewska-Straus, *Chopin: fame resounding far and wide*, item 175. In Tomaszewski and Weber, *Diary in images*, p. 224, there is an illustration of the second portrait, commissioned by Jane Stirling, now in the Collegium Maius, Cracow.
69 Barlow, 'Encounters with Chopin', p. 248.
70 Eigeldinger, *Chopin: pianist and teacher*, p. 279, n.16.
71 Quoted by Strunk, in Léo, 'Musical life in Paris (1817–1848)', p. 259.
72 Azoury, *Chopin through his contemporaries*, p. 177.
73 See Hedley, *Chopin correspondence*, p. 166. Chopin to Fontana, 28 December 1838. 'Leo is a Jew!' Chopin exclaims. This letter, written from Valldemosa, describes Chopin's trials as he tries to deal with his personal affairs from Mallorca, and awaits the release of his Pleyel piano from customs.
74 Hedley, *Chopin correspondence*, p. 247.
75 For Sophie Léo, see Eigeldinger, *Chopin vu par ses élèves*, pp. 352–3, and the 'Translator's Note' by W. Oliver Strunk, in Léo, 'Musical life in Paris (1817–1848)', p. 259.
76 Léo, 'Musical life in Paris (1817–1848)', p. 402. Sophie Léo's personal assessment of Chopin appears on pp. 401–3 here; it was, of course, not published until after the composer's death. See also p. 401 for references to Liszt, Thalberg, and Hallé.
77 Hallé, *Life and letters*, p. 32, continuing on p. 33 with a description by Hallé of Chopin and their friendship. The reference to 'Mallet' is to the Parisian banking family of that name; in 1840, on Hallé's arrival in Paris, he and Chopin were both invited to dinner by 'Mallet', presumably Adolphe-Jacques Mallet, Régent de la Banque de France. See Niecks, *Chopin*, vol.2, p. 171. Guizot's connections with the Mallets are touched on in Guizot, *Lettres à sa fille, Henriette*, pp. 270, 271, 303, 667, 695, 756, 758, 809, 860, 862.
78 Strunk, in Léo, 'Musical life in Paris (1817–1848)', p. 259. Chopin's published correspondence includes letters between Gryzmała and Auguste Léo.
79 For this paragraph, see Samson, *Chopin*, p. 252.
80 *Revue et gazette musicale*, 20 February 1848, in English translation from Atwood, *Pianist from Warsaw*, pp. 244–5.
81 This paragraph relies on Samson, *Chopin*, pp. 252–4.
82 See Hallé, *Life and letters*, p. 229.

3 London 1848
Chopin in London

Between Chopin's first visit to London in 1837 and his second in 1848, his reputation in Britain seems to have grown. Friends such as Franz Liszt, whose correspondence is peppered with references to artists whom he was promoting, took up the cudgels on Chopin's behalf. Thus, when in London in 1840, Liszt remarked in a letter to Marie d'Agoult on 29 May that 'Wessel, who has published Chopin's collected works and is losing more than 200 louis on them, has come to ask me to play some of his pieces, to make them known. As yet, no one has dared risk it.' Liszt promised to play Chopin's études, mazurkas, and nocturnes when the occasion arose. 'You can tell him that when you see him', Liszt added. 'I am delighted to be able to do him this small service . . . This will encourage Wessel to buy other manuscripts from him. The poor publisher is rather tired of publishing without selling.'[1]

Although Chopin's music was not well known, except in purely musical circles, his reputation has preceded him to London,[2] even though, writes Niecks, 'Billet, Osborne, Kalkbrenner, Hallé, and especially Thalberg, who came about the same time across the channel, caused more curiosity.'[3]

Chopin's arrival in the capital on 20 April 1848, Maunday Thursday, had been heralded by Chorley in the *Athenaeum*. In the issue of 8 April (no.1067, p. 374) he comments that 'among the most recent arrivals from Paris' are the violinist Friedrich Hermann and the pianist George Osborne. However, he continues, 'the amateurs and professors of the pianoforte will hear with still greater interest that M. Chopin is expected, if not already here.' Perhaps, indeed, he may 'remain in England'. 'M. Chopin's visit', adds Chorley, 'is an event for which we heartily thank the French Republic.' Three weeks later, in its issue of 29 April, the *Athenaeum* (no.1070, p. 444) reported that Chopin, Jenny Lind, and Kalkbrenner were all in London.

According to Arthur Hedley, Chopin brought a large number of letters of introduction with him to London; most were delivered to their addressees, but Chopin kept the one to Samuel Carter Hall, journalist and writer, and editor of the *Art-Union: Monthly Journal of the Fine Arts* (from 1849 known as the *Art Journal*). In his letter to Hall, Charles Gavard, the French writer and diplomat, observes that 'Chopin is very modest and is afraid that certain persons might try to exploit his name – at least so it seems to me. I would ask you to take care of him in that respect – no one can advise him better than you, and if it is felt that some newspapers should write about him, let it be a paper like yours.'[4]

Among others, three letters of introduction, dated 11 April 1848, were written in Paris on behalf of Chopin by Dimitri de Obrescoff, whose wife Natalia was a friend of Jane Stirling, and greatly admired by Chopin; her daughter, Princess Catherine de Souzzo, was one of his pupils and the dedicatee of his Fantasia in F minor (Op.49). One letter was addressed to the wife of Baron Philip Graf von Brunnow, Russian diplomat, Ambassador in London of the Russian Imperial Court; the second, it seems, to Henry Bingham Baring, the politician; and the third, apparently, to Robert Henry Herbert, 12th Earl of Pembroke and 9th Earl of Montgomery.[5]

Opinions varied on the character and extent of Chopin's musical reputation in England in 1848. Niecks observes that

> in those days, and for a long time after, the appreciation and cultivation of Chopin's music was in England confined to a select few. Mr. Hipkins told me that he 'had to struggle for years to gain adherents to Chopin's music, while enduring the good-humoured banter of Sterndale Bennett and J W Davison.'[6]

The battle fought in the *Musical World* in 1841 illustrates the prevailing difference of opinion; hostilities began on 28 October with a criticism of the Four Mazurkas (Op.41) which described Chopin (among many negative observations) as 'a dealer in the most absurd and hyperbolical extravagances'.[7] Chopin's publishers, Wessel & Stapleton, protested against this criticism, and adduced the opinions of numerous musicians in support of their own views. A vigorous correspondence ensued.[8]

Two years later, in 1843, Wessel & Stapleton published *An essay on the works of Frederic Chopin*, by the music critic J.W. Davison, in which he strongly supported the composer against his critics.[9] Indeed his language is effusive, almost embarrassingly so:

> Chopin does not carry off your feelings by storm, and leave you in a mingled maze of wonder and dismay; he lulls your senses in the most delicious repose, intoxicates them with bewitching and unceasing melody, clad in the richest and most exquisite harmony – a harmony which abounds in striking and original features, in new and unexpected combinations
>
> (p. 2).

Davison considers Chopin's concertos, studies, and mazurkas – those 'charming bagatelles' which have been made widely known in England by the eminent pianists 'who enthusiastically admire, and universally recommend them to their pupils' (p. 4).[10]

As for the nocturnes, 'to hear one of these eloquent streams of pure loveliness ... is the very transcendency of musical delight' (p. 5). Chopin's polonaises 'are remarkable for a boldness of phraseology, a decision of character, a masterly continuousness of purpose, and a sparkling brilliancy of passage' (p. 5). Waltzes, ballades, scherzos, impromptus, preludes, rondos, and the Sonata in B flat minor (Op.35) are similarly praised. The 'strange delight' we experience from Chopin's music, Davison continues, 'may in part be traced to the melancholy which invests it as a garment – and which is mystically sympathetic with our own peculiar temperaments. It makes us dream of a happy past – mourn over a sad present – and yearn for an undefined future' (p. 12). Furthermore,

> Chopin has the peculiar gift (so rarely granted to musicians) of attracting the attention and exciting the admiration of philosophers and poets, as well as the votaries of his own art; it would be difficult to name a writer of any note in Paris, who is not an intense worshipper of his genius.

'Indeed', concludes Davison, 'one can hardly turn to a romance of the present day, without finding some allusion to him' (p. 13).

An instance of this can be found in Balzac's novel *Ursule Mirouët* (1841), in which Chopin is singled out for praise, along with the book's heroine:

> In all music there is, besides the thought of the composer, the soul of the performer . . . Chopin proves, for that unresponsive instrument the piano, the truth of this fact, already proved by Paganini on the violin. That fine genius is less a musician than a soul which makes itself felt, and communicates itself through all species of music, even simple chords.

Ursula, Balzac adds, 'by her exquisite and sensitive organization, belonged to this rare class of beings'.[11]

On the Continent, writes Davison, Chopin's esteem could be gathered from the 'demand for his works', notably in Germany, and by the 'unanimous and enthusiastic testimony' of such musicians as Berlioz, Czerny, Liszt, Mendelssohn, Meyerbeer, Moscheles, and Schumann (pp. 17–18). After tabulating Chopin's works by style and levels of difficulty, Davison points to the 'arrangements of every description [which] have been eagerly demanded by the public', and which amateur musicians play with eagerness and delight (p. 17). Chopin, says Davison, 'lulls your senses in the most delicious repose, intoxicates them with bewitching and unceasing melody, clad in the richest and most exquisite harmony'. Although 'it would be difficult to name a writer of any note in Paris, who is not an intense worshipper of his genius', Chopin remains 'the most modest and retiring of beings . . . [who] has won the suffrage of all his brother artists, who look upon him as a star for wise men to follow, as an idol for universal worship' (p. 13).

A key role in the dissemination of Chopin's music in England was taken by his publishers. Frederick Stapleton, Christian Wessel's partner, had heard Chopin play in Paris, and persuaded Wessel to buy everything he could of Chopin's compositions.[12] Later, Cramer, Beale & Co were to publish Chopin's work extensively. All was dependent upon the growing popularity of the piano in a domestic setting, and the market for sheet music.[13] 'The now commonplace presence in parlour or drawing room of the instrument', writes Victoria Cooper, 'led to an unprecedented expansion of the piano repertoire, including arrangements of recent operas, earlier oratorios, and classical works; accompaniments to vocal or instrumental music; and solos.'[14] In Victorian literature, the portrayal of the piano in the home was a sign of women's accomplishment, education, and social status, and it appeared as a symbol in novels such as *David Copperfield*, *Jane Eyre*, and *Pride and Prejudice*. Sometimes, a specific manufacturer was named: Jane Fairfax's piano in *Emma* is a Broadwood, as is Amelia Sedley's in *Vanity Fair*.[15] Depictions of domestic interiors show the piano, and the piano teacher, as an essential part of the 'polite' Victorian interior. A Scottish example of this is the drawing by John Harden of his family home in Queen Street, Edinburgh, not far from the Hopetoun Rooms in which Chopin played.[16]

Travel between Paris and London had become much easier since Chopin visited England in 1837. Ferries across the English Channel now plied between Dieppe and Newhaven, Calais and Dover, and Boulogne and Folkestone (see Plate 8).[17] Hotels were being built for travellers taking the ferries: Newhaven saw the construction of the London & Paris Hotel, finished in 1847, and in 1854 the Lord Warden Hotel in Dover, designed by Samuel Beazley, was completed (see Figure 3.1). Chopin travelled by train from Paris to Boulogne, and then by ferry to Folkestone, where he may have stopped at the Pavilion Hotel, opened by

Figure 3.1 Admiralty Pier, Dover, showing the Lord Warden Hotel. Engraving published by Rock and Co, London, 1869. Private collection

Figure 3.2 Pavilion Hotel, Folkestone. Published by W. Tiffen, engraved by J. Newman, circa 1850. Private collection

the South Eastern Railway Company in 1843 (see Figure 3.2).[18] Once in Britain, Wojciech Grzymała was to be Chopin's most frequent correspondent (see Figure 3.3). 'I crossed the Channel without being very sick', he told Grzymała, in a letter written from London on Good Friday, 'but I did not travel by the fast boat. nor with the new acquaintances I made on the train, for one had to take a launch in order to board the vessel at sea. I preferred to come by the ordinary route, and I arrived here at six o'clock as I had to rest a few hours at Folkestone.'[19]

Architecturally, the London which greeted Chopin in 1848 displayed evidence of the expansion of areas such as Mayfair, Piccadilly, and St James's, and including Regent Street and the Strand. Here it was, north of the River Thames, that Chopin was to live and spend much of his time when in the city (see Figure 3.4). Having reached London on Maunday Thursday, 20 April, he stayed first at No. 10 Bentinck Street, north-west of Cavendish Square, which Jane Stirling and Mrs Erskine had arranged for him. Bentinck Street, now much altered, was begun in 1765 and takes its name from William Bentinck, 2nd Duke of Portland, on whose estate it lies – off Welbeck Street, and north of Oxford Street (see Figure 3.5). The domestic character of the area can be seen from *John Tallis's London street views*, of 1838–40 (see Figure 3.6).[20]

The next day, Good Friday, Jane wrote excitedly to Franchomme from No. 44 Welbeck Street, telling him that Chopin had arrived the previous evening:

> votre Cher Voyageur est arrivé sans avoir de pas trop souffert du voyage – la traversée n'a pas été tout à fait tranquille, et il y avait de pluie – il était sur le

Figure 3.3 Wojciech Grzymała (1793–1871). Photograph by Etienne Carjat. Bibliothèque Polonaise, Paris. Akg-images/DeAgostini Picture Library/G. Dagli Orti

pont – mais grâce à Dieu il ne paraît pas enrhumé. Il nous arrivait hier soir – vous pouvait juger ce que c'était de le voir!

That day, Chopin had endured a long journey, said Jane, and hardly surprisingly, 'il est rentré fatigué.'[21] 'My good Mrs Erskine and her sister have thought of

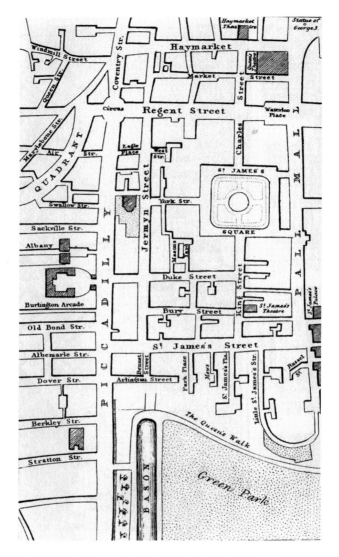

Figure 3.4 Piccadilly, London, and adjacent streets, from Jackson, John Tallis's London street views, 1838–1840 (2002 reprint), part 14, p. 68. Private collection

everything', Chopin told Gryzmała, 'even of my [special] drinking chocolate, and not merely for rooms for me . . . You can't imagine how kind they are – I have only just noticed that this paper I am writing on has my monogram [three Cs interlinked], and I have met with many similar delicate attentions.' But better rooms than those in Bentinck Street had become available elsewhere, and Chopin planned to move there within 'a day or two'.[22]

Figure 3.5 Bentinck Street, London. Pencil sketch by Thomas Colman Dibdin, circa 1850 (detail). London Metropolitan Archives

Meanwhile, he was off for the weekend. 'I am leaving town today as it is Good Friday and there is nothing to do here', he explained to Gryzmała. 'I am going to see some people belonging to the former King's entourage, who live outside London.'[23] Louis-Philippe and his family were at his time settling into Claremont, the country house near Esher in Surrey which the king had visited with Queen Victoria when in England in 1844, and it has been suggested that the friends with whom Chopin may have spent the weekend were the Count and Countess A. de Perthuis.[24] The count was aide-de-camp to Louis-Philippe. Chopin dedicated his Four Mazurkas (Op.24) to him, and his Sonata in B minor (Op.58) to his wife, Emilie. In Paris, on behalf of Louis-Philippe, Perthuis had helped to arrange Chopin's concerts at the Tuileries Palace.[25]

After his weekend away, Chopin moved on 23 April, Easter Sunday, to rooms in No. 48 Dover Street, off Piccadilly, a street originally laid out about 1683 and named after one of the speculators, Henry Jermyn, Lord Dover; although south of Oxford Street, it was only a stone's throw from Welbeck Street, to its north, where Jane Stirling and her sister lived. The house in which Chopin stayed is no more.[26] The composer was soon writing to his friends in Paris, telling them of his journey and his new life. 'Je suis aussi bien que possible, après la traversée, respirant cette fumée de charbon de terre', he informs Mlle de Rozières. 'Je tâche de me reposer. Mes lettres sont dans mon portefeuille; mon piano n'est pas encore deballé. J'ai

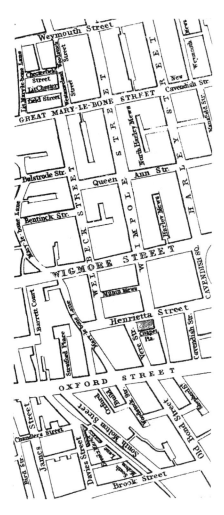

Figure 3.6 Wigmore Street, Welbeck Street, and Bentinck Street, London, from Jackson, *John Tallis's London street views, 1838–1840* (2002 reprint), part 50, p. 141. Private collection

écrit deux mots aux miens; veuillez je vous prie les envoyer.' Chopin describes Easter Monday as tranquil, his apartment as expensive, and asks Mlle de Rozières to address letters to him there.[27]

Apparently, the accommodation in Dover Street had been recommended to Chopin by Karol Sculczewski, London agent of the Hôtel Lambert, and since 1845 the secretary of the Literary Association of the Friends of Poland.[28] Born in 1814, Szulczewski had fought in Polish forces in battles against the Russians, and elsewhere, fleeing to Paris after the failure of the Polish uprisings.[29] In 1842, he moved to London, where, as an ardent patriot, he counted Lord Dudley Coutts Stuart and the Earl of Harrowby among his friends. Both Szulczewski and Stanisław Koźmian, who had been Chopin's factotum during his first visit to London, were to assist the composer during his seven months' stay in Britain.

'Here I am just settling down', Chopin wrote to his 'dearest friend' Franchomme from Dover Street, on 1 May. 'At last I have a room – a nice large one – in which I can breathe and play, and here comes the sun to see me today for the first time.'[30] Moreover, as Chopin later commented to Gryzmała, there are other advantages. 'I have three pianos', he wrote: 'In addition to my Pleyel I have a Broadwood and an Érard, but I have so far only been able to play on my own. At last I have good lodgings; but no sooner have I settled down than my landlord now wants to make me pay twice as much, or else accept another room.' Chopin is 'already paying twenty-six guineas a month', but at least he has an attractive place in which to teach:

> It is true that I have a large splendid drawing-room, and can give my lessons here. So far I have only five pupils. I don't yet know what I shall do. I shall probably stay here because the other room is neither so large nor so suitable. And once you have announced your address it is better not to change. The landlord's pretext for the change is that we have nothing in writing and so he may raise the rent.[31]

Soon, more pupils were to seek Chopin out, although, at a guinea a lesson, they provided him with little enough income.[32]

In fact, Chopin's rent was later increased to ten guineas a week, as he told Mlle de Rozières, although he acknowledged that he was living in 'one of the finest districts in London', in an apartment with 'a large drawing-room with three pianos' and 'a fine staircase'. 'I give a few lessons at home', he wrote. 'I have a few engagements to play at fashionable drawing-rooms – this brings in a few guineas which disappear in spite of all my economy.' 'I am aware of the expense', he confided, 'all the more since my Italian valet (the most typical Italian imaginable) sneers at my attempts at economy. He refuses to accompany me in the evening if I take a cab rather than a privately hired carriage. I have to put up with it all as I can't find anyone better.' Despite the fact that Chopin had been 'spitting blood these last few days', and had 'nothing but ices and lemonade', this had not prevented him from becoming 'acquainted somewhat with London society'. As he puts it: 'A host of *Ladies* whom I have been introduced to and whose names go in one ear and out the other as soon as they are mentioned.'[33]

What of the three pianos which were in Chopin's rooms in Dover Street? The Érard had been provided by Sébastien Érard who, on Chopin's arrival in London, had 'hastened to offer his services and . . . placed one of his pianos at [Chopin's] disposal'.[34] The Broadwood was Grand Pianoforte No. 17,093 (London, 1847); according to Hipkins's essay 'Chopin's pianoforte', in the catalogue of the Broadwood exhibits at the International Inventions Exhibition of 1885, this was sent to

No. 48 Dover Street and retained by Chopin 'throughout the season', apart from its removal once, 'on the occasion (May 10th) of his playing to Lady Blessington, at Gore House, Kensington'.[35] The Pleyel, referred to by Chopin as '*my Pleyel*' [sic], seems to have been Grand Pianoforte No. 13,819 (Paris, circa 1846), now in the Cobbe Collection, at Hatchlands, and brought by the composer from Paris (see Plate 9);[36] indeed Hipkins's widow reports that her late husband indicated that it was this Pleyel, not the Broadwood, which Chopin played at Gore House. Chopin, she writes,

> came to Broadwood through the recommendation and courtesy of the Pleyel House in Paris; he brought one of his Pleyel pianos with him, but only used it once, at an evening at the Countess of Blessington's at Kensington Gore, directly after his arrival. He immediately took to the Broadwood pianos, and after that occasion used them exclusively in England and Scotland, until in effect, his return to Paris in November of that year, 1848.[37]

On 15 August 1848, by then in Scotland, Chopin wrote to Camille Pleyel from Calder House, and mentioned the sale of his Pleyel. 'Before I left for Scotland, where I look forward to spending, if I can, a few quiet weeks', he said, 'I sent you a short note from London, when forwarding the £80 I received from Lady Trotter for your piano.'[38] Effectively, Chopin here seems to have been acting as an agent for Pleyel.[39]

Chopin's records of piano lessons at No. 48 Dover Street appear in his pocket diary for 1848, now in Warsaw.[40] The 'five pupils' mentioned by Chopin in his letter to Gryzmała on 13 May are identified by Arthur Hedley as 'Miss C Maberly, Lady Christopher, Mrs Wilde, Lady Parke and the Duchess of Rutland's daughter'[41] – this last a mistake for the Duchess of Sutherland's daughter, Lady Constance Leveson-Gower, who had seven lessons between 25 May and 6 July 1848.[42] The diary also shows that Catherine Maberley – the dedicatee of Chopin's Three Mazurkas (Op.56), and a friend of Jane Stirling – took five lessons between 10 May and 24 June, supplementing those she had in Paris.[43] Mrs Katherine Erskine, Jane Stirling's sister, who similarly had taken lessons from Chopin in Paris, had a further six from him in London, spread between 12 June and 4 July 1848.[44]

The names of other of Chopin's London students may be added to these, some speculative.[45] Notable amongst these is that of Lady Mary Cadogan, wife of the 4th Earl of Cadogan, whom Chopin met, with many other titled women, at a recital he gave at the London home of the Marquess of Douglas (son of the Duke and Duchess of Hamilton); Chopin refers to Lady Cadogan as 'my former pupil, now *dame de Compagnie* to the duchess of Cambridge'.[46] In London, Chopin continued to teach some of his Parisian pupils,[47] and he maintained his connections with the Rothschild family; his Waltz in C sharp minor (Op.64, no.2), which was played to acclaim in England and Scotland in 1848, was dedicated to Charlotte Rothschild.[48] Writing to Gryzmała on 2 June 1848, Chopin describes meeting

'Old Mme Rothschild' – one imagines Hannah, then aged sixty-five, widow of Nathaniel Meyer Rothschild. Chopin writes:

> She asked me how much I *cost* ["Combien coûtez-vous?"], as some lady who had heard me was making enquiries. Since Sutherland gave me twenty guineas, the fee fixed for me by Broadwood on whose piano I play, I answered, "Twenty guineas". She, obviously trying to be kind and helpful, replied that of course I play very beautifully.

Whereupon, she advised Chopin to 'take less, as one had to show greater "moderayshon" this season.' Chopin deduced from this that people 'are not so open-handed and money is tight everywhere. To please the middle class you need something sensational, some technical display which is out of my sphere.'[49]

There was also Lady Murray. In 1826, Mary Rigby (as she then was), married Sir John Archibald Murray, who became Lord Advocate and Lord of Session in Scotland. Chopin observed that Lady Murray, 'an important, well-known lady who is very fond of music', and his first pupil in London, 'spends most of her time in Edinburgh and exercises command over musical affairs'.[50] No details of Chopin's lessons with Lady Murray have survived, but on 18 July 1848 we find him in London sending a note to her: 'J'aurai l'honneur d'attendre Lady Murray aujourd'hui à 4h, si cela lui est agréable. Son très humble serviteur Chopin.'[51] The cellist Louis Drechsler also forms a link; a pupil of Auguste Franchomme, from Edinburgh, he came to see the composer in London. 'He seemed a good fellow and is very fond of you', he reported to Franchomme, from Calder House. 'He plays [the cello] with a local *grand dame*, Lady Murray, one of my sixty-year-old pupils.' Drechsler, who was born in Dessau, conducted the Gentlemen's Amateur Society concerts in Edinburgh, where he founded the Singverein, a male voice choir, in 1846. Chopin promised to visit Lady Murray at her 'fine castle' – namely Strachur, on Loch Fyne – which he duly did.[52]

Teaching had its problems, however, as Chopin explained to Wojciech Gryzmała in a letter of 8–17 July. Chopin acknowledges that he is 'already known in the right way in certain circles, but it takes time, and the season is already over'. What he lacks are guineas:

> They are awful liars here: as soon as they don't want anything they clear off to the country. One of my lady pupils has already left for the country, leaving nine lessons unpaid. Others, who are down for two lessons a week, usually miss a week, thus pretending to have more lessons than they really do. It does not surprise me, for they try to do too much – to do a little bit of everything.

Taking lessons from Chopin was nothing if not fashionable. 'One lady', the composer continued, 'came here from Liverpool to have lessons for a single week! I gave her five lessons – they don't play on Sundays – and sent her away happy!' As for Lady Peel, she wanted Chopin to give her daughter one lesson a week 'simply to be able to say that she has lessons from me. She will probably leave after two weeks.'[53] With such financial problems, let alone those related to publishing his work, it is hardly surprising that Chopin was attracted, despite his hesitations, to earning fees from the recital platform.[54]

As well as Louis-Philippe, the February Revolution of 1848 brought François Guizot – the foreign minister, and later prime minister of France – to England. Once he arrived, Guizot was in touch with Louis-Philippe at Claremont.[55] Henry Fowler Broadwood (who had, Chopin noted, 'splendid connections') thereupon 'received M. Guizot and his whole family in his house'.[56] Hallé, who had himself arrived in London that March, continued to teach former pupils who, like him, had fled Paris. 'Amongst them', he noted, 'there was the daughter of M. Guizot, who, fallen from his high estate, was living in a modest house in Pelham Crescent, Brompton.'[57] Late that May, Chopin met Guizot at a dinner. 'It was pitiful to see him', Chopin told Gryzmała. 'Although he was decked out with the Order of the Golden Fleece it was obvious that he suffers morally, even if he still has hopes.'[58] Guizot devoted the rest of his life to writing,[59] and to making his mark as 'the first great modern historian of France'.[60]

Once settled in London, Chopin began the extensive correspondence with friends and relatives in Poland and France, which provides us with an invaluable commentary on his time in Britain. Chopin was welcomed by both Poles and Britons alike. Moritz Karasowski – regarded by Adam Harasowski, it must be said, as an untrustworthy source[61] – writes in his biography of Chopin that on the composer's arrival the Polish emigrants in London arranged a dinner 'at which about forty of the most prominent members of the Polish colony were present'.[62] Karasowski indicates that 'after several toasts and speeches extolling Chopin as a musician and a patriot', the composer 'rose, and clinking his glass', spoke as follows:

> My dear countrymen: – The expressions I have just received of your attachment and devotion have touched me deeply. I should like to have been able to thank you in words, but, unfortunately, the gift of oratory has been denied me. I invite you to come with me to my house, and listen to the expression of my thanks on the piano.

This speech was received 'with a storm of applause', continues Karasowski. 'Every one rose and followed the artist. Although exhausted by the day's excitement, Chopin made a supreme effort, and, amid continuous applause, played till two in the morning.'[63]

As well as showing hospitality towards Guizot, Henry Fowler Broadwood welcomed Chopin into his London circle (see Figure 3.7). Chopin again played for the Broadwoods, as he had done in 1837, at No. 46 Bryanston Square, in this instance at an 'at home' on Wednesday 21 June 1848, when he was the guest of Mrs H. Fowler Broadwood at a 'small early party'.[64] By this time, James Shudi Broadwood had passed on the running of his firm to his elder son, Henry Fowler Broadwood, who divided his time between London and Lyne House, near Dorking, in

Figure 3.7 Henry Fowler Broadwood (1811–93). Undated portrait, by unknown photographer. Broadwood Trust. Surrey History Centre, Woking, Surrey

Surrey.[65] Broadwood', Chopin told his family in Warsaw, 'who is a real London Pleyel, has been my best and truest friend', and is 'universally beloved . . . He is, as you know, a very rich and well-educated man whose father transferred to him his property and factory and then retired to the country.' Chopin cites an example of his 'English courtesy':

> One morning he came to see me – I was worn out and told him that I had slept badly. In the evening when I came back from the Duchess of Somerset's what do I find but a new spring mattress and pillows on my bed! After a lot of questioning, my good Daniel (the name of my present servant) told me that Mr Broadwood had sent them, and had asked him to say nothing.[66]

An Old Harrovian, Broadwood was 'a man-about-town, courtier and politician', of whom it was said that he carried on 'two complementary existences, as pianoforte maker and as country squire and sportsman'.[67]

But all was not well with him. For whereas in public he continued to appear 'the prince of pianoforte makers', as Hallé called him, in private he must have been worried, as from 1845 the sales of Broadwood instruments rapidly declined.[68] For in addition to the 'French challenge', notably from Érard, the bestselling Broadwood square pianos and grands were going out of fashion. In particular, Henry Fowler Broadwood's reluctance to use the single cast-iron frame, and the technique of overstringing, meant that the firm did not move with the times.[69] That said, although Broadwoods failed to obtain the Gold Medal for piano manufacture at the Great Exhibition of 1851 (which went to Érard), the firm did win awards at the International Exhibition in South Kensington of 1862, the Paris Exhibition of 1867, and the International Inventions Exhibition in London of 1885.[70]

This last exhibition had a catalogue of Broadwood exhibits which had been prepared under the care of A.J. Hipkins, including a section entitled 'Chopin's pianoforte', which describes the Broadwood pianos used by Chopin in 1848 (see Figure 3.8).[71] Alfred James Hipkins, writer on music and musical instruments, was noted for his entries on the keyboard and related topics in the first edition of Grove's *Dictionary of music and musicians* (1879–89), and in the ninth edition of the *Encyclopaedia Britannica* (1875–89).[72] In 1896, he published *A description and history of the pianoforte*. Hipkins began his career at the age of fourteen, in 1840, as an apprentice piano tuner at Broadwoods', working for the firm for the rest of his life, and meeting Chopin and Jane Stirling there in 1848; indeed, he may have been the first English pianist to devote entire recitals to the Polish composer.

Hipkins casts many sidelights on Chopin's period in Britain, a selection of which were brought together and published by his daughter, Edith J. Hipkins, in the book *How Chopin played*, of 1937; in 1926, Edith, who was a painter, had presented her portrait of her father (1898) to the National Portrait Gallery, London. Signficantly, as he lived until 1903, A.J. Hipkins was able personally to give information to two early Chopin biographers: Joseph Bennett, whose book *Frederic Chopin* came out initially in 1884–5,[73] and Frederick Niecks, for his life of Chopin, first published in 1888.[74] Hipkins' role at Broadwoods, however, was problematical, as he used his influence to prevent the adoption of new design features which might have kept the firm's pianos competitive. He was inclined

Figure 3.8 Alfred James Hipkins (1826–1903). Undated portrait, by unknown photographer. Broadwood Trust, from Wainwright, *Broadwood by appointment* (1982), p. 217. Private collection

to keep the Broadwoods as they were, producing the sound he had admired in Chopin's playing.[75]

According to Hipkins, the 'recollection of the Broadwood piano and its responsiveness to his sensitive touch remained with Chopin, so that when he returned to London in the April of 1848 one of the first visits he paid was to Broadwoods' warehouse in Great Pulteney Street'. This was Hipkins' first meeting with the composer. 'He paid many subsequent visits', Hipkins wrote, 'and it was on those occasions I heard him play. It was the first near experience I had of genius.'[76] On one occasion Chopin came with Jane Stirling and Frederick Beale, of the publishers Cramer & Co, to play the two waltzes in C sharp minor and A flat major, respectively (Op.64, nos 2 and 3), just completed, although Hipkins best recalls him playing the *Andante spianato* (Op.22).[77] At Broadwoods', to save him fatigue, Chopin was carried upstairs. Hipkins' admiration for Chopin as a pianist was boundless:

> His *fortissimo* was the full pure tone without noise, a harsh inelastic note being to him painful. His *nuances* were modifications of that tone, decreasing to the faintest yet always distinct *pianissimo*. His singing *legatissimo* touch was marvellous. The wide, extended arpeggios in the bass were transfused by touch and pedal into their corresponding sustained chords, and swelled or diminished like waves in an ocean of sound.

Hipkins observes that, despite the passage of fifty-one years (he was writing in 1899) 'very strong impressions remain on the memory'. 'I remember Chopin, his look, his manner and his incomparable playing', he writes, 'as vividly as if my meeting him had been last year.'[78]

Chopin was frequently at the Broadwood showrooms, says Hipkins, and 'immediately took to the Broadwood pianos', but his 'weakened breathing power' meant that he had to be carried upstairs. He was

> of middle height, with a pleasant face, a mass of fair curly hair like an angel, and agreeable manners. But he was something of a dandy, very particular about the cut and colour of his clothes. He was painstaking in the choice of pianos he was to play upon anywhere, as he was in his dress, his hair, his gloves, his French.

In England, in 1848, Hipkins remarks, 'his compositions were almost unknown. Every time I heard him play, the pieces were strange to me, and I had to rush across Regent Street to Wessel, his English publisher, to discover what I had been hearing.'[79]

As for Chopin's choice of pianos, he 'especially liked Broadwood's Boudoir cottage pianos of that date, two-stringed, but very sweet instruments, and he found pleasure in playing on them'. The Broadwood Grand Pianoforte which he chose for his London and Manchester concerts (No. 17,047) is dated 1847, and is the property of the Royal Academy of Music, London, on permanent loan to The Cobbe Collection Trust, Hatchlands, Surrey (see Plate 10).[80] Its case is of rosewood, veneered on laminated oak, and a brass plaque on the lid indicates that Chopin used the piano for his London recitals in 1848.[81] A name label bears the words

Patent
Repetition Grand Pianoforte
John Broadwood & Sons
Manufacturers to Her Majesty
33 Great Pulteney Street, Golden Square
London

The other Broadwood pianos used by Chopin are lost to view; according to Hipkins, the composer used Grand Pianoforte No. 17,093 (circa 1847) in his lodgings in No. 48 Dover Street, and at Gore House, and Grand Pianoforte No. 17,001 (circa 1847) for his concerts in Glasgow and Edinburgh. 'All these instruments were chosen by Chopin himself in our warehouse', Hipkins explains, 'and on such visits he was accompanied by his friends and pupils, Miss Stirling and M Tellefsen.'[82]

Henry Fothergill Chorley,[83] as well as J.W. Davison,[84] was prominent among the English music critics who gave voice to their views on Chopin (see Figure 3.9). Chorley, as we have seen, met Chopin in Paris and was music critic for

London 1848: Chopin in London   75

Figure 3.9 James William Davison (1813–85). Pencil sketch by G.D. Davison, from a daguerreotype, circa 1857, from Davison, *From Mendelssohn to Wagner* (1912), frontispiece. British Library, London

the *Athenaeum* from 1833 to 1868, and author of *Thirty years' musical recollections* (1862). Those whom Chorley entertained at his London home, No. 15 Victoria Square, included Charles Hallé (see Figure 3.10). Chorley, said Hallé, was 'a man of strong views, fearless in his criticism, perfectly honest', although 'often unconsciously swayed by personal antipathies or sympathies'.[85] Chorley, indeed, may have been 'unconsciously swayed' by his personal sympathy for Chopin. For instance, the *Athenaeum*, 6 May 1848 (no.1071, p. 467), includes an essay by Chorley entitled 'Deux Valses pour la Piano, par F. Chopin', which promotes Chopin's recently completed waltzes, Op.64, in D flat major and C sharp minor

Figure 3.10 Charles Hallé (1819–95). Frontispiece (1890) from Hallé and Hallé, *Life and Letters of Sir Charles Hallé* (1896). Private collection

(nos 1 and 2; no.3, in A flat major, is not mentioned). These waltzes, Chorley writes, have 'more originality and style than many a heap of notes calling itself sonata or concerto by [a] contemporary composer, thinking to claim honours as a classical writer'. Chopin, Chorley concludes,

> is distinctly, gracefully, poetically natural; and, therefore, as we long ago said, when there was small idea of his ever coming to England, well worth studying

in his writings. Those are fortunate who have means of gaining an insight into the matter, by hearing the composer perform his own compositions.

Other London publications reporting on Chopin's stay in London include the *Daily News*, the *Examiner*, the *Illustrated London News*, *John Bull*, the *Morning Post*, and *Musical Opinion*.[86] Subsequent commentaries are found in the memoirs of Willert Beale, William Kuhe, and other contemporaries (such as Cox, Diehl, Kemble, and Moscheles).[87]

Music critics and journalists avidly recorded the comings and goings of foreign musicians, who had long been attracted to London's cultural life. Prominent among visiting composers were Berlioz and Weber, and also Mendelssohn, who travelled to London ten times between 1837 and 1847. In 1848, as Niecks put it,

> England was just then heroically enduring an artistic invasion such as had never been seen before; not only from France, but also from Germany and other musical countries arrived day after day musicians who had found that their occupation was gone on the Continent, where people could think of nothing but politics and revolutions.[88]

Hallé, after leaving Paris for England, told his parents in a letter of 27 April 1848 how difficult life can be for pianists:

> I have been here in London for three weeks, striving hard to make a new position, and I hope I shall succeed; pupils I already have, although as yet they are not many. The competition is very keen, for, besides the native musicians, there are at present here – Thalberg, Chopin, Kalkbrenner, Pixis, Osborne, Prudent, Pillet [i.e., Billet], and a lot of other pianists besides myself who have all, through necessity, been driven to England, and we shall probably end by devouring one another.[89]

It was into this jungle that Chopin had stepped.

In addition to pianists, of course, opera singers migrated to London. Two opera houses were dominant at that time: Her Majesty's Theatre, Haymarket (until 1837 known as the King's Theatre), and the Royal Italian Opera House, Covent Garden (until 1847 known as the Theatre Royal) (see Figure 3.11). The connection between Chopin's music and opera has often been noted, although, despite the urging of friends, he never himself wrote an opera. According to Niecks, he told his pupil, the Russian pianist Vera Rubio, 'You must sing if you wish to play', and made her take singing lessons and go to Italian opera – this last, Rubio maintained, 'Chopin regarded as positively necessary for a pianoforte-player.'[90] In the London of 1848, Chopin had ample opportunity to indulge his enthusiasm, as the competition between Her Majesty's and Covent Garden gave rise to a flurry of activity.

The changes in the operatic scene in London since Chopin's visit of 1837 were extensive.[91] In the intervening years Her Majesty's Theatre, in the Haymarket, had presented such significant new works as Donizetti's *Lucia di Lammermoor*

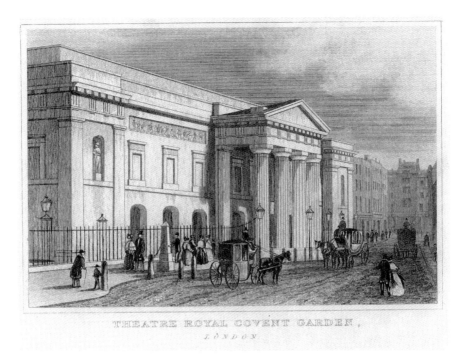

Figure 3.11 Theatre Royal, Covent Garden, London. Engraving of exterior from Dugdale, *England and Wales delineated* (circa 1848). Private collection

(1838), *Linda di Chamounix*, and *Don Pasquale* (both 1843), and Verdi's *Ernani* (1845), *Nabucco* (in a version renamed *Nino*, set in ancient Egypt), and *I Lombardi* (both 1846). But changes were afoot. The stage at Her Majesty's was dominated by such singers as Fanny Persiani, Grisi, Mario, Tamburini, and Lablache. At the end of 1846, however – influenced by the conductor Michael Costa and by Persiani's husband, the composer Giuseppe Persiani – most of the company left Her Majesty's to set up on their own at Covent Garden Theatre. Remodelled by the architect of the original building, Sir Robert Smirke, this then became known as the Royal Italian Opera (see Figure 3.12).[92]

Competition between Her Majesty's Theatre and Covent Garden at the time of Chopin's second London visit was intense:

> The manager at Her Majesty's, Benjamin Lumley, secured Jenny Lind and mounted Verdi's only opera written for London, *I masnadieri*, besides giving Italian versions of Meyerbeer's *Robert le diable* and Donizetti's *La Fille du régiment* and *La Favorite* (all 1847). Subsequent Verdi premières here were *I due Foscari* (1847), *Attila* (1848) and finally, after a forced three-year closure of the theatre, *La traviata* (1856).[93]

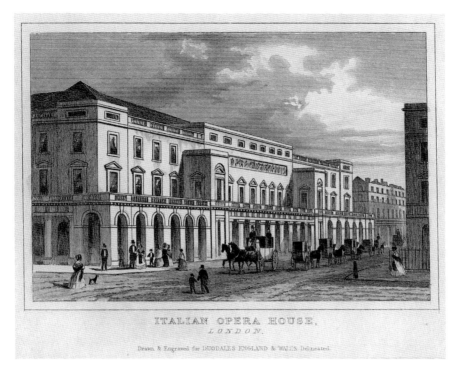

Figure 3.12 Italian Opera House, London. Engraving of exterior from Dugdale, *England and Wales delineated* (circa 1848). Private collection

Meanwhile,

> Covent Garden capitalised on the Meyerbeer fever with his *Gli Ugonotti* (1848) and Italian versions of *Le Prophète* (1849) and *L'Etoile du Nord* (1855), also giving *Benevenuto Cellini* (1853; under Berlioz) and the London premières of *Rigoletto* (1853) and *Il trovatore* (1855), the latter with Pauline Viardot.

Alas, after only nine seasons as the Royal Italian Opera, Covent Garden Theatre burned to the ground in 1856,[94] to be rebuilt over the next two years by the architect E.M. Barry.[95] Musically, Covent Garden was considered better than Her Majesty's, its orchestra under Costa being regarded as one of the most polished in Europe.[96] On the other hand, until the reconstruction of Covent Garden Theatre, Her Majesty's was regarded as the most beautiful opera house in London.[97]

Chopin was alert to the rivalries between the two theatres, and the comings-and-goings of singers between Paris and London. 'Since fashionable custom is more important in London than any conceivable art', he told his family in 1846, writing from Nohant, 'next season promises to be interesting.'[98] Once in London, Chopin was able to benefit from the rich fare available at both Covent Garden and Her Majesty's.[99] One of the leading performers at Covent Garden was Pauline Viardot, whose appearances during the 1848 season included *I Capuleti e i Montecchi*, *Don Giovanni*, *Les Huguenots*, and *La sonnambula*;[100] Chopin remarked, however, that Viardot had 'no great success here as she is with Grisi and Alboni who are very popular'.[101] At Her Majesty's, Jenny Lind also sang *La sonnambula*, as well as *Lucia di Lammermoor*, both of which Chopin heard; after seeing *Lucia di Lammermoor*, Chopin commented that Lind was 'very good' and 'arouses the greatest enthusiasm'.[102] Clearly, Chopin admired both women: Viardot, he thought 'very charming', and added, perhaps surprisingly, that 'she was so gracious as to sing my Mazurkas at a concert held in her theatre [i.e., Covent Garden] – without my asking.' Chopin also regarded Lind as 'charming', and a 'singer of genius'.[103]

Among other friends from Paris whom Chopin met in London was Mrs Harriet Grote, wife of George Grote, MP, and friend and biographer of Ary Scheffer, who lived at No. 4 Eccleston Street, until she moved to No. 12 Savile Row in May 1848.[104] Mrs Grote – a supporter of John Ella and his institution for chamber music, the Musical Union – entertained both Mendelssohn and Jenny Lind.[105] 'The social life of the Grotes during the eighteen forties centred round the world of music', writes M.L. Clarke, biographer of George Grote. 'Mrs Grote was devoted to music, and was herself a good pianist and a fair performer on the cello.' She was involved in the politics of the musical world, and liked to entertain musicians and invite them to her rural retreat at Burnham Beeches, Buckinghamshire.[106]

The Grotes had met Mendelssohn in 1844, and they remained in close touch with him until his death three years later; he visited the Grotes at Burnham in 1844, and again in 1847.[107] Mrs Grote's friendship with Jenny Lind rose partly out of her Swedish connections, for one of Mrs Grote's sisters had a Swedish husband, and had long been a friend of Jenny's in Stockholm. Mrs Grote was 'instrumental in persuading Jenny Lind to come to England in 1847 to sing in the opera at Her Majesty's Theatre, and it was at the Grotes' house that she stayed when she first arrived'.[108] Lady Eastlake, in her book *Mrs Grote: a sketch*, reports that Mrs Grote 'formed the highest opinion of [Jenny Lind's] powers and told her she was "every inch a prima donna".'[109] On one occasion, 'the Grotes received her in their own residence in Eccleston Street, at the door of which the benevolent hostel stood to welcome her, with no less a celebrity at her side than Felix Mendelssohn, then on his second visit to England, and about to bring out his 'Elijah' at Exeter Hall.'[110] 'Those who personally knew the great and gifted Felix Mendelssohn Bartholdy', Lady Eastlake continues, 'will readily believe . . . that the warmest friendship should have been formed between him and the Grotes.'[111]

Chopin followed firmly in the footsteps of Mendelssohn and Lind in Mrs Grote's patronage. With the return to England of Jenny Lind for the 1848 opera season, Mrs Grote reported, their house 'was once more the scene of brilliant musical doings: Chopin, Thalberg, Dorus Gras, shining also among our "stars".' Although, she added, 'the lamented Mendelssohn was no longer with us.'[112] One day Chopin and Jenny had tea with Mrs Grote,[113] who in June hosted a recital in her house in Savile Row 'where Dorus Gras sang and Chopin played'.[114]

Chopin had affectionate recollections of his hostess, whom he had met in Paris at Mme Marliani's, and who introduced him to Jenny Lind. He thought Mrs Grote 'highly educated', and

> a very kind person, although a great radical and quite a character. She receives a crowd of interesting people – dukes, lords, scholars – in short, all the fashionable celebrities. She speaks in a deep voice and does not wrap up the truth in cotton-wool. Someone was asked his opinion of her: 'How do you find Mrs Grote?' and replied: 'I find her *grotesque*.'

Notwithstanding, Mrs Grote proved her kind-heartedness by asking Chopin, Jenny Lind, and Mrs Adelaide Sartoris to visit her country estate at Burnham Beeches, but the composer was unable to go.[115]

Two other invitations were significant. On one occasion, Chopin records that he and Jenny Lind were invited to Mrs Grote's home – 'only the two of us, and we remained at the piano from nine o'clock until one in the morning'.[116] On the other occasion, the attendance of Queen Victoria at Her Majesty's Theatre, when Jenny Lind had just reached London, led to a rush for tickets. After calling on Mrs Grote, Chopin was invited into her first-floor box;[117] but, realising that climbing the stairs would make him breathless, the manager sent him 'a ticket for one of the best stalls, with the compliments of Mlle Lind and Mrs Grote'. As for the opera itself: 'The performance was most brilliant.'[118]

As in 1837, whilst in London in 1848, Chopin took the opportunity of seeing his publishers, namely Cramer, Beale & Co, at No. 201 Regent Street (at the corner of Conduit Street), and Wessel & Co, at No. 229 Regent Street (at the corner of Hanover Street) (see Figure 3.13).[119] Most notably, that year, Chopin published in London the three waltzes of Op.64. The first two, as we have seen, were warmly praised by Chorley, and published by Cramer, Beale & Co;[120] later in 1848, Cramer, Beale & Co brought out the third of the waltzes, in A flat major.[121] Wessel & Co also published an edition of them in 1848.[122] It is a complex story, not excluding piracy, but it is clear that these waltzes were enthusiastically received when Chopin performed them on his visit to Britain,[123] and that they stand among the peaks of his compositions.

Overarching Chopin's time in Britain was his desperate health. On 18 April 1848, the day before he left Paris for London, Chopin had written anxiously to Dr Molin, his French homeopathic doctor: 'I do not want to leave Paris without seeing you and taking your prescriptions with me. So I would ask you to spare me a minute on your rounds today.'[124] Hardly surprisingly, when in London, he turned to homeopathy for his medical treatment. Homeopathy had been introduced in 1832 by Frederick Hervey Quinn, the first homeopathic physician in England.[125] In London, Chopin was treated by Dr Henry V. Malan, physician to the Marylebone Homeopathic Dispensary.[126] In 1841–2, he spent eighteen months at the Hahnemanns' clinic in Paris, where Jane Stirling and Katherine Erskine

Figure 3.13 Premises of Cramer, Beale & Co, No. 201 Regent Street, at the corner of Conduit Street, London, from *Grand panorama of London, Regent Street to Westminster Abbey*, by Leighton and Sanderson, 1849 (1966 reprint). Private collection

were patients.[127] It was Dr Malan who treated Chopin daily as he lay ill at No. 4 St James's Place, prior to his concert in Guildhall on his return to London from Edinburgh.[128]

Chopin's letters are full of references to his illness, and his courage in struggling against it is evident. Despite his medical travails, he maintained a lively correspondence. Indeed his emotional dependence upon friends in Paris and elsewhere, and family in Poland, led to almost obsessional letter-writing, for which posterity is the beneficiary. Although his composing seems to have virtually ceased, his letters show that Chopin's social and musical activity was extensive, as he taught, gave recitals, and satisfied the social demands of his hosts. The best record of Chopin's life in London and Scotland comes from his own pen.

Notes

1 Williams, *Franz Liszt: selected letters*, p. 141 (letter no.109). In note 17 here, Williams writes: 'Liszt included several of the Polish composer's works in his recital of 29 June [1840] at Willis's Rooms, thereby becoming the first pianist to play Chopin, in public,

London 1848: Chopin in London   83

in London.' The *Athenaeum* on 4 July 1840 reported that two of Chopin's mazurkas were 'exquisitely played' by Liszt on this occasion: 'Positive faëry-work upon the piano'. Quoted by Williams, *Portrait of Liszt*, p. 136.
2   Hedley, *Chopin*, pp. 103–4. Chopin never played either of his piano concertos in public during his visit to Britain. Ellsworth, 'The piano concerto in London concert life', pp. 175–6, 223–5, 287, lists only eleven performances of Chopin concertos between 2 June 1838 and 9 May 1849.
3   See Niecks, *Chopin*, vol.2, p. 278. See also the *Gazette musicale*, 2 April 1848, cited in Wierczyński, *Chopin*, p. 371.
4   Hedley, *Chopin correspondence*, p. 312; Hedley cites no source for his quotation. Wierczyński, *Chopin*, p. 371, adds that 'Chopin was also welcomed by a notice in the Musical world', but gives no details. For Hall, see the articles by Peter Mandler on Samuel Carter Hall, and Anna Maria Hall (née Fielding), respectively, in *Oxford DNB online*.
5   Hedley, *Chopin correspondence*, p. 312; Hedley cites no source for his quotation. Wierczyński, *Chopin*, p. 371, adds that 'Chopin was also welcomed by a notice in the Musical world', but gives no details. For Hall, see the articles by Peter Mandler on Samuel Carter Hall, and Anna Maria Hall (née Fielding), respectively, in *Oxford DNB online*.
6   Niecks, *Chopin*, vol.2, pp. 278–80.
7   Niecks, *Chopin*, vol.2, p. 279.
8   Niecks, *Chopin*, vol.2, p. 280.
9   Davison was music critic of *The Times* from 1846 to 1879, and wrote for the *Musical World*, of which he was editor. Wessel & Stapleton were also the publishers of the *Musical Examiner*, and a long quotation from this periodical concludes Davison's *Essay*. For ease of reference, pagination to the *Essay* is given in the text here. In later years, Davison changed his opinion of Chopin. Reasons for this are suggested by Niecks, *Chopin*, vol.2, p. 279, n.8, when he writes that 'it may have been due to the fear that the rising glory of Chopin might dim that of Mendelssohn; or Davison may have taken umbrage at Chopin's conduct in an affair related to Mendelssohn.'
10 Conversely, Hadden, *Chopin*, p. 139, remarks: 'Certainly his compositions were seldom taught. Teachers in those days, when selecting pieces for their pupils, limited themselves to standard classical works.'
11 Balzac, *Ursula* (trans. Wormeley), pp. 110–11. For the French text, see Balzac, *Ursule Mirouët*, p. 186.
12 Hadden, *Chopin*, p. 139. Later, Cramer, Beale & Co were to publish Chopin extensively. For the context of Chopin's publishing in England, see Kallberg, *Chopin at the boundaries*, pp. 200–14, and 'Frédéric Chopin and his publishers', exhibition catalogue, Department of Special Collections, University of Chicago Library, 1998. See Chapter 1, note 56, and below, note 122.
13 See Temperley, 'Domestic music in England, 1800–1860', p. 32. See also the section 'Domestic music and performance', in Cooper, *House of Novello*, pp. 21–7.
14 Cooper, *House of Novello*, p. 22.
15 See Burgan, 'Heroines at the piano', p. 45.
16 See Brown, *Harden drawings*, passim.
17 In France, most travellers still had to make their way from Paris to the Channel ports by stagecoach; in England, however, the South Eastern Railway Company had opened its line from Folkestone to London in 1843, and in 1844 the Company completed a six-mile rail link between Dover and Folkestone, so that passengers arriving in Dover from Calais could transfer to Folkestone to catch the train to London. See Bishop, *Folkestone*, p. 85. Gray, *South Eastern Railway*, p. 267, points out that the Amiens & Boulogne Railway opened as far as Boulogne on 17 April 1848 – a few days before Chopin travelled on it. Bucknall, *Boat trains and channel packets*, pp. 46–7, indicates

84   *London 1848: Chopin in London*

that although the railway line from Paris had arrived at Boulogne by 1848, it was not until 1851 that it reached the Ville station there (later renamed the Centrale).
18 See Simmons, *Victorian railway*, p. 38, and Carter, *British railway hotels*, pp. 28–9, 123. For the South Eastern Railway Company see Gray, *South Eastern Railway, passim*. Details of the steamers used by the Company are given in Duckworth and Langmuir, *Railway and other steamers*, pp. 127–32.
19 Hedley, *Chopin correspondence*, p. 313. Chopin to Grzymała, Good Friday [21 April 2008].
20 For Bentinck Street, see Cherry and Pevsner, *London 3: north west*, p. 631, and Weinreb, Hibbert, and Keay, *London encyclopaedia*, p. 59.
21 Ruhlmann, 'Chopin – Franchomme', p. 132, with a Polish translation on p. 133. The French MS of the complete letter is reproduced here as plate 8. For Welbeck Street, see Cherry and Pevsner, *London 3: north west*, pp. 654–5, and Weinreb, Hibbert, and Keay, *London encyclopaedia*, p. 994. No. 44 Welbeck Street is given as the address of Jane Stirling and Mrs Erskine on other occasions.
22 Hedley, *Chopin correspondence*, p. 313. Chopin to Grzymała, Good Friday [21 April 1848].
23 Hedley, *Chopin correspondence*, p. 313. Chopin to Grzymała, Good Friday [21 April 1848].
24 See Hoesick, *Chopin*, vol.3, pp. 158n, 160. Zamoyski, *Chopin*, p. 255, and *Chopin: prince of the romantics*, p. 267, accepts this. For Louis-Philippe's exile in England, and his life at Claremont, see Antoinetti, *Louis-Philippe*, pp. 925–37.
25 Szulc, *Chopin in Paris*, pp. 101, 302, 374–5. Szulc says Émilie was a pupil of Chopin, but gives no source.
26 See Bradley and Pevsner, *London 6: Westminster*, pp. 522–4; Colvin, *Dictionary*, pp. 1026–7; and Weinreb, Hibbert, and Keay, *London encyclopaedia*, pp. 245–6. Nos 43–48 Dover Street now consist of a block of offices and flats.
27 See the letter from Mlle de Rozières to Chopin, 24–9 April 1848, in TiFC (Warsaw), M/3255. This was sold at Sotheby's, London, 5 December 2003, lot 56, purchased by Marek Keller, and presented to TiFC (Warsaw), 6 May 2005. See *Ruch Muzyczny* (2005), no.13, p. 4. I owe this periodical reference to Zbigniew Skowron. The French quotation here is from the Sotheby's catalogue description.
28 According to Samson, *Chopin*, p. 254. A note about the redirection of mail, from Chopin to Szulczewski, of 24 April 1848 [Easter Monday], is in Sydow, *KFC*, vol.2, p. 241 (letter 620), and Sydow and Chainaye, *Chopin correspondance*, vol.3, p. 339 (letter 713).
29 Załuski, *Scottish autumn of Frederick Chopin*, p. 94. For further biographical information on Szulczewki see Mirska and Hordyński, *Chopin documents*, p. 346, n.185, and Niecks, *Chopin*, vol.2, p. 303, n.35. More generally, see Zamoyski, *Chopin*, pp. 255, 262, 269, 270, 334.
30 Hedley, *Chopin letters*, p. 314, and Niecks, *Chopin*, vol.2, p. 277.
31 Hedley, *Chopin correspondence*, p. 17. Chopin to Grzymała, 13 [May 1848].
32 As Chopin writes: 'I give a few lessons at home', in a letter to Mlle de Rozières, 1 June 1848 (Hedley, *Chopin correspondence*, p. 318); and 'I give a few lessons at home at a guinea a time', in a letter to Grzymała, 2 June [1848] (Hedley, *Chopin correspondence*, p. 319). According to Lowell Mason's diary, in June 1837 Moscheles was charging a guinea a lesson, and taught from 8 o'clock in the morning until 7 o'clock in the evening. 'He takes no time for rest and takes no lunch except what he takes in his carriage in going from one pupil to another.' Mason, *A Yankee musician in Europe*, p. 51.
33 Hedley, *Chopin correspondence*, p. 318. Chopin to Mlle de Rozières, 1 June 1848.
34 Hedley, *Chopin correspondence*, p. 315. Chopin to Gutmann, 6 May 1848. See 'Chopin: Pianos in Britain' in Willis, 'Chopin in Britain', vol.2, Appendix D, pp. 352–4.
35 Hipkins, *List of Broadwood exhibits*, p. 12. The essay entitled 'Chopin's pianoforte' is on pp. 12–13.
36 See Macintyre, 'Chopin's true sound', *passim*. Chopin's reference to '*my Pleyel*' is in Hedley, *Chopin correspondence*, p. 317. Chopin to Grzymała, 13 [May 1848].

According to Eigeldinger, 'Chopin and Pleyel', p. 394, the underlining here appears in Chopin's original Polish. It does not do so in either Sydow, *KFC*, vol.2, pp. 244–6 (letter 625) or Hedley's English translation of the letter. In his letter of 24–9 April 1848 to Mlle de Rozières (TiFC [Warsaw], M/3255), Chopin specifically refers to his piano as not yet unpacked after his Channel crossing. See note 27 above.

37 Hipkins, *How Chopin played*, p. 6. Hipkins' volume was assembled after his death by his daughter, Edith, and is not entirely reliable. See the entry on Hipkins in Eigeldinger's *Chopin: pianist and teacher*, p. 93, n.11, and *Chopin vu par ses élèves*, p. 130, n.11. Macintyre, 'Chopin's true sound', p. 26, says that Chopin played this Pleyel, not a Broadwood, at Gore House, but quotes no source.

38 Hedley, *Chopin correspondence*, p. 28. Chopin adds: 'Mr Mankowski, who was kind enough to undertake to convey this sum to you, is a very agreeable young nobleman – a friend of Koźmian – who adores music. I hope he succeeded in meeting you. I should so much like to hear about you from him and to learn how you are.'

39 See Macintyre, 'Chopin's true sound', *passim*. Margaret Trotter, and 'the Trotters' appear in Fanny Erskine's diary. See Barlow, 'Encounters with Chopin', *passim*. As quoted by Macintyre (p. 27), Alec Cobbe 'believes that Margaret Trotter, who died unmarried, bequeathed the instrument to her grand-niece, Margaret Lindsay, who married Sir Lewis Majendie of Castle Hedingham, near Saffron Walden'. Eventually, it was bought by Alec Cobbe in 1988, and is now in the Cobbe Collection. See also the anonymous article, 'Grand historic find, a Chopin discovery: composer's own piano uncovered in Surrey collection', *BBC Music magazine* (May 2007), p. 8. The 'sale' of the piano to Lady Trotter is a puzzle. Had Chopin 'owned' the Pleyel, he surely would not have sent Camille Pleyel the £80 he received from selling it. He would have kept the money. The piano must have been loaned to Chopin by the Pleyel firm, whose pianos Chopin was promoting and selling, as an agent. Chopin's sale of Pleyels, earning him commission, is commented on by Eigeldinger, 'Chopin and Pleyel', p. 394. A letter of 6 June 1910, from Anne D. Houstoun, at Johnstone Castle, to 'J Maynard Saunders, Esq', tells him that she has a Pleyel piano, autographed by Chopin in 1848, and 'a pencil sketch of Chopin by Winterhalter'. See BnF (Paris), Vma.4334 (7).

40 TiFC (Warsaw), M/378, Chopin's pocket diary for 1848. Deciphering Chopin's handwriting in his diary can be difficult. Students whose names appear in it between 10 May and 21 July 1848 include Lady Mary Kristofer, Cooper, Erskine, Maberly, Park/Parke/Parker, Duchess of Sutherland, Wedgwood, and Lady Wild/Wylde. This list is not comprehensive. No diary for 1837 belonging to Chopin seems to have survived.

41 Hedley, *Chopin correspondence*, p. 317, n.1. Chopin to Gryzmała, 13 [May 1848].

42 On 2 June [1848], Chopin tells Gryzmała: 'I give Sutherland's daughter one lesson a week' (Hedley, *Chopin correspondence*, p. 319). The Duke of Sutherland's payment to Chopin of seven guineas for lessons for his daughter, Lady Constance Leveson-Gower, is recorded in the Duke's account book, January 1845 – June 1855, in Staffordshire Record Office, Stafford, D593/R/18/1. James Yorke kindly gave me this reference. See also, Yorke, *Lancaster House*, pp. 98, 186, n.50 (Chapter 3).

43 For the publication of the Two Nocturnes (Op.55), dedicated to Jane Stirling, and the Three Mazurkas (Op.56), dedicated to Catherine Maberly, see Eigeldinger, *Chopin vu par ses élèves*, p. 233.

44 For Mrs Erskine see Wróblewska-Straus, 'Jane Wilhelmina Stirling's letters to Ludwika Jędrzejewicz', p. 62, n.2. Striking omissions from Chopin's diary are any references to lessons given to Jane Stirling or Tellefsen.

45 For Chopin's students generally see Eigeldinger, *Chopin vu par ses élèves*, *passim*, and the sources cited there. For further lists of his pupils see, particularly, Bronarski, 'Les élèves de Chopin', *passim*; Holland, 'Chopin's teaching and his students', pp. 84–140; and Jaeger, 'Quelques nouveaux noms d'élèves de Chopin', *passim*.

46 Opieński, *Chopin's letters*, pp. 370–1 (letter 261). Chopin to his family in Warsaw, 19 August 1848. In Hedley's translation of this letter (*Chopin correspondence*,

pp. 331–40), the names of several ladies, including Lady Cadogan's, are omitted on p. 333.

47 Although Chopin's Parisian pupil Mlle la Comtesse Émilie de Flauhaut had married Lord Shelburne in 1843, as his second wife, and now lived in England, there is no evidence that she had lessons from Chopin in London. However, she wrote to him from Lansdowne House asking for two tickets for his recital at Mrs Sartoris' house on Friday 23 June 1848. See the three letters in TiFC (Warsaw), M/432/l.k.II.p. 2, M/432/2.k.II.p. 2, and M/433/2.k.II.p. 2.

48 Charlotte de Rothschild was also the dedicatee of Chopin's Ballade, no. 4, in F minor (Op.52), first published in 1842.

49 Hedley, *Chopin correspondence*, p. 320.

50 Hedley, *Chopin correspondence*, p. 326. Chopin to Gryzmała, [End of July 1848], and Hedley, *Chopin correspondence*, p. 337. Chopin to his family in Warsaw, [10–19 August 1848]. For Lady Murray's meeting in Britain in 1858 with the Polish pianist Cecylia Działyńska, see Eigeldinger, *Chopin vu par ses élèves*, p. 138, n.29.

51 Sonkei Kaku Library, Maeda Ikutoku Kai Foundation, Tokyo, cited in Wróblewska-Straus, 'Jane Wilhelmina Stirling's letters to Ludwika Jędrzejewicz', p. 63, n.4.

52 Hedley, *Chopin correspondence*, p. 327. Chopin to Franchomme, 11 August [1848]. For Drechsler, see Baptie, *Musical Scotland*, p. 47.

53 Hedley, *Chopin correspondence*, pp. 325–6. Chopin to Gryzmała, 8–17 July [1848]. 'Lady Peel' was surely Julia (née Floyd), wife of Sir Robert Peel, 2nd Bt, formerly prime minister (1834–5). The Peels had seven children, five sons and two daughters: the daughters were Julia (1821–93) and Eliza (1832–83). In 1848 Julia was already the Countess of Jersey, so Chopin's actual or prospective pupil was probably Eliza. See also the entry by John Prest on Sir Robert Peel, 2nd Bt, in *Oxford DNB online*. Chopin's pocket diary for 1848 in TiFC (Warsaw) contains no reference to any pupil who had five lessons in one week, and the student from Liverpool remains unidentified.

54 As, for instance, he wrote from Calder House: 'They want me to play at Edinburgh in the first days of October. If it means making some money, and if I have the strength, I shall certainly do it, for I don't know how I am going to manage this winter.' Hedley, *Chopin correspondence*, p. 339. Chopin to his family in Warsaw, [10–19 August 1848].

55 Johnson, *Guizot*, p. 261. For a more recent comprehensive view of Guizot, see Theis, *François Guizot*, passim.

56 Hedley, *Chopin correspondence*, pp. 335–6. Chopin to his family in Warsaw, [10–19 August 1848]. The arrival of Guizot's family in Bryanston Square on 3 March is recorded in Theis, *François Guizot*, p. 469.

57 Hallé, *Autobiography*, pp. 118–19. In April that year, according to William Atwood, Chopin visited Guizot at his London home. See Atwood, *Parisian worlds*, pp. 73, 93. No documentation is given.

58 Hedley, *Chopin correspondence*, p. 321. Chopin to Gryzmała, 2 June, [1848].

59 For Scheffer's portrait of Guizot see Ewals, *Ary Scheffer (1795–1858): gevierd romanticus*, pp. 170–2, and Ewals, *Ary Scheffer (1795–1858)*, p. 41.

60 Johnson, *Guizot*, p. 320.

61 See Harasowski, *The skein of legends around Chopin*, pp. 63–81, which is a chapter entitled 'A weaver of legends caught red-handed'.

62 Karasowski, *Chopin*, pp. 345–6.

63 Niecks was unable to find verification of this episode, and is justly cautious about accepting Karasowski's authority. See Niecks, *Chopin*, vol.2, p. 282.

64 The invitation to Chopin is in TiFC (Warsaw), M/436.k.II.p. 2. A letter to Chopin in Paris from Henry Fowler Broadwood, No. 33 Great Pulteney Street, dated 1 February 1849, is in TiFC (Warsaw), M/434.k.II.p. 2.

65 See the entry on Henry Fowler Broadwood by Charles Mould in *Oxford DNB online*, and Wainwright, *Broadwood by appointment*, passim. See also the chapter, 'John Broadwood and Sons', in Burnett, *Company of pianos*, pp. 44–66.

66 Hedley, *Chopin correspondence*, pp. 335–6. Chopin to his family in Warsaw [10–19 August 1848]. This letter goes on to refer to Broadwood's arrangements for Chopin's rail travel to Edinburgh.
67 Wainwright, *Broadwood by appointment*, pp. 131, 139.
68 Wainwright, *Broadwood by appointment*, p. 165.
69 Entry on Henry Fowler Broadwood by Charles Mould in *Oxford DNB online*. For the context of the history of the Broadwood firm see, e.g., Ehrlich, *The piano*, especially pp. 34–41.
70 For the exhibitions, see Wainwright, *Broadwood by appointment*, pp. 185, 187 (1862), 192 (1867), and 210, 222 (1885).
71 The authorship of the catalogue is not given, but Hipkins' daughter, Edith, ascribes it to her father in *How Chopin played*, p. 36. A typescript of the essay 'Chopin's pianoforte' is in the Broadwood Archives, Surrey History Centre (Woking), 2185/JB/83/82.
72 For A.J. Hipkins, see the entries on him by Cyril Ehrlich in *Grove music online* and Anne Pimlott Baker in *Oxford DNB online*. Eigeldinger (*Chopin: pianist and teacher*, p. 93, n.11, and *Chopin vu par ses élèves*, p. 130, n.11) discusses Hipkins' career, and the publication of Edith Hipkins' book, *How Chopin played*, and its sources.
73 For Bennett, see Arthur D. Walker's entry on him in *Grove music online*.
74 Bennett, in his *Frederic Chopin*, p. 51, writes: 'We are indebted to the great kindness of Mr A J Hipkins, of the firm of Broadwood and Sons, for a most interesting paper on Chopin in England. The communication needs neither preface nor comment. It is clear, full, and authoritative as to the matter of which it treats.' Similarly, in his *Chopin* (vol.1, p. vii), Niecks acknowledges Hipkins' contribution to the publications of Bennett and Hueffer, as well as his own; when he covers Chopin's visit to England and Scotland in chapter 31, vol.2 (pp. 277–306), Niecks thanks Hipkins for 'reading the proof-sheets of this chapter' (p. 277n). On p. 57, Bennett quotes John Muir Wood's personal comments on Jane Stirling, Mrs Houston, and Chopin's Glasgow concert.
75 Parakilas, *Piano roles*, pp. 403–4. Eventually, about the time of Hipkins' death in 1903, Parakilas explains, tradition and progress went their separate ways, and 'even the most conservative of piano makers, like Broadwood and Érard, came to accept changes that had been introduced to the design of grand pianos half a century earlier.'
76 Hipkins, *How Chopin played*, p. 4. A footnote glosses the reference to 'the Broadwood piano' thus: 'The Boudoir cottage piano – Pleyel bought one as a model for Paris'. Broadwood's premises in Great Pulteney Street are referred to in Foreman, *London: a musical gazetteer*, p. 332, and shown in the map on p. 331.
77 Hipkins, *How Chopin played*, p. 5.
78 Hipkins, *How Chopin played*, pp. 5–6.
79 Hipkins, *How Chopin played*, pp. 6–7.
80 See Cobbe, *Composer instruments*, pp. 59–61. Richard Burnett identifies the 1846 trichord Broadwood grand at Finchcocks (No. 16,582) as of the same specification as the model played by Chopin at his London concerts. He adds: 'The "Chopin" Broadwood, however, was not Chopin's favourite instrument. He much preferred the Broadwood bichord cottage grands, because of the lovely una corda, and the delicate and intimate tone colour of the instruments.' See Burnett, *Company of pianos*, p. 196, n.2, and the illustration on p. 55.
81 Harding, *The piano-forte*, pp. 399–400, shows a price list of pianos from John Broadwood and Sons, dated January 1840. The cases, in ascending price, were described as Mahogany, Elegant, and Rosewood. The cheapest piano was 38 guineas, the most expensive 155 guineas.
82 Hipkins, *List of Broadwood exhibits*, pp. 12–13. Broadwood pianos of Chopin's date are listed in Clinkscale, *Makers of the piano*, vol.2, pp. 47–61, but the only one with possible Chopin connections here is the Broadwood grand at Gargunnock, p. 55 (EP 278). In his piece, 'Backstage notes', in *The New Yorker* of 23 November 1998 (p. 32), Jay Fielden writes of a recent concert at Lincoln Center when Emanuel Ax played

88   *London 1848: Chopin in London*

'an Empire-style pianoforte, manufactured in London by John Broadwood & Sons in 1840'. As Ax 'stormed into Chopin's Second Piano Concerto, the vapors that often seem to surround the arch-Romantic vanished, and the audience heard what it might have been like when the composer himself was at the keyboard'. That said, writes Fielden, 'the vintage instrument could be described as sounding like a harpsichord on steroids.' It was being sold from a 'piano emporium across the street from Lincoln Center, called Klavierhaus'. The price: $100,000.

83 For Chorley, see Robert Bledsoe, *Chorley, passim*, and Bledsoe's articles on Chorley in *Grove music online*, and *Oxford DNB online*.
84 For Davison, see the entries on him by Leanne Langley in *Grove music online* and John Warrack in *Oxford DNB online*, and Richard Kitson, 'James William Davison,' *passim*.
85 See Rigby, *Hallé*, pp. 68–9.
86 For musical periodicals, see Leanne Langley's publications, notably 'The musical press in 19th-century England', 'Music', and 'The English musical journal in the early nineteenth century'.
87 See Chapter 4 of *Chopin in Britain*.
88 Niecks, *Chopin*, vol.2, p. 278.
89 Hallé, *Life and letters*, p. 229. For Hallé in London in 1848, see Beale, *Hallé*, pp. 38–43.
90 Niecks, *Chopin*, vol.2, p. 187.
91 The following section is based largely on Langley, 'Italian opera and the English press', p. 2.
92 Colvin, *Dictionary*, p. 932.
93 Langley, 'Italian opera and the English press', p. 2. For observations on George Hogarth's perception of Jenny Lind, Mario, and Grisi in 1847 and 1848, see Langley, 'Italian opera and the English press', p. 7.
94 Langley, 'Italian opera and the English press', p. 2.
95 Colvin, *Dictionary*, p. 932.
96 For Sir Michael Costa, see the entries on him in *Grove music online*, by Nigel Burton and Keith Horner, and in *Oxford DNB online*, by J.A.F. Maitland, revised by John Warrack.
97 Nalbach, *The King's Theatre*, pp. 85, 92–3. The description of the King's Theatre (i.e., Her Majesty's Theatre) in Chopin's day is on pp. 85–93. Chorley's comments on the London opera scene in 1848 are considered in Bledsoe, *Chorley*, pp. 162–3.
98 Hedley, *Chopin correspondence*, pp. 268–9. Chopin to his family in Warsaw, 11 October 1846. For tabulation of the repertoire of Covent Garden and Her Majesty's Theatre, see Hall-Witt, *Fashionable acts*, pp. 298–9. See also Chorley, *Thirty years' musical recollections*, vol.2, pp. 22, 29.
99 See the conspectus of London operatic life at this time in White, *History of English opera*, especially pp. 260–301. For the 1848 season in Covent Garden, see Rosenthal, *Two centuries of opera at Covent Garden*, pp. 65–84, and the analysis on pp. 679–81; and for Her Majesty's Theatre, see Lumley, *Reminiscences of the opera*, pp. 206–29. Lumley's book is dedicated to Mrs Grote.
100 Rosenthal, *Two centuries of opera at Covent Garden*, pp. 679–80.
101 Hedley, *Chopin correspondence*, p. 321. Chopin to Gryzmała, 2 June [1848]. But see Chorley's comments on Viardot in his *Thirty years' musical recollections*, vol.2, pp. 45–60. Viardot's London season of 1848 is covered in Steen, *Enchantress of nations*, pp. 153–67.
102 Hedley, *Chopin correspondence*, p. 321. Chopin to Gryzmała, 2 June [1848]. For Chopin's enthusiasm for Lind's performance in *La sonnambula* during his London stay, see Hedley, *Chopin correspondence*, pp. 314–15. Chopin to Gryzmała, 4 [May 1848]; Hedley, *Chopin correspondence*, p. 317. Chopin to Gryzmała, 13 [May 1848]; and Hedley, *Chopin correspondence*, pp. 334–5. Chopin to his family in Warsaw, [10–19

August 1848]. Lady Blessington told Hans Christian Andersen, when he visited Gore House, that she was 'captivated' by Jenny Lind, and the 'purity' of her performance in *La sonnambula*. 'The tears stood in her eyes while she spoke of it', Andersen reported. See Sadleir, *Strange life of Lady Blessington*, p. 320. Thomas Carlyle, who heard a performance by Lind in *La sonnambula*, in August 1848, described it as 'a chosen bit of nonsense from beginning to end'. Quoted in Ashton, *Thomas and Jane Carlyle*, p. 288.
103 Both these accolades are in Hedley, *Chopin correspondence*, pp. 318–19. Chopin to Mlle de Rozières, 1 June 1848.
104 Grote, *George Grote*, p. 185. See also Clarke, *George Grote*, pp. 83–4. For the Grotes generally, see the articles by Joseph Hamburger on George Grote and Harriet Grote, respectively, in *Oxford DNB online*. For No. 12 Savile Row, part of a development (1732–5) by the 3rd Earl of Burlington, see Bradley and Pevsner, *London 6: Westminster*, p. 569; *Survey of London*, vol.31, *The Parish of St James Westminster*, part 2, North of Piccadilly (1963), p. 524; and Weinreb, Hibbert, and Keay, *London encyclopaedia*, p. 823. For the blue plaque to George Grote, see Cole, *Lived in London*, p. 425, and the map on p. 424.
105 For Ella, see Bashford, *Pursuit of high culture*, pp. 150–1.
106 Clarke, *George Grote*, p. 81.
107 Clarke, *George Grote*, p. 81.
108 Clarke, *George Grote*, pp. 81, 82. Presumably this was at No. 4 Eccleston Street Maja Trochimczyk draws attention to Chopin's comments on Jenny Lind's Swedish character in 'Chopin and the "Polish race"', p. 306, n.8.
109 Eastlake, *Mrs Grote: a sketch*, p. 89.
110 Eastlake, *Mrs Grote: a sketch*, p. 90. Mendelssohn and Lind are considered on pp. 89–97. The words 'second visit' must be a slip here. The premiere was at Birmingham in 1846. Mrs Grote's projected biography of Jenny Lind was never completed. But see the chapter, 'Mrs Grote and Jenny Lind', in Lewin, *Lewin letters*, vol.1, pp. 375–86. It is noted on p. 375 here that Mrs Grote met Jenny Lind in Frankfurt, in September 1845.
111 Eastlake, *Mrs Grote: a sketch*, p. 94. During a provincial tour, accompanied by Mrs Grote, Jenny Lind visited Newcastle, where they stayed with Joseph Grote, brother of George Grote. Joseph's brother-in-law, a young captain in the Indian army, Claudius Harris, was also living at the house, and he was 'entirely, mastered by the charm and goodness of the wonderful singer'. Holland and Rockstro, *Jenny Lind the artist*, p. 387. Their romance is considered here on pp. 387–91.
112 Grote, *George Grote*, p. 185. Lind's time with the Grotes in Paris and Amiens in 1849 is chronicled here on pp. 192–4. An autograph notebook recording Lind's performances, inscribed by her on the flyleaf "Annotations-Bok för Jenny Lind", in Swedish, containing her list of performances from 25 September 1846 in Frankfurt, to 19 December 1851 in Philadelphia, is described in the catalogue of Sotheby's sale of musical manuscripts in London, 19 May 2006 (L06402, lot 92). Included are her performances in London and elsewhere in Britain in 1847, 1848, and 1849. It was sold for a hammer price, with buyer's premium, of £4,320.
113 Holland and Rockstro, *Jenny Lind*, p. 262.
114 Mrs Grote to Mrs Frances von Koch, 24 July 1848, in Lewin, *Lewin letters*, vol.2, p. 62.
115 Hedley, *Chopin correspondence*, pp. 334–5. Chopin to his family in Warsaw, [10–19 August 1848].
116 Hedley, *Chopin correspondence*, p. 335. Chopin to his family in Warsaw, [10–19 August 1848]. An attempt to prove that Chopin and Jenny Lind had 'a secret romance of dramatic proportions' [sic] is the basis of Jorgensen, *Chopin and the Swedish nightingale* (2003).
117 Hedley, *Chopin correspondence*, p. 334. Chopin to his family in Warsaw, [10–19 August 1848]. Jennifer Hall-Witt points out (*Fashionable acts*, p. 182) that 'Queen

90   London 1848: Chopin in London

Victoria attended Her Majesty's Theatre twenty-seven times [in 1847], including all sixteen of Jenny Lind's performances, but patronized Covent Garden only nine times.'

118 Hedley, *Chopin correspondence*, p. 334. Chopin to his family in Warsaw, [10–19 August 1848]. Jennifer Hall-Witt indicates (*Fashionable acts*, pp. 160, 302) that Benjamin Lumley's book *Reminiscences of the opera* (1864) 'was almost entirely written by Harriet Grote, with some assistance from John Palgrave Simpson and John Oxenford, both writers. Lumley wrote the preface and probably some of the footnotes' (p. 302).
119 For Cramer, Beale & Co's premises, see Lewis Foreman, *London: a musical gazetteer*, p. 317. Both Wessel and 'Verrey' are given the address of No. 229 Regent Street in *Kelly's directory, London 1848*. Details of the partnerships, and locations, of 'Cramer' and 'Wessel' appear, respectively, in Humphries and Smith, *Music publishing in the British Isles*, pp. 120–1, 363, 328; and Parkinson, *Victorian music publishers*, pp. 62–3, 285–6.
120 See Grabowski, 'Publication des valses, Op.64', *passim*. See also Brown, 'Chopin and his English publisher', pp. 368–9.
121 Niecks, *Chopin* vol.2, p. 287, n.15.
122 See Grabowski, 'Publication des valses, Op.64', pp. 56, 59. For Wessel, see 'Frédéric Chopin and his publishers', exhibition catalogue, Department of Special Collections, University of Chicago Library, 1998, case 11, and the entry on Christian Rudolf Wessel, by Alexis Chitty and Peter Ward Jones, in *Grove music online*.
123 See Chapter 4 of *Chopin in Britain*.
124 Hedley, *Chopin correspondence*, p. 312. Chopin to Molin, [18 April 1848]. For Molin, see the Introduction and Conclusion of *Chopin in Britain*. For Chopin's treatment by Molin in Paris, see Atwood, *Parisian worlds*, pp. 348–9.
125 See the article on Quin by G.C. Boase and Bernard Leary in *Oxford DNB online*. After taking his MD at Edinburgh in 1820, Quin built up a successful practice amongst the Euopean aristocracy in Naples before returning to London. Patronized in part for his social acceptability, Quin started the British Homeopathic Society (later the Faculty of Homeopathy) in 1844, and chiefly through his efforts the London Homeopathic Hospital (later the Royal London Homeopathic Hospital) was founded in 1849 in Golden Square, Soho; it moved to Great Ormond Street in 1859. See Rankin, 'Professional organisation and the development of medical knowledge', pp. 46–7, for material in this paragraph; the quotation is on p. 47. Anne Thackeray Ritchie refers to Quin in a letter to Mrs Anne Carmichael-Smyth, Friday 26 February 1846. See Shankman, Bloom and Maynard, *Anne Thackeray Ritchie: journals and letters*, letter 6, pp. 18, 299, n.4.
126 For Dr Malan, see Chapter 10 of *Chopin in Britain*.
127 Handley, *Homeopathic love story*, p. 204.
128 See Hedley, *Chopin correspondence*, p. 350. Chopin to Gryzmała, 17–18 [November 1848].

Plate 1 Ary Scheffer (1795–1873). Self-portrait, 1838. Rijksmuseum, Amsterdam. Akg-images/Quint & Lox

Plate 2 Landing at Dover from the steam packet. Painting attributed to Michael William Sharp, circa 1826. Copyright National Maritime Museum, Greenwich, London

Plate 3 Sablonière Hôtel, Leicester Square, London. Watercolour by Charles John Smith, circa 1830. London Metropolitan Archives

Plate 4 Bryanston Square, London. Entrance doorway to No. 46 on west side. James T. Parkinson, architect, circa 1811. Photograph: Peter Willis, 2003

Plate 5 Pauline Viardot (1821–1910). Portrait by Carl Timoleon von Neff, circa 1842. Akg-images/RIA Nowosti

Plate 6 Hôtel Lambert, Île St-Louis, Paris. External view from across the Seine. Photograph from website *www.insecula.com* (2006)

Plate 7 Érard Grand Pianoforte No. 713 (London, 1843), purchased by Jane Stirling in 1843, and perhaps at Keir when Chopin stayed there in 1848. Cobbe Collection, Hatchlands, Surrey. Photograph: Salvatore Arancio

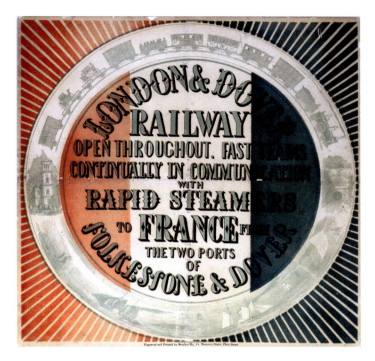

Plate 8 Poster for the South Eastern Railway Company, circa 1845, advertising cross-Channel services between London and France, via Folkestone and Dover. National Railway Museum, York

Plate 9 Pleyel Grand Pianoforte No. 13,819 (Paris, circa 1848), brought from Paris to London by Chopin, April 1848. Cobbe Collection, Hatchlands, Surrey. Photograph: Salvatore Arancio

Plate 10 Broadwood Grand Pianoforte No. 17,047 (London, 1847), played by Chopin in 1848 in London recitals. Royal Academy of Music, London, on Permanent Loan to the Cobbe Collection, Hatchlands, Surrey. Photograph: Salvatore Arancio

Plate 11 No. 99 Eaton Place, London. Exterior, showing plaque commemorating Chopin's recital there on Friday 23 June 1848. Photograph: Peter Willis, 2008

Plate 12 No. 99 Eaton Place, London. Detail of plaque commemorating Chopin's recital there on Friday 23 June 1848. Photograph: Peter Willis, 2008

Plate 13 Jemima Blackburn (née Wedderburn). *A rehearsal*. Watercolour, 1844, showing music-making, under Ella's direction, at the home of her uncle, Sir George Clerk, with the Earl of Falmouth fourth from right, playing the violin or viola. Copyright National Portrait Gallery, London

Plate 14 Alfred, Count D'Orsay (1801–52). Portrait by Sir George Hayter, 1839. Copyright National Portrait Gallery, London

Plate 15 No. 35 St Andrew Square, Edinburgh (formerly the Douglas Hotel). Exterior facing St Andrew Square. Photograph: Paul Zanre, 2007

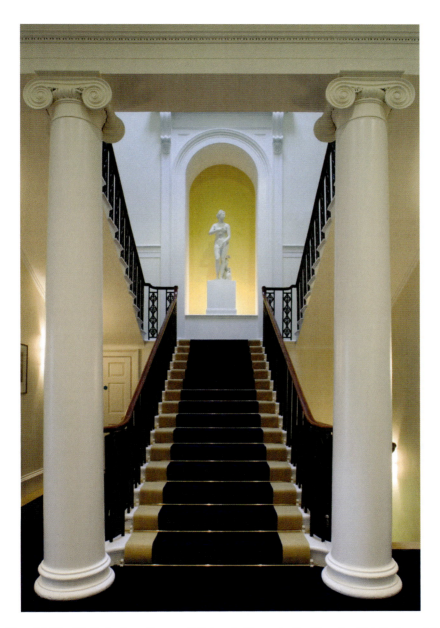

Plate 16 No. 35 St Andrew Square, Edinburgh (formerly the Douglas Hotel). Imperial staircase leading off entrance hall. Photograph: Paul Zanre, 2007

Plate 17 No. 10 Warriston Crescent, Edinburgh, with plaque on right commemorating Chopin's stay in 1848. Courtesy of Miss Jane Kellett. Photograph: Peter Willis, 1998. The plaque reads:

FRYDERYK CHOPIN
1810–1849 POLISH COMPOSER
STAYED HERE ON THE OCCASION
OF HIS CONCERT IN EDINBURGH
ON THE 4TH OCTOBER 1848
TO COMMEMORATE THE HUNDREDTH
ANNIVERSARY OF THIS EVENT THIS PLAQUE
WAS PLACED BY THE POLISH COMMUNITY
AND THEIR SCOTTISH FRIENDS IN 1948

Plate 18 Keir House, Perthshire. Entrance, designed by David Hamilton (1820), resited in 1969. Photograph: Peter Willis, 2008

Plate 19 Pleyel Grand Pianoforte No. 1,318 (Paris, circa 1827), mahogany, owned by Sarah, Duchess of Hamilton, now at Lennoxlove, East Lothian, and formerly at Hamilton Palace, where it may have been played by Chopin in 1848. Courtesy the Duke of Hamilton

Plate 20 Strachur House, Argyll. Central block, from west-south-west, with entrance porch added after Chopin's time. Copyright Historic Environment Scotland (HES), Edinburgh

Plate 21 Strachur House, Argyll. Entrance hall and staircase. Copyright Historic Environment Scotland (HES), Edinburgh

4 London 1848
Recitals

'Chopin seems to have gone to a great many parties of various kinds', wrote his biographer Frederick Niecks, 'but he could not always be prevailed upon to give the company a taste of his artistic quality.' As an instance of this, Niecks notes that Brinley Richards, the Welsh pianist and composer, saw Chopin 'at an evening party at the house of the politician Milner Gibson, where he did not play, although he was asked to do so'.[1] Similarly, when Chopin attended an evening event on 6 May 1848 at George Grote's home, he did not perform, although the next month, as we have seen, he did play at a concert arranged by Mrs Grote, with the Belgian soprano Julie Dorus-Gras as singer.[2] The actor William Macready was less successful: he arranged a dinner in Chopin's honour, at which he was to have met Thackeray, Berlioz, Adelaide Procter, Julius Benedict, and other notables, but the composer never turned up.[3]

Chopin's ill health meant he was regarded, notably in France, as a composer 'de chambre de malade' who displayed the pallor of the grave as through music he displayed his suffering.[4] The flavour of such private performances is well captured by the Italian writer and critic Pier Angelo Fiorentino, in the *supplément* to the *Dictionnaire de la conversation et de la lecture* (1868), where he describes meeting Chopin in London 'chez un des écrivains les plus distingués de la presse anglaise'. He sets the scene:

> Nous étions dix ou douze tout au plus dans un petit salon discret, confortable, propice également à la causerie ou au recueillement. Chopin remplaça Mme Viardot au piano, et nous plongea dans un ravissement ineffable. Je ne sais ce qu'il nous joua; je ne sais combaien de temps dura notre extase: nous n'étions plus sur la terre; il nous avait transportés dans des régions inconnues, dans un milieu de flamme d'azur, où l'âme dégagée des liens corporels vogue vers l'infini. Ce fut, hélas! le chant du cygne.[5]

The description here of Chopin and Pauline Viardot, performing at the home of a London writer, with Chopin's music recalling a swan's song, evokes a powerful image.

The 'écrivain' referred to by Fiorentino may well have been H.F. Chorley; according to Bledsoe, Chopin had 'played at parties at Chorley's house'.[6] This was No. 15 Victoria Square, Lower Grosvenor Place, described by Elizabeth Barrett Browning as 'enchanted'.[7] Victoria Square was built in 1838–42 as a speculation by the architect Sir Matthew Wyatt; the houses are stuccoed, with giant Corinthian pilasters, and 'pepper-pot' corners.[8] Sir Charles Hallé, after writing about Mrs Sartoris' house at No. 99 Eaton Place, continues:

> Another house, the tiniest in London perhaps, but a real gem, to which I repaired often with great pleasure, was that of Henry F Chorley, the musical critic and contributor to the 'Athenaeum'. I was always sure to find interesting men there, and met Cockburn and Coleridge, who both rose to be Lord Chief Justices of England, for the first time under his roof.[9]

Hallé also encountered Chopin at Chorley's house, and heard the composer play there on several occasions.[10]

Another house famous for its celebrated guests was No. 24 Cheyne Row, Chelsea, the home of Thomas and Jane Welsh Carlyle (see Figure 4.1). A modest, four-storey brick building of three bays, it was Carlyle's home from 1834 until his death in 1881; it was established as a museum in 1895, restored by C.R. Ashbee, and passed to the National Trust in 1936.[11] Here, Jane Welsh Carlyle 'conducted a sparkling tea-table salon, attended by European refugees, American visitors, radicals, journalists, politicians, men about town, and their joint friends, rising women critics, and novelists'.[12] Chopin played for the Carlyles at Cheyne Row, in 1848. 'Even Carlyle', writes Rosemary Ashton, 'whose musical taste seems to have

"A Chelsea Interior" (Thomas and Jane Carlyle at home), by Robert Tait, 1857, detail

Figure 4.1 24 Cheyne Row, London. Detail from *A Chelsea interior*, by Robert Scott Tait, 1857. National Trust Picture Library/Michael Boys

been restricted more or less to Scottish ballads, thought him "a wonderful Musician".[13] On 7 July, Jane Welsh Carlyle seems to have attended the *matinée musicale* at Lord Falmouth's.[14] In mid-July, she told her cousin, Helen Welsh, 'that she had heard Chopin twice, and that he had visited Cheyne Row'.[15] The same month, Jane Carlyle wrote ecstatically to Jane Stirling: 'Oh, how I wish he understood English! How I wish I could open my heart to him!'[16] Others who heard Chopin at Cheyne Row included Ralph Waldo Emerson,[17] and perhaps Charles Dickens, whose portrait was painted by Ary Scheffer when the novelist was on an extended visit to Paris in 1855.[18]

Lady Anne Antrobus, wife of Sr Edmund Antrobus, 2nd Bt, was another of Chopin's hosts.[19] The Antrobuses' London house was at No. 146 Piccadilly; the banker Lionel de Rothschild lived at No. 148 Piccadilly,[20] and Rothschild's wife, Charlotte, indicates in her diary that Chopin played at Lady Antrobus' home on 12 May 1848. 'Chopin came into the room with great effort', Mme de Rothschild writes:

> he looked ghostlike, could hardly speak, and with every word his eyes filled with tears, his frail body twitched convulsively; he is extraordinarily thin, and yet it seemed to me as if there was not a bone in his body . . . I cannot tell how much I wondered at the unsurpassable delicacy of playing, which no other fingers could match, and his glittering interpretation; one could truly have imagined one was hearing shimmering pearls falling gentle onto the keys. Such soft, gentle, delicate, tender, sweet playing has surely never been perfected before.[21]

As a friend, patron and pupil of Chopin in Paris, Charlotte de Rothschild was nothing if not an admirer of the composer.[22]

Chopin's visits to the houses of Mrs Grote and the Broadwoods, Chorley, the Carlyles, and the Antrobuses, when he played in a domestic setting, without advertisement or tickets, are typical of others he made during 1848.[23] We do not know if and when he was paid on such occasions, but surely he must have performed without recompense many times. The sum of 20 guineas, which Chopin told 'Old Mme Rothschild' was his standard fee,[24] was his charge for his performance at Stafford House, for the Sutherlands, and he makes clear that there were two other occasions on which he received the same payment: at the Marquess of Douglas's, No. 13 Connaught Place,[25] and at the Countess of Gainsborough's, in Chandos Street, Cavendish Square.[26] On 2 June 1848, Chopin told Grzymała that he was having dinner that night with Lady Gainsborough, a former Lady of the Bedchamber to Queen Victoria, and that she was 'very charming to [him]'. 'She gave a *matinée* and introduced me to the leading society ladies', Chopin wrote.[27] The Duchess of Somerset, who lived at Somerset House, Park Lane, was also 'very charming',[28] and invited Chopin 'to her evening parties where the son of Don Carlos [the Spanish Pretender] spends most of his time . . . But the Duke is close-fisted', added Chopin, 'so they don't pay.'[29] The Duke and Duchess of Cambridge were other friends of the pianist, and lived at No. 94 Piccadilly, originally designed by Matthew Brettingham, later the Army and Navy Club (the 'In and Out').[30] Other possible hosts in London include Sir William Stirling Maxwell (as he became) at No. 38 Clarges Street,[31] and 'Madam Bunsen', wife of the Prussian Minister at the Court of St James's, at No. 4 Carlton House Terrace.[32]

Stafford House (now Lancaster House), Monday 15 May 1848

Chopin, with Lablache, Mario, Tamburini, and Benedict

Chopin's first concert, as distinct from domestic recital, was in the grand setting of Stafford House (now Lancaster House), the London home of the Duke and Duchess of Sutherland, on 15 May 1848. The Duchess of Sutherland, Mistress of the Robes to Queen Victoria, was wife of the 2nd Duke, and a Polish sympathizer. The subject of a celebrated portrait by Winterhalter, she was a leader of London society, and a notable supporter of liberal and philanthropic causes (see Figure 4.2).[33] The Sutherlands' Scottish seat was Dunrobin Castle, Sutherland, and Stafford House their London home.[34]

Stafford House was begun in 1825 as a royal residence for the Duke of York, and was first named York House; on the Duke's death in 1827, it was bought by the 2nd Marquess of Stafford (later the 1st Duke of Sutherland), and renamed Stafford House (see Figure 4.3). The original architects were Benjamin Dean Wyatt and Philip Wyatt, and in 1833–6 an attic storey was added by Sir Robert Smirke. In 1833, the 2nd Duke called back Benjamin Dean Wyatt for the decoration of the state rooms, with Smirke completing minor ones, and then, in 1839–41, Sir Charles Barry altered or finished several state rooms. The style is French, and sumptuous, with the ground floor dominated by a stair hall with a dramatic staircase rising to first-floor level. Throughout, paintings and sculpture are integrated into the decorative scheme, though since Chopin's time Stafford House has lost its great Sutherland collection of pictures. In 1912, the house was bought by Sir William Lever for use by the London Museum, and renamed Lancaster House. It was restored in 1952–3 by the British Government as a location for conferences and hospitality.[35]

The Duke and Duchess were both supporters of Polish refugees, with the Duke serving as vice-president of the Literary Association of the Friends of Poland. For her part, the Duchess on 5 June 1841 had held a concert at Stafford House in aid of the Polish cause, at which the performers were Julius Benedict, Adelaide Kemble, and Franz Liszt, an arm in a sling. Writing in the *Athenaeum* on 19 June 1841 (no.71, p. 478), Chorley pronounced that this 'Polish *matinée* will long be spoken of as the most brilliant entertainment of its kind within our memory'.[36] It was a success to be repeated when Chopin played at the house.

The occasion for this was the baptism of the Sutherlands' daughter, Lady Alexandrina Leveson-Gower, in the private chapel at Buckingham Palace on 15 May 1848; Queen Victoria herself was one of the godparents, and the guest of honour that evening at a dinner for eighty people at Stafford House.[37] The splendour

Figure 4.2 Harriet Elizabeth Georgina Leveson-Gower, Duchess of Sutherland (1806–68). Portrait by Winterhalter, 1849. Private Collection. Scottish National Portrait Gallery, Edinburgh

96   London 1848: recitals

Figure 4.3 Stafford (now Lancaster) House, St James's, London. Watercolour of west front, by Thomas Hosmer Shepherd, circa 1845, showing additional storey of 1833–8. Museum of London

of the occasion was not lost on the Queen; as she remarked to the Duchess of Sutherland on this or a similar occasion: 'I come from my house to your palace.'[38]

A concert followed. The *Morning Post* on 18 May 1848 (p. 6) explains that it featured the singers Lablache, Mario, and Tamburini, and the pianists Benedict and Chopin.[39] Chopin's playing, commented the *Illustrated London News* on 20 May, 'created a great sensation', while Julius Benedict accompanied the three singers 'admirably' as they sang the trio from Rossini's *William Tell*.[40] Furthermore, Benedict, having played with Liszt at Stafford House seven years before, now teamed up with Chopin in playing a Mozart duet (see Figure 4.4). 'More than thirty years after', Niecks reports, 'Sir Julius still had a clear recollection of "the great pains Chopin insisted should be taken in rehearsing it, to make the rendering of it at the concert as perfect as possible".'[41]

Chopin, as a soloist, seems to have played mazurkas at Stafford House, and he alludes in his letters to his wish for royal patronage. 'Her Majesty spoke a few very gracious words to me', he told Mlle de Rozières, on 1 June. 'I doubt, however, whether I shall be playing at Court, as a period of Court-mourning, lasting until the 22nd or 24th, has just begun for one of Her Majesty's aunts.'[42] In August, writing to his family from Scotland, Chopin describes how the Duchess of Sutherland introduced him to the Queen, who 'was gracious and spoke with me twice. Prince Albert moved closer to the piano. Everyone said that these are rare

Figure 4.4 Sir Julius Benedict (1804–85). Portrait from the *Illustrated London News*, 13 June 1885, p. 607. Private collection

favours.'[43] Unfortunately, no opportunity to play at Buckingham Palace ever came to him; the Queen, recording the concert in her diary, made only vague references to 'pretty music' and 'some pianists playing'.[44]

Despite such disappointment, Chopin waxed eloquent about the interior of Stafford House. 'I should like to describe to you the Duchess's palace, but it is beyond me', he writes. 'All those who know', he continues, 'say that the Queen of England herself has not such a residence. All the royal palaces and castles are ancient and splendid, but have not the taste and elegance of Stafford House.' Here, for instance, are 'splendid paintings, statues, galleries, carpets, all most beautifully laid out and with the most wonderful effects of perspective'. Nor could he forget 'the Queen standing on the stairs in the most dazzling light, covered with all her diamonds and orders – and the noblemen, wearing the Garter, descending the stairs with the greatest elegance, conversing in groups, halting on the various landings from every point of which there is something fresh to be admired'.[45]

Chopin told Gryzmała that he was paid 20 guineas for performing at Stafford House, and that 'this was the fee fixed for me by Broadwood on whose piano I play.'[46] The Broadwood used at Stafford House may have been Grand Pianoforte No. 17,047 (London, 1847), used by Chopin for his recitals at Mrs Sartoris' and the Earl of Falmouth's, and his concerts in Manchester and at Guildhall, and now in the Cobbe Collection at Hatchlands. We cannot tell. Chopin's connections with the Sutherlands continued. 'I give Sutherland's daughter one lesson a week', Chopin told Gryzmała on 2 June [1848].[47] This would have been Lady Constance Leveson-Gower, later Duchess of Westminster. According to Chopin's pocket diary, Lady Constance had seven weekly piano lessons between 25 May and 6 July 1848;[48] other manuscript sources indicate that he was paid seven guineas for them, and confirm that he received 20 guineas for the Stafford House concert itself.[49]

Chopin partly attributed his failure to receive royal patronage after the recital in Stafford House to his own lack of initiative. He made no 'special effort', he told his parents, writing from Scotland. 'Not only did I not try, but I did not call on the Court music-director, or rather the person who organises the Queen's concerts and conducts the Philharmonic Society orchestra (the leading concerts here, which correspond to those of the Paris Conservatoire).' Moreover, Chopin caused offence by declining an invitation to play from the Philharmonic Society orchestra itself, despite calling it 'a great favour, or rather a distinction, for everyone who comes her applies for it. Neither Kalkbrenner nor Hallé have played this year, in spite of all their efforts.' Chopin regarded one rehearsal ('a public one to which people are admitted with free tickets') as inadequate. He could withstand any criticism from the press, who after all (with the exception of Davison in *The Times*) had given 'good notices' of his *matinées*.[50]

Mrs Sartoris', No. 99 Eaton Place, Belgravia, Friday 23 June 1848

Chopin, with Mario and Alary

In 1842, the soprano Adelaide Kemble, daughter of Charles Kemble, and sister of Fanny Kemble, married Edward John Sartoris – a wealthy man of fashion, with aspirations to become a Member of Parliament – and on 23 December that year retired from the stage (see Figure 4.5). The loss to English opera was considerable.[51] 'My sister perpetually reminded me of Pasta', Fanny Kemble wrote, 'and, had she remained a few years longer in her profession, would, I think, have equalled her.'[52] The previous year, on 29 June 1841, Adelaide Kemble and Liszt had performed together at the house of Mr and Mrs George Grote at No. 4 Eccleston Street, an event described by Moscheles as 'really thrilling'.[53] Later that year,

London 1848: recitals 99

Figure 4.5 Adelaide Kemble (Mrs Sartoris) (1814–79). Albumen print by Camille Silvy, 1860.
Copyright National Portrait Gallery, London

Liszt invited Kemble to join him on a Rhineland tour, which proved a great success, and paved the way for her triumphant debut in *Norma* at Covent Garden that November. The conductor was Julius Benedict. 'Miss Kemble', Chorley wrote in the *Athenaeum*, 'was as completely in her part, musically and dramatically . . . as any among the glorious line of her predecessors.'[54] Moscheles, too, was full of praise, describing her as 'gifted with a glorious voice, which she uses with equal success in Italian bravuras, German Leider, or old classical music'.[55] After her retirement, Kemble continued to sing in private gatherings, she and her husband often linking up with Moscheles and his wife.[56] In 1844, after Mendelssohn had joined them following his final Philharmonic concert, Mrs Moscheles reported that Adelaide Kemble 'was in splendid voice. Our guests were so grateful and happy, not happier than the hostess herself, for those were golden hours indeed!'[57]

When, therefore, Mrs Sartoris held a *matinée musicale* featuring Frederick Chopin, she was continuing an established tradition in her life. Eaton Place, Belgravia, built by Thomas Cubitt and completed in 1850, consists of a broad street of grand houses.[58] Mrs Sartoris's former home, No. 99, is still in existence, although it is now converted into apartments (see Plate 11). It is stuccoed, classical in detail, with a projecting Doric porch in the centre, and a corbelled balustrade above which connects to a neighbouring residence. The ground floor is rusticated, with a basement below. Where the building turns the corner into West Eaton Place, there is a Blue Plaque commemorating Chopin's concert (see Plate 12). It reads:

FRYDERYK
CHOPIN
1810–1849
GAVE HIS FIRST
LONDON CONCERT
IN THIS HOUSE
JUNE 23 1848

In fact, this was not Chopin's first London concert, as his performance in Stafford House had taken place earlier, on 15 May 1848; but it was his first 'public' concert, in the sense that it was a recital for which members of the public could purchase tickets.[59]

The *Athenaeum* once again drew its readers' attention to Chopin's presence in London in its issue of 10 June 1848 (no.1076, p. 588), when it mentioned 'a pleasant rumour that possibly [Chopin] may be shortly heard in public – a *matinée or concert* being "in projection", his health permitting'. The rumour was confirmed by an advertisement in *The Times* of Thursday 15 June which indicated that the *matinée musicale* would begin at 3 o'clock, and that a 'limited number of tickets, one guinea each, with full particulars', were obtainable from Cranmer, Beale & Co at their premises at No. 201 Regent Street. One hundred and fifty were sold (see Figure 4.6). That Saturday, 17 June, the *Athenaeum* (no.1077, p. 613) announced that 'M. Chopin's *Matinée* (another attraction of the choicest possible quality) will be held on Friday next.'[60] A flyer, confirming the details, indicated that Chopin 'will perform several of his latest compositions'.

Chopin's friendship with, and admiration for, Adelaide Sartoris, whom he knew in Paris, is well attested. Now, 'she has been taken up by the whole of London society and is received everywhere, while everyone comes to her house', Chopin writes.[61] 'I feel quite at home with her; she is perfectly natural – she knows of all

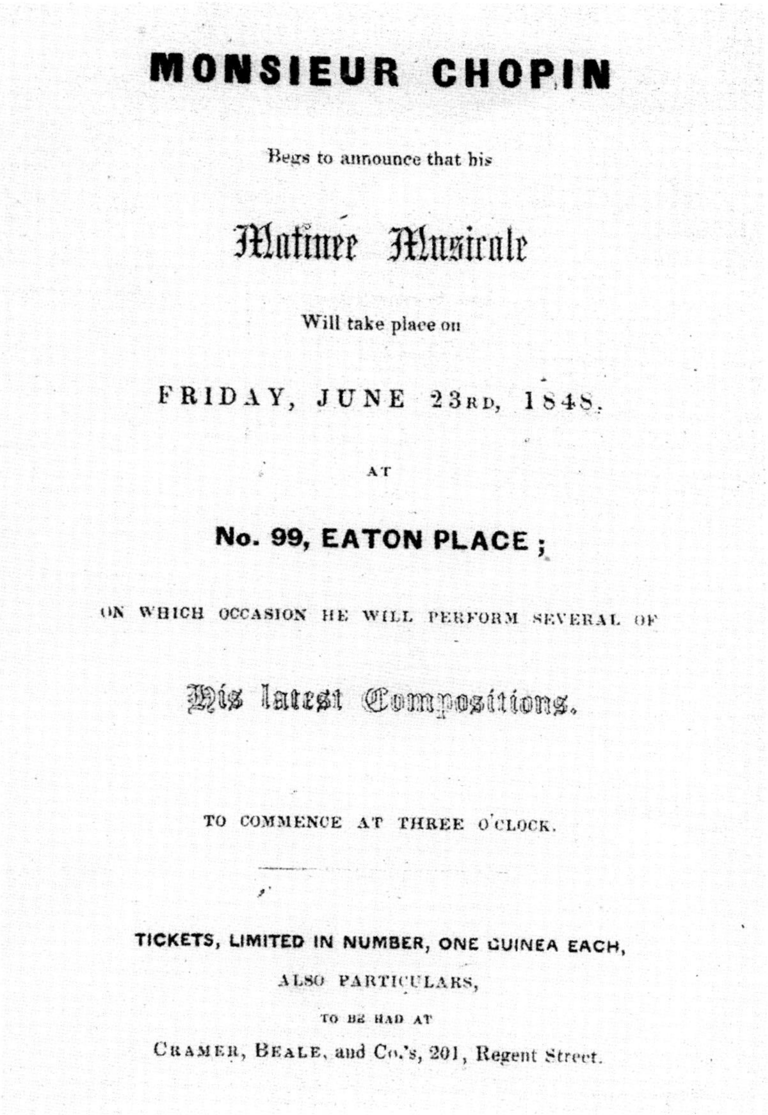

MONSIEUR CHOPIN

Begs to announce that his

Matinée Musicale

Will take place on

FRIDAY, JUNE 23RD, 1848.

AT

No. 99, EATON PLACE ;

ON WHICH OCCASION HE WILL PERFORM SEVERAL OF

His latest Compositions.

TO COMMENCE AT THREE O'CLOCK.

TICKETS, LIMITED IN NUMBER, ONE GUINEA EACH,

ALSO PARTICULARS,

TO BE HAD AT

CRAMER, BEALE, and Co.'s, 201, Regent Street.

Figure 4.6 Publicity for Chopin's *matinée musicale* at Mrs Sartoris' house, from Tomaszewski and Weber, *Diary in images* (1990), p. 238, and Mirska and Hordyński, *Chopin na obczyźnie* (1965), p. 286

my little private faults from our common friends – Dessauer and Liszt, for example.' The 'common friends' included the Thun-Hohenstein family, whom Chopin and his parents visited in 1835 at Tetschen, near the Polish frontier, and with

102 *London 1848: recitals*

whom Mrs Sartoris had also stayed.[62] There was also Charles Hallé. To Adelaide Sartoris, Hallé observed, 'I owe some of the greatest pleasures I have enjoyed in London'. She 'was indeed a rare woman', he continues,

> and her somewhat taciturn husband a man of vast intelligence. Both were musicians to the core, intensely enthusiastic, and of sound judgment. Their house reminded me strongly of the 'salon' of Armand Bertin in Paris, for it was the rendezvous of most of the remarkable people in London: poets, painters, musicians, all feeling equally at home, and all finding something to interest them.

Hallé is then specific:

> It is to Mrs Sartoris that I owe my first acquaintance with Browning, Thackeray, Dickens, Leighton, Watts, Wilkie Collins, and a host of other celebrities; and it will always be my pride to have enjoyed their affectionate and intimate friendship till death removed them both.

Here, at Mrs Sartoris' and at Chorley's houses, Hallé noted, he had the 'privilege and happiness' to hear Chopin play several times.[63]

Before his *soirées*, Chopin visited the Broadwood showroom in Great Pulteney Street to try out the pianos, and paid the cost of the hire with free tickets.[64] An ex-pupil from Paris, who wrote personally to Chopin asking for two tickets for the recital, was Lady Shelburne, formerly Mlle la Comtesse Emile de Flahault, to whom Chopin dedicated his Bolero in C major (Op.19);[65] her father-in-law, Lord Lansdowne, Chopin wrote, 'is himself very fond of music and every season gives a grand vocal concert at his own house'.[66] Among the listeners at Mrs Sartoris' house, to whom Chopin 'gave much pleasure', notes the *Musical World*, Jenny Lind 'seems to be the most enthusiastic'.[67]

Chopin shared the recital with the Italian tenor Giovanni Mario, who was accompanied at the piano by Giulio Alary. As can be seen from the programme (see Figure 4.7), Chopin played his own compositions, in four sets, described, respectively, as 'ANDANTE (Op.22), precedé d'un Largo', 'ANDANTE SOSTENUTO, 13me et 14 Etude', 'NOCTURNE, BERCEUSE, IMPROMPTU', and 'MAZURKA, BALLADE, VALSE'. Readily identifiable here is Op.22, which is the *Grande Polonaise brillante précédée d'un Andante spianato*;[68] the *Andante spianato* was one of Chopin's favourite recital pieces, and was probably included in his Glasgow concert, if not elsewhere, during his visit to Britain.

An account of Chopin's performance at Mrs Sartoris', written by Henry Fothergill Chorley, appeared in the *Athenaeum* of 1 July (no.1079, p. 660).[69] Chorley was unrestrained in expressing his admiration for the composer, whose 'peculiar' treatment of the piano, his fingering, and other 'innovations', all 'charm by the ease and grace which, though superfine, are totally distinct from affectation'. As for Chopin's own compositions, 'no musician . . . can be indifferent to their exquisite and peculiar charm.' Another member of the audience, Charles Salaman – English pianist, conductor, composer, writer and teacher – later observed that he would

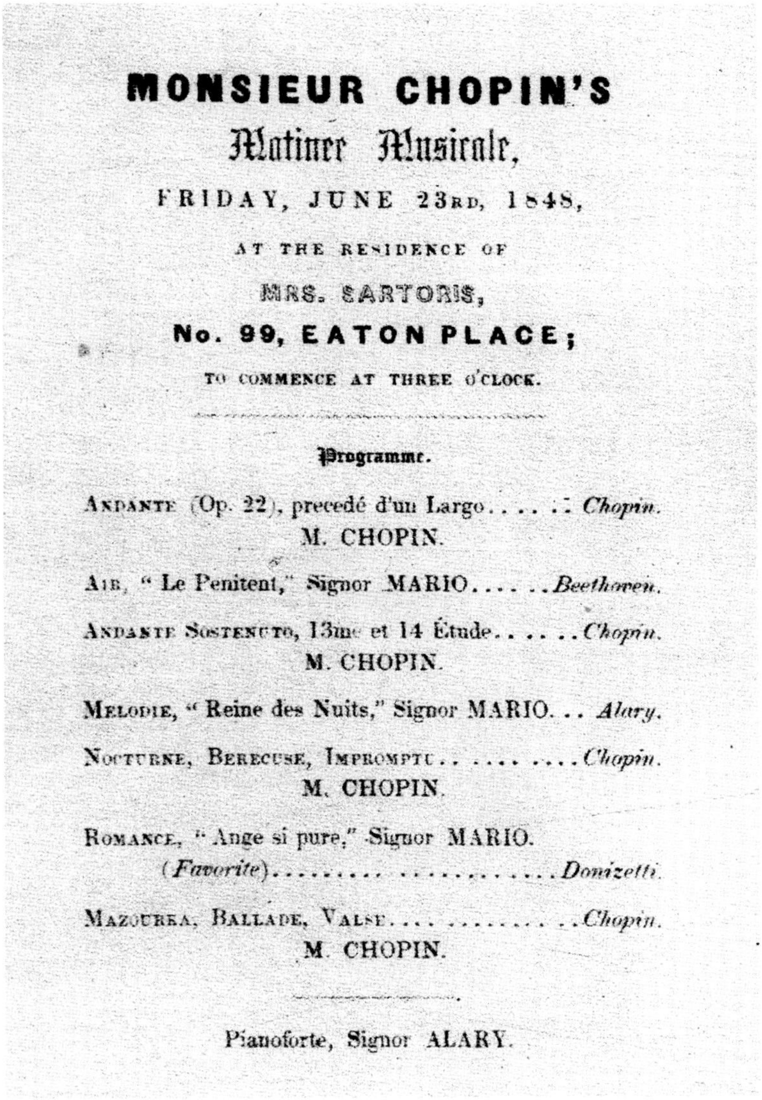

> **MONSIEUR CHOPIN'S**
> Matinée Musicale,
> FRIDAY, JUNE 23RD, 1848,
> AT THE RESIDENCE OF
> MRS. SARTORIS,
> **No. 99, EATON PLACE;**
> TO COMMENCE AT THREE O'CLOCK.
>
> Programme.
>
> ANDANTE (Op. 22), precedé d'un Largo ..... *Chopin*.
>   M. CHOPIN.
>
> AIR, " Le Penitent," Signor MARIO ...... *Beethoven*.
>
> ANDANTE SOSTENUTO, 13me et 14 Étude ...... *Chopin*.
>   M. CHOPIN.
>
> MELODIE, " Reine des Nuits," Signor MARIO ... *Alary*.
>
> NOCTURNE, BERCEUSE, IMPROMPTU .... *Chopin*.
>   M. CHOPIN.
>
> ROMANCE, " Ange si pure," Signor MARIO.
>   (*Favorite*) .... *Donizetti*.
>
> MAZOURKA, BALLADE, VALSE .... *Chopin*.
>   M. CHOPIN.
>
> Pianoforte, Signor ALARY.

Figure 4.7 Programme for Chopin's *matinée musicale* at Mrs Sartoris' house, from Mirska and Hordyński, *Chopin na obczyźnie* (1965), p. 286

never forget Chopin's playing, especially of the Waltz in D flat (Op.64, no.1). 'I remember every bar, how he played it', he recalled, 'and the appearance of his long, attenuated fingers during the time he was playing. He seemed quite exhausted.'[70]

Neither Chorley nor Salaman makes mention of the Italian tenor Giovanni Mario, who is listed in the printed programme as singing 'Le Penitent', by

Beethoven, 'Reine des nuits', by Alary, and 'Ange si pure', from Donizetti's opera, *La Favorite*. Chopin, however, refers to Mario in a letter to Mlle de Rozières, dated 30 June 1848, in which he describes the recital. 'Mrs Sartoris (Miss Kemble) lent me her house', he wrote. 'I had a select audience of 150 at one guinea, as I did not want to crowd the rooms. All the tickets were sold the day before.' As for Mario, 'He is the fashionable society vocalist *par excellence* – there is no lady in quite the same position.'[71] Chopin had known Mario in Paris, where they had both been members of the Rothschilds' circle,[72] and Mario had sung the title role in *Robert le diable* at the Opéra.

A striking, and comprehensive, description of the recital at Mrs Sartoris' is given by the pianist, administrator, and composer Wilhelm Kuhe, in his book *My musical recollections* (1896) (see Figure 4.8). In Kuhe's opinion, Chopin 'was known to only a very limited number of music-lovers in this country', whereas in Paris his concerts 'were anticipated with the keenest interest, and his compositions were already the delight of all the pianoforte-players in France and Germany; and Mendelssohn, Schumann, and Liszt led the van of his admirers'. In England, by contrast, the sale of his works 'was by no means large, and they were seldom taught'.[73]

The audience at Mrs Sartoris', therefore, represented an enlightened minority. 'At the end of the apartment, on a slightly raised platform, stood a splendid grand piano, specially prepared by Messrs Broadwood for Chopin's delicate touch.' This was Grand Pianoforte No. 17,047 (London, 1847), now in the Cobbe Collection at Hatchlands (see Plate 10).[74] Kuhe would never forget the 'impression made upon [him] by the mere appearance of this great artist'. He continues:

> His figure was attenuated to such a degree that he looked almost transparent; indeed, so weak was he that at a party given about that time at Chorley's, when my wife was present, he had to be carried upstairs, being too feeble to walk.

'No sooner, however, did his supple fingers begin to sweep the keyboard', Kuhe writes,

> than it was evident that a revelation of refined and poetical playing awaited us. His wondrous touch, the perfect finish of his execution, I can only suggest. Let me merely say that the performance was to me the most perfect example of poetry in sound which ever greeted my ears.

Kuhe, like Charles Salaman, was particularly struck with the Waltz in D flat major (Op.64, no.1), the so-called 'Minute Waltz'. He claimed this was 'still in manuscript, but so many enquiries for it followed Chopin's recital that Messrs Cramer, Beale & Co, who had purchased the copyright, were obliged to hurry on its publication, and it actually appeared two days after the manuscript left the composer's hands'.[75]

Unlike other commentators, Kuhe records the contribution of Giovanni Mario, who, singing in the intervals between the pianoforte pieces, 'looked extremely

Figure 4.8 Wilhelm Kuhe (1823–1912). Photograph by Richard Bentley & Son, 1896. Frontispiece to Kuhe, *My musical recollections* (1896). Private collection

handsome in his velvet coat, presenting a strong contrast to the deathlike appearance of the great pianist, and singing as he alone could sing' (see Figure 4.9). Nevertheless, Kuhe observes, 'the occasion was not altogether without a certain gloom. Everyone felt that the genius who held us spellbound would not long be spared to the world.'[76]

Figure 4.9 Giovanni Matteo Mario, Cavaliere de Candia (1810–83). Undated portrait lithograph by Cäcilie Brandt. Private collection

Although Kuhe does not mention Giulio Alary, the *Examiner* of 8 July 1848 notes that Mario was 'accompanied by that consummate musician, Signor Alary' (see Figure 4.10).[77] Mario had sung one of Alary's songs. 'Reine des nuits', presumably accompanied on the piano by the composer. Mario and Alary were

Figure 4.10 Un Secret: paroles de Alfred de Musset, musique de G. Alary, p. 1 of score. London: Chappell, [n.d.]. Private collection

friends in Paris, and *No. 13 of The Album Mario*, consisting of the 'most popular French songs', included the song 'Le secret', or 'Un secret', a setting by Alary of words by Alfred de Musset (see Figure 4.11).[78] On May 1836, both Chopin and Alary had performed at the Parisian salon of the Duke and Duchess Decazes, and

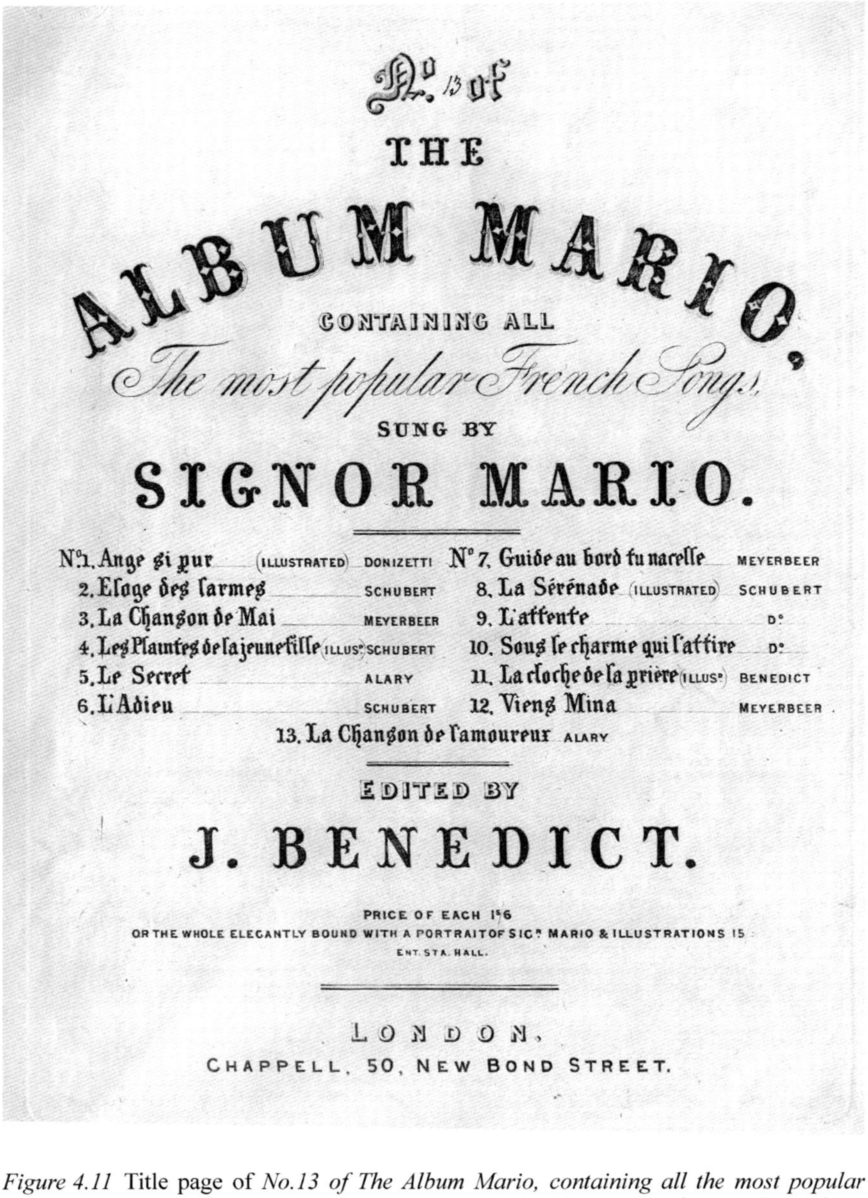

No. 13 of
THE
ALBUM MARIO,
CONTAINING ALL
The most popular French Songs,
SUNG BY
SIGNOR MARIO.

No. 1. Ange si pur	(ILLUSTRATED) DONIZETTI	No. 7. Guide au bord tu nacelle	MEYERBEER
2. Eloge des larmes	SCHUBERT	8. La Sérénade (ILLUSTRATED)	SCHUBERT
3. La Chanson de Mai	MEYERBEER	9. L'attente	D°.
4. Les Plaintes de la jeune fille (ILLUS.)	SCHUBERT	10. Sous le charme qui l'attire	D°.
5. Le Secret	ALARY	11. La cloche de la prière (ILLUS.)	BENEDICT
6. L'Adieu	SCHUBERT	12. Viens Mina	MEYERBEER

13. La Chanson de l'amoureux ALARY

EDITED BY
J. BENEDICT.

PRICE OF EACH 1/6
OR THE WHOLE ELEGANTLY BOUND WITH A PORTRAIT OF SIG. MARIO & ILLUSTRATIONS 15/
ENT. STA. HALL.

LONDON,
CHAPPELL, 50, NEW BOND STREET.

Figure 4.11 Title page of *No.13 of The Album Mario, containing all the most popular French songs, sung by Signor Mario*, edited by J. Benedict. London: Chappell, [n.d.]. Private collection

Alary was an accompanist at Chopin's concert in 1848 at the Salons Pleyel (just before he left for London), at which the singers were Antonia Molina Sitchès de Mendi and Edouard Robert.[79] In 1851, when Alary's opera *Sardanapale* was given its premiere in St Petersburg, the principal roles were taken by Mario, Grisi, and Giorgio Ronconi.[80]

At the close of his review of Chopin's *matinée musicale* at Mrs Sartoris' house, in the *Athenaeum* of 1 July 1848 (no.1079, p. 660), Chorley urged Chopin to give further concerts. 'It is to be hoped that M. Chopin will play again', he wrote, 'and the next time some of his more developed compositions . . . Few of his audience will be at all contented by a single hearing.' Adelaide Sartoris may well have hoped to repeat her success, but her life, like Chopin's, was about to change. 'In October 1849, the year following Chopin's recital', explains Ann Blainey, 'Edward [Sartoris] moved his household out of London. He sublet No. 99 Eaton Place and took a three-year lease on Knuston Hall, not far from Wellingborough in Northamptonshire.'[81] Mrs Sartoris' London salon was no more.

Earl of Falmouth's, No. 2 St James's Square, Friday 7 July 1848

Chopin, with Pauline Viardot and Antonia de Mendi

Chopin's second *matinée musicale* took place at the Earl of Falmouth's London house, No. 2 St James's Square (see Figure 4.12).[82] The junction of the square with Charles Street was the former site of Ossulston House, built in the 1670s, and owned by the Bennet family, later Lords Ossulston; this was demolished by 1753, and replaced by two houses known as Nos 1 and 2 St James's Square.[83] No. 1 was built by the 2nd Earl of Dartmouth, and No. 2 (where Chopin played) by Hugh Boscawen, 2nd Viscount Falmouth, with an entrance front of four bays, and a main cornice with three storeys below and an attic storey above. The house was owned, and mostly occupied, by the Boscawen family, until 1923, the year in which it was sold by Viscount Falmouth to the Canada Life Assurance Company. At the time substantially unaltered, it was destroyed by German bombing on the night of 14 October 1940 (see Figure 4.13).[84]

George Henry Boscawen, 5th Viscount Falmouth and 2nd Earl of Falmouth, had succeeded to the title in 1841 on the death of his father, the 1st Earl, and had an acknowledged musical pedigree.[85] 'In 1845, not long after the vogue for "house concerts" had begun', Christina Bashford points out, 'two specialist chamber-music clubs, the Beethoven Quartett Society and the Musical Union, were established, giving concerts in Harley Street and Mortimer Streets respectively.'[86] The Earl of Falmouth was involved in both of these clubs. John Ella, who played in a quartet led by Falmouth, described him as 'a most excellent amateur violin player'.[87] A watercolour of 1848 by Jemima Blackburn shows the Earl playing a violin or viola, at a rehearsal under John Ella's direction at the home of Sir John Clerk, of Penicuik, 6th Bt, in Park Street, London (see Plate 13).[88] Falmouth owned a fine collection of Italian instruments, as well as an extensive library of chamber music.[89]

Figure 4.12 St James's Square, London. Photograph of exterior of No. 2 (left) and No. 1 (right), circa 1934–8. Copyright The Canada Life Insurance Company, from *Survey of London: the Parish of St James, Westminster*, part 1 (1960), plate 164a

Chopin had been introduced to Falmouth by Henry Fowler Broadwood, and was fond of him.[90] 'Lord Falmouth is a great music-lover', Chopin told his family in Warsaw,

> wealthy, a bachelor and nobleman, who offered me the use of his mansion in St James's Square for my concert. He was most amiable – to see him in the street you wouldn't say he had threepence; and at home he has a crowd of lackeys better dressed than himself. I knew his niece in Paris, but I only saw her at a concert in London.[91]

The *matinée musicale* was advertised in *The Times* on Thursday 6 July 1848 to take place on Friday 7 July at four o'clock – the day before the celebration of the Earl's 37th birthday, on the Saturday, at his country seat, Tregothan House, Devon.[92] Again, as with the recital at Mrs Sartoris's, tickets, 'limited in number', were sold by Cramer, Beale & Co. But the recital itself was different, as the programme makes clear, in that Chopin shared the stage not with Mario but with Pauline Viardot, and her cousin, Mlle Antonia de Mendi, the mezzo-soprano who had performed with Chopin at his last concert in the Salons Pleyel in Paris.

Figure 4.13 St James's Square, London. Photograph of No. 2, after direct hit by bombing, 14 October 1940, from Forrest, *St James's Square* (2001), p. 145

Chopin again played the Broadwood Grande Pianoforte No. 17,047 (1847), now in the Cobbe Collection, at Hatchlands, which had been hired for his recital in Eaton Place.[93] Chopin's programme for the Falmouth recital lists similar pieces to those he performed for Mrs Sartoris (see Figure 4.14). He played four sets – the Andante Sostenuto and scherzo (Op.31); three études; a nocturne and the berceuse; and preludes, mazurkas, a ballade, and waltzes.[94] Chorley reported in the *Athenaeum* on 15 July (no.1081, p. 708) that 'Chopin played better at his second than his at his first *Matinée* – not with more delicacy (that could hardly be), but with more force and *brio*.' Chorley especially welcomed 'two among what may be called M. Chopin's more serious compositions', namely his Scherzo in B flat minor (Op.31), and his Étude in C sharp minor (Op.25, no.7). Chorley's views were endorsed by other publications.[95] All pointed to the recital as a fashionable event. *John Bull* admired Chopin's 'wonderful powers of execution', while the *Illustrated London News* praised not only his 'original genius as a composer, but his novel and striking style as an executant'. The *London Daily News* also lauded Chopin as composer and performer, adding that his music 'is characterised by freedom of thought, varied expression, and a kind of romantic melancholy'.

Unlike Chorley, the writers of these opinions pay scant attention to the contribution of Pauline Viardot and Antonia de Mendi to the success of the recital. Earlier, in the *Athenaeum* of 20 May 1848 (no.1073, p. 516), Chorley had already expressed his admiration for Viardot, when he reported on 'an excellent concert'

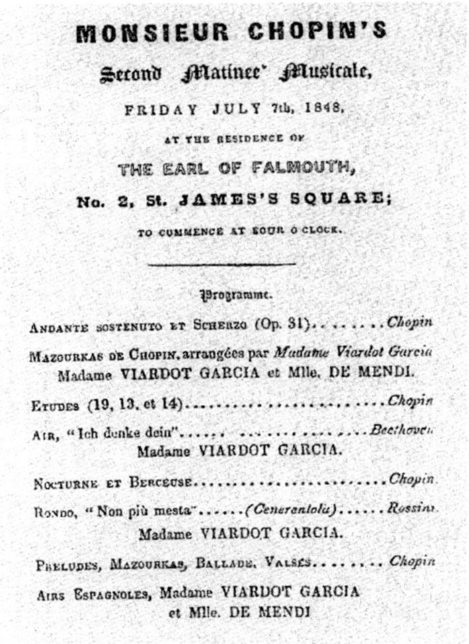

MONSIEUR CHOPIN'S
Second Matinée Musicale,

FRIDAY JULY 7th, 1848,

AT THE RESIDENCE OF

THE EARL OF FALMOUTH,

No. 2, St. JAMES'S SQUARE;

TO COMMENCE AT FOUR O'CLOCK.

Programme.

ANDANTE SOSTENUTO ET SCHERZO (Op. 31)........*Chopin*

MAZOURKAS DE CHOPIN, arrangées par *Madame Viardot Garcia*
   Madame VIARDOT GARCIA et Mlle. DE MENDI.

ETUDES (19, 13, et 14)........................*Chopin*

AIR, "Ich denke dein"...................*Beethoven*
   Madame VIARDOT GARCIA.

NOCTURNE ET BERCEUSE........................*Chopin*

RONDO, "Non più mesta"......(*Cenerentola*)......*Rossini*
   Madame VIARDOT GARCIA.

PRELUDES, MAZOURKAS, BALLADE, VALSES.........*Chopin*

AIRS ESPAGNOLES, Madame VIARDOT GARCIA
   et Mlle. DE MENDI

Figure 4.14 Programme for Chopin's *matinée musicale* at the Earl of Falmouth's house, Friday 7 July 1848. Mirska and Hordyński, *Chopin na obczyźnie* (1965), p. 288

at Covent Garden which featured Viardot and Charles Hallé. Now, at Lord Falmouth's, Viardot sang the rondo, 'Non più mesta', from Rossini's *Le Cenerentola*, and Beethoven's song, 'Ich denke dein'. With de Mendi, Viardot also performed Spanish airs, and her own song-settings of Chopin mazurkas; Viardot often sang these in London, and they became so popular that she published twelve of them, in two sets of six, in 1864 and circa 1888.[96] 'Increasing experience', wrote Chorley, 'disposes us more and more to consider [Viardot] as the greatest artist of her time.'[97]

Jane Welsh Carlyle, who may have been at the recital at Lord Falmouth's, wrote enthusiastically to Jane Stirling shortly afterwards, enclosing a poem entitled 'Chopin playing', by her friend Anthony Coningham Sterling, a retired army captain, with whom she apparently attended the *matinée*.[98] Jane admitted that she thought the poem was '*prose run mad*', and on reflection may have regretted her suggestion that Jane Stirling translate it into French for Chopin's benefit. However, her opinion of the composer was unequivocal. 'I never liked any music so well', she wrote. 'I cannot fancy but that every piece he composes must leave him with many fewer days to live.'

Countess of Blessington's, Gore House, Kensington, 10 May 1848

In 1848, Gore House, Kensington, on the site of the present Royal Albert Hall, was the home of Marguerite Gardiner, Countess of Blessington, literary hostess, memoirist, novelist (see Figure 4.15), and notable friend of Alfred, Count D'Orsay, one of the foremost dandies of the time (see Plate 14).[99] The Countess's second husband, the 1st Earl of Blessington, had died in 1829. Thereafter, distinguished men of arts, letters, and fashion, were attracted to her soirées, first at Seamore Place, Park Lane, from 1830, and then for thirteen years at Gore House, to which

Figure 4.15 Marguerite, Countess of Blessington (1789–1849). Mezzotint by William Giller, published by J. McCormick, after Edmund Thomas Parris, 1835.

Copyright National Portrait Gallery, London

she moved in 1836. Here, she gathered around her a salon of prominent literary and political figures, including Edward Bulwer-Lytton, Benjamin Disraeli, Charles Dickens, and William Makepeace Thackeray. And here it was that Chopin played for her. Lady Blessington was the author of novels and of personal reminiscences, including *Conversations of Lord Byron with the Countess of Blessington* (1834), *The idler in Italy* (1839), and *The idler in France* (1841). However, her financial position worsened, and in 1849, to escape her creditors, she and D'Orsay fled to Paris, where both died.

Built in the 1750s, Gore House was a three-storey brick mansion, with a central canted porch, facing Kensington Gore (see Figure 4.16).[100] From 1808 to 1821, when it was occupied by William Wilberforce, it was often visited by leading evangelicals. Fifteen years later, very different meetings were taking place there. D'Orsay, who was married to, but separated from, Lady Blessington's stepdaughter, lived for a while in one of the smaller houses near Gore House until, in 1839, he moved in with the Countess. The interiors of Gore House were sumptuous. The library, decorated with green furnishings and white and gilt bookshelves, formed the social centre of the house, and was lit by windows from both the garden and street fronts. When, after Lady Blessington's and D'Orsay's flight to France, the contents of Gore House were sold, over a period of twelve days, enormous crowds flocked there. It was demolished in 1857.[101]

Among musicians entertained at Gore House were Franz Liszt and Charles Hallé. Liszt visited during his stays in 1840 and 1841,[102] and in 1843, when Charles Hallé met Count d'Orsay for the first time, he found him a 'brilliant and

Figure 4.16 Gore House, Kensington, elevation towards Kensington Gore. Watercolour by Thomas Hosmer Shepherd, circa 1840s. Kensington Central Library

eccentric *roi des modes*'. Subsequently, Hallé wrote, he was 'invited to several small evening parties at Gore House, made delightful by Lady Blessington's grace and D'Orsay's wit' (see Figure 4.17).[103]

Chopin's experience of first encountering D'Orsay was similarly genial. On 6 May 1848, soon after arriving in London, Chopin wrote to Adolf Gutmann and told him that he had been to Gore House to meet Count D'Orsay, taking with him a letter from Princess Marcelina Czartoryska. As Chopin puts it: 'I have called on Mr D'Orsay who received me very civilly in spite of the delay in delivering my letter. Please thank the Princess [Czartoryska] for me.'[104] Four days later, on 10 May, Chopin played at Gore House, though we have no description of the event.[105] According to Hipkins, as reported by his daughter, it was the only occasion on which Chopin used the Pleyel piano he had brought from Paris.[106]

Henry Chorley had fond memories of Lady Blessington at both Seamore Place and Gore House;[107] indeed, he seems to have been smitten with her. 'She was a steady friend, through good report and evil report, for those to whom she professed friendship', he wrote.[108] 'Her society included distinguished men of all ranks and all classes, – statesman, ambassadors, foreign grandees . . . actors,

Figure 4.17 'Women in politics. Lady Blessington's Salon at Gore House, Kensington', circa 1840s. Print from drawing by 'Johnson'. Westminster City Archives

musicians, painters, poets, historians, men of science.' 'For all', Chorley added, 'she had the same attentive natural courtesy.'[109] Chorley had reason to be grateful. Lady Blessington's 'thoughtful kindness . . . to a young and untried man of letters such as Chorley, at the outset of his career', writes Henry Hewlett, 'was of the utmost value to him'.[110]

All told, Chopin looked back on his recitals at Gore House, and other domestic settings, with some misgivings. At least they provided a limited income. 'I gave two matinées', he told Franchomme, 'which appear to have given pleasure but were a nuisance, none the less.'[111] But they enabled him to afford the 'spacious lodging absolutely necessary, and a carriage and man-servant'. Whereas, as he told Mme de Rothschild, his fee for informal performances was 20 guineas, his earnings at his *matinées musicales* were more substantial: at Mrs Sartoris', Chopin made 150 guineas,[112] and at Lord Falmouth's he hoped to clear at least 100 guineas.[113] London was expensive. 'From the money I have made', Chopin explained to Gryzmała, 'I may have only 200 guineas (5,000 francs) left after deducting the cost of my lodgings and carriages. In Italy one could live a year on that, but not six months here.'[114]

By July, Chopin's stay in London was drawing to an end. Teaching, and the income it provided, was drying up; it was the close of the social season, and his aristocratic pupils were leaving the city for the country. Chopin was coming under increasing pressure from Jane Stirling and Mrs Katherine Erskine (his 'kind Scots ladies') to visit Scotland. Lord Torphichen, one of their brothers-in-law, and laird of Calder House, in Midlothian, had also urged him to go. 'In London I was always at [the Stirling sisters'] house and I could not refuse their invitation to come here', he told his family in Warsaw later, writing from Calder House, 'especially as there is nothing for me to do in London and I need a rest; and as Lord Torphichen gave me a cordial invitation.'[115] At this point, John Muir Wood enters the story.

Unsurprisingly, Henry Fowler Broadwood learnt of Chopin's plans. According to Muir Wood's son, Herbert Kemlo Wood, his father happened to be in London at the time, and Broadwood asked him to accompany Chopin on his rail journey to Edinburgh.[116] Chopin and Muir Wood already knew each other. Born in Edinburgh in 1805, Muir Wood was a pianist, music seller, publisher, impresario, and pioneer photographer (see Figure 4.18).[117] He was also one of a dynasty. His father, Andrew Wood, an Edinburgh piano-maker and music publisher, had entered into partnership with John Muir in 1797 and, on Muir's death in 1818, entered into a second partnership with one George Small.[118] The firm of Muir, Wood & Co (later Wood & Co), established in Waterloo Place, Edinburgh, published sheet music, and manufactured square pianos, organs, harps and drums. In 1829, Muir Wood's father died, and he joined his brother George in the family business. In 1848, Muir Wood and George Wood set up a branch of the family firm in Buchanan Street, Glasgow, and Muir Wood moved to Glasgow to manage it. Muir Wood continued to play a leading part in Scottish musical life, notably through his publications, research into the history of Scottish music, and the organization of concerts.[119]

Muir Wood himself had been trained as a pianist, and took lessons from Kalkbrenner when he visited Edinburgh in 1814.[120] In 1826, Muir Wood travelled

Figure 4.18 John Muir Wood (1805–92). Photograph by Muir Wood of himself holding a photographic printing frame. Scottish National Photography Collection. Scottish National Portrait Gallery, Edinburgh

to Paris, where he was taught by one of the most celebrated piano teachers of the day, Johann Peter Pixis.[121] The next year, supported by his family, Muir Wood became a pupil in Vienna of Carl Czerny, a former student of Beethoven, and a teacher of Liszt. Muir Wood remarked that his friendship in Vienna lay 'principally among the Poles who are in general very clever and know several languages . . . They almost all play some instrument, and are well acquainted with the theory of music.' Furthermore, during his time in Paris and Vienna, Muir Wood 'achieved an excellent command of four languages', and was able to pursue an interest in science which was later to prove essential to his practice of photography.[122]

Returning to Scotland in 1828, Muir Wood taught the piano, and he and George Wood gave concerts for many years;[123] in addition, he acted as an impresario, arranging concerts by well-known performers, such as Liszt, and a visit to Glasgow by Sir Charles Hallé and the Hallé Orchestra. But Muir Wood retained his connections with the Continent, and in 1835 or 1836, while visiting Frankfurt am Main, and staying with the Polish violinist Karol Lipiński, he met Chopin for the first time.[124] Indeed, it has been suggested that Muir Wood had learnt to speak Polish, and that he and Chopin joined in playing a piano duet together.[125] As Herbert Kemlo Wood, explains:

> Chopin stopped [in Frankfurt] on his way from Carlsbad to Paris in 1835 and was met by Lipiński and was taken to his rooms, where there was naturally a great deal of music making. Chopin, finding a good piano, played away willingly, Lipiński and my father played together, and then Chopin suggested a piano duet and made my father join him in one by Mozart.

It was, Kemlo Wood adds, 'an event soon forgotten in his crowded career'.[126]

During the following decade, John Muir Wood developed his interest in photography. His knowledge of it, Sara Stevenson writes, 'may date from his friendship in the 1840s with the eye surgeon Dr Jasper MacAldin who shared his knowledge of optics and chemistry. Muir Wood's subjects were portraits and landscapes of Scotland, England, Ireland, France, Belgium and Germany.'[127] In Edinburgh, Muir Wood was set within a group of pioneers of photography, who included David Octavius Hill and Robert Adamson. Muir Wood never sold or exhibited his work, and seems to have abandoned photography in 1852 or so, after the introduction of glass plates. Alas, he seems not to have taken portraits of Chopin, or other musicians he knew, although a photograph of about 1850 near Fingal's Cave, on the island of Staffa, in which a seated figure may be Muir Wood himself, could be seen as a homage to Mendelssohn.[128]

Muir Wood, then, seemed to be an appropriate companion for Chopin as he journeyed to Edinburgh. The composer's pocket diary shows that he left Euston Station, London, by the 9 a.m. train on Saturday 5 August 1848.[129] Designed by Robert Stephenson for the London & Birmingham Railway, Euston had been opened in 1837. Philip Hardwick, the Elder, was architect for the screen in front of the station consisting of lodges and a central Doric portico, through which passengers entered and departed. Next, Hardwick added two hotels, the Victoria (opened 1839) and the Adelaide (opened 1840), on either side of the portico, and Chopin may have patronized them when he passed through Euston in 1848 (see Figure 4.19).[130]

Figure 4.19 London & Birmingham Railway Terminus, Euston Square, London. Drawn by Thomas Hosmer Shepherd, engraved by H. Bond, circa 1848. Private collection

Arriving at the station, Chopin told his family in Warsaw, he

> found on the platform for Edinburgh a gentleman who introduced himself from Broadwood and gave me two tickets instead of one for seats in my compartment – the second one for the seat opposite, so that no one might be in my way. Besides that he arranged for a certain Mr Wood (an acquaintance of Broadwood's) to be in the same carriage. He knew me (having seen me in 1836 at the Lipińskis' in Frankfort!). He has music shops in Edinburgh and Glasgow.

Furthermore, Broadwood had arranged for Chopin's servant Daniel – 'who is better behaved than many gentleman, and better looking than many Englishmen' – to be seated in the same compartment.[131] Thus cosseted, Chopin left London at the start of his Scottish adventure.

Notes

1 Niecks, *Chopin*, vol.2, p. 281. See TiFC (Warsaw), M/441.k.II.p. 2, which is an 'At Home' card, addressed to Chopin, from Mrs Milner Gibson at No. 50 Wilton Crescent,

120   London 1848: recitals

London, for Monday 10 July 1848. A letter to Chopin of 1 August 1848 from Mrs Milner Gibson invites him 'souper chez moi' the following Sunday. See TiFC (Warsaw), M/442.k.II.p. 2. Mrs [Susannah] Arethusa Gibson was a London hostess and political activist. Her husband, Thomas Milner Gibson, was an English politician and Member of Parliament.

2 Letter from Mrs Grote to Mrs Frances von Koch, 24 July 1848, in Lewin, *Lewin letters*, vol.2, p. 62. The party of 6 May is recorded in Hueffer, *Musical studies*, p. 59, and Hueffer, 'Chopin', p. 391.

3 Hadden, *Chopin*, p. 136, based on Niecks, *Chopin*, vol.2, p. 281.

4 For background to Chopin's recitals in 1848, see Samson, 'Myth and reality: a biographical introduction', in Samson, *Cambridge companion to Chopin*, pp. 1–8; Janet Ritterman, 'Piano music and the public concert, 1800–1850', *passim*; and Ritterman and Weber, 'Origins of the piano recital in England, 1830–1870', *passim*. For 'soloists', 'chamber musicians', and 'private aristocratic and royal concerts', see Rohr, *Careers of English musicians, 1750–1850*, pp. 113–19. Individual Chopin recitals in London are considered in Atwood, *Pianist from Warsaw*, pp. 160–70. Agresta's article 'Chopin in music criticism in nineteenth-century England', consists of an introduction to an anthology of sixty – five published writings on Chopin. However, none refers to his visit to England in 1837, and only six appeared within his spell in England and Scotland in 1848 – three from the *Athenaeum*, and three from the *Musical World*. Related articles by Agresta are 'Aspect de la réception de Chopin en angleterre pendant les années 1840', and 'Chopin in England'.

5 Fiorentino, 'Chopin', p. 427. This publication is rare: the French text quoted here is from the copy in the Bibliothèque Mazarine, Paris, where I was able to examine it thanks to the good offices of the late Andrew Fairbairn. Niecks, *Chopin*, vol.2, p. 282, proffers the following English translation:

> We were at most ten or twelve in a homely, comfortable little *salon*, equally propitious to conversation and contemplation. Chopin took the place of Madame Viardot at the piano, and plunged us into ineffable raptures. I do not know what he played to us; I do not know how long our ecstasy lasted: we were no longer on earth; he had transported us into unknown regions, into a sphere of flame and azure, where the soul, freed from all corporeal bonds, floats towards the infinite. This was, alas! the song of the swan.

Fiorentino was precipitate, proceeding immediately to explain that Chopin returned to Paris to die, but making no reference to his intervening period in England and Scotland.

6 Bledsoe, *Chorley*, p. 178.
7 Bledsoe, *Chorley*, p. 144.
8 See Bradley and Pevsner, *London 6: Westminster*, pp. 757–8; Colvin, *Dictionary*, p. 1192; and Weinreb, Hibbert, and Keay, *London encyclopaedia*, p. 975.
9 Hallé, *Autobiography*, p. 118, and Rigby, *Hallé*, pp. 68–9.
10 Hallé, *Autobiography*, p. 56. In his consideration of Chopin, on pp. 55–7, Hallé mentions listening to Chopin playing in London in 1848 at both Mrs Sartoris' and Chorley's, but nowhere else. In particular, Hallé notes hearing for the first time 'the beautiful waltzes, Op.62, recently composed and published, which have since become the most popular of his smaller pieces' (p. 56). Surely, 'Op.62' here is a mistake for 'Op.64'?
11 See Cherry and Pevsner, *London 3: north west*, p. 576, and *Carlyle's House, London*, The National Trust, revised edition (London, 1998). In the Carlyles' day, the house was known as No. 5 Cheyne Row. According to *Carlyle's House, London*, p. 20, the piano and stool in the sitting room or parlour were brought to London in 1842 from Templand, Dumfriesshire, the home of Mrs Carlyle's mother, who died that year. The piano, an upright, replaced an earlier one, and can be seen to the left of Robert Scott

Tait's *A Chelsea interior*, of 1857. *Carlyle's House catalogue* (1895), reprinted by the Saltire Society, contains references to the pianos on pp. 39 and 42, with an illustration on p. 53.
12 See the article on Jane Baillie Welsh Carlyle by Kenneth Fielding and David Sorensen in *Oxford DNB online*.
13 Ashton, *Thomas and Jane Carlyle*, p. 288.
14 See Hedley, *Chopin correspondence*, p. 323.
15 Ashton, *Thomas and Jane Carlyle*, p. 288.
16 See Hedley, *Chopin correspondence*, p. 323. For a version of this text, see National Library of Scotland (Edinburgh), MS Acc.9227, uncatalogued letter. See also later in this chapter, note 98. There is some uncertainty here: was the letter addressed to Chopin's friend Jane Stirling, or to Jane Sterling, sister of John Sterling, who was the subject of a biography by Carlyle? On 4 August 1850, Jane Stirling called unexpectedly at Cheyne Row, her visit prompting firm reactions from both Carlyles. See Bone, *Jane Stirling*, p. 100.
17 Richardson, *Emerson*, p. 144. Emerson's visit to Scotland, to see Carlyle at Craigenputtock, is considered in Christiansen, *The visitors*, pp. 86–90. Christiansen, on p. 117, notes that Emerson's response to Chopin was 'cloth-eared'.
18 There seems to be no proof that Dickens heard Chopin play, although the composer listed the novelist among the 'distinguished personalities' he met. See Hedley, *Chopin correspondence*, p. 333. Chopin to his family in Warsaw, [10–19 August 1848].
19 There is no entry in the *Oxford DNB online* for Sir Edward Antrobus, Bt. The address No. 146 Piccadilly is taken from *Kelly's directory, London 1848*. Dasent, *Piccadilly*, pp. 287–8, describes Antrobus as 'a partner in Coutts's, and the second of the great banking firm to settle in the neighbourhood'.
20 The interior of No. 146 Piccadilly can be seen in a photograph of 1899 in the Historic England Archive (formerly National Monuments Record), Swindon (negative BL 15503). For No. 148 Piccadilly, see Dasent, *Piccadilly*, pp. 289–93, and Ferguson, *World's banker*, pp. 556, 996.
21 Quoted by Jorgensen, *Chopin and the Swedish nightingale*, p. 56.
22 See Ferguson, *World's banker*, pp. 363–5.
23 See the discussion of Chopin's recitals in Atwood, *Pianist from Warsaw*, pp. 160–70.
24 Hedley, *Chopin correspondence*, p. 320. Chopin to Grzymała, 2 June [1848]. 'Old Mme Rothschild' would have been Hannah Barent de Rothschild (née Cohen) (1783–1850), mother of Lionel Nathan de Rothschild. See Chapter 2 of *Chopin in Britain*, note 36.
25 The address given in *Kelly's directory, London 1848*. Reference to Chopin's performance for Douglas is in Hedley, *Chopin correspondence*, p. 333. Chopin to his family in Warsaw, [10–19 August 1848]. The Marquess of Douglas was the courtesy title given to the elder son of the Duke and Duchess of Hamilton. His mother, the Duchess of Hamilton, the châtelaine of Hamilton Palace, had met Chopin in Paris.
26 Chopin notes that, of these three recitals, his performance for the Countess of Gainsborough was the 'first in order of date'. See Hedley, *Chopin correspondence*, p. 333. Chopin to his family in Warsaw, [10–19 August 1848].
27 Hedley, *Chopin correspondence*, p. 319. Chopin to Grzymała, 2 June [1848]. According to Chopin, Dr Malan's wife was a niece of Lady Gainsborough. See Hedley, *Chopin correspondence*, p. 350. Chopin to Grzymała, 17–18 [November 1848].
28 Somerset House, which was demolished in 1915, is described and illustrated in *Survey of London*, vol.40, *The Grosvenor Estate in Mayfair*, part 2, *The buildings* (1980), pp. 285–7, and plate 45a, and plate 14b in vol.39. The Duchess of Somerset remained in the house until her death in 1880.
29 Hedley, *Chopin correspondence*, p. 319. Chopin to Grzymała, 2 June [1848].
30 See Bradley and Pevsner, *London 6: Westminster*, pp. 562–3, and Colvin, *Dictionary*, p. 157. Formerly known as Egremont House, and then Cambridge House, the original

122 London 1848: recitals

building has been greatly altered. In 1829, the house had assumed semi-royal status when it became the residence of the Duke of Cambridge, seventh son of George III. See Dasent, *Piccadilly*, pp. 81, 85, 93–5. The sale of the 'In and Out' is recorded in *The Times*, 13 January 1999, p. 30, with an asking price of £50 million. Subsequently, the club moved to No. 4 St James's Square.

31 William Stirling's address is taken from *Kelly's directory, London 1848*. 'I made his acquaintance in London', says Chopin. Hedley, *Chopin correspondence*, p. 319. Chopin to Grzymała, 2 June [1848].

32 An invitation card addressed to Chopin from 'Madame Bunsen' to an 'at home' at 10 o'clock on Friday 16 June [1848] is in TiFC (Warsaw), M/435.k.II.p. 2. The Bunsens' address at No. 4 Carlton House Terrace is given in *Kelly's directory, London 1848*. A concert and exhibition was held at the Polish Embassy, London, on 20 April 1948, entitled 'Frederick Chopin in London', marking the centenary of Chopin's arrival on that day in 1848. The pianist Henryk Sztompka, from Warsaw, performed 'those works of Chopin which the composer played in London during the summer of 1848', at Stafford House, Mrs Sartoris', and the Earl of Falmouth's. The piano, lent by Broadwood and Son, was that used by Chopin 'at all the above concerts', namely the Broadwood Grand Pianoforte No. 17,047 (London, 1847), now at Hatchlands. The exhibition, accompanying the concert, consisted of material from the Instytut Fryderyka Chopina, Warsaw, and from Arthur Hedley's collection. See the copy of the programme in the Broadwood Archives, Surrey History Centre (Woking), 2185/JB/83/22.

33 For the Duchess of Sutherland, see the article on her by K.D. Reynolds in *Oxford DNB online*.

34 For Stafford House (under 'Lancaster House'), see Bradley and Pevsner, *London 6: Westminster*, pp. 589–91; Colvin, *Dictionary*, pp. 101, 174, 937, 1173; Weinreb, Hibbert, and Keay, *London encyclopaedia*, p. 473; and Yorke, *Lancaster House, passim*.

35 This paragraph is based on Bradley and Pevsner, *London 6: Westminster*, pp. 189–91. For the richness of the interiors at Stafford House, see the illustrations to Yorke, *Lancaster House, passim*.

36 See Pocknell, 'Franz Liszt's and Adelaide Kemble's symbiotic relations', p. 67, using the late Pauline Pocknell's transcripts of quotations from the *Athenaeum*.

37 Atwood, *Pianist from Warsaw*, pp. 162–4, gives a description of the concert, on which part of the following text is based. See also Yorke, *Lancaster House*, p. 109, and plate 83. Alas, Lady Alexandrina died in infancy.

38 Yorke, *Lancaster House*, p. 11, citing Gower, *My reminiscences*, p. 6.

39 Oliver Davies kindly alerted me to this quotation. As we see, Adelaide Kemble, although she performed at Stafford House with Liszt in 1841, did not sing there on this occasion.

40 Quoted from Atwood, *Pianist from Warsaw*, p. 245.

41 Niecks, *Chopin*, vol.2, p. 281. On the same page, Niecks notes that 'John Ella heard Chopin play at Benedict's'. Julius Benedict was not knighted until 1871.

42 Hedley, *Chopin correspondence*, p. 318.

43 Hedley, *Chopin correspondence*, p. 332. Chopin to his family in Warsaw, [10–19 August 1848].

44 The remarks by the Queen are taken from Yorke, *Lancaster House*, p. 109, citing Queen Victoria's journals, 15 May 1848, Royal Archives, Windsor Castle.

45 Hedley, *Chopin correspondence*, p. 320. Chopin to Grzymała, 2 June [1848].

46 Hipkins makes no mention of the use by Chopin of a Broadwood at Stafford House in his essay 'Chopin's pianoforte', *International inventions exhibition* (1885), pp. 12–13.

47 Hedley, *Chopin correspondence*, p. 319.

48 TiFC (Warsaw), M/378, Chopin's MS pocket diary for 1848.

49 James Yorke kindly told me that in the Duke of Sutherland's account book, January 1845 – June 1855, in Staffordshire Record Office, Stafford, there are records of

payments to Chopin both for the piano lessons for Lady Constance Leveson-Gower (D593/R/18/1), and for the concert at Stafford House (D593/R/2/42/3). See also Yorke, *Lancaster House*, pp. 98, 109, 186, n.50 (Chapter 3), 187, nn.94–96 (Chapter 3).

50 Hedley, *Chopin correspondence*, pp. 332–3. Chopin to his family in Warsaw, [10–19 August 1848].

51 For Adelaide Kemble, see the articles on her by W.H. Husk, revised by George Biddlecombe, in *Grove music online*, and by L.M. Middleton, revised by K.D. Reynolds, in *Oxford DNB online*.

52 Quoted by Pocknell, 'Franz Liszt's and Adelaide Kemble's symbiotic relations', p. 77, from (Fanny) Kemble, *Records of later life*, vol.2, p. 293. For the context of these remarks, see Rosenthal, *Two centuries of opera at Covent Garden*, p. 59, and p. 67 of the late Pauline Pocknell's article. In the following section I use her transcripts of quotations from the *Athenaeum*.

53 Moscheles, *Recent music and musicians*, p. 282.

54 *Athenaeum*, no.332, 6 November 1841, p. 860, quoted by Pocknell, 'Franz Liszt's and Adelaide Kemble's symbiotic relations", pp. 72–3. For this and subsequent performances by Kemble, see Rosenthal, *Two centuries of opera at Covent Garden*, pp. 53–4.

55 Moscheles, *Recent music and musicians*, p. 282.

56 Pocknell, 'Franz Liszt's and Adelaide Kemble's symbiotic relations', p. 78.

57 Quoted in Moscheles, *Recent music and musicians*, p. 301.

58 See Bradley and Pevsner, *London 6: Westminster*, p. 745, and plate 80; Colvin, *Dictionary*, p. 290; and Weinreb, Hibbert, and Keay, *London encyclopaedia*, p. 263. For the architectural context, see Hobhouse, *Thomas Cubitt, passim*, and the article on Cubitt by Hermione Hobhouse in *Oxford DNB online*.

59 According to the caption to a photograph illustrating 'The President's letter', The Chopin Society (London), Newsletter, Spring 2008, pp. 11–14 [13], the plaque at No. 99 Eaton Place was unveiled on 23 June 1949. This photograph shows the pianist Natalia Karp, Colonel Evelyn Broadwood, and Arthur Hedley on that day. For Chopin's blue plaques at No. 99 Eaton Place, and No. 4 St James's Place, see Rennison, *London blue plaque guide*, p. 40, and Sumeray, *Discovering London plaques*, p. 44. They are also referred to on p. 147 of the Chopin entry in Sadie, *Calling on the composer*, pp. 140–9. The blue plaque at No. 4 St James's Place is described in Cole, *Lived in London*, pp. 474–5, and its position shown in the map on p. 466. The location of the plaques can be seen in Sumeray, *Track the plaque*, pp. 33, 46.

60 Quoted from Bennett, *Chopin*, pp. 53–4.

61 Hedley, *Chopin correspondence*, p. 331. Chopin to his family in Warsaw, [10–19 August 1848]. In this letter Chopin mistakenly refers to Mrs Sartoris as '*née* Fanny Kemble'.

62 Hedley, *Chopin correspondence*, p. 335. Chopin to his family in Warsaw, [10–19 August 1848].

63 Hallé, *Autobiography*, pp. 56, 118. Three letters written by Mrs Sartoris to Chopin in 1848, about his visits to No. 99 Eaton Place, are in TiFC (Warsaw), M/437.k.II.p. 2, M/438.k.II,p. 2, and M/439.k.II.p. 2.

64 Wainwright, *Broadwood by appointment*, p. 161.

65 TiFC (Warsaw), M/432/1.k.II.p. 2. Her letter, written on the day of the concert, was sent from Lansdowne House. Two other letters from Lady Shelburne to Chopin, also of 1848, are in TiFC (Warsaw), M/432/2.k.II.p. 2, and M/433/2.k.II.p. 2.

66 Hedley, *Chopin correspondence*, p. 334. Chopin to his family in Warsaw, [10–19 August 1848].

67 Niecks, *Chopin*, vol.2, p. 285, cites the *Musical World*, 8 July 1848. But, as Niecks says in note 11 on that page, the reporter of the *Musical World* was wrong to suggest that Chopin played twice at Mrs Sartoris'. Chopin's second *matinée musicale* at Lord Falmouth's on 7 July was held on the afternoon before the article in the *Musical*

124 London 1848: recitals

World appeared. It has to be said that the reporter admitted: 'We were not present at either, and, therefore, have nothing to say on the subject.' For Jenny Lind's attendance at Chopin's recital at Mrs Sartoris', see Holland and Rockstro, *Jenny Lind the artist*, pp. 324–5.

68 See Brown, *Index of Chopin's works*, pp. 63 (no.58), 92–3 (no.88).

69 The text is given in Atwood, *Pianist from Warsaw*, pp. 245–7; on p. 245, Atwood gives accounts of the concert from the *Illustrated London News* (1 July 1848), and on pp. 247–8 from the *Examiner* (8 July 1848).

70 Report of a meeting of the London Musical Association, 5 April 1880, quoted in Niecks, *Chopin*, vol.2, p. 286. See Salaman, 'Pianists of the past', pp. 327–8, and the article on the two waltzes in the *Athenaeum*, no.1071, 6 May 1848, p. 467. See also Grabowski, 'Publication des valses, Op.64', *passim*. Lenz regarded the three waltzes in Op.64 as Chopin's best. See 'Panorama de l'oeuvre de Chopin', in Lenz, *Les grands virtuoses du piano* (Eigeldinger), p. 174. They are Op.64, no.1, in D flat major (the so-called 'Minute Waltz'), Op.64, no.2, in C sharp minor, and Op.64, no.3, in A flat major. See Brown, *Index of Chopin's works*, pp. 170–1 (no.164).

71 Hedley, *Chopin correspondence*, p. 322. For Mario and Grisi, see Forbes, *Mario and Grisi*, pp. 98–9.

72 See Hedley, *Chopin correspondence*, p. 227. Joseph Filtsch to his parents in Hungary, Paris, [20] January 1843.

73 Kuhe, *My musical recollections*, pp. 111–12.

74 See Cobbe, *Three hundred years of composers' instruments*, pp. 52–5.

75 Kuhe, *My musical recollections*, pp. 113–14. Kuhe's recollection is incorrect. All three waltzes in Op.64 had already been published in Leipzig and Paris.

76 Kuhe, *My musical recollections*, p. 114.

77 Quoted in Atwood, *Pianist from Warsaw*, p. 24

78 For Alary in Paris see Atwood, *Pianist from Warsaw*, pp. 108, 157, 228, 247, 279, n.35.

79 See Atwood, *Pianist from Warsaw*, pp. 107, 108, 155–7. The programme of Chopin's last Parisian concert appears on p. 157.

80 Forbes, *Mario and Grisi*, p. 117.

81 Blainey, *Fanny and Adelaide*, p. 238. Knuston Hall is now an Adult Residential College, run by Northamptonshire County Council.

82 For St James's Square, see Bradley and Pevsner, *London 6: Westminster*, pp. 624–5; Forrest, *St James's Square*, especially pp. 99, 144, and plate 57; *Survey of London*, vol.29, *The Parish of St James, Westminster*, part 1 (1960), pp. 77–83; and Weinreb, Hibbert, and Keay, *London encyclopaedia*, pp. 770–1. I am grateful for help to the present Earl of Falmouth, Angela Broome (Royal Institution of Cornwall, Truro), and Alison Campbell (Cornwall Record Office, Truro).

83 See Dasent, *St James's Square*, pp. 84–9, 223, 224. On p. 88 there is a pen-and-ink drawing of Falmouth's house.

84 The illustration here is taken from Forrest, *St James's Square*, p. 145; although this is credited on p. vii to the Imperial War Museum, the Museum has been unable to locate it. Subsequently, Nos 1 and 2 were replaced in 1954–6 by premises designed by Mewès and Davis for the Westminster Bank, which had bought the site in 1950. In 1995–9, Nos 1 and 2 were succeeded by a building designed by the architects Sheppard, Robson and Partners. See Ward, *London County Council bomb damage maps*, p. 111.

85 For Lord Falmouth's musical activities, see Bashford, *Pursuit of high culture*, pp. 68, 108, 116, 150, 157, 184, 200, 280–1.

86 Bashford, 'Learning to listen', p. 29.

87 Bashford, *Pursuit of high culture*, p. 108.

88 Bashford, *Pursuit of high culture*, pp. 150–1.

89 Bashford, *Pursuit of high culture*, p. 108.

90 Hedley, *Chopin correspondence*, p. 336. Chopin to his family in Warsaw, [10–19 August 1848].

91 Hedley, *Chopin correspondence*, p. 331. Chopin to his family in Warsaw, [10–19 August 1848]. Who was Falmouth's niece whom Chopin knew in Paris?
92 Lord Falmouth could hardly have attended both events. The celebrations at Tregothnan on Saturday 8 July are described in the *Royal Cornwall Gazette*, 14 July 1848, p. 2, columns 6–7. I owe this reference to Angela Broome, Librarian Archivist, Courtney Library, Royal Institution of Cornwall, Truro.
93 Wainwright, *Broadwood by appointment*, p. 161.
94 A 'commemoration recital', by Jan Ekier (from Warsaw), was given on Tuesday 15 November 1960 at 8 p.m. in the premises of the Arts Council of Great Britain, No. 4 St James's Square, London. Entitled 'Chopin in London, 1848', it included works performed at Chopin's concert at Lord Falmouth's, and marked twenty years since the destruction by German bombing of No. 2 St James's Square, two doors away, on the night of 14 October 1940. The piano used was the same Broadwood Grand Pianoforte No. 17,047 played by Chopin at the original *matinée*. See the copy of the programme, with an introduction by Arthur Hedley, in Surrey History Centre (Woking), 2185/JB/83/22.
95 The texts of the following reviews are taken from Atwood, *Pianist from Warsaw*, pp. 248–51.
96 Chopin notes in letter to Grzymała, 13 [May 1848], that Viardot sang his mazurkas at Covent Garden, 'without my asking her' (Hedley, *Chopin correspondence*, p. 316). As Chorley makes clear, Viardot was using a Spanish text. For Viardot's settings of Chopin mazurkas, see Guillot, 'Une interprétation des oeuvres de Chopin en France', *passim*; and Schuster, 'Six mazurkas de Frédéric Chopin', *passim*. For a recent edition, see Rose, *Chopin – Viardot: twelve mazurkas for voice and piano* [1988]. According to Hedley, *Chopin correspondence*, p. 361n, 'the most popular and effective was her arrangement of the Mazurka in D, Op.33, no.2'. This appears as no.II in Rose's edition, with the title 'Aime-moi'. For Viardot's settings of Chopin's music, see also Berger, 'Histoire d'une amitié', pp. 144–7. For Chorley's relationship with Viardot, see Waddington, 'Henry Chorley, Pauline Viardot, and Turgenev', *passim*.
97 *Athenaeum*, 15 July 1848 (no.1081, p. 708).
98 National Library of Scotland (Edinburgh), MS Acc.9227, uncatalogued letter. It is undated but headed 'Monday', which may well be 10 July 1848, i.e., the Monday following Chopin's concert 'the other day' at Lord Falmouth's, on Friday 7 July 1848. The underlining is in the original manuscript. See also earlier in this chapter, note 16. A version of the letter is in Hedley, *Chopin correspondence*, p. 323, where Hedley notes that 'the English text of this letter appears to be lost.' The letter ends, engagingly: 'I have sprained one of my great toes! and it is all black the poor toe and as large as two natural ones.' Hedley gives no indication of the contents of the poem which Jane Welsh Carlyle encloses. It is in fact thirty-eight lines long, and describes Chopin as a 'pale wizard'. A transcription, which benefited from the eagle eye of Tom Craik, is given in Willis, 'Chopin in Britain', vol.1, p. 160 (http://etheses.dur.ac.uk/1386/).
99 For the Countess of Blessington and the Count D'Orsay, see Sadleir, *Blessington – D'Orsay, passim*; Sadleir, *Strange life of Lady Blessington, passim*; and the article on 'Marguerite Gardiner' by William H. Scheuerle in *Oxford DNB online*.
100 For Gore House, see Cherry and Pevsner, *London 3: north west*, p. 488; *Survey of London*, vol.38, *The museums area of South Kensington and Westminster* (1975), pp. 11–13, and plate 78b; and Weinreb, Hibbert, and Keay, *London encyclopaedia*, pp. 332–3. For their advice on Gore House I am grateful to Alison Kenney, of the City of Westminster Archives Centre, and Amber Baylis, of the Royal Borough of Kensington and Chelsea Libraries and Arts Service.
101 The richness of the interior is described in Connely, *Count D'Orsay*, pp. 241–2. An eye-witness account of the sale is in Weinreb, Hibbert, and Keay, *London encyclopaedia*, p. 333.

126 *London 1848: recitals*

102 Williams, *Franz Liszt. Selected letters*, p. 141. See also Williams' comments on Liszt and Gore House on p. 955, and Allsobrook's remarks in *Liszt: my travelling circus life*, pp. 23–5.
103 Hallé, *Autobiography*, p. 101.
104 Hedley, *Chopin correspondence*, p. 315. Chopin to Gutmann, 6 May 1848.
105 The date of 10 May 1848 is given in Hipkins's essay 'Chopin's pianoforte', *International inventions exhibition* (1885), p. 12.
106 Hipkins, *How Chopin played*, p. 6. Or was it Broadwood Grand Pianoforte No. 17,093 (London, circa 1847)? This is given in Hipkins's essay 'Chopin's pianoforte', *International inventions exhibition* (1885), p. 12.
107 Hewlett, *Chorley*, vol.2, pp. 173–90. Surprisingly, Chorley makes no mention of musicians here.
108 Hewlett, *Chorley*, vol.2, pp. 173–4. An expanded version of this quotation appears in Sadleir, *Blessington – D'Orsay* (1933 edition), pp. 382–3.
109 Chorley, *Thirty years' musical recollections*, vol.1, p. 81.
110 Hewlett, *Chorley*, vol.2, p. 183.
111 Hedley, *Chopin correspondence*, p. 327. Chopin to Franchomme, 6–11 August [1848].
112 Hedley, *Chopin correspondence*, p. 322. Chopin to Mlle de Rozières, 30 June 1848.
113 Hedley, *Chopin correspondence*, p. 324. Chopin to Grzymała, 8–17 July [1848].
114 Hedley, *Chopin correspondence*, p. 331. Chopin to his family in Warsaw, [10–19 August 1848].
115 Hedley, Chopin correspondence, p. 336. Chopin to his family in Warsaw, [10–19 August 1848].
116 Wood, 'Chopin in Britain, I', p. 12. Herbert Kemlo Wood (1866–1953), was the son of John Muir Wood and Helen Kemlo Stephen. See his obituary in the *Glasgow Herald*, 11 May 1953.
117 For generous advice and information on John Muir Wood I am grateful to Paul Muir Wood, and to Duncan Fraser, who showed me the Muir Wood photographs at the Scottish National Portrait Gallery, Edinburgh. For John Muir Wood's life, see Stevenson, Lawson, and Gray, *Photography of John Muir Wood*, pp. 7–31, which draws on research by Paul Muir Wood, and material in his archives, and the obituary of John Muir Wood in the *Musical Herald*, 1 August 1892, p. 249. His death is also commented on, by the Revd J. Woodfall Ebsworth, in *Notes and Queries*, 8th series, vol.2 (9 July 1892), p. 40.
118 Andrew Wood named his son John Muir Wood after his late partner, John Muir. For various partnerships of the Wood family, and the addresses of their business premises in Edinburgh and Glasgow, see Humphries and Smith, *Music publishing in the British Isles*, pp. 339–40, and Parkinson, *Victorian music publishers*, pp. 300–1.
119 For the context of Muir Wood's publications, see Farmer, *History of music in Scotland*, pp. 357, 428.
120 For John Muir Wood in Edinburgh, see notably Cranmer, 'Music retailing in late 18th- and early 19th-century Edinburgh', *passim*, and Cranmer, 'Concert life', *passim*.
121 Stevenson, Lawson, and Gray, *Photography of John Muir Wood*, p. 7.
122 Stevenson, Lawson, and Gray, *Photography of John Muir Wood*, pp. 7–8. Quotations here are from the archives of Paul Muir Wood, used with his permission.
123 Farmer, *History of music in Scotland*, p. 472.
124 Hedley, *Chopin correspondence*, p. 336. Chopin to his family in Warsaw, [10–19 August 1848].
125 Wood, 'Chopin in Britain, II', p. 6. See also Muir Wood's obituary in the *Musical Herald*, 1 August 1892, p. 249.
126 Wood, 'When Chopin was in Glasgow'.
127 Stevenson, *Light from the dark room*, p. 124. A portrait of Dr Aldrin by John Muir Wood, circa 1850, is in the Scottish National Portrait Gallery, Edinburgh. For John

Muir Wood as a photographer, see Stevenson, Lawson, and Gray, *Photography of John Muir Wood*, passim, and Lawson, 'Photographs by John Muir Wood', *passim*. Muir Wood's legacy consists of some 900 prints and negatives, taken mostly in the 1840s and 1850s.

128 Scottish National Portrait Gallery, Edinburgh. This was included in the exhibition, 'John Muir Wood and the origins of landscape photography in Scotland', Scottish National Portrait Gallery, Edinburgh, 2008.

129 Editorial comment, Hedley, *Chopin correspondence*, p. 327, citing Chopin's MS pocket diary for 1848, TiFC (Warsaw), M/378. See also TiFC (Warsaw), M/378/4, folded card (in Chopin's hand?), 'London and Birmingham/Euston Square Station/Convoie de 9 heures'.

130 See Cherry and Pevsner, *London 4: north*, pp. 361–2, and Weinreb, Hibbert, and Keay, *London encyclopaedia*, pp. 277–8. The sumptuous great hall at Euston, designed by Philip Hardwick, the Younger, was not opened until 27 May 1849. Alas, none of these buildings now remains. Against strong opposition, most of Euston was demolished in the early 1960s to make way for a new station.

131 See Hedley, *Chopin correspondence*, p. 336. Chopin to his family in Warsaw, [10–19 August 1848]. For details of contemporary trains see Lambert, *Illustrated London News*, *passim*, which is used by Nowaczyk, 'Chopin mknął do Szkocji', *passim*. Chopin took the west route from London to Edinburgh, via Carlisle; it was not possible to travel on the east coast route entirely by train until the completion of the Royal Border Bridge over the Tweed at Berwick in 1850. A favoured journey between London and Edinburgh at this time was by ship.

5   Edinburgh

Chopin reached Edinburgh at about 9 p.m. that evening, Saturday 5 August, having taken twelve hours to travel from Euston via Birmingham and Carlisle.[1] When he stepped off the train, he found a city of great contrasts, in which poverty and high culture existed side by side. Shepherd's engravings, notably in his book *Modern Athens* (1829–31), show the rugged life of the Old Town set against the classical splendours of the New Town. Between the two, overlooked by Edinburgh Castle, lay Princes Street and the Mound, on which Playfair's Royal Institution (now the Royal Scottish Academy) had been completed in 1835 (see Figure 5.1).[2] Further east, on Princes Street, the Scott Monument, designed by George Meikle Kemp, had been finished in 1845, and recorded by such photographers as William Donaldson Clark, and Hill and Adamson (see Figs 5.2 and 5.3).[3] 'In the sunny months of the years 1843 to 1847', as one writer expresses it, 'Edinburgh saw an extraordinary experiment in art.' Hill and Adamson

> set precedents and standards, shaping the art of calotype photography, invented by W H Fox Talbot, and experimenting with its difficulties and possibilities . . . They looked at the landscape, principally of Edinburgh; they watched the Scott Monument being built and the railways enter the city.'[4]

In addition, engraved maps of Edinburgh proliferated, and images of the notable men and women in Scottish cultural life were captured in print and photograph.[5]

Among those who met Chopin on the station platform in Edinburgh were Jane Stirling, and Dr Adam Lyschiński and his wife. Miss Stirling was born on 15 July 1804 at Kippenross, near Dunblane, Perthshire, the seat of her father, John Stirling, 6th of Kippendavie,[6] and died at Calder House on 6 February 1859.[7] Raeburn painted a striking portrait of father and daughter (see Figure 5.4). The family were a branch of the Stirlings of Keir, and Jane's mother, formerly Mary Graham, gave birth to thirteen children, seven sons and six daughters, of whom Jane was the youngest. Jane's sister Katherine, her constant companion in later years, was born in 1891, and died in London on 4 March 1868.[8] She married James Erskine, of Linlathen, in 1811, only to be widowed five years later; according to Audrey Bone, she had four daughters, but 'each died within four days of birth', before she was widowed in 1816.[9] A photograph of the two sisters, surely taken after

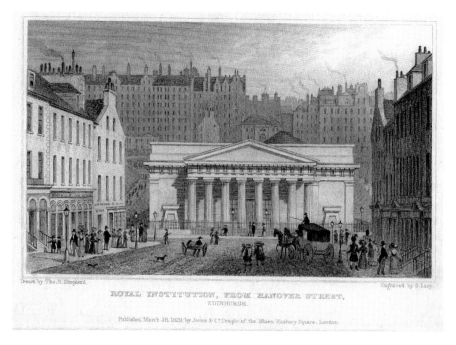

Figure 5.1 Edinburgh, New Town. The Royal Institution (now the Royal Scottish Academy) seen from Hanover Street, looking beyond it to the Mound and the Old Town. Drawn by Thomas Hosmer Shepherd, engraved by S. Lacy, from *Modern Athens* (1829/31). Private collection

Chopin's death, shows Jane as 'Chopin's widow' (see Figure 5.5). The Stirling family, then as now prominent in Perthshire, had acquired considerable wealth through trade in Jamaica.

The two 'kind Scots ladies', who had taken care of Chopin in Paris, would now be devoted to his welfare in Scotland.[10] The most familiar portrait of Jane Stirling is the lithograph by Achille Devéria which shows her with Lady Frances Ann [Fanny] Bruce, daughter of the 7th Earl of Elgin (see Figure 2.6), but this fails to capture Jane's beauty. Ary Scheffer, however, succeeded in doing so. Thomas Erskine, of Linlathen, explains that Scheffer used Jane as a model for his painting *Le Christ consolateur* (1837).[11] Here, Erskine notes, Scheffer 'presented in one of the figures [i.e., the Virgin Mary] his ideal of female beauty, and was struck on being first introduced to Miss Stirling to find in her the almost exact embodiment of that ideal. She was introduced afterwards in many of his pictures.'[12]

Another relative, Miss May Stirling, wrote:

> I had a great admiration for my great-aunt Jane. It was a great pleasure to watch her tall graceful figure as she moved about the room . . . She was

130 *Edinburgh*

Figure 5.2 Edinburgh. Princes Street, the Scott Monument, and the Royal Institution (now the Royal Scottish Academy). Albumen print by William Donaldson Clark, circa 1858. Scottish National Photography Collection. Scottish National Portrait Gallery, Edinburgh

certainly a striking looking woman, and clever, and she had moreover a very winning way of speaking: my Aunt Jane took us more than once to the studio of Ary Scheffer in whose pictures her own features are so often to be traced, notably that of Christ and the Maries. I only remember distinctly in the crowd the Princess Czartoriska [sic] who was fresh from Polish troubles that made her the central figure of the party.[13]

Jane's beauty is apparent in Scheffer's portrait of her, with Mrs Katherine Erskine, and their niece, Mrs William Houston (née Marion Douglas Russell, of Woodside), of perhaps 1844 (see Figure 5.6), which has the same wistful look we see in the lost drawing, seemingly of her, and attributed to Scheffer, maybe of the same date (see Figure 5.7).[14] For her part, Jane commissioned a portrait of Chopin from Scheffer,[15] and one or two portraits of the composer from Franz-Xaver Winterhalter, including one of 1847 which is now in the Collegium Maius, Cracow.[16] After Chopin's death, Jane bought the Pleyel piano originally hired by Chopin in Paris, and sent it to his family in Warsaw.[17]

The mid-1840s had seen Jane's purchase of an Érard grand piano, now at Hatchlands,[18] Chopin's dedication of the Two Nocturnes (Op.55), in F minor and

Edinburgh 131

Figure 5.3 Edinburgh. The Scott Monument, newly completed, April 1845. Photograph by David Octavius Hill and Robert Adamson. Scottish National Photography Collection. Scottish National Portrait Gallery, Edinburgh

E flat major respectively, to 'Mademoiselle J.W. Stirling', first published in 1844, and the start of lessons with him (see Figure 5.8).[19] Evidence of Chopin's teaching includes Jane Stirling's copy of his complete works, annotated by the composer, and subsequently edited by Jean-Jacques Eigeldinger and Jean-Michel Nectoux.[20]

Figure 5.4 John Stirling, of Kippendavie (1742–1816) and his youngest daughter, Jane Wilhelmina Stirling (1804–59), by Sir Henry Raeburn, circa 1810–14. Collection of the National Trust for Scotland. Scottish National Portrait Gallery, Edinburgh

Edinburgh 133

Figure 5.5 Jane Stirling (left), with Mrs Katherine Erskine, of Linlathen. Photograph, provided by Mme Ganche, from Bone, *Jane Wilhelmina Stirling* (1960), opposite p. 89. Private collection

Dr Adam Lyschiński, one of the people who met Chopin on the platform in Edinburgh[21] – when, his wife told Niecks, he addressed Chopin in Polish[22] – seems to have been the Stirling family physician. Lyschiński, a Pole and a homeopath, was educated at Edinburgh University, where he graduated MD in 1837,[23] and in the same year became a Licentiate of the Royal College of Surgeons (LRCS) of Edinburgh. He was a medical officer in the Edinburgh Homeopathic Dispensary (together with Dr Dionysus Wielobycki) at No. 5 St James's Square, which was instituted in 1841.[24] Indeed, Edinburgh was in the forefront of homeopathic medicine: Frederick Hervey Foster Quin, who had founded the British Homeopathic Society (later the Faculty of Homeopathy) in 1844, had taken his MD at Edinburgh in 1820, and Edinburgh medical graduates had started the *British Journal of Homeopathy* (now known simply as *Homeopathy*) in 1843.[25]

At mid-century, musical activity in Edinburgh and Glasgow was flourishing. On a domestic level, music-making was prospering in the home, at least among the well-to-do (see Figure 5.9). Edinburgh concert life owed much of its success to the founding in 1819 of the Professional Society of Musicians, H.G. Farmer explains, which concentrated on the great orchestral works of the time.[26] In 1835, the Edinburgh Musical Association was formed, and 'in addition to these

Figure 5.6 Jane Stirling (centre), with Mrs Katherine Erskine, of Linlathen (right), and their niece Mrs William Houston (née Marion Douglas Russell, of Woodside). Portrait by Ary Scheffer, 1844. Private collection. Scottish National Portrait Gallery, Edinburgh

professional concerts there were dozens of others run by entrepreneurs or societies.'[27] New halls were erected in Scottish cities – the Assembly Rooms, Aberdeen (1820), the City Hall, Glasgow (1841), the Music Hall, Edinburgh (1843), and the Queen's Rooms, Glasgow (1850) – which encouraged both choral and orchestral performances. Both Edinburgh and Glasgow benefited from the series of concerts arranged by George Wood, John Muir Wood, and others.[28] Among the celebrated performers in Edinburgh were Moscheles (1828), and Paganini, who in 1831 gave ten concerts in the Assembly Rooms, and in 1833 one in the Adelphi Theatre, and another in the Hopetoun Rooms, Queen Street.[29] On his tour of Scotland in 1841, Liszt also played in the Hopetoun Rooms, where he attracted a capacity audience of four hundred, and 'all the ladies came out.'[30] Opera was not neglected. In Edinburgh, during the 1830s, the productions at the Caledonian Theatre and the Theatre Royal included Mozart's *Le nozze di Figaro* and *Don Giovanni*, Rossini's *Il barbiere di Siviglia*, Weber's *Der Freishütz*, and Bellini's *La sonnambula*.[31]

Initially, Chopin stayed at the Douglas Hotel in St Andrew Square, one of a group of buildings marking the east end of George Street, the central axis in James Craig's eighteenth-century plan of the New Town of Edinburgh; Raskin's plan of

Figure 5.7 Jane Stirling (?). Photograph of lost drawing attributed to Ary Scheffer, ?1844. Location unknown. Image recorded in reference section, Scottish National Portrait Gallery, Edinburgh

1851 shows it, and other locations with Chopin connections (see Figure 5.10). The centrepiece, and for long the head office of the Royal Bank of Scotland, is the free-standing house designed by William Chambers in 1771 for Sir Laurence Dundas.[32] As can be seen in Shepherd's engraving of 1829, two houses,

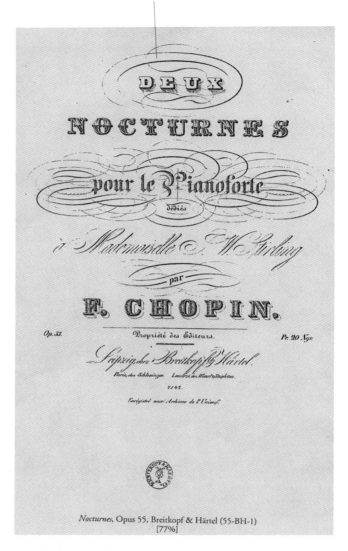

Figure 5.8 Chopin, title page of Deux Nocturnes (Op.55), dedicated to 'Mademoiselle J W Stirling'. Leipzig: Breitkopf & Härtel, 1844 (German first edition). Platzman, *Chicago catalogue* 1, p. 178. University of Chicago Library

Nos 35 and 37 St Andrew Square, flanked the forecourt. First to be constructed was No. 35, to the north, built in 1769 by Craig for Andrew Crosbie, of Holm (see Figure 5.11). The architect Andrew Elliot was engaged in 1819 by the Royal Bank of Scotland to convert the house into their head office, and in 1830 it became the Douglas Hotel; the hotel was later altered and extended, and is now again used by

Figure 5.9 John Harden (1772–1847). Pen and ink drawing of his wife Jessy at the piano in No. 28 Queen Street, Edinburgh, with her sons and a female relative, 1805. National Library of Scotland, Edinburgh, MS 8866, II.33b

the Royal Bank of Scotland (see Plate 15), Elliot's entrance hall – with its imperial staircase, with Ionic columns on the ground floor and Corinthian on the upper, and lit by a ribbed dome, set on wreathed pendentives – remains much as Chopin would have known it (see Plate 16).

Despite its attractions, Chopin found the Douglas Hotel 'unbearable' (Niecks' word) and stayed there only a day and a half, after which Dr Lyschiński put him up in his own home. This was No. 10 Warriston Crescent, Edinburgh, a stone terrace house on the Warriston estate laid out in 1809–20 by the architect James Gillespie Graham (see Plate 17).[33] The house, which still exists, is of two storeys to the street, but – as the land slopes steeply – there is a third (basement) storey on the garden side. The disposition of the rooms now seems to be much as it was when Chopin was there. The Lyschińskis' children were sent away to stay with a friend, and Chopin had to be satisfied with their nursery on the first floor as his bedroom, with an adjoining room for his servant, Daniel. The room in which Chopin

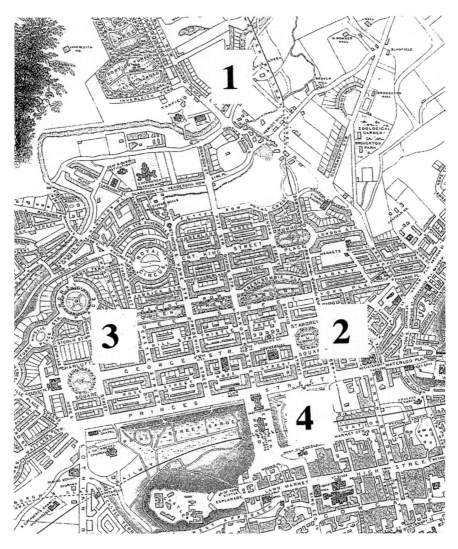

Figure 5.10 Edinburgh, New Town. Detail of plan, drawn and engraved by John Rapkin, with illustrations drawn and engraved by H. Winkles, with additional indication of places connected with Chopin's visit to Edinburgh in 1848. Published by John Tallis & Co, London and New York, [1851] (2003 facsimile). Private collection.

1 10 Warriston Crescent
2 Douglas Hotel, St Andrew Square
3 Hopetoun Rooms, Queen Street
4 Scott Monument, Princes Street

played the piano was probably the sitting room, overlooking the street.[34] No. 10 Warriston Crescent became Chopin's pied-à-terre in Edinburgh during his visit to Scotland, and he stayed there several times, including the night of his Edinburgh concert in the Hopetoun Rooms on 4 October 1848. This stay is commemorated by a plaque on the wall of No. 10 Warriston Crescent, facing the street,[35] and by a bronze bust of Chopin by the Polish sculptor Józef Markiewicz in the Usher Hall, Edinburgh. Originally given to the Chopin Circle in Edinburgh by the Chopin Society in Warsaw, this was presented to the City of Edinburgh at a concert by the Scottish National Orchestra at the Usher Hall on 28 February 1975.[36]

The day after Chopin's arrival, a neighbour of the Lyschińskis, Miss Mary Paterson, who lived next door at No. 11 Warriston Crescent, placed a carriage at their disposal.[37] Mrs Lyschińska therefore took Chopin out for a drive, and showed him the sights of the city, including the Scott Monument, and the music shop of John Muir Wood's father, Andrew Wood, at No. 12 Waterloo Place. Chopin found Edinburgh a 'most handsome town', and was intrigued to hear, as he passed a music shop, a blind man playing one of his mazurkas.[38]

Frederick Niecks, on Mrs Lyschińska's authority, describes life with her family. 'Chopin rose very late in the day', he says, 'and in the morning had soup in his room. His hair was curled daily by the servant, and his shirts, boots, and other things were of the neatest – in fact, he was a *petit-maître*, more vain in dress than any woman.' So far as his health was concerned, it was a familiar story: 'Chopin was so weak that Dr Lyschiński had always to carry him upstairs. After dinner he sat before the fire, often shivering with cold. Then all on a sudden he would cross the room, seat himself at the piano, and play himself warm';[39] according to Hipkins, he would use 'the old square piano in preference to the new and modern grand, standing in the same room'.[40] Chopin, Niecks adds, 'could bear neither dictation nor contradiction: if you told him to go to the fire, he would go to the other end of the room where the piano stood. Indeed, he was imperious.'[41]

As evidence of this, Niecks explains that Chopin once asked Mrs Lyschińska to sing, but she declined. 'At this he was astonished and quite angry. "Doctor, would you take it amiss if I were to force your wife to do it?" The idea of a woman refusing him anything seemed to him preposterous.' Mrs Lyschińska told Niecks that 'Chopin was gallant to all ladies alike, but thinks that he had no heart. She used to tease him about women, saying, for instance, that Miss Stirling was a particular friend of his. He replied that he had no particular friends among the ladies, that he gave to all an equal share of his attention.' Mrs Lyschińska ventured further. ' "Not even George Sand then", she asked, "is a particular friend?" "Not even George Sand", was the reply.'[42]

Further confirmation of Chopin's connections with the Lyschińskis is provided by the autograph score of the song 'Wiosna' (apparently written in 1838, and published posthumously as Op.74, no.2), which is signed by Chopin and inscribed 'Warriston Crescent 1848'.[43] The song has an intriguing history,[44] even including a miniature version.[45] Chopin kept up his connections with Dr Lyschiński even after he had left Scotland for London. Again, Jane Stirling was in the wings. Writing to him at 10 Warriston Crescent, from No. 4 St James's Place, on 3 November 1848,

Figure 5.11 Edinburgh, New Town. East side of St Andrew Square, showing the Douglas Hotel (directly behind coach). Engraving by Thomas Hosmer Shepherd and J. Johnstone, from *Modern Athens* (1829/31). Private collection

Chopin asked Dr Lyschiński to forward an enclosed letter to Jane Stirling at Barnton (see Figure 5.12).[46]

This was a reference to Barnton House, Midlothian, an estate on the northern outskirts of Edinburgh, set in extensive woodland, said by Small in his *Castles and mansions of the Lothians* (1893) to amount to nearly 600 acres. In Chopin's day, Barnton was owned by William Ramsay, of Barnton, whose wife, Mary, was daughter of Lord Torphichen, and thus a niece of Jane Stirling. Barnton House had been remodelled in the castle style, following designs by Robert Adam (see Figure 5.13). Later, the Glaswegian architect David Hamilton added a porch, circa 1810.[47] Although it is not known if Chopin visited Barnton, Jane Stirling stayed there both before and after the composer's death. William Ramsay, of Barnton, died on 14 March 1850, and ten letters sent from Barnton by Jane Stirling to Chopin's sister, Ludwika Jędrzejewicz, are all dated between 10 October 1850 and 26 August 1854.[48] In the first of these, written as Jane prepares to leave for Paris to attend the solemnities marking the first anniversary of Chopin's death, it is clear that the health of Mary Ramsay, recently widowed and still living at Barnton, was giving her great concern.[49] Barnton House was demolished circa 1920, but gate piers and remnants of the curtain wall remain, and part of the former parkland has

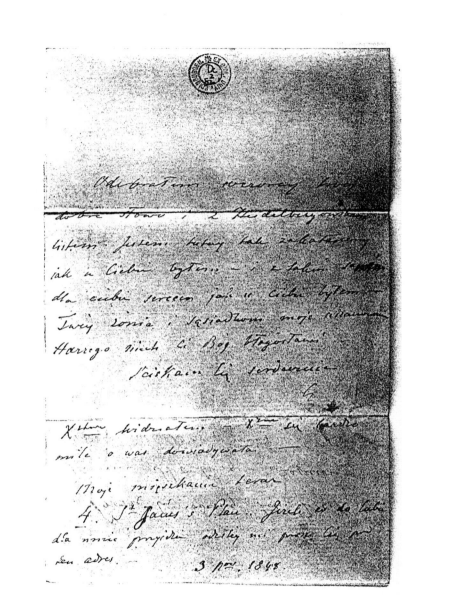

Figure 5.12 Chopin. Recto of autograph letter in Polish of 3 November 1848 sent by Chopin from No. 4 St James's Place, London, to 'Dr Lishinski' at No. 10 Warriston Crescent, Edinburgh, asking him to forward an enclosed note to Jane Stirling at Barnton. Special Collections, Edinburgh University Library, Dc.2/82/1

Figure 5.13 Barnton House, Edinburgh. View from Small, *Castles and mansions of the Lothians* (1883). Mitchell Library, Glasgow

become the Bruntsfield Links Golfing Society, and the Royal Burgess Golfing Society.[50]

Notes

1. For overviews of Chopin's Scottish visit see Załuski, *Scottish autumn of Frederick Chopin, passim*; Bone, *Jane Stirling*, pp. 63–92; and Fiske, *Scotland in music*, pp. 149–55. T. Ratcliffe Barnett's chapter, 'The broken butterfly: Chopin in Scotland', *Scottish pilgrimage*, pp. 11–20, ends with verses from Alfred Noyes' poem, 'The death of Chopin'. Barnett notes (p. 11) that the description of Chopin as a 'butterfly' emanates from Liszt. A discussion of this essay appears in a 1943 review of Barnett's book by Alan Dent, reprinted as the chapter 'Chopin – and the lang Scots miles', *Nocturnes and rhapsodies*, pp. 184–8. See also Janice Galloway and Iwo Załuski, 'Chopin's Scottish swansong', BBC Radio 3, first broadcast on Saturday 26 May 2007, from 12.15 to 1 p.m. More recently, see Nowaczyk, 'Chopin mknął do Szkocji', *passim*. I owe this reference to Zbigniew Skowron.
2. Playfair's National Gallery of Scotland (1850–7) was not yet started.
3. For photography in Edinburgh during the 1840s, generally, see Stevenson and Forbes, *A companion guide to photography in the National Galleries of Scotland*, especially pp. 24–6, 28 (John Muir Wood), 15–23, 65 (Hill and Adamson).
4. *Year of photography at the National Galleries of Scotland* (Edinburgh: National Galleries of Scotland, 2002), n.p.
5. John Muir Wood, for example, took many portrait photographs, including George Wood (his brother and business partner), and Helen Kemlo Stephen (his wife). See

Stevenson, Lawson, and Gray, *Photography of John Muir Wood*, pp. 34–5. My attempts to find a portrait of Chopin among Muir Wood's unidentified photographs at the Scottish National Portrait Gallery, failed. Duncan Forbes, senior curator at the gallery, kindly showed me these.
6 Although John Stirling was 'of Kippendavie', and had inherited the estate in 1775, he moved from there to live at Kippenross, a few miles away. It is a complex story, but a summary can be found in McKerracher, *Street and place names of Dunblane and district*, pp. 36–8. See also Bone, *Jane Stirling*, pp. 5–14.
7 Jane Stirling's will and inventory, granted probate on 4 April 1859, are in the National Archives of Scotland (Edinburgh), SC70/4/63, Edinburgh Sheriff Court Wills; and SC70/1/100, Edinburgh Sheriff Court Inventories, respectively. See www.scotlandspeople.gov.uk. See Willis, 'Chopin in Britain', vol.2, Appendix A: Jane Stirling: Family context, pp. 336–7, with its tabulation of the connections of Stirlings to Scottish country seats (http://etheses.dur.ac.uk/1386/). See also Fraser, *Stirlings of Keir, passim*. For a synopsis of Jane Stirling's links to Chopin, see particularly, Eigeldinger, *Chopin vu par ses élèves*, pp. 232–3, and 'Exemplaires Stirling', pp. 245–56, in the same volume.
8 Katherine Erskine's will and inventory, granted probate on 7 August 1868, are in the National Archives of Scotland (Edinburgh), SC70/4/116, Edinburgh Sheriff Court Wills; and SC70/1/140, Edinburgh Sheriff Court Inventories, respectively. See www.scotlandspeople.gov.uk
9 According to Bone, *Jane Stirling*, p. 8.
10 Hedley, *Chopin correspondence*, p. 336. Chopin to his family in Warsaw, [10–19 August 1848].
11 See Ewals, *Ary Scheffer: gevierd romanticus (1795–1858)*, pp. 200–3; Ewals, *Ary Scheffer (1795–1858)*, p. 48; and Morris, 'Ary Scheffer and his English circle', pp. 294–5.
12 Quoted in Niecks, *Chopin*, vol.2, p. 291. The supposition that Jane is the model for the Virgin Mary is mine.
13 Quoted in Bone, *Jane Stirling*, p. 104. The date of the letter was 22 November 1851, but Bone does not give the name of the addressee. Presumably, May Stirling was the granddaughter of one of Jane's brothers.
14 There is some debate as to whether the artists here were Ary or Henri Scheffer. For the lost drawing, see Morris, 'Ary Scheffer and his English circle', pp. 296–8.
15 For the Scheffer portrait, see Wróblewska-Straus, 'Jane Wilhelmina Stirling's letters to Ludwika Jędrzejewicz', p. 61, n.4.
16 See Tomaszewski and Weber, *Diary in images*, p. 224.
17 See, e.g., Samson, *Chopin*, p. 282.
18 See Cobbe, *Composer instruments*, pp. 51–3.
19 See Eigeldinger, *Chopin: pianist and teacher*, p. 180.
20 See Chopin, *Oeuvres pour piano (Stirling), passim*. It was subsequently held by Mrs Anne D. Houston, at Johnstone Castle.
21 Edinburgh had several stations. See Gifford, McWilliam, and Walker, *Edinburgh*, pp. 289–90, 369. See also, e.g., the various entries under 'Edinburgh' in Simmons and Biddle, *Oxford companion to British railway history*. Among many sources of information on Scottish stations is Biddle, *Britain's historic railway buildings*, pp. 597–712.
22 Niecks, *Chopin*, vol.2, p. 292. This is probably correct, as when Chopin wrote to Dr Lyschiński from London on 3 November 1848, he did so in Polish. See Special Collections, Edinburgh University Library, Dc.2/82/1.
23 The title of Lyschiński's MD dissertation was 'On Smallpox'. See *List of the graduates in medicine of the University of Edinburgh*, p. 112; alphabetical index of names, p. 41. We know from medical directories, registers, and related sources that Lyschiński acted as a medical officer on troopships in 1838–40. He became a registered medical practitioner in Scotland on 31 December 1858, following the passing of the Medical Act of that year, which introduced Medical Registration; prior to that date, there was no national register. The Medical Registers record him at No. 10 Warriston Crescent

until 1877; at No. 6 Dundas Street, Edinburgh, in 1878–82; then at No. 28 Blomfield Road, Shepherd's Bush, London, in 1883–96.
24 Dr Dionysius Wielobycki, also Polish, took his MD at Edinburgh University in 1843, the title of his dissertation being 'On Plica Polonica'. See *List of the graduates in medicine of the University of Edinburgh*, p. 133; alphabetical index of names, p. 70.
25 The *Homeopathic medical directory* for 1853 gives details of Scottish homeopathic dispensaries, and notes that the Edinburgh dispensary had treated 19,055 patients to 1 August 1852. It was supported by private contribution, and admission was free. I owe this reference to Bernard Leary. The degree of Doctor of Medicine (MD) from the four Scottish universities in the mid-nineteenth century had a mixed reputation; the University of St Andrews, for instance, was not alone in being criticized for granting MD degrees 'by post'. Between 1836 and 1862, the university awarded 1,885 such degrees. See Hamilton, *The healers*, p. 157.
26 See the coverage in Farmer, *History of music in Scotland*, *passim*, including opera in Edinburgh and Glasgow on pp. 415–17, and concerts on pp. 464–81. For a full list of Farmer's writings on Scottish music, see Farmer, *Bibliography*, *passim*.
27 For musical life in Edinburgh in the early 1800s, see Cranmer, 'Music retailing in late 18th- and early 19th-century Edinburgh', *passim*; Cranmer, 'Concert life', *passim*; and Eichner, 'Singing the songs of Scotland', *passim*.
28 Farmer, *History of music in Scotland*, pp. 472, 473. The cellist Louis Drechsler, a friend of Lady Murray, was highly esteemed in Edinburgh, where he conducted the Gentlemen's Amateur Society concerts, and founded the Singverein, a male voice choir, in 1846. See Baptie, *Musical Scotland*, p. 47, and Niecks, *Chopin*, vol.2, pp. 288–9.
29 See Macdonald, 'Paganini, Mendelssohn and Turner in Scotland', pp. 31–3, 35, 36–7.
30 Allsobrook, *Liszt: my travelling circus life*, p. 164. Liszt's performances in Scotland in 1841 are documented by Allsobrook on pp. 158–65.
31 Farmer, *History of music in Scotland*, p. 415. The Reid Chair of Music at the University of Edinburgh was established in 1838, when the first holder was John Thomson. At the time of Chopin's visit, the Reid Professor was John Donaldson, who occupied the chair from 1845 to 1865.
32 For the following description of the Douglas Hotel, see Gifford, McWilliam, and Walker, *Edinburgh*, pp. 324–5. See also Gow, 'Fit for an empress', *passim*. Renovation of No. 35 St Andrew Square by the Royal Bank of Scotland, as a conference centre, was completed in 2007 by Michael Laird Architects. I am grateful to Douglas Bell and Nicola McGowan, of the Royal Bank of Scotland, and Susan Horner and Roy Milne, of Michael Laird Architects, for arranging a visit to the building.
33 See Gifford, McWilliam and Walker, *Edinburgh*, pp. 580–1. In 1998, the occupant of No. 10 Warriston Crescent, Jane Kellett, kindly gave me access to the house, and information about Chopin's stay there.
34 Niecks, *Chopin*, vol.2, pp. 292–3.
35 For an advance notice of the unveiling of the plaque, see the *Evening News* (Edinburgh), Thursday 6 February 1975.
36 A report of the presentation of the bust appears in the *Evening News* (Edinburgh), Thursday 6 February 1975.
37 Niecks, *Chopin*, vol.2, p. 292. We know that Miss Paterson lived at No. 11 Warriston Crescent from the *Edinburgh and Leith 1848 street and trade directory*.
38 Hedley, *Chopin correspondence*, p. 336. Chopin to his family in Warsaw, [10–19 August 1848].
39 Niecks, *Chopin*, vol.2, p. 293.
40 Hipkins, *How Chopin played*, p. 8. This observation is based on information given to Edith Hipkins in 1906, when she met Mrs Lyschińska in London, describing her as 'a small dark-eyed vivacious woman over eighty'. Wainwright, *Broadwood by appointment*, p. 164, notes that Mrs Lyschińska recalled that Chopin 'would of an evening

retire into an adjoining room, where an old Broadwood square piano of her childhood stood, and play upon it with evident pleasure'. No source is given.
41 Niecks, *Chopin*, vol.2, p. 293.
42 Niecks, *Chopin*, vol.2, p. 293. Niecks adds: 'Had Mrs Lyschińska known the real state of matters between Chopin and George Sand, she certainly would not have asked that question.' Niecks' description is used as the basis of Hadden, *Chopin*, pp. 142–3. 'Mrs Lyschińska at that time was young and a singer', Edith Hipkins writes, 'and although of Scottish race, her husband had taught her some Polish airs, so when Chopin finally left he bestowed several personal relics upon her, including his gold sleeve-links, which she, in 1895 and again in 1906, brought to London in the vain quest for purchasers.' Hipkins, *How Chopin played*, p. 8.
43 His 'Wiosna' seems frequently to have been used by Chopin as a calling card. For an analysis of Chopin's nineteen songs, with complete Polish and English texts, and musical examples, see Jacobson, 'The songs', *passim*. 'Wiosna' ('Spring'), Op.74, no.2 (1838), with Polish words by Stefan Witwicki, and English translation, is considered on pp. 205–6. For Witwicki, see Rambeau, 'Chopin et son poète, Stefan Witwicki', *passim*.
44 Jacobson notes that 'Chopin himself, as well as Liszt, made a piano transcription of this song, and there are at least six manuscripts of Chopin's transcription ranging in date from April 1838 to September 1848. See Brown, *Index of Chopin's works*, pp. 121–2 (no.117), describing Chopin's pianoforte arrangement of 'Wiosna', as Andantino in G minor (Op.74, no.2). For the published version of 'Wiosna', see Kobylańska, *RUC*, vol.1, pp. 434–40 (nos 1101–12), with no.1110, signed by Chopin at Warriston Crescent in 1848, illustrated in vol.2, p. 200 (plate 77), and listed on p. 274; Kobylańska, *T-BW*, pp. 186–9; and Chomiński and Turło, *KDFC*, pp. 152, 158, 442–4. The Chopin entry by Michełowski and Samson in *Grove music online*, under 'solo songs', gives the date of composition of 'Wiosna' as 1838. Tomaszewski, *University of Edinburgh and Poland*, p. 36, writes: 'We agree with W. Hordyński that Chopin had written the song and dedicated it to the doctor's wife; and with Sophie Skorupska that the manuscript was acquired from the Lyschińskis by Cecily Działyńska when she visited Edinburgh in 1858.' For speculation about this, see the sources cited by Kobylańska, *RUC*, vol.1, pp. 438–9 (no.1110), and Kobylańska, *T-BW*, p. 188.
45 In 1833, Sophy Horsley wrote in a letter to Lucy Hutchins Callcott: 'Mendelssohn took my album with him the night of our glee-party, but you have no idea how many names he has got me.' According to Gotch, 'This truly amazing little book measures only 2 inches by 1½ inches and is less that ½ inch thick – yet it contains 137 names, most of them accompanied by bars of music, or tiny exquisite drawings. One page is covered by an entire song written by Chopin.' See Gotch, *Mendelssohn and his friends in Kensington*, p. 50, and note. This album was sold at Sotheby's Printed and Manuscript Music Sale in London on Thursday 9 December 1999 (L09213, lot 1), when the hammer price with buyer's premium was £24,150. The contents of the album, listed in the Sotheby's sale catalogue, make clear that Chopin's entry was a MS of the song 'Wiosna', signed by him, and 'transcribed for piano, on one stave, eighteen bars, 29 June 1848'. Manuscripts of three songs by Chopin are listed in a letter from Jane Stirling to Ludwika Jędrzejewicz in July 1852. See Wróblewska-Straus, 'Jane Wilhelmina Stirling's letters to Ludwika Jędrzejewicz', pp. 121, 123, n.15. For a performer's view of the songs, see the essay by the bass Doda Conrad, 'Chopin the song-writer', which followed a recital in New York in 1948. According to Conrad (pp. 45–6), during Hitler's rule of Poland, from 1939 to 1945, Chopin's songs were banned.
46 See Special Collections, Edinburgh University Library, Dc.2/82/1.
47 Colvin, *Dictionary*, pp. 54, 59, 472. See also Cant, *Villages of Edinburgh*, vol.1, pp. 58–9, and Gifford, McWilliam, and Walker, *Edinburgh*, p. 552. The extent of the woodland can be seen on the 1853 Ordnance Survey map. For Robert Adam's designs

for Barnton, see King, *Complete works of Robert and James Adam*, pp. 220, 223, and plate 315, and King, *Unbuilt Adam*, pp. 13, 23, 27, 138, 157, 158–9, 161, and plates 106, 165–9.
48 See Wróblewska-Straus, 'Jane Wilhelmina Stirling's letters to Ludwika Jędrzejewicz', especially the table on pp. 53–9. Of the ten letters Jane sent from Barnton, five are given here in full transcript.
49 This letter is summarized in Karłowicz, *Souvenirs*, p. 192 (letter 15).
50 Cant, *Villages of Edinburgh*, vol.1, p. 59.

6 Scottish Country Seats

Despite his increasingly debilitating illness, Chopin kept up an extensive correspondence as he travelled around Scotland, and fortuitously many of his letters have survived. He was cut off physically, but emotionally he remained attached to his family in Warsaw, and to Paris and his Parisian friends. George Sand and the problems of her daughter, Solange, recur in his letters, and his wistfulness for Nohant is never far away. As he moves from country seat to country seat, Chopin provides a running commentary on his concerts in Manchester, Glasgow, and Edinburgh, and gives us lively impressions of his hosts and their other visitors. Chopin's impressions of the Scottish landscape, Scots, and the life in Scottish country seats show him to be a perceptive critic. His letters also demonstrate his besetting ill health, as he struggles with nausea, coughing blood, and forms of delirium. It was an exciting time to be in Scotland, as the country was experiencing a surge in tourism,[1] notably enhanced by the development of the railways (see Figure 6.1).[2] The houses Chopin visited were mostly connected with Jane Stirling's family, and located in the Scottish Lowlands between Calder to the east and Strachur to the west (see Figure 6.2).[3] Edouard Ganche, in his book *Voyages avec Frédéric Chopin* (1934), with its section on 'Chopin en Ecosse', picks out three houses in particular: Calder, Keir, and Johnstone Castle.[4]

After his stay in the Douglas Hotel, and with Dr and Mrs Lyschiński in Warriston Crescent, Chopin went to the first of these, Calder House, at Mid Calder, west of Edinburgh.[5] Calder, since 1350 the seat of the Sandilands (later the Lords Torphichen), was to be Chopin's principal residence among Scottish country seats. Here, in 1556, John Knox is reputed to have celebrated Holy Communion for the first time in Scotland according to Presbyterian rites. The original L-plan of Calder House had been extended and altered several times, including the addition circa 1820 of a stair tower and a two-storey bow containing a staircase rising to the earlier Georgian front door. These features can be seen in two early nineteenth-century paintings of Calder by William Wilson (see Figs 6.3 and 6.4), and along with later alterations circa 1880 in the views published by McCall in *The history and antiquity of the parish of Mid Calder* of 1894. The first-floor drawing room, where Chopin may have entertained his host, still exists, its high windows offering fine views over the distant countryside.[6]

148 *Scottish country seats*

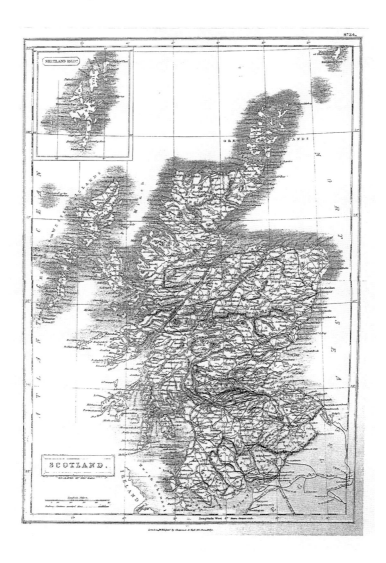

Figure 6.1 Map of Scotland, engraved by Sidney Hall (London, 1852–4). Private collection

The owner of Calder, James Sandilands, 10th Baron Torphichen, married Margaret Douglas Stirling, daughter of John Stirling, of Kipppendavie, and a sister of Jane Stirling and Mrs Katherine Erskine, in 1806, but by the time of Chopin's visit he was a widower. His wife had died in 1836, leaving four children – a son Robert (later the 11th Baron), John (who was in holy orders), James (captain in the 8th Hussars), and a daughter Mary, who in 1828 had married William Ramsay,

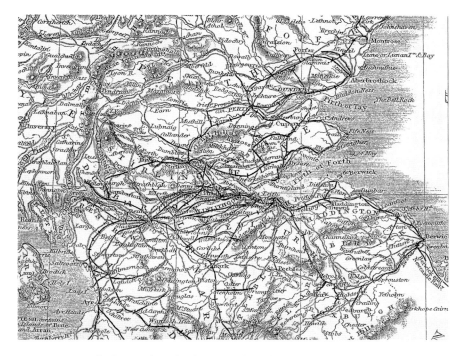

Figure 6.2 Detail of Map of Scotland, engraved by Sidney Hall, showing location of country seats related to Chopin's visit in 1848. Private collection

[Annotation: 1 Edinburgh 2 Calder House 3 Keir 4 Gargunnock 5 Wishaw 6 Johnstone Castle 7 Glasgow 8 Strachur 9 Kippenross 10 Hamilton Palace 11 Dunblane 12 Manchester]

of Barnton. In early life, Torphichen had been captain of an East Indiaman, and he lived until the age of ninety-two. His portrait by Ary Scheffer, painted in Paris, is dated 1849 (see Figure 6.5).[7]

On 14 July 1848, Lord Torphichen wrote to Chopin from Calder welcoming the composer, Jane Stirling and Mrs Erskine to the house;[8] later in July, Chopin told Grzymała that he had been invited to Scotland both by Torphichen and Lady Murray, of Strachur, 'an important, well-known lady who is very fond of music'.[9] The journey from Edinburgh to Calder was twelve miles. 'I got into the carriage which Lord Torphichen had sent for me. The carriage was driven in the English style, with the driver mounted on the horse [i.e., a postilion].' Chopin remarks that he had known his 'kind Scots ladies' for a long time in Paris, and they 'take such care' of him. 'In London I was always at their house and I could not refuse their invitation to come here', he added, 'especially as there is nothing for me to do in London and I need a rest; and as Lord Torphichen gave me a cordial invitation.'[10]

Chopin enjoyed Calder thoroughly, describing its interiors and exteriors with enthusiasm. 'The room I occupy has the most splendid view imaginable', he

Figure 6.3 Calder House, Midlothian. View of entrance front from across the River Almond (detail), by William Wilson, circa 1820s. Private collection. Scottish National Portrait Gallery, Edinburgh

Figure 6.4 Calder House, Midlothian. View of house and the Kirk of Calder (detail), by William Wilson, circa 1820s. Private collection. Scottish National Portrait Gallery, Edinburgh

Figure 6.5 James Sandilands, 10th Baron Torphichen (1770–1862). Portrait by Ary Scheffer, 1849. Private collection. Scottish National Portrait Gallery, Edinburgh

told his family in Warsaw, 'although this part of Scotland is not the *most* beautiful.' Jane Stirling and Mrs Erskine were nothing if not attentive. 'How kind my Scots ladies are to me here! I no sooner have time to wish for something than it is ready to hand – they even bring me the Paris newspapers every day. I have quiet, peace and comfort.' Torphichen had invited him for the whole of the next summer: 'I would not mind staying here all my life, but what would be the use?' In his room, which was well away from the others so that he could play and do as he pleased, he found a Broadwood piano, whilst 'in the drawing-room is a Pleyel, which Miss Stirling brought with her.'[11] Country-house life he found congenial: 'People are arriving all the time for a few days. The houses are most elegantly fitted up: libraries, horses, carriages to order, plenty of servants, etc.' As for Torphichen:

> Some evenings I play Scotch songs to the old lord – the good man hums the tunes to me and expresses his feelings in French as best he can. Although everyone in high society, especially the ladies, speaks French, the general conversation is usually in English and then I regret that I can't follow it; but I have neither the time nor the desire to learn the language. Anyhow, I understand everyday conversation.[12]

Moreover, as Chopin tells Pleyel, 'there is even a certain "red cap" phantom' at Calder, though 'he has not been seen for some time.'[13]

Chopin's day-to-day existence in Scotland was radically different from his hectic musical and social life in Paris and London, with its teaching, composing and

152 Scottish country seats

performing. Not that his students were forgotten. In a recently discovered letter of 12 August 1848, for example, we find Chopin writing from Calder House to an unnamed female pupil, sending a list of her lessons, apologizing for not meeting her at Eaton Square before leaving London, and thanking her for the excellent datura plant which she had sent him (see Figure 6.6). From Calder, Chopin also wrote to Henry Fowler Broadwood.[14]

When Chopin travelled to Scotland, he seems to have decided to leave No. 48 Dover Street for good; on returning to London at the end of October he stayed elsewhere. As an indication of this, he sold the Pleyel grand piano of circa 1846 (No. 13,819), which he had in Dover Street, and which he had brought with him from Paris. It is now in the Cobbe Collection at Hatchlands, Surrey. On 15 August, ten days after leaving the capital, he wrote to Camille Pleyel from Calder about the sale, and the £80 he had received for the piano from Lady Trotter (the mother of Margaret Trotter who, as 'Miss Trotter', appears as a student of Chopin).[15]

In spite of the pleasures of life at Calder, or perhaps because of them, Chopin confessed his inability to compose. Writing to Franchomme from Edinburgh and Calder, earlier that August, Chopin remarked that he 'should like to be paid an annuity for having composed nothing'. The park at Calder was 'very fine', his host 'excellent', and he himself 'as well as [he] may be'.[16] However, he had not

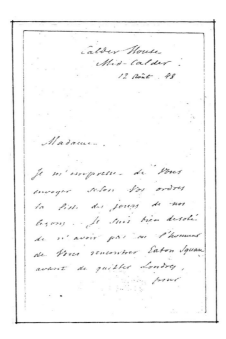

Figure 6.6 Letter from Chopin to unidentified female pupil, Calder House, 12 August 1848, recto. National Archives of Scotland (Edinburgh), Ogilvy of Inverquharity Papers, GD 205/47/11/1

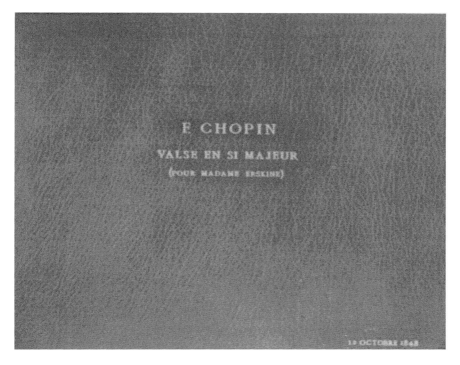

Figure 6.7 Leather cover for the copy of the first page of the lost MS of a Waltz in B major, entitled 'F. CHOPIN/VALSE IN SI MAJEUR/(POUR MADAME ERSKINE) / 12 OCTOBRE 1848'. TiFC (Warsaw), F 1791

had 'a decent musical idea', was 'out of [his] rut', and like 'a donkey at a fancy-dress ball – a violin E-string on a double-bass'. He added: 'I would like to compose just a little, if only to please the good ladies, Mrs Erskine and Miss Stirling. I have a Broadwood in my room and Miss Stirling's Pleyel in the drawing-room; plenty of paper and pens.' Yet creativity seemed to have deserted him.[17]

But not entirely. Despite Chopin's gloom, he was apparently able to complete one piece at Calder – a waltz in B major, discovered in manuscript by Arthur Hedley, dated 12 October 1848 (when Chopin would have been at the house) and inscribed '*pour Madame Erskine*' (see Figs 6.7 and 6.8). It is Chopin's only known composition during his visits to England and Scotland, and no details of it have emerged; it is now lost, and remains unpublished.[18]

Chopin was to visit Calder more than once over the summer and autumn of 1848, and on 16 October we find him writing from the house to the pianist Adolph Gutmann, in Heidelberg. 'I visit one lord after another', Chopin explains. 'Everywhere I meet, together with the heartiest goodwill and boundless hospitality, superb pianofortes, magnificent paintings, famous collections of books; there are

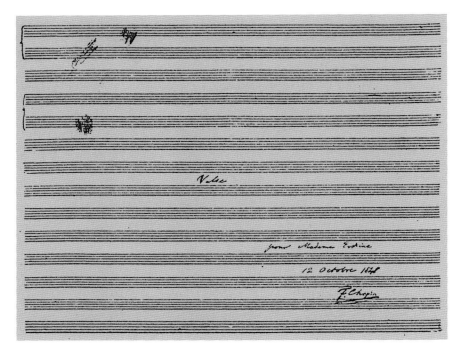

Figure 6.8 Copy of the first page of the lost MS of a Waltz in B major, inscribed by Chopin 'pour Madame Erskine', and dated 12 October 1848, when he was staying at Calder House. TiFC (Warsaw), F 1530

also hunting, dogs, dinners without end, cellars, for which I have less use.' Chopin's concerts in Manchester, Glasgow, and Edinburgh were now behind him, and he could look forward to returning to Paris. 'The cholera approaches; London is full of fogs and spleen, and in Paris there's no president.'[19]

Chopin's letters also give a lively picture of his visit to Keir House, near Dunblane, where his host was William Stirling – known as Sir William Stirling Maxwell, 9th Bt, after he succeeded to the baronetcy in 1865 – who had inherited the estate in 1847, on the death of his father, Archibald Stirling (see Figure 6.9). William was still a bachelor when Chopin stayed with him at Keir in 1848, and earlier in the year had entertained the composer at his London home at No. 38 Clarges Street.[20] He was born in 1818 at Kenmure House, Kirkintilloch, near Glasgow. A man of culture and literary distinction, he published his *Annals of the artists of Spain* in three volumes in 1848, and assembled a fine collection of art objects. At mid-century, the German art historian Dr Gustav Friedrich Waagen, Director of the Royal Gallery of Pictures in Berlin, toured British country houses, gathering material for his *Treasures of art in Great Britain* (1854), of which the supplementary volume, *Galleries and cabinets of art in Great Britain* (1857), includes a description of 'Objects of art at Keir'.[21]

Scottish country seats 155

Figure 6.9 Sir William Stirling Maxwell, 9th Bt (1818–78). Stipple engraving by William Holl, Junior, 1856 or later, after chalk drawing by George Richmond.
Copyright National Portrait Gallery, London

The house itself, originally erected in the eighteenth century, had been altered and extended by the architect David Hamilton between 1829 and 1835.[22] Apart from the remodelling of the dining room, the additions included a long gallery and a magnificent bow-windowed drawing room, as shown in Hamilton's scheme

156 Scottish country seats

of 1829, now in the possession of Keir Estates (see Figure 6.10); both the drawing room and the library would have made fine settings for a Chopin recital. The exterior effect of these changes can be seen in the view from the west in Fraser's *Stirlings of Keir* (see Figure 6.11), though by the time this was published in 1858 Stirling (with the assistance from 1849 of the architect, Alfred Jenoure) had moved the entrance from the east to the north, added a semi-elliptical bow to the east front, and expanded the library into the former entrance hall.[23] The exterior of the drawing room, however, remained unchanged, as is evident from a photograph of 1975. Keir house is now in foreign ownership, and the resiting of Hamilton's lodge and entrance gates in 1969, close to a major road, does nothing to encourage visitors (see Plate 18).

On 1 October we find Chopin writing to Wojciech Grzymała from Keir, where the window of his room overlooks 'a most lovely view of Stirling Castle . . . and of the mountains and lakes and splendid parks – in short, one of the finest views in Scotland'.[24] His host, whom he met in London, is 'a rich bachelor and has here numerous fine pictures . . . He has travelled widely and has been in the East: he

Figure 6.10 Keir House, Perthshire. Drawing by David Hamilton of the south elevation (1829), showing the drawing room extension to the left. Copyright Historic Environment Scotland (HES), Edinburgh

Figure 6.11 Keir House, Perthshire. 'Keir – 1837', from Fraser, *Stirlings of Keir* (1858), showing to the left the three-bay extensions to the house by David Hamilton, from 1829. National Library of Scotland, Edinburgh

is an intelligent man. Whenever members of English society are visiting Scotland they come to see him. He keeps open house and there are usually about thirty people to lunch.' The appeal to Chopin of attractive aristocratic women persists. 'Various celebrated beauties are also here just now (Mrs Norton left a few days ago), and dukes and lords.[25] They were more numerous than usual this year as the Queen was in Scotland and passed this way unexpectedly yesterday by train.'

Chopin bemoans the weakness of his health. 'I cannot compose anything', he tells Grzymała, 'not because I have no desire to, but because of material obstacles, since I have to hop along another branch every week. But what else can I do?'[26] He has a 'host of invitations', but his illness means that he cannot accept those to such houses as the Duchess of Argyll's [Inveraray] and Lady Belhaven's [Wishaw]. The routine of life at Keir can be stressful. 'Nowadays, for instance, I am not fit for anything during the whole morning, until two o'clock [lunch] – and after that, when I have dressed, everything irritates me and I go on gasping until dinner-time. Dinner over, I have to remain at table with the menfolk, *watching* them talk and *listening* to them drinking.' Afterwards, Daniel carries Chopin upstairs to his bedroom. Then, writes Chopin, he 'helps me to undress, puts me to bed, leaves a candle, and then I am free to gasp and dream until morning, when it starts all over again'. Hardly is he used to one setting than he has to go somewhere else. 'My Scots ladies give me no peace', he moans. Although apparently Jane

158   Scottish country seats

Stirling and Mrs Erskine were not staying at Keir. 'They either turn up to fetch me or cart me around to their families . . . They will suffocate me out of *kindness* and I, out of *politeness*, will not refuse to let them do it.'

From Keir, Chopin was in touch with his friend and pupil Mlle Marie de Rozières, a pianist and sometime governess to Solange Dudevant-Sand (see Figure 6.12). 'I find here many people who seem to like music and plague me to play', he wrote. 'Out of politeness I do so, but every time with fresh regrets, swearing I will not be caught again.'[27] The piano Chopin may have played at Keir was an Érard grand (No. 713), now in the Cobbe Collection at Hatchlands (see Plate 7).[28] It is dated 1843, with a case of mahogany veneer on oak, and was supplied by the makers to Jane Stirling in 1843 – the year she may have met Chopin – and chosen for her, in London, by Jules Benedict. Subsequently, the piano has had a colourful history, and it was sold to Alec Cobbe by the present Archibald Stirling, of Keir, in 1997.[29]

After Calder and Keir, Johnstone Castle was for Ganche 'la troisième et dernière station importante de Chopin en Ecosse'.[30] Chopin stayed at Johnstone, situated to the west of Glasgow, in September 1848, before and after his Glasgow concert.[31] His hosts were Ludovic Houston, 6th of Johnstone, and his wife Ann, eldest sister of Jane Stirling.[32] The original part of the house dated from the sixteenth century, but it had been extended circa 1812 by Ludovic's father, George Houston. Its castle style, suggesting that the architect may have been James Gillespie Graham, can be seen in the prospect from Ramsay's *Views in Renfrewshire* (1839) (see Figure 6.13), and in Thomas Annan's photograph in Millar's *Castles and manors*

Figure 6.12 Marie de Rozières (1805–65). Drawing by George Sand. Musée Carnavalet, Paris. Mirska and Hordyński, *Chopin na obczyźnie* (1965), p. 216

Figure 6.13 Johnstone Castle, Johnstone, Renfrewshire. Engraving by William H. Lizars, from Ramsay, *Views in Renfrewshire* (1839). Mitchell Library, Glasgow

of Renfrewshire and Buteshire (1889) (see Figure 6.14). During World War II, Johnstone was used as a prisoner-of-war camp, and as a billet for Polish servicemen. It was demolished in 1956, and little more than a tower now remains (see Figure 6.15). A plaque affixed to nearby railings records Chopin's visit.

Chopin told Wojciech Grzymała that Johnstone is 'very fine and luxurious, and is kept up on a grand scale'.[33] As usual, his fellow-guests both fascinate and appal him. 'They are all cousins here, male and female, belonging to great families with great names which no one on the Continent has ever heard of', he wrote. 'The whole conversation is conducted on genealogical lines.' Nonetheless, Chopin continues. 'they are very good and kind and I receive every possible attention. There is a varied crowd of old ladies and seventy to eighty-year old lords, but no young people – they are away shooting.' Chopin asks Grzymała his forgiveness for 'writing all this rubbish; you know what a torture it sometimes is for me to write – the pen burns my fingers, my hair falls over my eyes, and I can't write what I would like to – so I scribble a lot of useless nonsense'. The letter, completed on 9 September, ends: 'I haven't written to Solange or to Rozières. I shall do so when I feel my nerves less on edge.' Indeed, according to Gavoty, Chopin wrote to Solange that day, telling her of his weird experience when playing his

Figure 6.14 Johnstone Castle, Johnstone, Renfrewshire. Photograph by Thomas Annan, from Millar, *Castles and manors of Renfrewshire and Buteshire* (1889). Thomas Annan Collection, Glasgow City Libraries

Sonata in B flat minor (Op.35) for some British friends.[34] He also dropped a line to Camille Pleyel, recommending Thomas Tellefsen (who seems to have been at Johnstone Castle at the time) to him.[35]

Chopin's letters give little more than hints of any musical activities at Johnstone. In entertaining the owners and their friends, Chopin would have had access to the Pleyel Grand Pianoforte No. 13,716 (Paris, 1847), which belonged to Jane Stirling.[36] Later in 1848, on 15 November, Chopin signed it, and it is now in the Collegium Maius in Cracow (see Plate 34).[37]

Chopin gives us details of a 'strange accident' which he experienced at Johnstone Castle, and which might have cost him his life. As the composer told Grzymała:

> We were driving to see some neighbours on the coast. The carriage I was in was a coupé, with a very handsome pair of young thoroughbred English horses. One horse began to rear; he caught his foot and then started to bolt, taking the other horse with him. As they were tearing down a slope in the park, the reins snapped and the coachman was thrown from his seat (he received a very nasty bruising). The carriage was smashed to bits as it was flung against tree after tree: we should have gone over a precipice if the vehicle had not

Figure 6.15 Johnstone Castle, Renfrewshire. Remains, 2008. Photograph: Peter Willis, 2008

been stopped at length by a tree. One of the horses tore itself free and bolted madly, but the other fell with the carriage on top of it. The windows were smashed by branches.

Miraculously, Chopin survived. 'Luckily I was unhurt', he continues,

> apart from having my legs bruised from the jolting I had received. My manservant had jumped out smartly, and only the carriage was demolished and the horses wounded. People who saw it all from a distance cried out that two men were killed, when they saw one thrown out and the other lying on the ground. Before the horse could move I was able to crawl out of the carriage unhurt, but none of those who saw what had happened, or we ourselves, could understand how we had escaped being smashed to pieces.

Death seemed to beckon. 'I confess that I was calm as I saw my last hour approaching', Chopin admitted, 'but the thought of broken legs and hands appals me. To be a cripple would put the finishing touch to me.'[38]

Chopin told Grzymała, in a letter of 4–9 September 1848, that he would stay a week at Johnstone Castle, 'and then go to Lady Murray's, in a still more beautiful district, where I shall spend another week'.[39] This was Strachur House. He returned to Johnstone in time for his concert in Glasgow on the afternoon of

162   Scottish country seats

Figure 6.16 Milliken House, Renfrewshire. Engraving by William H. Lizars from Ramsay, *Views in Renfrewshire* (1839). Mitchell Library, Glasgow

Wednesday, 27 September. That evening there was a dinner at Johnstone, which must have been the highlight of Chopin's time there, as the guests included Lord and Lady Murray, Lord Torphichen, Prince Aleksander Czartoryski, and his wife Princess Marcelina; their son, Prince Marcel, was also staying at the castle. The next day, Chopin reports, Lord and Lady Murray, and Lord Torphichen, 'could not find praise enough for Princess Marcelina'.[40]

Not far from Johnstone Castle are two other houses with Stirling family connections, for which James Gillespie Graham also acted as architect: Milliken, Renfrewshire, and Wishaw, Lanarkshire. Gillespie Graham's client at Milliken, Sir William Napier, Bt, was a relative of the Houstons of Johnstone, and it is not impossible that Chopin visited Millilken when staying at Johnstone nearby (see Figs 6.16 and 6.17).[41] We are on firmer ground with Wishaw, Motherwell, which was the seat of Lord and Lady Belhaven and Stenton. In 1825, the earlier house was enlarged and remodelled in the castle style by Gillespie Graham, and as such appears in Neale's *Views of noblemen's and gentlemen's seats in Scotland*, of circa 1830 (see Figure 6.18).[42] It was demolished in 1853. Lady Belhaven was among the thirty or so guests at Keir in October 1848, and that month we find Chopin telling Mlle de Rozières that 'if it is fine I shall go to the Duchess of Argyll's at

Figure 6.17 Milliken House, Renfrewshire. Photograph by Annan, from *The old country houses of the old Glasgow gentry*, 2nd edition (1878). Mitchell Library, Glasgow

Figure 6.18 Wishaw House, Lanarkshire. Engraving from Neale, *Views of noblemen's and gentlemen's seats in Scotland* (circa 1830). Private collection

164 Scottish country seats

Inveraray on Loch Fyne, and to Lady Belhaven's [at Wishaw], one of the largest places in the country.'[43] Chopin seems never to have gone to Inveraray, but a fortnight later, on 16 October, he was writing to Lady Belhaven from Calder: 'Madam, if I may still take advantage of your invitation, on which day may I have the honour of presenting my respects at Wishaw? I am leaving Calder House today for Edinburgh . . . I shall stay three days at Warriston Crescent.'[44] He then must have gone to Wishaw, for at the end of the month he comments to Grzymała: 'I wrote to you while I was at Wishaw, at Lady Belhaven's, but my letter was so despairing, so awful, that it was just as well I did not send it.'[45]

On the other hand, Chopin found that 'country-house life in high society is really very interesting. They have nothing like it on the Continent.'[46] Jane Stirling and Katherine Erskine made sure that Chopin visited other houses with owners connected to the Stirling family. Although Chopin declined the chance of going to Kippenross (see Figure 6.19), Jane Stirling's birthplace, a few miles from Keir, because of the rain,[47] he may have visited Kippendavie, whence Jane's family came;[48] Gargunnock House, the seat of John Stirling, 2nd of Gargunnock, son of Jane Stirling's brother, Charles (see Figure 6.20);[49] Glenbervie House, Stirlingshire,[50] and possibly Eglinton Castle, Ayrshire.[51]

The grandest of the Scottish country seats visited by Chopin was Hamilton Palace, where, as at Strachur, he was independent of his 'good Scots ladies'. Hamilton had been enlarged by Alexander, 10th Duke of Hamilton, who extended the north front between 1822 and 1828 to the classical designs of David Hamilton, the Glasgow architect who had altered and extended Keir (see Figure 6.21). These

Figure 6.19 Kippenross House, Perthshire, birthplace of Jane Stirling in 1804, now extensively altered. Photograph: Peter Willis, 2008

Figure 6.20 Gargunnock House, Stirlingshire. Pencil drawing by W.F. Lyon, 1870. Copyright Historic Environment Scotland (HES), Edinburgh

Figure 6.21 Hamilton Palace, Lanarkshire. Engraving by Joseph Swan, from a painting by John Fleming, from Swan, *Select views on the River Clyde* (1830). Private collection

interpreted proposals by the Neapolitan architect Francesco Saponieri.[52] Internally, opulence reigned. In 1854, the German art historian Gustav Waagen, in his book, *Galleries and cabinets of art in Great Britain*, described the interior of the palace as Chopin must have found it six years previously. The Duke of Hamilton, Waagen noted, combined 'in equal measure a love of art with a love of splendour and was an especial lover of beautiful and rare marbles'. Furthermore, 'as a full crimson predominated in the carpets, a deep brown in the woods of the furniture, and a black Irish marble, as deep in colour as the *nero antico*, in the specimens of marble, the general effect was that of the most massive and truly princely splendour.'[53] Hamilton Palace was demolished in 1919.

Chopin went to Hamilton for a few days towards the end of October 1848, following his Edinburgh concert and a visit to Wishaw. His hosts were the 10th Duke and his wife, the Duchess, formerly Susan Euphemia, second daughter of William Beckford of Fonthill (see Figure 6.22). Beckford was a keen musician, and his daughter shared his enthusiasm, playing both the piano and the cello. In 1828, Beckford gave her a Pleyel grand, No. 1,318 (Paris, circa 1827), now at Lennoxlove House, which Chopin may have played at Hamilton (see Plate 19);[54] significantly, the Duchess's portraits by Willes Maddox, at Lennoxlove and Brodick Castle, show her seated at a grand piano. Although Chopin told his family

Figure 6.22 Susan Euphemia (née Beckford), Duchess of Hamilton (1786–1859). Portrait by Willes Maddox, circa 1845. Private Collection, Scotland. Scottish National Portrait Gallery, Edinburgh

in Warsaw that he 'used to know' the Duchess of Hamilton in Paris,[55] she was not, apparently, one of his pupils. However, she was a patroness of the arts, and 'her musical interests were well known. Probably during a visit to Italy in 1821, she was made an honorary member of the Philharmonic Academy', and a Latin diploma she received is also at Lennoxlove. Among the Duchess's collection of musical scores there are manuscripts of eleven cello sonatas by Boccherini, five of which exist only at Lennoxlove.[56]

Despite the Duchess's enthusiasm, Chopin found the lack of appreciation of music at Hamilton Palace somewhat galling. 'By "art" they mean here painting, sculpture and architecture', he told Gryzmała. 'Music is not an art, and is not called by that name; and if you say "artist" these English [*sic*] think you mean a painter, sculptor or architect. But music is a *profession*, not an art, and no one ever calls any musician an artist or uses the word in such a sense in print.' Furthermore, Chopin was exasperated by the ladies' habits – whether the lady be playing 'most dreadful tunes' on an accordion, or accompanying herself '*standing* at the piano while she sings a French romance with an English accent'.[57] Among the guests at Hamilton were the Prince of Lucca, and the Prince and Princess of Parma;[58] the Princess told Chopin that one of the ladies '*whistled* for her, with guitar accompaniment'.[59] Chopin adds: 'Every comment ends with the words: "Leik water", meaning 'that the music flows like water. I have never yet played to an Englishwoman without her saying: "Leik WATER!!" They all look at their hands and play wrong notes most soulfully. What a queer lot! God preserve them!'[60]

Returned to Edinburgh from Hamilton, Chopin informs Grzymała that Lord Dudley Stuart had written and asked him to play on 16 November at 'a benefit-concert for the Poles, to be given before the ball begins'. Chopin is staying with Dr Lyschiński, who is giving him 'homeopathic treatment'. Should the weather improve, Chopin says, he will return to Hamilton and 'go from there to the Isle of Arran (the whole of which belongs to them) and stay with the Baden princess who has married their son, the Marquis of Douglas'. The Marquess – at whose London home Chopin had already played – lived at Brodick Castle, on Arran. 'But I already know that nothing will come of all this', Chopin remarks.[61] He was right. Chopin's visit to Brodick never materialized.

He did, however, go to Strachur House, situated in the far reaches of Argyll, on the east side of Loch Fyne. Writing to his family on 10–19 August 1848, Chopin referred to the invitation to visit Scotland which he had received from Mary Murray, sixty years old, and 'the first pupil [he] had in London', whom he had promised to visit 'in a few weeks' time'. Lady Murray, Chopin commented, 'spends most of her time in Edinburgh and exercises command over musical affairs. Lady Murray lives in a most beautiful district on the sea-coast. In fact one has to cross the sea to get there.'[62] 'One has to sail across Loch Long (one of the prettiest Lochs here) and go along the west coast of Scotland', Chopin wrote.[63] One could either go by steamer down Loch Long, the Firth of Clyde, round Bute, and up to Loch Fyne; or else cross Loch Long, and travel by coach to Strachur. It marked the most northerly point on Chopin's Scottish travels.

Chopin's host, Sir John Archibald Murray, was called to the Scottish bar in 1800, became a Member of Parliament in 1826, and in 1839 left Parliament for the Court of Session (see Figure 6.23).[64] He was knighted and took his seat on the bench as Lord Murray. A generous patron of the arts, Murray held a special position in Edinburgh and London society: Sir Walter Scott records enjoyable evenings spent at Murray's house in Edinburgh, and Harriet Martineau praised his and Lady Murray's tea parties at Westminster when he was Lord Advocate.[65]

Strachur itself, begun before the 1780s, is a classically inspired house built by General John Campbell, of Strachur, and originally called Strachur Park, set in extensive gardens.[66] Following the death of Campbell's widow, the house was let to a series of tenants, including Lord Murray, from circa 1838 to circa 1862. Strachur is three storeys high and five bays wide, with lower wings added to the gables. On the main front, a rectilinear central porch, plastered and balustraded, has been replaced by an early twentieth-century version, with rounded ends. The garden front is dominated by a three-storey central bow, with a crenellated parapet (see Plate 20). The drawing room, with its fine detailing and semi-circular bow, and overlooking the garden, would have provided an admirable setting for Chopin's informal recitals (see Plate 21). In Edinburgh, so at Strachur, the Murrays were renowned hosts, but we can only speculate about Chopin's time there.

Figure 6.23 Sir John Archibald Murray (?1778–1859), Scottish judge, Lord Advocate, and Lord of Session. Portrait by Sir John Watson Gordon, 1856. Scottish National Portrait Gallery, Edinburgh

Chopin's favourite pupil was the German pianist and composer Adolphe Gutmann. Writing to Gutmann in Heidelberg on 16 October 1848, as he approached the end of his tour of Scottish country seats, Chopin reflected on the experience: 'Ever since you last wrote to me, I have been in Scotland, Walter Scott's beautiful country, among all the memories and reminders of Mary Stuart, of the Charleses, etc.' Everything in Scotland, says Chopin, is 'doubly brilliant, except the sun, which is the same now as always'. Winter is approaching, and he is apprehensive. 'What will happen to me', he writes, 'I don't yet know.'[67]

Notes

1 See the chapter 'Transport and tourism, 1800–1850', in Durie, *Scotland for the holidays*, pp. 44–64, and the coverage of coaches, steamers, and trains, in Grenier, *Tourism and identity in Scotland, passim*.
2 See Wood, *Building railways*, pp. 13–14, and pp. 14–16 for subsequent development of the railways in Scotland at this time. A fuller treatment is in Thomas, *Scotland: the Lowlands and the Borders, passim*.
3 Graphic illustrations of the routes of the railways in Britain appear in Freeman and Aldcroft, *Atlas of British railway history, passim*. For details of the architects and country seats in this chapter, in addition to the sources cited in individual endnotes, see the *Dictionary of Scottish architects* (www.scottisharchitects.org.uk), and the Royal Commission on the Ancient and Historical Monuments of Scotland (www.rcahms.gov.uk), notably CANMORE (www.canmore.rchams.gov.uk), and the published RCAHMS printed volumes.
4 Ganche, *Voyages avec Frédéric Chopin*, pp. 91–115. In 1930, Ganche and his wife had made a tour of Scottish country houses with Chopin connections. Ganche accords each of the three houses a description and a single photograph: Calder on pp. 96–101, Keir on pp. 106–9, and Johnstone on pp. 109–15.
5 See the architectural descriptions of Calder House in Jaques and McKean, *West Lothian*, pp. 98–9; McWilliam, *Lothian*, pp. 324–5; and Small, *Castles and mansions of the Lothians*, vol.1 (1883). Mid Calder moved from the old county of Midlothian to West Lothian following local government reorganization in 1974. Chopin's links with Calder House inspired the play *Chopin in Midcalder*, by Raymond Raszkowski Ross, at the Edinburgh Festival Fringe in 2003, when it was performed by 'theatre objektiv' at the Netherbow Theatre. See Ross, 'My hallucinatory sojourn in Chopin's Caledonia', p. 6. Ross writes: 'The play isn't a narrative account . . . but rather a hallucinatory evocation of Chopin's short, troubled life.' Eleanor Morris kindly drew this reference to my attention.
6 I am grateful to the present (15th) Lord Torphichen and Lady Torphichen for their hospitality at Calder House, and for their help and advice on Chopin's visit there, and his relationship with Jane Stirling and Mrs Katherine Erskine. For Calder and the Torphichens, see M'Call, *History and antiquities of the parish of Mid-Calder, passim*. 'A pedigree of the family of Sandilands of Calder, Lords Torphichen', appears on pp. 42–3. A copy of this book, inscribed on 10 August 1930 to Édouard Ganche by the 13th Lord Torphichen, and Lady Torphichen, is in BJ (Cracow), 584094.III. Correspondence between Lord Torphichen and Ganche of 1931–4 is in BnF (Paris), Dossiers Ganche (Édouard), Vma.4334 (7).
7 A letter of Jane Stirling, of 13 February 1848, summarized in Karłowicz, *Souvenirs*, p. 142, notes that Lord Torphichen currently is having his portrait painted in Scheffer's studio. Ewals, *Ary Scheffer: sa vie et son oeuvre*, p. 439, states that this was exhibited (no.62) in the Scheffer exhibition held in Paris in 1859. Here, and in Kolb, *Ary Scheffer*, p. 493, the date of the portrait is given as 1847.

170   *Scottish country seats*

8   Karłowicz, *Souvenirs*, p. 182, the first of two summaries of letters sent to Chopin from Calder House by Lord Torphichen about the composer's arrival and stay there. In the second, dated 25 August 1848, Torphichen expresses regret that he had missed seeing Chopin in Edinburgh. 'Il languit après lui, ainsi qu'après sa marveilleuse musique', as Karłowicz puts it. Torphichen hopes that Chopin will return to Calder House the next summer. See *Chopin studies* (Warsaw), vol.1 (1985), p. 61, n.3, and Harasowski's coverage of Karłowicz in *Skein of legends around Chopin*, pp. 114–17, and plates 46–8.
9   Hedley, *Chopin correspondence*, p. 326. Chopin to Grzymała, [End of July 1848].
10   Hedley, *Chopin correspondence*, p. 336. Chopin to his family in Warsaw, [10–19 August 1848]. Subsequent quotations are from this letter. Chopin underestimates Lord Torphichen's age here, when he calls him a 'seventy-year-old Scot'. Born on 21 July 1770, he would have celebrated his seventy-eighth birthday the month before Chopin's first visit to Calder House, in August 1848.
11   Chopin gained 10% commission on his sale of a Pleyel to Jane Stirling, as recorded by Eigeldinger, 'Chopin and Pleyel', p. 394. Notably, 'the sale price was increased to secure the commission without diminishing the piano maker's profits.' See also Eigeldinger's later article, 'Chopin et la manufacture Pleyel', pp. 105–6.
12   Hedley, *Chopin correspondence*, p. 337. Chopin to his family in Warsaw, [10–19 August 1848].
13   Hedley, *Chopin correspondence*, p. 329. Chopin to Camille Pleyel, 15 August 1848. De Pourtales, *Polonaise*, p. 301, translates this as: 'There is even a little Red Riding Hood in the form of a ghost. But I have not yet seen her.' This calls to mind the 'terrors and phantoms' which Chopin saw in the cloisters at Valldemossa, described by George Sand in her *Histoire de ma vie*. See Sand, *Story of my life*, p. 1091. See also the draft memoir on Chopin sent from Paris by Solange Clésinger to Princess Marcelina Czartoryska, 18 September [?circa 1850], in which she describes this event. It was sold at Sotheby's Printed and Manuscript Music Sale in London on Thursday 9 December 1999 (L09213, lot 63), when the hammer price, with buyer's premium, was £2,875.
14   NAS (Edinburgh), Ogilvy of Inverquharity Papers, GD 205/47/11/1. A transcript of the original French text is in Willis, 'Chopin in Britain' (www.etheses.dur.ac.uk/1386), vol.2, pp. 350–1. The letter to Henry Fowler Broadwood is in Surrey History Centre, Woking, Broadwood Album. To my knowledge, both these letters are unpublished.
15   Hedley, *Chopin correspondence*, p. 328. Chopin to Pleyel, 15 August 1848. See Cobbe, *Composer instruments*, pp. 58–9; and Cobbe, *Three hundred years of composers' instruments*, pp. 48–51. This piano has been identified by Jean-Jacques Eigeldinger and Alec Cobbe as the one which Chopin sold. See Macintyre, 'Chopin's true sound', *passim*. As Chopin sent the payment direct to Pleyel, it suggests that Chopin never owned the piano.
16   Hedley, *Chopin correspondence*, pp. 327–8. Chopin to Franchomme, 6–11 August [1848].
17   Earlier in his life Chopin had composed an Écossaise in B flat major (1827), now lost, and Three Écossaises by him were published posthumously as part of Op.72 (nos 3–5). See Brown, *Index of Chopin's works*, pp. 19 (note to no.17), and 10–11 (no.12); Kobylańska, *RUC*, vol.l, pp. 420–4; Kobylańska, *T-BW*, pp. 178–9; and Chomiński and Turło, *KDFC*, pp. 80–1, with the illustration of a title page for 'Três Escocesas' (Op.72, no.3), published in Brazil in 1957, as plate 69. The Chopin entry by Michełowski and Samson in *Grove music online* gives the date of composition of the Three Écossaises as circa 1829.
18   Its discovery in 1952 by Arthur Hedley is noted in Brown, *Index of Chopin's works*, p. 172 (no.166). Photocopies of the first page of the MS, and of the leather cover for it, are catalogued in Kobylańska, *RUC*, vol.1, p. 516 (no.1245), and Kobylańska, *T – BW*, p. 241 (no.3). The original MS is now lost, but (according to a note on the back of the photocopy of the first page) Hedley offered it to the Fryderyck Chopin Museum,

Warsaw, on 10 March 1960. Grażyna Michniewicz, of the Fryderyk Chopin Museum, tells me that, in the 1960s, when Hedley's collection was divided between the Collection of A.M. Ferrà at Valldemosa, Mallorca, and the Frederyk Chopin Museum (partly sold, partly given by Hedley), this waltz was not included. The MS title page is now lost, its most recent recorded location being in the collection of W. Westley Mannings, in London. See the 'Works' section in the entry on Chopin by Kornel Michałowski and Jim Samson in *Grove music online*. I am grateful to Grażyna Michniewicz and John Rink for information about this waltz, and to Zbigniew Skowron for translating Kobylańska's catalogue entry in *RUC*, vol.1, p. 516 (no.1245).

19 Opieński, *Chopin's letters*, pp. 388–9 (letter 266). Chopin to Gutmann, 16 Oct[ober], 1848. Hedley does not publish this letter, but he comments on it in an editorial note, *Chopin correspondence*, p. 347. See also below, note 67.

20 See the entry on Sir William Stirling Maxwell by Hilary Macartney in *Oxford DNB online*. William's father, Archibald Stirling (1769–1847), was 14th of Keir and 11th of Cawder. William Stirling's London address is taken from *Kelly's directory, London 1848*.

21 On pp. 443–58. For the context of Stirling Maxwell's art-historical writings, see Howarth, *Invention of Spain*, particularly p. 131.

22 For architectural descriptions of Keir see Rowan, 'Keir, Perthshire', *passim*; Gifford and Walker, *Stirling and central Scotland*, pp. 542–4; McKean, *Stirling and the Trossachs*, p. 78; and McKerracher, *Street and place names of Dunblane and district*, pp. 34–5. See also Colvin, *Dictionary*, p. 473.

23 Clearly, Fraser's *Stirlings of Keir* shows the house after Chopin's visit, not as the composer would have experienced it. The richness of the interior can be seen in Christie's sale catalogue, *The property of Archibald Stirling of Keir*, 22–4 May 1995, when its contents were sold.

24 Hedley, *Chopin correspondence*, pp. 342–5. Chopin to Grzymała, 1 October 1848. Subsequent quotations in this paragraph are from this letter.

25 The 'Mrs Norton' here is the poet Caroline Norton (née Sheridan) (1808–77), the Hon Mrs George Norton, who married Sir William Stirling Maxwell in 1877, after the death of his first wife in 1875.

26 Hedley, *Chopin correspondence*, p. 344. Chopin to Grzymała, 1 October 1848. Subsequent quotations in this paragraph are from this letter.

27 Hedley, *Chopin correspondence*, p. 345. Chopin to Mlle de Rozières, 2 October 1848.

28 See Cobbe, *Composer instruments*, pp. 51–3. Inside the piano is the inscription: 'Benedict for Miss Stirling. Pearson.' Alec Cobbe here discusses the provenance of the piano, and suggests that, having been purchased in London, it was 'presumably despatched' to Jane Stirling in Paris. 'In December 1847', he writes, 'the instrument was probably back in Britain, for Chopin is recorded as arriving for dinner in Paris to try out a further new Érard instrument of Jane Stirling's.' However, rather than this to-ing and fro-ing, is it not more likely that Jane Stirling bought two Érards, one in Paris and another in London?

29 See the chapter 'Jane Stirling's Érard', in Cobbe, *Chopin's swansong*, pp. 28–37; and 'Jane Stirling's grand piano', in Cobbe, *Three hundred years of composers' instruments*, pp. 56–9. Ganche, *Voyages avec Frédéric Chopin*, p. 107, refers to seeing this piano at Keir in 1930, and quotes the inscription on a metal plate on the piano dating it 1841; he notes that it was 'played upon by Frédéric Chopin when he stayed at Keir, in October 1848'.

30 Ganche, *Voyages avec Frédéric Chopin*, p. 109. Ganche then quotes a letter of Jane Stirling, of 23 July 1851, indicating that, in 1848, Chopin spent several weeks with her elder sister, Mrs Houston, at Johnstone Castle. This letter, sent from No. 12 rue du Château-Neuf, Saint-Germain-en-Laye, to Chopin's sister Ludwika Jędrzejewicz, appears in Ganche, *Dans le souvenir de Frédéric Chopin*, pp. 130–1. Ganche, *Voyages*

172 Scottish country seats

avec Frédéric Chopin, p. 107. Ganche's visit to Keir (pp. 106–9) took place after his pilgrimage to Dunblane Cathedral, to see Jane Stirling's supposed grave (pp. 102–5), and a brief stop near Kippenross to pay homage to her there (p. 105). Ganche, *Dans le souvenir de Frédéric Chopin*, contains a chapter, 'Jane Stirling et sa correspondance', pp. 101–49. For the relationship between the Stirling family and Keir, Kippendavie (now Ryland Lodge), and Kippenross, see McKerracher, *Street and place names of Dunblane and district*, pp. 34–8.

31 For descriptions see 'Johnston Castle' in Ramsay, *Views of Renfrewshire* (1839), and 'Johnstone Castle' in Millar, *Castles and mansions of Renfrewshire and Buteshire* (1889). For Gillespie Graham at Wishaw and Milliken, see Colvin, *Dictionary*, p. 443.

32 Ludovic Houston died in 1862, when he was succeeded by his nephew George Ludovic Houston, 7th of Johnstone, who passed away in 1931, having retired to Cyprus; his wife, and later widow, Mrs Anne Douglas Houston, was great-niece of Jane Stirling, the dedicatee of Ganche's *Voyages avec Frédéric Chopin*, and the source of many Chopin-related items in Ganche's Chopin collection in Lyons.

33 Hedley, *Chopin correspondence*, pp. 340–1. Chopin to Grzymała, [4–9 September 1848].

34 See Gavoty, *Chopin* (French edition), pp. 299–300, and Gavoty, *Chopin* (English edition), p. 233.

35 Hedley, Chopin, p. 110. For the original French text, see Sydow and Chainaye, *Chopin correspondance*, vol.3, p. 386 (letter 736), and for a Polish translation, see Sydow, *KFC*, vol.2, p. 442 (letter 640).

36 It was obtained by Ganche from Mrs Anne D. Houston. In a letter of 6 June 1910, Mrs Houston wrote from Johnstone to 'J. Maynard Saunders, Esq', who had published a letter about Jane Stirling and Chopin in the *Glasgow Herald*, and noted: 'You may be interested to know that I have in my possession a grand piano chosen for Miss Stirling by Chopin, and bearing his autograph and the date 1848. It is a Pleyel, and still in very good condition.' See BnF (Paris), Vma.4334 (7).

37 Collegium Maius (Cracow), MUJ 6887–30/VIII. The piano bears the signature 'Fr. Chopin / 15 novembre 1848'.

38 Hedley, *Chopin correspondence*, pp. 341–2. Chopin to Grzymała, [4–9 September 1848]. Jourdan, *Nocturne*, p. 246, says that the Stirling sisters were in a second coupé, but gives no source.

39 Hedley, *Chopin correspondence*, p. 340. Chopin to Grzymała, [4–9 September 1848].

40 Hedley, *Chopin correspondence*, p. 343. Chopin to Grzymała, 1 October [1848].

41 Colvin, *Dictionary*, p. 443, notes that Milliken was built in 1825, and demolished circa 1935.

42 For Wishaw see Colvin, *Dictionary*, pp. 194, 443. Additions were made by William Burn in 1858.

43 Hedley, *Chopin correspondence*, p. 345. Chopin to Mlle de Rozières, 2 October 1848.

44 Hedley, *Chopin correspondence*, p. 347. Chopin to Lady Belhaven, 16 October 1848.

45 Hedley, *Chopin correspondence*, p. 349. Chopin to Grzymała, 30 October [1848].

46 Hedley, *Chopin correspondence*, p. 345. Chopin to Mlle de Rozières, 2 October 1848.

47 See Ganche, *Voyages avec Frédéric Chopin*, p. 105, and Ganche, *Dans le souvenir de Frédéric Chopin*, pp. 120–1. At Kippenross, the classical character of the original house of circa 1770, enlarged by the architect William Stirling in 1809, remains, although it has been altered by a variety of architects, including Robert Rowand Anderson. See Colvin, *Dictionary*, pp. 813, 987; Gifford and Walker, *Stirling and central Scotland*, pp. 564–5; McKean, *Stirling and the Trossachs*, p. 79; and McKerracher, *Street and place names of Dunblane and district*, pp. 37–8.

48 Kippendavie, reconstructed from 1816 by William Stirling, is now called Ryland Lodge, divided into apartments, and hidden in suburban Dunblane. See McKerracher, *Street and place names of Dunblane and district*, pp. 36–7.

49 Jane Stirling's brother, Charles Stirling, 1st of Gargunnock, had died in 1839, and was succeeded by his son, John. For the architecture of Gargunnock, see Gifford and Walker, *Stirling and central Scotland*, pp. 515–16, and McKean, *Stirling and the Trossachs*, p. 127. Gargunnock House is now let, on behalf of trustees, by the Landmark Trust. There is a grand piano at Gargunnock which rumour has it may have been played by Chopin. It is by John Broadwood and Sons, London, and described inside as 'Short/Drawing Room/Grand/No. 725'. The number 'WT 7521' occurs on the frame inside the piano. The lid of the keyboard bears the words: 'Manufactured for / PATERSON & SONS, / EDINBURGH & GLASGOW'. This suggests that the piano was manufactured in the 1850s – too late for Chopin. Tellefsen wrote to his parents in Norway from Gargunnock, on 15 July 1849. See Tellefsen, *Thomas Tellefsens familiebreve*, pp. 114–15.

50 Glenbervie House (formerly called Woodside) was the home of Jane Stirling's brother, Sylvester Douglas Stirling, of Glenbervie (1803–46). He was succeeded by his son, Charles Douglas Stirling, of Glenbervie (1840–56). After her husband's death (by drowning) in 1846, his widow Anne Craigie Stirling demolished the existing Glenbervie House, and rebuilt it. Tellefsen wrote to his parents in Norway from Glenbervie in August 1848. See Tellefsen, *Thomas Tellefsen familiebreve*, pp. 107–8.

51 For Eglinton Castle, see Colvin, *Dictionary*, pp. 59, 110, 472, 786. In Tellefsen, *Thomas Tellefsen familiebreve*, pp. 122–3, there is a letter of 17 August headed 'Eagleton Slot', which may refer to Eglinton. A letter from Tellefsen to his parents from Hamilton Palace, 27 July 1851, appears here on pp. 128–9, and another from Stirling, 24 September 1857, on p. 151.

52 The architectural splendour of Hamilton can be seen in Gow, *Scotland's lost houses*, pp. 26–41, and Gow, *Scottish houses and gardens*, pp. 128–47. See also Tait, 'Hamilton Palace', *passim*, and Colvin, *Dictionary*, pp. 194, 435, 473, 952. After the demolition of Hamilton Palace in 1919, archives and some contents of the palace were transferred to the Hamilton family seat of Lennoxlove. Many of the art treasures from Hamilton had been dispersed in 1882.

53 Waagen, *Galleries and cabinets of art in Great Britain*, quoted by Gow, *Scotland's lost houses*, p. 32, and Gow, *Scottish houses and gardens*, p. 141.

54 See 'Lennoxlove. Treasures of Lennoxlove', exhibit 13. The piano bears the wording: 'Médaille d'or Exposition de 1827 / Ignace Pleyel & Cie. paris / Rue Cadet No. 9'.

55 Hedley, *Chopin correspondence*, p. 333. Chopin to his family in Warsaw, [10–19 August 1848].

56 See 'Lennoxlove. Treasures of Lennoxlove', exhibit 111. Boccherini spent the latter part of his life in Spain. During a visit to Portugal in 1787, he met William Beckford, whose daughter Susan, later Duchess of Hamilton, had been born in France the previous year.

57 Hedley, *Chopin correspondence*, pp. 347–8. Chopin to Grzymała, 21 October [1848].

58 Chopin's reference to the Prince of Lucca is puzzling. Charles II, Duke of Parma, was Duke of Lucca from 1824, until he succeeded as Duke of Parma in 1847. In this year the Duchy of Lucca was annexed to the Grand Duchy of Tuscany. But who was 'Prince of Lucca' in 1848?

59 Jane Stirling's guitar is in the Collegium Maius (Cracow), MUJ 6888–31/VIII. It was made in Naples by Gennaro Fabricatore in 1823, and was acquired by Ganche from Mrs Ann D. Houston; the wooden guitar case still has labels affixed to it for its transport by the London & North Eastern Railway from Johnstone Castle to Lyons. As an instrument, of course, the guitar has emotional appeal for the heroine. A Polish example of this from the pen of Maria Wirtemberska, a contemporary of Chopin and Jane Stirling, is found in Wirtemberska, *Malvina, or the heart's intuition*, page 35: 'Having uttered this short prayer Malvina felt stronger. She opened her window and wishing to divert herself picked up her guitar and went out onto the terrace that encircled the

house.' This novel was first published, in Polish, in 1816. Wirtemberska was daughter of Prince Adam Kazimierz Czartoryski and his wife Princess Isabela Czartoryska. Ursula Phillips kindly alerted me to her English translation of this book.
60 Hedley, *Chopin correspondence*, p. 348 Chopin to Grzymała, 21 October [1848].
61 Hedley, *Chopin correspondence*, p. 348. Chopin to Grzymala, 30 October [1848]. The 'Baden princess' was Princess Marie of Baden (1817–88), who had married the Marquess of Douglas (later 11th Duke of Hamilton) in 1843. She was a cousin of Napoleon.
62 Hedley, *Chopin correspondence*, p. 337. Chopin to his family in Warsaw, [10–19 August 1848]. *The Edinburgh and Leith street and trade directory, 1848–1849*, p. 93, gives Lord Murray's Edinburgh address as No. 11 Great Stuart Street.
63 Hedley, *Chopin correspondence*, p. 341. Chopin to Grzymala, [4–9 September 1848].
64 The following paragraph is largely derived from the entry on Sir John Archibald Murray by Gordon F. Millar in *Oxford DNB online*.
65 The Murrays' London address is given in *Kelly's directory, London 1848* as No. 36 St James's Street, but no evidence has been found that Chopin played there.
66 For architectural descriptions of Strachur House see RCAHMS, *Mid Argyll and Cowal* (1992), pp. 358–65; Walker, *Argyll and Bute*, pp. 466–70; and Walker, *Argyll and the islands*, pp. 13–14. The RCAHMS volume contains numerous photographs of the interior of Strachur.
67 Opieński, *Chopin's letters*, pp. 388–9 (letter 266). Chopin to Gutmann, 16 Oct[ober] 1848. Hedley does not publish this letter, but he comments on it in an editorial note, *Chopin correspondence*, p. 347. See also above, note 19.

Plate 22 Julie Schwabe (1819–96). Portrait by Ary Scheffer, before 1858. Copyright Roehampton University Library and Special Collections

Plate 23 Johanna Maria (Jenny) Lind (1820–87), and Marietta Alboni, Countess Pepoli (née Maria Anna Marzia) (1824–94). Hand-coloured, half-plate daguerrotype, 1848, by William Edward Kilburn. Copyright National Portrait Gallery, London

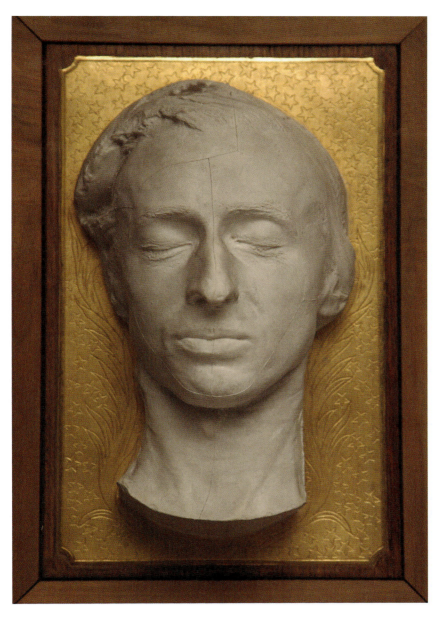

Plate 24 Chopin. Plaster death mask, based on original by Auguste Clésinger, Paris, 1849. Gift of Miss Susan Fisher Scott to the Royal Manchester College of Music, 1910. Royal Northern College of Music, Manchester. Photograph: Michael Pollard, 2008

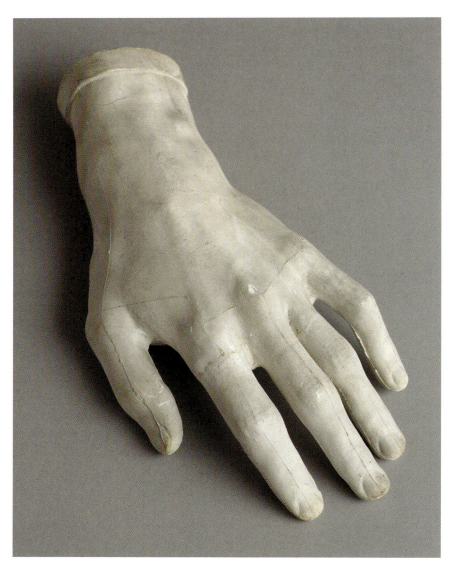

Plate 25 Chopin. Plaster left hand, based on original by Auguste Clésinger, Paris, 1849. Gift of Miss Susan Fisher Scott to the Royal Manchester College of Music, 1910. Royal Northern College of Music, Manchester. Photograph: Michael Pollard, 2008

Plate 26 Chopin. Detail of bronze statue by Ludwika Nitschowa. Gift of the Frederick Chopin Society of Poland, to the Royal Northern College of Music, Manchester, 1973. Royal Northern College of Music, Manchester. Photograph: Michael Pollard, 2010

Plate 27 Chopin. Bronze statue by Ludwika Nitschowa. Gift of the Frederick Chopin Society of Poland, to the Royal Northern College of Music, Manchester, 1973. Royal Northern College of Music, Manchester. Photograph: Michael Pollard, 2010

Plate 28 Chopin. Bronze statue by Robert Sobociński, Deansgate, Manchester, unveiled 2011. Photograph: Michael Pollard, 2014

Plate 29 Chopin. Bronze head by Józef Markiewicz, presented by the Frederick Chopin Society of Warsaw, to the citizens of Edinburgh, Friday 28 February 1975. Usher Hall, Edinburgh. Photograph: Paul Zanre, 2014

Plate 30 Chopin. Setting of bronze head by Józef Markiewicz, Usher Hall, Edinburgh. Photograph: Paul Zanre, 2014

Plate 31 Exterior of No. 4 St James's Place, London, showing plaque commemorating Chopin's stay there before his Guildhall concert on 16 November 1848. Photograph: Peter Willis, 2008

Plate 32 Exterior of No. 4 St James's Place, London. Photograph: Peter Willis, 2008

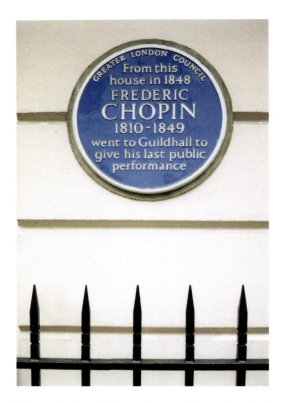

Plate 33 Detail of plaque at No. 4 St James's Place. Photograph: Peter Willis, 2008

Plate 34 Pleyel Grand Pianoforte No. 13,716 (Paris, 1848), inscribed 'Frederic Chopin 15 Novembre 1848', of rosewood inlaid with veins of copper. Collegium Maius (Cracow), MUJ 6887: 1945. Akg-images/De Agostini Picture Library/A. Dagli Orti

Plate 35 Sir James Clark, 1st Bt (1788–1870), Physician in Ordinary to Queen Victoria, by Hope James Stewart, 1849. Scottish National Portrait Gallery, Edinburgh

Plate 36 Chopin's grave, and monument by Auguste Clésinger, 1849 (detail). Cemetery of Père Lachaise, Paris. Akg-images/De Agostini Picture Library/G. Dagli Orti Permissions for the reproduction of illustrations in Chopin in Britain have been obtained and are listed on p. xxiv.

7 Manchester
Concert in Gentlemen's Concert Hall, Monday 28 August 1848

Although tickets were sold for Chopin's recitals at Mrs Sartoris' and the Earl of Falmouth's, their settings were domestic rather than public, and it was only after reaching Scotland that he performed in concert halls in Britain. Apart from playing privately for his Scottish hosts, Chopin gave three public performances during this time: the first (which took him briefly back to England) in Manchester, the second at the Merchants' Hall in Glasgow, and the third at the Hopetoun Rooms in Edinburgh.[1]

The identity of the pieces played by Chopin in these concerts has long been a matter of debate. Invitations, advertisements, and programmes give no more than an impression of intent, considering the composer's well-known reluctance to perform in public, and his difficulties in deciding what to play. Often as not, the final decision was left until the last minute.

Thus in Manchester, Chopin's changes necessitated the printing of a supplementary programme by the Directors of the Gentlemen's Concert Society, whereas in Glasgow, John Muir Wood, the organizer, similarly suffered in his efforts to make Chopin commit himself. One of Muir Wood's sons, Herbert Kemlo Wood, writing in *The voice of Poland* in 1943, explains that Chopin at Glasgow 'could not make up his mind about the programme' and 'preferred to play as the spirit moved him and often changed his mind'.[2] It was the same problem in both Edinburgh and Glasgow, where his habit was to put down 'Études, Nocturnes, Mazurkas', and 'he would play of these what he felt inclined to do.' On the day before he was to perform in Edinburgh, he told Grzymała that he still had not 'seen the hall or settled the programme'.[3] At both the Glasgow and Edinburgh concerts, Herbert Kemlo Wood adds, the audiences 'were almost entirely made up of Chopin's aristocratic friends, principally ladies of whom he always had a devoted following'.[4]

In Manchester, however, Chopin was supported by a different section of the public. On 19 August 1848, barely two weeks after he arrived in Scotland, Chopin was writing from Calder House and telling his family of his forthcoming concert in Manchester, 'at which Italians from London will sing' and for which he was to be paid £60, 'which is not to be turned down'. He was to travel the 200 miles from Edinburgh by train, which, he noted, was a journey of eight hours.[5] In all likelihood this would have taken him on the Caledonian Railway to Carlisle, where he would have changed to the London & North Western Railway, arriving

176 *Manchester: Gentlemen's Concert Hall*

in Manchester either at Salford Station, New Bailey Street, or at London Road Station, now known as Piccadilly.

Manchester, bustling industrial city and centre of commerce, had a lively musical life (see Figure 7.1). In Manchester, Chopin explained, 'some kind friends are awaiting me, wealthy manufacturers who have Neukomm staying with them.' Also in the city was Mrs Mary Rich, whom Chopin knew in Paris as one of 'three Scotch ladies', and 'a great friend of both myself and the Stirlings and Erskines'.[6] The 'kind friends' in Manchester were Salis Schwabe and his wife Julie Schwabe, who had recently moved from Rusholme House, on the southern outskirts of the city, to Crumpsall House, to the north. Crumpsall was a classical mansion with outbuildings, set in open landscape with a prominent lake (see Figure 7.2); it has since been demolished to make way for a housing estate. In addition, the Schwabes owned Glyn Garth, Llandegfan, Isle of Anglesey, a mid-nineteenth-century house in Elizabethan style overlooking the Menai Strait (see Figure 7.3).[7]

Jenny Lind was also a friend of the Schwabes, and the previous year had made her first appearances in Manchester, on 28 August 1847 as Amina in *La sonnambula*, and on 2 September as Maria in Donizetti's *La figlia del reggimento*. Between these performances, on 31 August, reports William Axon, 'she was serenaded by the Leidertafel at Rusholme House, the residence of Mrs Salis Schwabe, whose guest she was.' Engagingly, during her stay Lind 'was often seen riding on horseback in the direction of Didsbury'.[8] She visited Manchester once more in 1848, appearing as Lucia in *Lucia di Lammermoor* on 9 September, and again

Figure 7.1 View of Manchester. Engraving by C. Reiss, Hildburghausen [1842]. Private collection

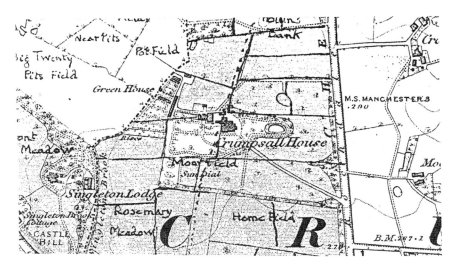

Figure 7.2 Crumpsall House, Lancashire. Detail from Ordnance Survey, 1847–8. Manchester City Libraries

Figure 7.3 Glyn Garth Anglesey. View from the Menai Straits, from Thomas Catherall, *Views in north Wales* (Chester and Bangor, circa 1850). Courtesy Thomas Wright

as Amina two days later. In this, and in her preceding visit in 1847, she was supported by the Italian bass Luigi Lablache.[9]

Salis Schwabe's likeness can be seen in a bust by William Bally (see Figure 7.4), and his wife's in a portrait by Ary Scheffer (see Plate 22).[10] Salis Schwabe and his brother Adolf ran a calico factory at Rhodes, Middleton, outside Manchester. Chopin knew the Schwabes from cultural life in Paris, where they consorted with Auguste and Sophie Léo, Fanny Erskine, Jane Stirling and Mrs Katherine Erskine, Mrs Mary Rich, and musicians such as Charles Hallé and Thomas Tellefsen.[11]

Chopin has given us a thumbnail sketch of the Schwabes. Writing to Wojciech Grzymała, from Johnstone, he explained that when in Manchester he

> lived in the suburbs as there is too much smoke in town: all the rich people have their houses outside the town. I was staying with my good friend Schwabe – you may have seen him at [Auguste] Léo's. He is a leading manufacturer and owns the tallest chimney in Manchester – it cost him £5,000. He is a friend of Cobden's and a great free-trader himself. He is a Jew – or rather a Protestant convert like Léo. His wife is particularly kind. They insisted on my staying longer, as Jenny Lind is arriving there this week and will also be staying with them.

Figure 7.4 Salis Schwabe (1800–53). Bust by William Bally, circa 1853. Old Grammar School, Middleton, Manchester. Courtesy Middleton Civic Association. Photograph: Alan Seabright, 2003

Chopin added that the Schwabes and Jenny Lind are 'great friends'. 'While I was there', he continued, 'we also had that dear Mrs Rich, whom you saw at my place with Miss Stirling.' He met, too, Auguste Léo, brother of the Mancunian Hermann Léo, who was in Manchester 'on business'.[12]

Sigismond Neukomm, the Austrian composer, pianist and scholar, lived with the Schwabes for several months during the late summer and autumn of 1848, and he and Chopin seem to have been there together.[13] Among others whom Chopin encountered in Manchester, possibly at the Schwabes', was Fanny Erskine, to whom he gave a manuscript of the song 'Wiosna', inscribed *'souvenir de Crumpsal House/à Mademoiselle Fanny Erskine/F Chopin / 1, Sept. 1848'* (see Figure 7.5).[14] The date here indicates that Chopin did not leave Manchester until early September; several days later, on 4–9 September, he was writing to Gryzmała from Johnstone Castle.[15]

Chopin's description of the Schwabes does not do justice to the remarkable Julie Schwabe who, following her husband's death in 1853, carried on her cultural and philanthropic activities in Manchester before moving to Naples, where she launched a one-woman campaign to raise funds to establish schools. Widowed at the age of thirty-four, Julie was left with seven children and a huge fortune. She was regarded as a 'prophetess of liberal education', with a strong sense of social justice, and was involved in the Froebel system of teaching children.[16] Friends and visitors, in Manchester and at Glyn Garth, included not only the radicals John Bright and Richard Cobden, but also Geraldine Jewsbury, Mrs Gaskell, and the

Figure 7.5 Chopin. Autograph of song 'Wiosna', with Polish words by Witwicki, inscribed 'souvenir de Crumpsal House à Mademoiselle Fanny Erskine', and dated 1 September 1848. Fitzwilliam Museum, Cambridge [from Harasowski, *The skein of legends around Chopin* (1967), plate 89]

prison reformer Thomas Wright.[17] As Edward Morris points out, 'Geraldine Jewsbury was also a guest of the Schwabes, visiting them frequently in 1848–1849 to hear her friend Sigismond Neuikomm play the organ.'[18] Additionally, Julie and Salis Schwabe 'provided the link between the Manchester cotton manufacturers as patrons of Scheffer and Scheffer's English political and literary admirers'.[19] As such, they were part of a wider community of supporters of French art.[20]

Chopin's Manchester recital took place in the Concert Hall, the venue used by the Gentlemen's Concert Society, which was founded in Manchester in 1777.[21] As Benjamin Love explained, in *The hand-book of Manchester* (1842):

> There are six hundred subscribers at five guineas, who have each two tickets, one for his own admission, and the other transferable to ladies, or to gentlemen residing six miles distant. So great is the number of applications for admission as members, that as many as three hundred names are usually on the books; and persons have frequently to wait three years and upwards before their chance by rotation arrives, the members being limited in number.
>
> To gratify the critical taste of Manchester, which is admitted to be of a high order, the first talent is always engaged. The orchestra consists of upwards of sixty performers. Admittance to the concerts is not purchaseable, and no person can enter except by a subscriber's ticket.

Love adds that there are 'no fixed evenings of performance', concerts being regulated by the availability of 'English or Foreign professional talent'.[22]

In 1831 the society opened the Concert Hall in Lower Mosley Street, in the centre of Manchester, on part of the site now occupied by the Midland Hotel, and diagonally opposite St Peter's Church, built by James Wyatt in 1788–94, but demolished in 1907.[23] The Concert Hall (later known as the Gentlemen's Concert Hall) was designed by Richard Lane, the leading Manchester architect practising in the Greek Revival style during the 1820s and 1830s, whose distinguished public buildings in the city included the Friends' Meeting House (1828–31) and Manchester Corn Exchange (1836).[24]

The Concert Hall (demolished in 1897–8) consisted of a rectangular block with an entrance portico of six unfluted Corinthian columns, leading into a square entrance hall with stairs giving access to the auditorium on the first floor; the outer bays of the entrance facade, framed by engaged columns, flanked a recessed central section (see Figs 7.6 and 7.7). With its high modelling, and allusions to Stuart and Revett's *The antiquities of Athens* (1762), notes Clare Hartwell, it looks as if Lane 'selected several appropriate motifs and brought them together in a striking and original composition'.[25] The interior of the Concert Hall, Love remarked in 1842, was 'fitted up with a splendour which is in accordance with the musical spirit for which Manchester is celebrated'. He continued: 'This concert room, for elegance of design and superb appearance, may vie with any in Europe, and presents, on full dress evenings, a brilliant scene of the beauty and fashion of Manchester and its environs; whilst the performances, generally, for correctness of execution, are acknowledged to be unsurpassed by any out of

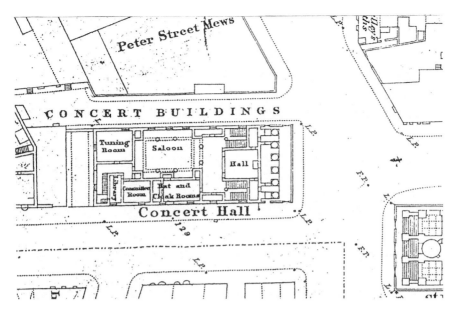

Figure 7.6 Gentlemen's Concert Hall, between Peter Street and Mosley Street, Manchester, with St Peter's Church to the right. Ground-floor plan, from Ordnance Survey, 1849–51. Manchester City Libraries

Figure 7.7 Gentlemen's Concert Hall, Peter Street, Manchester, with portico of St Peter's Church on left. Engraving by John Fothergill, 1832. Manchester City Libraries

the metropolis.'[26] Charles Hallé concurred: 'Few towns are in possession of such a beautiful hall, one in which music can be thoroughly and socially enjoyed' (see Figure 7.8).[27] One observer put it more colourfully, observing that it was 'decorated in white and gold and panelled in rich mahogany, with a 60 ft high elliptical dome soaring above an auditorium where audiences attended concerts in full evening dress'.[28]

Apart from Chopin, other celebrated pianists who had performed in Manchester included John Field, who gave two concerts in the city in July 1832, for which he received 50 guineas, 'certainly the largest fee he received during the whole of his visit to England'.[29] Franz Liszt played in the Theatre Royal as a boy prodigy in 1824 and 1825, visiting the city with his father. He returned in 1840, and gave two concerts, the second on a Broadwood in the Athenaeum; his own Érard, which travelled with him, was already on its way to Ireland.[30]

News of Chopin's forthcoming performance in Manchester appeared in an advertisement in the *Manchester Guardian* on 9 August 1848, in which the Directors of the Concert Hall

> beg to announce to the Subscribers, that a DRESS CONCERT has been fixed for Monday the 28th of August next, for which the following Performers have

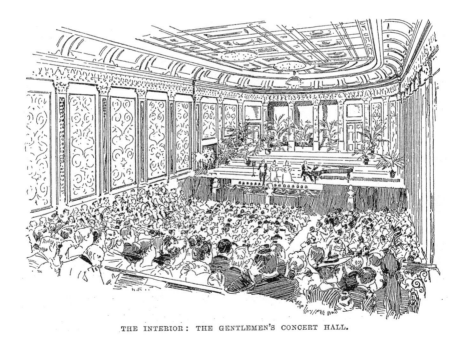

THE INTERIOR: THE GENTLEMEN'S CONCERT HALL.

Figure 7.8 Gentlemen's Concert Hall, Peter Street, Manchester. Interior from William Arthur Shaw, *Manchester old and new* . . . (London: Cassell [1896]), vol.3, p. 36. Manchester City Libraries

been engaged: – Signora ALBONI, Signora CORBARI, Signor SALVI, and Mons. CHOPIN.[31]

The concert was held at 7 p.m. and, as can be seen, the three singers were all Italian – the contralto Marietta Alboni, Amelia Corbari, 'seconda donna', and the tenor Lorenzo Salvi. The leader of the orchestra was the Edinburgh-born violinist Charles Alexander Seymour, who was then active in Manchester musical circles.[32] Alboni, regarded as the most celebrated of the artists at the Manchester concert (see Plate 23), had made her debut at Bologna in 1842, appeared at La Scala the same year, and in Vienna in 1843, and spent the winter of 1844–5 in St Petersburg with Antonio Tamburini and Pauline Viardot.[33] During the next two years she toured Germany and eastern Europe, making a triumphant London debut on 6 April 1847 as Arsace in Rossini's *Semiramide* to open the first season of the Royal Italian Opera in Covent Garden, where Corbari and Salvi also sang that year. Later in 1847, Alboni made her Parisian debut at the Théâtre-Italien, again singing Arsace, as well as the title role in *La Cenerentola*. In 1848 she returned to Covent Garden to sing Urbain in *Les Huguenots*.[34] Alboni's performance in Manchester was part of a concert tour of the Italian singers arranged by the impresario and composer Thomas Willert Beale;[35] the three performed items from operas by Verdi, Puccini, Rossini, Bellini, and Donizetti, and the orchestra played the overtures to Weber's *Der Freishütz*, Beethoven's *Prometheus*, and Rossini's *Il barbiere di Siviglia*.

The instrument played by Chopin in Manchester was the Broadwood Patent Repetition Grand Pianoforte No. 17047 (London 1847), which has a rosewood case, veneered on laminated oak, and is now owned by the Royal Academy of Music, on permanent loan to the Cobbe Collection, Hatchlands, Surrey (see Plate 10).[36] Chopin had already used this piano for his London recitals at Mrs Sartoris' and the Earl of Falmouth's, and was to play it again at Guildhall on 16 November. It also may have been employed by Chopin at Stafford House, and other private engagements in London.

The concert in Manchester was divided into two parts, and Chopin performed once in the first part, and once in the second (see Figure 7.9). On the day of the concert, a 'notice' issued by the Directors of the Gentlemen's Society indicated that Chopin's advertised programme had been superseded (see Figure 7.10), although all the pieces were still his own compositions:[37]

Part First: Nocturne et Berceuse
Part Second: Mazourka, Ballade, et Valse

was changed to

First Part: Andante and Scherzo
Second Part: Nocturne, Études, et Berceuse

CONCERT HALL, MANCHESTER.

MONDAY EVENING, AUGUST TWENTY-EIGHTH, 1848.

DRESS CONCERT.

MISCELLANEOUS.

Part First.

OVERTURE............................." Ruler of Spirits "..*Weber*.
TERZETTINO......Signora Alboni, Signora Corbari, and Signor Salvi......" Io t'amava "......(Nabuco)......*Verdi*
RECIT. è CAVATINA......Signora Corbari......" Come provar "......(La Cantatrice Villane)......*Pacini*.
ROMANZA.........Signor Salvi........." Ciel pietoso "........(Uberto).........*Verdi*.
NOCTURNE et BERCEUSE—PIANO-FORTE.................Mons. Chopin.................*Chopin*.
CAVATINA è FINALE............Signora Alboni............" Non più mesta "..........(Cenerentola)..........*Rossini*
DUETTO......Signora Corbari and Signor Salvi......" Vieni in Roma "......(Norma)......*Bellini*.

An Interval of **Twenty** Minutes.

It is particularly requested that Parties in promenading round the Hall will keep to the right.

Part Second.

OVERTURE ...." Prometheus "..............................*Beethoven*.
DUETTO...............Signora Alboni and Signora Corbari............." La Regatta Veneziano "..............*Rossini*
ROMANZA..........Signor Salvi.........." Una furtiva lagrima ".........(L'Elisir d'Amore).. ......*Donizetti*.
MAZOURKA, BALLADE, et VALSE—PIANO-FORTE.........Mons. Chopin.........*Chopin*.
DUETTO..........Signora Alboni and Signor Salvi........." Un soave non so che ".......(Cenerentola).........*Rossini*
ARIA............Signora Corbari........." Oh, dischiuso ".........(Nino).........*Verdi*.
TYROLIENNE..............Signora Alboni............." In questo semplice "..............(Betly)............*Donizetti*
TRIO...Signora Alboni, Signora Corbari, and Signor Salvi..." Cruda sorte "...(Ricciardo è Zoraide)...*Rossini*.
OVERTURE................." Il Barbiere di Siviglia "..................*Rossini*.

Leader of the Orchestra..................................Mr. Seymour.

TO COMMENCE AT SEVEN O'CLOCK PRECISELY.

☞ *The Committee earnestly request the co-operation of the Subscribers in maintaining silence during the Performances*

Subscribers are informed that the 15th Rule will be strictly enforced:—" That no gentleman residing in or within six miles of Manchester is considered as a stranger, or admissible to either Public or Private Concerts without being previously elected a Subscriber ; and that gentlemen who have permanent places of business in Manchester are considered as residents."

No Gentleman will be admitted except in Evening Dress, with either White or Black Cravat.

Carriages, in setting down and taking up Company, are to have their horses' heads towards Oxford-street.

Cave and Sever, Printers, 18, St. Ann's-street, Manchester.

Figure 7.9 Programme for Dress Concert, Gentlemen's Concert Hall, Peter Street, Manchester, Monday 28 August 1848, from Brookshaw, *Concerning Chopin in Manchester* (1951), between pp. 22 and 23. Manchester City Libraries

As part of Willert Beale's 'troupe', the Irish musician George Osborne regularly provided piano support for the singers, and he did so on this occasion, the *Manchester Guardian* reporting on 30 August that 'several of the vocal pieces were accompanied by Mr. Osborne, an able composer and pianist.'[38]

NOTICE.

The Directors beg to inform the Subscribers that Mons. CHOPIN will substitute the following pieces for those inserted in the Programme, viz :—

In the First Part,

ANDANTE and SCHERZO ....*Chopin.*

In the Second Part,

NOCTURNE, ETUDES, et BERCEUSE ....*Chopin.*

CONCERT HALL,
August 28*th,* 1848.

Figure 7.10 Notice of substitutions by Chopin in the programme of the Manchester concert, from Brookshaw, *Concerning Chopin in Manchester* (1951), between pp. 22 and 23. Manchester City Libraries

What of the reception of this event? The *Manchester Guardian*, again on 30 August, notes that the concert

> was the most brilliant and interesting which the directors have given during the season; and there was a larger audience than we remember to have seen here since the celebrated Grisi and Alboni concert in September last. Of course, the lustrous-eyed and liquid-voiced Alboni was the chief attraction of the concert.

To some members of the audience, however, Chopin was of as much, if not more, interest as Marietta Alboni, for 'he was preceded by a high musical reputation.' His physical appearance, the *Manchester Guardian* continued, was striking:

> He is very spare in frame, and there is an almost painful air of feebleness in his appearance and gait. This vanishes when he seats himself at the instrument, in which he seems for the time perfectly absorbed. Chopin's music and his style of performance partake of the same leading characteristics – refinement rather than vigour – subtle elaboration rather than simple comprehensiveness in composition – an elegant, rapid touch, rather than a firm, nervous grasp of the instrument.

However, the salon rather than the concert hall is his appropriate milieu:

> Both his compositions and his playing appear to be the perfection of chamber music – fit to be associated with the most refined instrumental quartets and quartet-playing – but wanting breadth and obviousness of design and executive power to be effective in a large concert hall.

Nonetheless, the critic continues, Chopin 'was warmly applauded by many of the most accomplished amateurs in the town, and he received an encore in his last piece, a compliment thus accorded to each of the four London artists who appeared at this concert'.[39]

Other publications were equally enthusiastic, though with reservations.[40] The *Manchester Courier and Lancashire General Advertiser* on 30 August praised Chopin's 'chasteness and purity of style' and his 'delicate sensibility of expression', and observed that the concert hall 'was filled to overflowing by a most brilliant audience'.[41] The *Musical World* (maybe its editor, J.W. Davison) was not so completely won over. Chopin it averred, in an article on 9 September,

> certainly played with great finish – too much so, perhaps, and might have deserved the name of *finesse* rather – and his delicacy and expression are unmistakeable; but I missed the astonishing power of Leopold de Meyer, the vigour of Thalberg, the dash of Herz, or the grace of Sterndale Bennett.

Even so, the review concluded, 'Chopin is assuredly a great pianist, and no one can hear him without receiving some amount of delectation.'[42]

The critic in the *Manchester Examiner* was able to obtain a ticket for the concert only 'with the greatest difficulty . . . so great was the desire to hear Alboni'. His impressions of Chopin were mixed: he 'does not quite come up to our idea of a first-rate pianist; it is true he plays very difficult music (provoking one almost to say with Dr. Johnson, "would that it were impossible!") with beautiful delicacy and precision of finger but there is no melody or meaning in it'. Chopin's practice of playing only his own work did not always endear him to his audiences, and the *Manchester Examiner*'s writer was not alone in finding Chopin's compositions unappealing. Rather than play one of Beethoven's sonatas, he observed, it is a pity that performers of his ability think it incumbent on them to astonish rather than please their audiences with *concertos* written by themselves, apparently for the express purpose of cramming into them elaborate passages, chromatiques and next-to-impossible cadenzas, all of which have no beauty in themselves, but should only be sparingly used to relieve what would be otherwise, perhaps, too monotonous a concord of sweet sounds.[43]

One wonders what this critic would have thought of Liszt!

George Osborne, who accompanied the singers at Chopin's Manchester concert, had lived in Paris from 1831 to 1843 and been a pupil of Fétis, Pixis, and Kalkbrenner, as well as a teacher of Hallé (see Figure 7.11).[44] A friend of Berlioz, as well as Chopin, Osborne had drawn fashionable audiences to his Parisian concerts, had accompanied Chopin in a performance of his F minor piano concerto in 1832, and in the same year had been one of six pianists (including Chopin) who performed together in the Salons Pleyel.[45] In 1843 he returned to England, where he played, taught, and composed chamber and violin music, overtures, and two operas. He made frequent trips back to Paris, where his patrons were drawn from the aristocracy and intellectual society, including in particular wealthy Irishmen and Englishmen living in France.[46]

In 1880 Osborne presented a lecture to the Musical Association in London, entitled 'Reminiscences of Fredrick [*sic*] Chopin', which provides us with a fascinating glimpse of Chopin's life in Paris in the 1830s and 1840s; the previous year, Osborne had given the Association a paper on Berlioz. Now he offered his views on Chopin as musician and as personal friend. He explains that, on tour with Alboni in 1848, he

> met Chopin at Manchester, where he was announced to play at a grand concert without orchestra. He begged I should not be present. 'You, my dear Osborne', said he, 'who have heard me so often in Paris, remain with those impressions. My playing will be lost in such a large room, and my compositions will be ineffective. Your presence at the concert will be painful both to you and me.

Despite Chopin's entreaty, Osborne – apart from accompanying Alboni, Corbari and Salvi, at the piano – made a point of listening to Chopin play:

> I was present, unknown to him, in a remote corner of the room, where I helped to cheer and applaud him. I heard him then for the last time, when his prediction was fulfilled in part, for his playing was too delicate to create enthusiasm, and I felt truly sorry for him.

Having said this, Osborne adds, Chopin's 'performance at that concert, however, has not effaced those pleasurable and vivid emotions which I hope ever to retain of his playing and of himself'.[47]

Figure 7.11 George Alexander Osborne (1806–93). Undated lithograph by Charles Motte, from drawing by Achille Devéria. Royal College of Music, London

On 4 August 1848 Hermann Léo – brother of Auguste Léo, whose salon Chopin frequented in Paris – wrote to Charles Hallé, inviting him to come to Manchester,[48] and it is probable, though not certain, that Hallé was present at Chopin's concert later that month. Hallé, too, was a supporter of Broadwoods. In his *Autobiography*, Hallé writes: 'I had the pleasure . . . to welcome [Chopin] to Manchester, where he played at one of the concerts of the society called the Gentlemen's Concerts [*sic*] in the month of August. It was then painfully evident that his end was drawing near; a year later he was no more.' What did Hallé mean when he said that he offered a 'welcome' to Chopin? Did they meet when Chopin was staying with the Schwabes? If Hallé attended Chopin's Manchester recital, he would surely have specifically said so.[49]

One puzzle remains about Chopin's visit to Manchester: did he perform twice? If he did so, the most likely location for a private recital was Crumpsall House. Jenny Lind had sung there, and we know that Chopin frequently played for his hosts in Scottish country seats. At Crumpsall, says Susanna Brookshaw, author of *Concerning Chopin in Manchester*, a pioneering study of Chopin's visit, Chopin

> was in congenial surroundings amongst people he liked, and what was often done from a sense of duty or obligation, would, one feels sure, be done as a pleasure in this instance, if only to recall happier days in Paris, when he and his friends met for music at Léo's house. There must have been a piano provided for his use in his own room or elsewhere, in order that he might prepare for the concert.

To Brookshaw, 'the belief that he played at Crumpsall House grows to absolute certainty', and she urges to 'let the mind's eye dwell for a moment upon a picture of Chopin playing after dinner in the drawing-room.' Perhaps it was on such an occasion at Crumpsall that a curious happening occurred.[50]

In 1974, in his book *Frédéric Chopin*, Bernard Gavoty noted that on 29 August, the day after his performance in the Gentlemen's Concert Hall, Chopin performed his Sonata in B flat minor (Op.35) in a salon in Manchester. Having played the allegro and scherzo, Chopin 'left the room, coming back to the audience a few minutes later to play the march and finale, without pause. The next day, the critic of the *Manchester Guardian*, who had been invited as a friend, wrote in astonishment at this brief interruption.'[51] Was he ill? Chopin was asked on the spot. The answer, Gavoty claimed, lay in a letter from Chopin to Solange Clésinger of 9 September 1848. In this letter, which Gavoty owned, Chopin wrote:

> A strange thing happened to me while I was playing my Sonata in B flat Minor for some British friends. I had played the allegro and the scherzo successfully, and I was going to attack the march when, suddenly, I saw the cursed creatures that one lugubrious night appeared to me at the monastery rising from the case of the piano. I had to go out for a moment to collect myself, after which I resumed playing without saying a word to anyone.

Gavoty commented: 'Chopin did not talk about his music; after he created it, he lived it.'[52] Is it significant that the third of the four movements of this sonata is known as the Funeral March?[53]

After Chopin's return to Scotland, in late August or early September, those who provide us with further links to Manchester include Salis and Julie Schwabe, and Sandy Scott (see Figure 7.12). From 1851 to 1857, Alexander John Scott was the first principal of Owens College, later the University of Manchester.[54] The Schwabes were also friends of both Scott and Thomas Erskine, of Linlathen, a cousin of Jane Stirling; in 1847, before he moved to Manchester, Scott had given lectures to Salis Schwabe's employees at his factory at Rhodes.[55] Scott (known as Sandy) was born in 1805, the son of a minister in the Church of Scotland. He graduated MA at the University of Glasgow in 1824, and was licensed by the presbytery of Paisley. He became tutor to the family of Thomas Erskine, of Linlathen, who had recently published two books, *Remarks on the internal evidence for the truth of revealed religion* (1820) and *An essay on faith* (1822). Scott was in sympathy with both works, and he and Erskine became lifelong friends. Theologically unconventional, Scott was deposed from the ministry in 1831, and for the next fifteen years used the tiny Woolwich chapel as his base for teaching and preaching.[56]

When working at Woolwich, from 1831 to 1846, Scott travelled to the Continent, notably to Switzerland and France, and it was during these years that he

Figure 7.12 Revd Alexander John (Sandy) Scott (1805–66). Portrait from Hair, *Regent Square* (1898), opposite p. 86. Private collection

seems to have met both Ary Scheffer and Chopin; indeed, it has been suggested that Scott may have been assembling material for a biography of the composer. Clearly, Jane Stirling, as a relative and close friend of Thomas Erskine, of Linlathen, would have been able to offer him significant help. In 1910, Scott's daughter, Miss Susan Fisher Scott, presented plaster casts of Chopin's death mask, and of his left hand, to the Royal Manchester College of Music (now the Royal Northern College of Music), and it is not impossible that both of these were given to Sandy Scott by Jane Stirling (see Plates 24 and 25).[57] The sculptor was Auguste Clésinger, who had married Solange Dudevant-Sand, daughter of George Sand, in 1847, and whose work included a bust of Sand (1847) and Chopin's head on the composer's grave in the Père Lachaise cemetery in Paris (1850). In 1973, the Frederick Chopin Society of Poland presented the Royal Northern College of Music with a full-length bronze statue of Chopin by the Polish sculptor Ludwika Nitschowa, to mark the 125th anniversary of Chopin's concert in Manchester in 1848 (see Plates 26 and 27).[58] In 2011, a bronze sculpture of Chopin seated at a piano, by the Polish artist Robert Sobociński, was unveiled in central Manchester (see Plate 28).

Salis Schwabe died at Glyn Garth on 23 July 1853, at the age of fifty-three.[59] After her husband's death, Mrs Julie Schwabe continued to entertain in her Welsh home. In 1857, the year of the Manchester Exhibition of Art Treasures, visitors included Ary Scheffer, who stayed first at Crumpsall House for three weeks and then at Glyn Garth. Here, wrote Mrs Grote, 'were present, in ample store, all those elements in which an imaginative, sentimental, and affectionate soul, like that of Scheffer, might find delectation and refreshment', including 'the picturesque mountain scenery of Carnarvonshire, the sight of the shipping gliding abour in the "Menai"; [and] the novel spectacle of the Welsh people, busy, yet not toil-worn'.[60]

Notes

1. An expansion of material contained in this chapter can be found in my book *Chopin in Manchester* (Newcastle upon Tyne: Elysium Press, 2011), which is based on my article, 'Chopin's recital in the Gentlemen's Concert Hall, Monday 28 August 1848', *Manchester Sounds*, vol.8 (2009–10), pp. 84–119.
2. Wood, 'Chopin in Britain, II', p. 6. Wood says that this letter is in his possession.
3. Quoted by Wood, 'Chopin in Britain, II', p. 6. See Hedley, *Chopin correspondence*, p. 346. Chopin to Grzymała, 3 October [1848].
4. Wood, 'Chopin in Britain, II', p. 6.
5. Hedley, *Chopin correspondence*, p. 339. Chopin to his family in Warsaw, 10–19 August 1848.
6. Hedley, *Chopin correspondence*, p. 339. Chopin to his family in Warsaw, 10–19 August 1848.
7. See the views of Crumpsall and Glyn Garth in Willis, *Chopin in Manchester*, plates 4, 5, 9, and 10.
8. Axon, *Annals of Manchester*, p. 241.
9. Axon, *Annals of Manchester*, p. 247. These last visits to Manchester by Jenny Lind, therefore, were after Chopin's concert there.
10. To my knowledge, the bust and the Scheffer painting were first published in my *Chopin in Manchester*, plates 6 and 7.

11 For the Schwabes and Scheffer, see Albisetti, 'Inevitable Schwabes', *passim*, and Morris, 'Ary Scheffer and his English circle', *passim*. Scheffer and the Schwabes are touched on in Morris, *French art in nineteenth-century Britain*, and Morris, 'Provincial internationalism'.
12 Hedley, *Chopin correspondence*, p. 340. Chopin to Grzymała [4–9 September 1848].
13 See Neukomm references in Hedley, *Chopin correspondence*, pp. 190–1, 326–7, 339.
14 For 'Wiosna', see above, Chapter 5, n.43.
15 Hedley, *Chopin correspondence*, p. 340. Chopin to Grzymała [4–9 September 1848].
16 See Peter Weston, *The Froebel Educational Institute: the origins and history of the college* (Roehampton: University of Surrey, 2002), pp. 4–5.
17 Gérin, *Elizabeth Gaskell*, p. 145. For Mrs Gaskell's correspondence with the Schwabes, see Chapple and Pollard, *Letters of Mrs Gaskell*, nos 113, 121, 122, 128, 162. Letters to Ann Scott, wife of A.J. Scott, appear as nos 437, 628.
18 Morris, 'Ary Scheffer and his English circle', p. 306.
19 Morris, 'Ary Scheffer and his English circle', p. 307.
20 See Morris, *French art in nineteenth-century Britain*, *passim*.
21 For the Gentlemen's Concert Society, see the material in the Henry Watson Music Library, Manchester Central Library, including R.780.68.Me.68.MIC, containing minutes, 1830–1920; and R.780.69.Me.68.MIC, containing the programmes of the Gentlemen's concerts, 1840–9. For wider consideration of the Gentlemen's concerts, see Allis, 'Gentlemen's concerts, Manchester, 1777–1920'; Gick, 'Chamber music concerts in Manchester, 1838–1844'; and Gick, 'Concert life in Manchester, 1800–1848'. The early years of the society are considered in Burchell, *Polite or commercial concerts?*, pp. 255–60. Beale, *Hallé*, contains many references to the Gentlemen's concerts, in the text and bibliography.
22 Love, *The hand-book of Manchester*, pp. 274–5.
23 For the St Peter's Square area, see Hartwell, Hyde, and Pevsner, *Lancashire: Manchester and the south-east*, pp. 322–4, 332–3.
24 For architectural descriptions of the Gentlemen's Concert Hall, see Hartwell and Wyke, *Making Manchester*, pp. 14, 18, 20, 23–4. For Lane, see Clare Hartwell, 'Manchester and the golden age of Pericles: Richard Lane, architect', in Hartwell and Wyke, *Making Manchester*, pp. 18–35.
25 Hartwell, 'Manchester and the Golden Age of Pericles', p. 23
26 Love, *The hand-book of Manchester*, pp. 274–5.
27 Quoted by Hartwell, 'Manchester and the Golden Age of Pericles', p. 24.
28 Jackson, 'New music festival', p.XII. Jackson gives no source for this. Allis, 'Gentlemen's concerts, Manchester, 1777–1920', p. 51, notes that a leaflet of 1852, describing the hall, observes that 'on the advice of the architect, Mr J. White, the decoration was changed from severe Greek into chaste Italian.'
29 Piggott, *John Field*, p. 51.
30 See Wright, *Liszt and England*, *passim*, and two articles by the same author, 'Master Liszt in England' and 'Liszt in Manchester'; also Allsobrook, *Liszt: my travelling circus life*, pp. 8, 114–16, 124–5. By this time the Athenaeum, promoting adult education, was the occupant of Manchester's first 'palazzo' building (1836–7), designed by Sir Charles Barry.
31 Text taken from Niecks, *Chopin*, vol.2, p. 294. The pioneering publications here are Susan Brookshaw's *Concerning Chopin in Manchester*, *passim*, and the article in which she summarizes her findings, 'Concerning Chopin in Manchester', *passim*. Brookshaw also deals with Chopin in her article 'Chopin's Jane Stirling', *Musical Opinion* (April 1948), pp. 254–5.
32 For Seymour see Brown and Stratton, *British musical biography*, p. 366.
33 This paragraph draws on the entry on Alboni by Elizabeth Forbes in *Grove music online*. For Chorley's views on Alboni, see his *Thirty years' musical recollections*, vol.2, pp. 8–13.

34 For Alboni, Corbari, and Salvi at Covent Garden in 1847–9, see Rosenthal, *Two centuries of opera at Covent Garden*, pp. 72–84.
35 See the entry on Beale by Michael Musgrave in *Oxford DNB online*.
36 See above, Chapter 3, n.80, and Cobbe, *Three hundred years of composers' pianos*, pp. 52–5.
37 The original programme, and its supplementary 'notice', are reproduced in Willis, *Chopin in Manchester*, plates 18 and 19.
38 *Manchester Guardian*, 30 August 1848, quoted in Atwood, *Pianist from Warsaw*, p. 253.
39 *Manchester Guardian*, 30 August 1848, quoted in Atwood, *Pianist from Warsaw*, p. 253.
40 Reviews of the concert in the *Manchester Courier and Lancashire General Advertiser* (30 August), the *Manchester Guardian* (30 August), the *Manchester Examiner* (5 September), and the *Musical World* (9 September), are given (with some elisions) in Atwood, *Pianist from Warsaw*, pp. 251–3. Not all later commentators on Chopin's Manchester concert take account of the changes Chopin made to his original programme.
41 Niecks, *Chopin*, vol.2, p. 295, with an extended text in Atwood, *Pianist from Warsaw*, p. 251. The suggestion made in a review of the Manchester concert in the *Manchester Times* (5 September 1848, p. 5d), that the Athenaeum in Manchester might have provided a better performance space for Chopin, is cited by Gick, 'Concert life in Manchester,1800–1848', p. 327, n.39.
42 *Musical World*, 9 September 1848, quoted in Atwood, *Pianist from Warsaw*, p. 252.
43 *Manchester Examiner*, 5 September 1848, quoted in Atwood, *Pianist from Warsaw*, pp. 251–2.
44 For Osborne, see Hunt, 'George Alexander Osborne', *passim*. Osborne's 'Le castillan, bolero' (1841) was dedicated to Chopin. I am grateful to Una Hunt for advice on Osborne; she has issued a piano CD entitled *Shower of pearls: the music of George Alexander Osborne* (RTé lyric fm, 2004).
45 See Niecks, *Chopin*, vol.1, p. 241.
46 See the entry on Osborne by R.H. Legge, revised by Rosemary Firmin, in *Oxford DNB online*, and Jean Mongrédien's article on Osborne in *Grove music online*.
47 Osborne, 'Reminiscences of Fredrick Chopin', p. 101, partly reprinted in Niecks, *Chopin*, vol.2, p. 295. Osborne was speaking and writing over thirty years after the Manchester concert, so his memory may have played him false.
48 Hallé, *Life and letters*, p. 230. Allis, 'Gentlemen's concerts, Manchester, 1777–1920', p. 55, refers to Hermann Léo and 'Liedertafel' – a singing party with guest musicians.
49 See Hallé, *Autobiography*, pp. 56–7.
50 Brookshaw, *Concerning Chopin in Manchester*, p. 18.
51 Gavoty, *Chopin* (French edition), pp. 298–300, and Gavoty, *Chopin* (English edition), pp. 232–3. This is reiterated on p. 418, n.3 of the French edition, and in a note on p. 330 of the English edition.
52 Gavoty, *Chopin* (English edition), p. 233. The French text of the letter is on p. 299 of the French edition, and the English translation (by Martin Sokolinsky) on p. 233 of the English edition. Gavoty indicates that he bought the letter in London, but its present whereabouts are unknown. The date of 9 September 1848 suggests that the letter, if authentic, was written at Johnstone Castle, where Chopin was then staying with the Houstons. If there were, indeed, a second recital by Chopin during his Manchester visit, it may well have been at Crumpsall House, for the Schwabes?
53 I am grateful to Jeffrey Kallberg for alerting me to this incident. For fuller details see Kallberg, 'La Marche de Chopin', *passim*; and Kallberg, 'Chopin's march, Chopin's death', pp. 22–3. The authenticity of the letter is considered here in note 59, and in note 58 references are given to George Sand's description in her *Oeuvres autobiographiques* of the 'cursed creatures' which Chopin saw in the Carthusian monastery at Valldemosa. See also Boczkowska, 'Chopin's ghosts', *passim*, but particularly p. 205, n.5.
54 For material in this paragraph, see the article by J. Philip Newell on Alexander John Scott in *Oxford DNB online*, and Newell's PhD thesis, 'A.J. Scott and his circle'. See

194   *Manchester: Gentlemen's Concert Hall*

     also Newell, *Listening for the heartbeat of God*, pp. 62–73, and Wilkinson, *Christian socialism*, pp. 21–2, leading into a consideration of Mrs Gaskell. Scott's appointment at Manchester is recorded in Fiddes, *Chapters in the history of Owens College and of Manchester University*, p. 29.

55 On 8 October and 20 October 1847, respectively, A.J. Scott gave two lectures at the Mechanics' Institute, Rhodes, 'to the workpeople of Mr. Salis Schwabe', with the titles 'On education', and 'The foundations of society, moral and economical'. See Thompson, *Owens College*, p. 653.

56 The quotations in this paragraph, and below, are taken from Newell's entry on Scott in *Oxford DNB online*. See also, e.g., Ashton, *Little Germany*, notably pp. 178–9, 207. In 1846, the Scott family moved to No. 40 Gloucester Crescent, Regent's Park, 'which became a regular meeting place for many of his literary friends, now including Thackeray, Ruskin, Francis Newman, and the controversial actress Fanny Kemble'. From 1848 to 1851, Scott was Professor of English Language and Literature at University College London, and one of the founders of Bedford College, 'the first centre of higher education for women in Britain based on the principles of religious freedom'; the fledgling Owens College, Manchester, to which Scott moved in 1851, was also free of religious tests. Here, Scott continued 'to pursue the development of education for the working classes, and in 1858, along with others, he founded the Manchester Working Men's College', and established connections with the wider artistic, intellectual, political, and socially committed community in Manchester.

57 For the gift of the casts, see the archives at RNCM (Manchester), RMCM/C/2/1. For a list of masks, and Chopin's hands, see Burger, *Chopin*, p. 339. For Clésinger's masks of Chopin, see Wróblewska-Straus, 'Jane Wilhelmina Stirling's letters to Ludwika Jędrzejewicz', pp. 74–5. Three plates of the Manchester death mask, taken by the Manchester photographer F.W. Schmidt (not 'Schmitt', as Ganche has it), are in Ganche, *Souffrances de Frédéric Chopin*, 6th edition (1935), frontispiece, and opposite pp. 128, 192. See the discussion of this mask, and Jane Stirling's connection with it, in R.J. Forbes, 'The death-mask of Chopin', *Manchester Guardian*, Wednesday 22 February 1933. In 1881, Princess Marcelina Czartoryska presented a death mask of Chopin by Clésinger to The Princes Czartoryski Museum, Cracow. It is illustrated in *The Princes Czartoryski Museum: a history of the collections* (Cracow, 2001), plate 288 (p. 174).

58 It is set on a marble base, and is described and illustrated in Wyke, *Public sculpture of Greater Manchester*, pp. 49–50. Another cast of this, unveiled in 1985, is in the park at Sanniki Palace, and illustrated in Juàrez and Sławińska-Dahlig, *Chopin's Poland*, p. 210.

59 As Axon, *Annals of Manchester*, p. 264, records: 'Mr. Salis Schwabe died at Glyn Garth, on the Menai Straits, July 23 [1853], in his 54th year. He was buried at Harpurhey Cemetery July 30, and was followed to the grave by the Bishop of Manchester and many of the leading persons of the city.'

60 Grote, *Memoir of the life of Ary Scheffer*, p. 117. Scheffer's visit to Crumpsall House and Glyn Garth is considered here on pp. 115–19.

8 Glasgow
Concert in Merchants' Hall,
Wednesday 27 September 1848

Musical life in Glasgow in the 1840s was becoming increasingly lively. In 1845, with the production of Balfe's *The Bohemian Girl* in the City Theatre, Glasgow awoke to opera; three years later, in 1848, the pace was set with the presentation of *La figlia del reggimento* and *La sonnambula*, featuring Jenny Lind, Luigi Lablache, and the French tenor Gustave-Hippolyte Roger.[1] The demand for venues for musical events led to the erection in Glasgow of the City Hall, designed by the architect George Murray (1841), to be followed by the Queen's Rooms, by Charles Wilson (1856). Choral and orchestral societies prospered, and in 1844 the reputed first complete performance of Handel's *Messiah* in Scotland was given in the City Hall. John Muir Wood and his brother George Wood both gave series of concerts. Opera singers were often engaged to perform in the concert hall as well as the theatre, while among instrumentalists Moscheles (1828), Paganini (1831), and Liszt (1841) paved the way for Chopin's appearance in 1848.[2]

Staying with the Houstons at Johnstone Castle, immediately prior to his Glasgow concert, Chopin received two letters: one from Grzymała, in Paris, telling Chopin of his visit to the *Gymnase musicale* with Solange Dudevant-Sand, and a second from Prince Alexander Czartoryski and Princess Marcelina, in Edinburgh, announcing that they had arrived and would be glad to see him. Chopin acted immediately. 'Although tired', he told Grzymała, 'I jumped into the train and caught them still in Edinburgh. Princess Marcelina is kindness itself, just as she was last year. I revived somewhat under the influence of their Polish spirit, and it gave me strength to play at Glasgow where a few score of the nobility drove in to hear me.' The weather was good, and the Prince and Princess travelled to Glasgow by train, bringing with them their son Marcel, then seven years old or so, and 'growing into a fine boy'. 'He can sing my compositions', Chopin adds, in parenthesis, 'and if anyone doesn't play them quite correctly he sings to show them how.'[3] In visiting Scotland, the Czartoryskis were reaffirming the family's long-standing connections to the country, and a commitment to cultural life which had earned them the title of 'the Medici of Poland'.[4]

The night before Chopin was due to perform in Glasgow, Ludovic and Ann Houston apparently entertained two sisters at Johnstone Castle. One was the 'lady now resident in Bedford' we have already met.[5] She was 'a member of a well-known Scottish family, who had the privilege of receiving some lessons from

Chopin when she was in Paris in 1846', after being introduced to the composer by Jane Stirling. On 18 March 1903 she wrote to J. Cuthbert Hadden, the Scottish organist, writer on music, and author of the book *Chopin* (1903), describing her experience of a visit to Johnstone. 'I was invited, with one of my sisters, to meet him', she wrote. 'He was then in a most suffering state, but nevertheless he was so kind as to play to us that evening in his own matchless style. We four were his only auditors. It was at such times, and not in a concert-room, that he poured himself out.' The next morning, 'on a cold ungenial day, we accompanied him to Glasgow' and heard 'that memorable recital'.[6]

Chopin's concert took place in the Merchants' Hall. Architecturally, the early nineteenth century had seen the centre of Glasgow transformed, with the establishment of the New Town (or Merchant City as it became known) laid out in a beaux-arts manner, with straight streets terminating in major classical buildings.[7] The Merchants' Hall was set in the City and County Buildings in Wilson Street, an entire block which originally incorporated the county offices and sheriff court (see Figure 8.1); the architects, chosen in 1841 after a competition, were William Clark and George Bell. Regrettably, as the building is now partially demolished, it is only possible to speculate on the character of the interior of the Merchants' Hall in Chopin' day. Its facade, on Hutcheson Street, however, still stands (see Figure 8.2).[8]

The organizer of Chopin's *matinée musicale* was John Muir Wood, and his advertisement for the concert announces that it was to be held on Wednesday

Figure 8.1 Glasgow, the Merchant City. County Buildings, Wilson Street, by Robert Carrick, 1852, showing the Merchants' Hall, Hutcheson Street, to the left. Mitchell Library, Glasgow

Figure 8.2 Merchants' Hall, Hutcheson Street, Glasgow. Undated lithograph by Maclure and Macdonald, from *View of the Merchants House of Glasgow* (1866), p. 443. Mitchell Library, Glasgow

27 September at 2.30 p.m., under the patronage of ten titled ladies from the Scots aristocracy (see Figure 8.3). Tickets were 'limited in number', obtainable from Muir Wood's premises at No. 42 Buchanan Street, at 'Half-a-Guinea each'. No mention is made, surprisingly, of the singer Mme Giulietta de Margueritttes, nor of John Muir Wood as her accompanist.

Muir Wood's effort to attract a distinguished audience for Chopin was not without success. Reporting on the concert the next day, the *Glasgow Courier* of 28 September noted that it was 'numerously attended by the beauty and fashion, indeed the very élite of our west end'.[9] Chopin's *matinée musicale*, the *Glasgow Herald* observed on 29 September, was given 'under the patronage of the most distinguished ladies of the nobility and gentry of the West of Scotland'; among those listed by Muir Wood are the Duchess of Argyll (chatelaine of Inveraray) and her sister Lady Blantyre, and Lady Belhaven (Chopin's hostess at Wishaw). At half-past two, when the concert was due to start, 'a large concourse of carriages began to draw up in Hutcheson Street and the streets adjoining. The audience which was not large, was exceedingly distinguished.'[10]

The programme for the concert, issued by John Muir Wood, lists four contributions by Chopin, interspersed with three songs from Mme Adelasio de

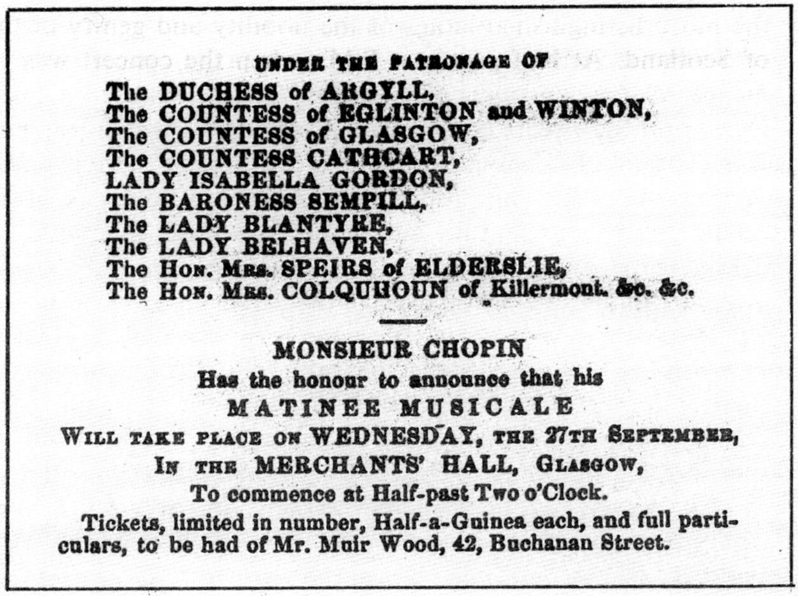

> UNDER THE PATRONAGE OF
> The DUCHESS of ARGYLL,
> The COUNTESS of EGLINTON and WINTON,
> The COUNTESS of GLASGOW,
> The COUNTESS CATHCART,
> LADY ISABELLA GORDON,
> The BARONESS SEMPILL,
> The LADY BLANTYRE,
> The LADY BELHAVEN,
> The Hon. Mrs. SPEIRS of ELDERSLIE,
> The Hon. Mrs. COLQUHOUN of Killermont. &c. &c.
>
> MONSIEUR CHOPIN
> Has the honour to announce that his
> MATINEE MUSICALE
> WILL TAKE PLACE ON WEDNESDAY, THE 27TH SEPTEMBER,
> IN THE MERCHANTS' HALL, GLASGOW,
> To commence at Half-past Two o'Clock.
> Tickets, limited in number, Half-a-Guinea each, and full particulars, to be had of Mr. Muir Wood, 42, Buchanan Street.

Figure 8.3 Advertisement for Chopin's *matinée musicale* in the Merchants' Hall, Glasgow, on Wednesday 27 September 1848, from Bone, *Jane Wilhelmina Stirling* (1960), plate opposite p. 76. Private collection

Marguerittes: 'La camelia' and 'La notte e bella' by Pietro Gugliemi, and 'Le Lac' by Lamartine, set to music by Louis Niedermeyer.[11] The *Glasgow Herald* on 29 September indicated that although Mme Adelasio 'showed much vocal ability', she 'evinced a certain lack of enthusiasm with which we were not at all charmed'.[12] The *Glasgow Courier* of 28 September was more positive, observing that she 'has a beautiful voice which she manages with great ease and occasional brilliancy. She sang several airs with much taste and great acceptance.' As for Chopin, his 'treatment of the piano-forte is peculiar to himself, and his style blends in beautiful harmony and perfection the elegant, the picturesque and the humorous . . . [Chopin] produces without extraordinary effort, not only pleasing but new musical delights.' All the pieces were 'rapturously applauded, and the audience separated with expressions of the highest gratification'.[13] All this was achieved by Chopin on the Broadwood Grand Pianoforte No. 17,001 (London, circa 1847), which he used later in his recital in the Hopetoun Rooms in Edinburgh.[14]

What pieces, then, did Chopin play in Glasgow? When John Muir Wood visited Chopin in Johnstone Castle to discuss the programme with him, he found the composer indecisive. Julius Seligmann, onetime President of the Glasgow Society of Musicians, endorses this impression. 'Mr Muir Wood managed the special arrangements of the concert', he wrote, 'and I distinctly remember him telling me that he never had so much difficulty in arranging a concert as on this occasion. Chopin constantly changed his mind.' Muir Wood had to go out to see him several times at Johnstone, 'but scarcely had he returned to Glasgow when he was summoned back to alter something'.[15]

A copy of the concert programme, which may have been annotated by John Muir Wood himself, enables us to speculate about the pieces Chopin chose to play:

> Andante [?], and Impromptu in F sharp major (Op.36)
> Études (Op.25)
> Nocturnes in C sharp minor and D flat major (Op.27)
> Nocturnes in F minor and E flat minor (Op.55)
> Berceuse in D flat major (Op.57)
> Mazurkas in A minor, A flat major, and F sharp minor (Op.59)
> *Polonaise fantaisie* in A flat major (Op.61)
> Preludes (Op.28)
> Ballade in F major (Op.38)
> Mazurkas in B flat major, A minor, F minor, A flat major, and C major (Op.7)
> Waltzes in D flat major, C sharp minor, and A flat major (Op.64)[16]

We do not know which of these Chopin performed, as accounts of the concert are not specific. But we may hazard guesses.[17]

The most problematic identification is that of the first piece, the *Andante* (puzzlingly identified in ink as 'No 8' on the surviving programme), which may have been the *Andante spianato* in G major, which forms an introduction to the Polonaise in E flat major (Op.22); Hipkins told Frederick Niecks that Chopin frequently played this *Andante* in his recitals, and indeed he may have done so later in the Hopetoun Rooms in Edinburgh.[18] However, Jeffrey Kallberg has proposed that the ink inscription 'No 8' suggests that the first piece is the 8th Prelude of Op.28 in F sharp minor, partly because 'the parallel tonalities of the Prelude and the Impromptu . . . make a more logical join . . . than would follow from the linking of the *Andante spianato* and the Impromptu'.[19] As to mazurkas, the 'lady now resident in Bedford' told Hadden that she could not 'recall distinctly anything but the marvellous brilliancy of the well-known Mazurka (Op.7), and the equally familiar Valses (Op.64), the second of which is so pathetic'. The impression on her was profound: 'I never saw Chopin again, but his tones still ring in my ears.'[20] Seligmann remembers Chopin playing his Mazurka in B flat major (Op.7, no.1), which he encored 'with quite different nuances' from those of the first time around.[21] Two of the nocturnes (Op.55) were those dedicated to Jane Stirling, and one imagines that Chopin included them for her, and that she and her sister, Mrs Katherine Erskine, attended the concert after staying at Johnstone Castle the previous night.[22]

It is impossible to say if Chopin's choice of repertoire was affected by his failing health, but his Glasgow audience were well aware of his illness. 'It goes to my heart to think of Chopin in his miserable state handed about among those kind and well-meaning, but tormenting, friends, and forced to appear in public', observed the lady from Bedford.[23] Seligmann stressed the affects of Chopin's illness upon his playing: 'His touch was very feeble, and while the finish, grace, elegance, and delicacy of his performances were greatly admired by the audience, the want of power made his playing somewhat monotonous.'[24] Another 'enthusiastic member of that Glasgow audience', George Russell Alexander, whose father was proprietor of the Theatre Royal in Glasgow, was struck by Chopin's 'pale, cadaverous appearance'. 'My emotion', Alexander comments, 'was so great that two or three times I was compelled to retire from the room to recover myself. I have heard all the best and most celebrated stars of the musical firmament, but never one has left such an impression on my mind.'[25] All told, comments Hadden, the general effect produced by Chopin upon his listeners in Glasgow was of a virtuoso 'who seemed to them all to be dying on his feet'.[26]

Despite the enthusiasm which greeted Chopin's performance, not all was sweetness and light. Hadden, taking his cue from Niecks, reports that the profits from the concert were 'said to have been exactly £60, a ridiculously low sum when we compare it with the earnings of later-day *virtuosi*; nay, still more ridiculously low when we recall the fact that for two concerts in Glasgow sixteen years before this Paganini had £1400.'[27] To Muir Wood, the attendance had been disappointing. 'I was then a comparative stranger in Glasgow', he wrote, 'but I was told that so many private carriages had never been seen at any concert in the town.' But this was deceptive. 'In fact it was country people who turned out with a few of the *élite* of Glasgow society. Being a morning [*sic*] concert, the citizens were busy otherwise, and half-a-guinea was considered too high a sum for their wives and daughters.'[28] To this, Niecks wryly observed that 'no doubt Chopin's playing and compositions must have been to the good Glasgow citizens of that day what caviare is to the general.'[29]

One final witness to Chopin's Glasgow recital must be called. This is the journalist and poet James Hedderwick (see Figure 8.4), who in 1842 established the *Glasgow Citizen*, a weekly, and in 1864 the *Glasgow Evening Citizen*, a successful daily which claimed at one point to have the largest circulation of any newspaper in the west of Scotland.[30] Four years before Chopin's visit to Glasgow, Hedderwick had published his first volume of poems. In recognition of his literary and editorial work, Hedderwick was awarded the honorary degree of Doctor of Laws by the University of Glasgow in 1878, and in 1891, as 'James Hedderwick, LL D', he published a volume of memoirs entitled *Backward glances, or some personal recollections*.

Here, under the heading 'An accidental treat', Hedderwick describes Chopin's Glasgow recital.[31] 'What's up?', he begins. 'A carriage-and-four at the entrance to the Merchants' Hall in Hutcheson Street!' A policeman tells him that it is "a Mr Chopin giving a concert". Hedderwick continues:

> On entering the hall, I found it about one-third full. The audience was aristocratic. Prince Czartoryski, a man whose name was patriotically associated with the Polish struggle for independence, was present; so likewise were

Figure 8.4 James Hedderwick (1814–97). Photograph by Dawsons from Hedderwick, *Backward glances, or some personal recollections* (1891), frontispiece. Private collection

some representatives of the ducal house of Hamilton; while sitting near were Lord and Lady Blantyre, the latter a perfectly beautiful woman, and worthy of her lineage as one of the daughters of the Queen's favourite Duchess of Sutherland. Others of the neighbouring nobility and gentry were observable;

and I fancied that many of the ladies might have had finishing lessons in music from the great and fashionable pianist in Paris.

'It was obvious, indeed', Hedderwick adds, 'that a number of the audience were personal friends of M. Chopin.'

Soon, Hedderwick's attention was 'attracted to a little fragile-looking man, in pale-grey suit, including frock-coat of identical tint and texture, moving about among the company, conversing with different groups, and occasionally consulting his watch, which seemed to be

> In shape no bigger than an agate stone
> On the forefinger of an alderman.[32]

Here was 'the musical genius' they had all come to hear:

> Whiskerless, beardless, fair of hair, and pale and thin of face, his appearance was interesting and conspicuous; and when, after a final glance at his miniature horologe [*sic*], he ascended the platform and placed himself at the instrument of which he was so renowned a master, he at once commanded attention.

Hedderwick compares Chopin with other pianists he had seen and heard: Thalberg, 'sitting with serene countenance while banging out some air with clear articulation and power, in the midst of perpetual coruscations of the most magnificent *fioriture*'; Liszt, 'tossing his fair hair excitedly, and tearing the wild soul of music from the ecstatic keys'; and Dohler, 'with his hammer-strokes, and a rapidity which took away one's breath'. But, says Hedderwick, 'the manner of Chopin was different'. His description of Chopin is poetic, not to say mawkish:

> No man has composed pianoforte music of more technical difficulty. Yet with what consummate sweetness and ease did he unravel the wonderful varieties and complexities of sound! It was a drawing-room entertainment, more *piano* than *forte*, though not without occasional episodes of both strength and grandeur.

Chopin, adds Hedderwick,

> took the audience, as it were, into his confidence, and whispered to them of zephyrs and moonlight rather than of cataracts and thunder. Of the whirl of liquid notes he wove garlands of pearls. The movements and combinations were calculated to excite and bewilder. They were strange, fantastic, wandering, incomprehensible, but less fitted, on the whole, for the popular concert hall than for the *salon* of a private mansion.

It was evident to Hedderwick – writing, it must be said, over forty years later – that Chopin 'was early marked for doom'. Thus, 'his compositions live and will live;

but he himself, with all his fine aspirations, was in a little while to be laid where neither applause nor criticism, neither glory nor trouble of any kind, could come.'

After Chopin's concert during the afternoon came the dinner at Johnstone Castle, where the guests included Lord and Lady Murray, Lord Torphichen, and Prince Aleksander and Princess Marcelina, with their son, Marcel, who duly returned to the Continent via Glasgow and London, looking at Loch Lomond en route. Writing to Grzymała from Keir the next weekend, Chopin again says how uplifted he felt at meeting the Czartoryskis once more. 'You can't imagine how that day brought new life to me', he explained. 'But I'm already depressed again – this fog!'[33]

The demolition of Johnstone Castle in 1956 means that we cannot easily imagine the building as Chopin experienced it. However, Édouard Ganche, after his visit to Johnstone in 1930, which he described in his book *Voyages avec Frédéric Chopin* (1934), waxes lyrical as he imagines Chopin at dinner there in 1848:

> Au rez-de-chaussée se trouve une admirable salle à manger rectangulaire, lambrissée de bois cirés, d'une patine rutilante, et ornée dans ses panneaux des portraits peints des maîtres successifs.

Dining, in his imagination, were Prince and Princess Czartoryski, Lord and Lady Murray, Lord Torphichen, and Jane Stirling and Mrs Katherine Erskine. As Ganche pictures the scene:

> Sous les lumières abondantes des lustres, dans la décoration de fête de cette belle salle pas trop spacieuse pour rester agréable et familiale, Frédéric Chopin se vit entouré par une assemblée choisie où pour son plus grand contentement secret l'élément polonais était hautement représenté.

Here, in the country of Walter Scott, Ganche writes, took place 'le banquet idéal de la musique et de l'amour, car toutes les personnes présentes aimaient Chopin, admiraient et honoraient la toute-puissance de son double génie de créateur et d'interprète'.[34]

Chopin planned to go back to see the Murrays at Strachur after his Glasgow concert;[35] however, his next stop was a visit to William Stirling at Keir, whence he reported to Grzymała that he had left Strachur 'a week ago' (that is, before the concert), and he seems never to have returned.[36] On 3 October, Chopin was back in Edinburgh.[37]

Notes

1 Farmer, *History of music in Scotland*, pp. 416–17.
2 Farmer, *History of music in Scotland*, pp. 471–2.
3 Hedley, *Chopin correspondence*, p. 343. Chopin to Grzymała, 1 October [1848]. See also Niecks, *Chopin*, vol.2, pp. 299–301.
4 For the Czartoryskis' connections with Scotland, see the editor's introduction in McLeod, *From Charlotte Square to Fingal's Cave*, pp. xiv – xxv.
5 See Chapter 2, note 57.

6 Hadden, *Chopin*, p. 147. 'We four', in all likelihood, were Ludovic and Ann Houston, and the two sisters. On p. 148, n.1, Hadden quotes another, undated, letter from the same lady. Her recollections of a lesson with Chopin in Paris are in a letter she wrote to Hadden on 27 March 1903, quoted in his *Chopin*, pp. 185–8. Harasowski, in his *Skein of legends around Chopin*, does not include Hadden's *Chopin* among the forty-two books he analyses.
7 For the Merchant City, see McKean, Walker, and Walker, *Central Glasgow*, pp. 70–7; and Williamson, Riches and Higgs, *Glasgow*, pp. 154–91.
8 For the Merchants' Hall, see McKean, Walker, and Walker, *Central Glasgow*, pp. 75–6; Williamson, Riches, and Higgs, *Glasgow*, pp. 165, 181, and the map on p. 155; and *Dictionary of Scottish architects online*, under 'Clarke & Bell', and 'City and County Buildings and second Merchants' House', respectively.
9 Quoted by Atwood, *Pianist from Warsaw*, pp. 254–5.
10 Quoted by Atwood, *Pianist from Warsaw*, pp. 253–4. For John Muir Wood's comments on this concert, Jane Stirling, Mrs Houston, and Chopin's visit to Britain generally, see Bennett, *Chopin*, p. 57.
11 See Herbert Kemlo Wood, 'When Chopin was in Glasgow: today's centenary of recital', *Glasgow Herald*, 27 September 1948. Herbert Kemlo Wood's obituary is in the *Glasgow Herald*, 11 May 1953.
12 Quoted by Atwood, *Pianist from Warsaw*, p. 254.
13 Quoted by Atwood, *Pianist from Warsaw*, p. 255. See also Niecks, *Chopin*, vol.2, pp. 296–7. Niecks adds on p. 297: 'Clearly this critic [from the *Glasgow Courier*] was not without judgment, although his literary taste and skill leave much to be desired. That there were real Chopin enthusiasts in Glasgow is proved by an effusion, full of praise and admiration, which the editor received from a correspondent and inserted on September 30, two days after the above criticism.'
14 See Chapter 9, note 15.
15 Quoted by Hadden, *Chopin*, p. 146. Seligmann here mistakenly refers to Milliken Park, but Hadden corrects him in a note. Hadden, whose book *Chopin* was first published in 1903, had been given Seligmann's written impressions 'ten years ago' – that is 45 years after Chopin's Glasgow concert.
16 Opus numbers are taken from Brown, *Index of Chopin's works*, *passim*. Item 5 in the programme lists six pieces: 'Nos 27, 59, & 61' (which is the Polonaise-fantaisie in A flat major), and 'Op. 27 & 55', and 'Op. 57'. I assume that the 'Nos' listed here refer to the opus numbers. Herbert Kemlo Wood, 'Chopin in Britain, II', p. 6, writes: 'Chopin could not make up his mind about his programme, he preferred to play as the spirit moved him and often changed his mind. This accounts for the absence of Opus numbers on the printed programme. The pieces played are identified only from manuscript jottings in my father's handwriting on the programme in my possession.'
17 For the interpretation of the programme, see, e.g., Niecks, *Chopin*, vol.2, pp. 296–7. See further speculations in Hedley, *Chopin*, p. 106, and comments on pp. 110–11.
18 Niecks, *Chopin*, vol.2, pp. 298–9.
19 Kallberg, *Chopin at the boundaries*, pp. 150–2. Would Chopin have been so concerned about the 'parallel tonalities'? In any case, he played preludes from Op.28 later in the concert. See also Kallberg, *Chopin at the boundaries*, p. 278, nn.37–9 (about Edinburgh).
20 Hadden, *Chopin*, pp. 147–8.
21 Hadden, *Chopin*, p. 146.
22 No firm evidence has been encountered to confirm that the Stirling sisters were at the Glasgow concert or at Johnstone Castle the previous evening. But surely they must have been.
23 Hadden, *Chopin*, p. 148n.
24 Hadden, *Chopin*, p. 146.

25 Hadden, *Chopin*, p. 147.
26 Hadden, *Chopin*, p. 147.
27 Hadden, *Chopin*, p. 144, reflecting Niecks, *Chopin*, vol.2, p. 296. Hedley, in an editorial note in *Chopin correspondence*, p. 342, says that 'Chopin cleared £90 by it', a statement he reiterates in his *Chopin*, p. 111. The reference to Paganini should be seen in the light of Hugh Macdonald's article, 'Paganini in Scotland', pp. 201–18, to which he kindly alerted me.
28 Quoted by Bennett, *Chopin*, p. 57. Niecks gives this quotation (unsourced) in *Chopin*, vol.2, p. 296, but changes 'country' to 'county'.
29 Niecks, *Chopin*, vol.2, p. 296.
30 See the entry on James Hedderwick by Daniel Finkelstein in *Oxford DNB online*.
31 The following quotations are taken from Hedderwick, *Backward glances*, pp. 199–202.
32 Shakespeare, *Romeo and Juliet*, I, iv, 55–6.
33 Hedley, *Chopin correspondence* p. 343. Chopin to Grzymała, 1 October [1848].
34 Ganche, *Voyages avec Frédéric Chopin*, pp. 110–11.
35 Hedley, *Chopin correspondence*, p. 339. Chopin to his family in Warsaw, [10–19 August 1848].
36 Hedley, *Chopin correspondence*, p. 342. Chopin to Grzymała, 1 October [1848].
37 Hedley, *Chopin correspondence*, p. 346. Chopin to Grzymała, 3 October [1848].

9 Edinburgh
Concert in Hopetoun Rooms, Wednesday 4 October 1848

In Edinburgh, Chopin stayed once more at No. 10 Warriston Crescent, with Dr and Mrs Lyschiński. It was the time of year for the Caledonian Rout. 'All this week', he explained to Mme de Rozières, 'there will be race-meetings, entertainments, balls, etc. The local fashionable set, the Hunt Committee, arrange these fêtes every year. All the local aristocracy puts in an appearance.'[1]

Writing to Grzymała on Tuesday 3 October, Chopin seems almost cheerful. 'Today the weather is fine, even warm', he writes, 'and I feel better. I am to play here tomorrow evening, but I have not seen the hall or settled the programme.' Meeting old friends must have lifted his spirits. 'Jenny Lind and Mrs Grote (I met the latter at the station) have been here and have gone off to give a performance in Glasgow.' After Glasgow, Lind was due to travel to Dublin. Also passing through Edinburgh, says Chopin, were 'Grisi, Mario and Alboni and all the others'.[2]

Chopin's *soirée musicale* took place the following day, Wednesday 4 October, at 8.30 p.m. in the Hopetoun Rooms (see Figure 9.1). Originally built as 'function rooms' for the British Hotel, at No. 72 Queen Street, and later changing hands frequently, these were often used by celebrated musicians visiting Edinburgh, such as Paganini in 1833,[3] and Liszt in 1841.[4] As the *Scotsman* noted at the time: 'M. Liszt is considered the greatest master of the pianoforte who has ever visited this city, and is, we believe, unequalled by any performer now living . . . What Paganini was on the violin, Liszt is on the pianoforte – possessing perfect execution, directed by the highest genius.'[5]

The Hopetoun Rooms, adjacent to Queen Street Gardens, were designed by Thomas Hamilton in the early 1820s (see Figure 9.2).[6] The *Scotsman*, marking the opening of the rooms in 1826, described them enthusiastically.[7] Their three elegant saloons, which could be used independently, had a vaulted ceiling, 'tastefully divided into compartments in plaster embellished with pateras'. Above, there was 'the most striking novelty' in the lighting, by glazed lanterns. The central hall was lit by a rectangular lantern, with twelve caryatids. All told, it was a fine setting for a concert, providing excellent facilities for the performer and a congenial space for the audience.[8] In 1834, as Barry's Hotel, writes Joe Rock, 'the rooms were re-decorated by D R Hay in shades of Etruscan Brown with imitation jasper for the columns and blue for the coffered panels in the soffit of the lantern, in

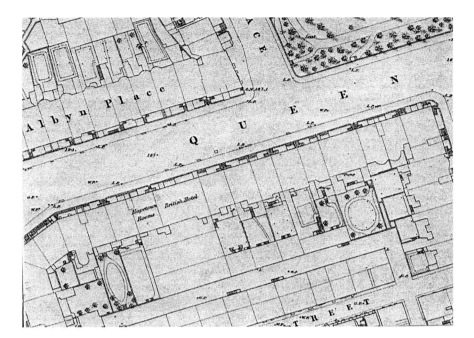

Figure 9.1 Ordnance Survey plan of Edinburgh (1849–53). Detail showing the Hopetoun Rooms and the British Hotel, Queen Street, and Queen Street Gardens (top right). National Library of Scotland, Edinburgh

imitation of the sky.'[9] Although the Hopetoun Rooms were demolished in 1967, by then part of The Mary Erskine School,[10] their character can be grasped from an undated sectional drawing (see Figure 9.3),[11] a sketch from the architect C.R. Cockerell's diary showing a lozenge-shaped hall with a domed ante-room at each end (see Figure 9.4), and photographs taken at the time of their destruction (see Figure 9.5).[12] An office building, Erskine House, now occupies the site, and a bronze plaque at the entrance in Queen Street commemorates Chopin's concert there. In 1975, a bronze head of Chopin by Józef Markiewicz was presented by the Frederick Chopin Society of Warsaw to the citizens of Edinburgh, as a memorial of the concert in the Hopetoun Rooms (see Plate 29). It is now in the Usher Hall, Edinburgh (see Plate 30).

Mrs Lyschińska told Frederick Niecks that 'Miss Stirling, who was afraid the hall might not be filled, bought fifty pounds' worth of tickets.'[13] As these were half-a-guinea each, her apprehension may have been justified, although this was the same price as had been charged in Glasgow; indeed, tickets at Chopin's recital at Mrs Sartoris' cost a guinea each, of which Cramer, Beale & Co sold a hundred and fifty. As Niecks put it, puzzlingly, 'Half-a-guinea had never been charged for

Figure 9.2 British Hotel, Queen Street, Edinburgh, which contained the Hopetoun Rooms, designed by Thomas Hamilton, circa 1825. The top storey was added in 1873 by MacGibbon and Ross, from Skinner, *A family unbroken* (1994), p. 34

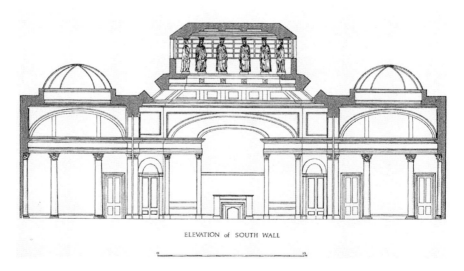

Figure 9.3 Hopetoun Rooms, Queen Street, Edinburgh. Section by Mairi Anna Birkland, from Rock, *Thomas Hamilton* (1984), p. 13

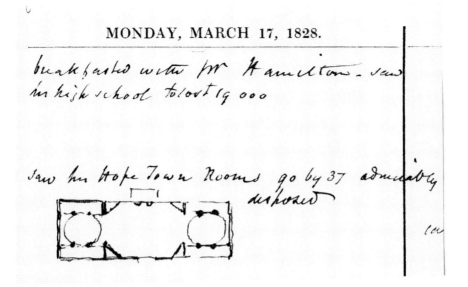

Figure 9.4 Hopetoun Rooms, Queen Street, Edinburgh. Sketch plan from C.R. Cockerell's diary, entry for Monday 17 March 1828, Series 7.9. CoC/10/3. Royal Institute of British Architects/British Architectural Library, London

Figure 9.5 Hopetoun Rooms, Queen Street, Edinburgh. Photograph of lantern, during demolition, 1967. Copyright Historic Environment Scotland (HES), Edinburgh

admission to a concert (which is probably overstating the case), and Chopin was little known.'[14] As in Glasgow, Chopin played the Broadwood Grand Pianoforte No. 17,001 (London, circa 1847).[15]

The programme, advertised in the *Scotsman* on Wednesday 4 October 1848 (the day of the concert), was similar to that for Chopin's Glasgow recital (see Figure 9.6). In Edinburgh, it was:

Andante et Impromptu
Études
Nocturnes et Berceuse
Grand[e] Valse Brillante
Andante precédé d'un Lango [*sic*]
Prelude, Ballade, Mazourkas et Valses

Tickets were available from Wood & Co, at No. 12 Waterloo Place, Edinburgh.

There was a significant difference from Chopin's Glasgow appearance: in Edinburgh he was the solo performer. He had never given a solo recital in a public

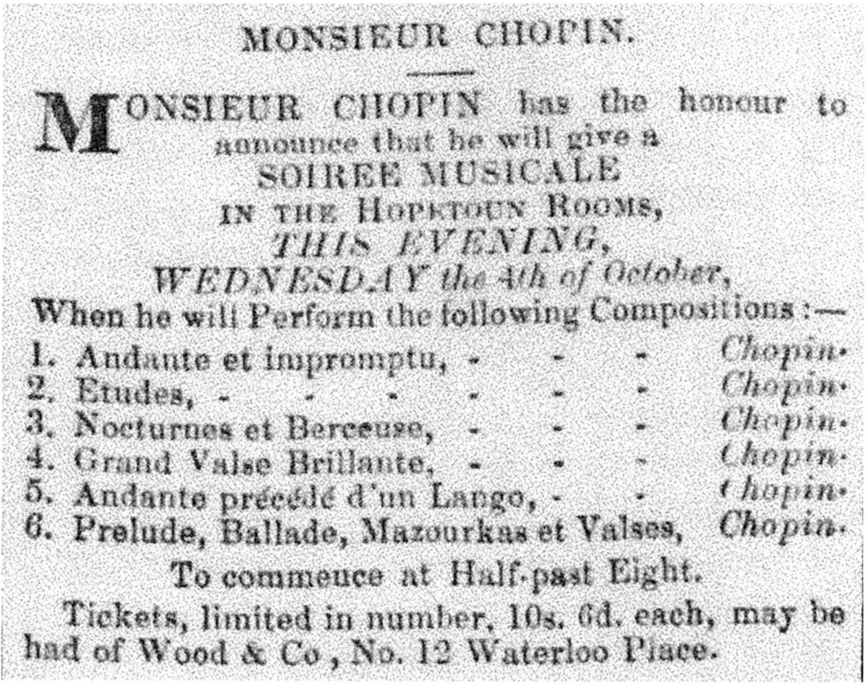

MONSIEUR CHOPIN.

MONSIEUR CHOPIN has the honour to announce that he will give a
SOIREE MUSICALE
IN THE HOPETOUN ROOMS,
THIS EVENING,
WEDNESDAY the 4th of October,
When he will Perform the following Compositions:—

1. Andante et impromptu, - - - *Chopin.*
2. Etudes, - - - - - - *Chopin.*
3. Nocturnes et Berceuse, - - - *Chopin.*
4. Grand Valse Brillante, - - - *Chopin.*
5. Andante précédé d'un Lango, - - *Chopin.*
6. Prelude, Ballade, Mazourkas et Valses, *Chopin.*

To commence at Half-past Eight.

Tickets, limited in number, 10s. 6d. each, may be had of Wood & Co, No. 12 Waterloo Place.

Figure 9.6 Advertisement for Chopin's *soirée musicale* in the Hopetoun Rooms, Edinburgh, on Wednesday 4 October 1848, from *The Scotsman*, 4 October 1848. Edinburgh City Library venue, at a time when to do so was still a rarity. It was a musical tradition not yet established.[16] In London, in the mid-to-late-1830s, Moscheles had pioneered classical *soirées*, and in the 1840s Sterndale Bennett established subscription concerts, which sowed the seeds of the 'recital', so-called.[17] This term owed its introduction within musical vocabulary to two solo concerts given by Liszt in London's Hanover Rooms in June 1840. These set the key features which were to define the 'recital' – 'performance from memory, a predominance of works for solo piano and few, or no, associate artists'.[18] In Edinburgh, Chopin was progressive enough to give a solo performance, and independent enough to limit himself to his own compositions.[19]

Although we cannot be sure of the exact pieces Chopin played in the Hopetoun Rooms, his Glasgow performance provides a guide.[20] Thus the Andante and Impromptu is likely to have been, as in the Merchants' Hall, the *Andante spianato* in G major (Op.22), and the Impromptu in F sharp major (Op.36). Similarly, following Glasgow, there was the Berceuse in D flat major (Op.57), and perhaps the Études from Op.25, and the two Nocturnes in F minor and E flat minor, respectively (Op.55), dedicated to Jane Stirling. Citing the *Edinburgh Evening Courant* and the *Musical World*, Niecks indicates that the Andante précédé d'un Largo consisted of 'a juxtaposition of two of [Chopin's] shorter compositions', but he does not suggest which.[21] Chopin introduces a striking addition in Edinburgh, however, with his inclusion of a Grande Valse Brillante, maybe the one in E flat major (Op.18). The debate continues. In 1947–8, Susan Brookshaw took up the challenge with her article in *Hinrichsen's musical year book*, entitled 'What did Chopin play in Edinburgh?', in which she provides further speculation.

There are signs that, although Chopin's recital in the Hopetoun Rooms was well received, the attendance was disappointing. Cuthbert Hadden proposes that the price of the tickets at half-a-guinea meant that the concert 'was attended almost solely by the nobility and the profession'.[22] Hadden was not surprised by this. 'Even if the charge for admission had been less than it was there would probably have been only a small audience', he wrote. 'Chopin was practically unknown in England; he was, we may say, wholly unknown in Scotland', so that Jane Stirling's fears 'were well-founded'. 'However much Chopin may have deplored her irksome attachment', Hadden concluded, 'she clearly proved a good friend to him while in the North.'[23] Furthermore, it is likely that some of Jane's friends and relatives, having heard Chopin play in Glasgow, may have decided not to go to his Edinburgh recital. And the Czartoryskis had already returned south.[24]

Reception of the concert itself by the press was positive. The *Scotsman* (7 October) observed that 'any pianist who undertakes to play alone to an audience for two hours, must, now-a-days, be a very remarkable one to succeed in sustaining attention and satisfying expectation. M. Chopin succeeded perfectly in both. He played his own music, which is that of a musician of genius. His playing of it was quite masterly in every respect.' The *Edinburgh Evening Courant* (7 October) indicated that there were Poles in the audience who recognized 'two Polish melodies'. 'That they went home to the hearts of such of the performer's compatriots as were present', the writer continues, 'was evident from the delight with which they hailed each forgotten melody with all its early associations, as it rang in their ears.' The *Edinburgh Advertiser* (6 October) endorsed the 'display of rank and beauty' to be seen in the Hopetoun Rooms on 'one of the most delightful musical evenings we have ever spent'. Indeed, it was a 'high compliment to the taste of the inhabitants of the Scottish metropolis', opined the *Caledonian Mercury* (12 October), that Chopin was induced to perform in the Hopetoun Rooms. 'This distinguished individual has for some weeks been resident in Scotland', said the columnist, 'and we trust that he has found amidst the magnificent scenery of the north, and the hospitality of the nobility and gentry, that repose for the exercise of his genius which the disturbed state of the Continent denies to men of the most peaceful habits and pursuits.'[25]

After his Edinburgh concert, Chopin spent a few days at Calder House, and later decided to accept Lady Belhaven's invitation to go to Wishaw. 'Madam', he wrote, on 16 October, 'if I may still take advantage of your invitation, on which day may I have the honour of presenting my respects at Wishaw? I am leaving Calder House today for Edinburgh . . . I shall stay three days at Warriston Crescent.' Writing at the same time to the pianist Adolphe Gutmann, in Heidelberg, Chopin tells him that his concert in Edinburgh seems to have gone well, yielding 'a little success and a little money'. Again he speaks of the 'red cap' ghost: 'It haunts the corridors at midnight with its red cap – I haunt them with my doubts and hesitations.' Following Wishaw, Chopin went to Hamilton Palace to stay with the Duke and Duchess of Hamilton.[26]

On 30 October, after his visit to the Hamiltons, Chopin told Grzymała that in Edinburgh 'cholera is on our doorstep.'[27] Composition was impossible. 'What has become of my art? and where have I squandered my heart?', Chopin laments. 'The critical point', as Jim Samson points out, 'is that whereas Sand had facilitated his creative work, Stirling suffocated it.'[28] At Hamilton Palace, the composer had respite from the attentions of Jane Stirling and Mrs Erskine, but once he was back in Edinburgh they sought him out at No. 10 Warriston Crescent. Here, too, Dr Lyschiński gave him 'homeopathic treatment'. 'My good Scots ladies, whom I have not seen for a week or two, will be coming here today', he complains. 'They would like me to stay longer and go trotting from one Scottish palace to another . . . They are kind-hearted but so tiresome!! – may God be with them!' The Stirling sisters were relentless in their pursuit. 'I get letters from them every day but I never answer a single one', he complains, 'and as soon as I go anywhere they come running after me if they possibly can.'

Small wonder that some people believed Chopin and Jane Stirling were to be married. 'But there must be some sort of physical attraction', Chopin writes, 'and the unmarried one is far too much like me. How can one kiss oneself?'[29] It is not a prospective wife, but his mother and sisters in Poland who are his principal concern: 'God fill their hearts always with happy thoughts!' As for Jane, Chopin considers himself 'nearer to a coffin than a bridal bed'. He tells Grzymała that he is returning to London, as Lord Dudley Stuart has asked him to play 'at a benefit-concert for the Poles, to be given before the ball begins'. The next day, 31 October, he took the train from Edinburgh to London, perhaps by the Scottish

Central Railway, which had started to run express trains between Perth and London (via Edinburgh) on the second of that month.[30] Chopin's Scottish adventure was at an end.

Notes

1. Hedley, *Chopin correspondence*, p. 346. Chopin to Mme de Rozières, 2 October 1848.
2. Hedley, *Chopin correspondence*, p. 346. Chopin to Grzymała, 3 October [1848].
3. See Macdonald, 'Paganini, Mendelssohn and Turner in Scotland', pp. 31–3, 35, 36–7.
4. Allsobrook, *Liszt: my travelling circus life*, p. 164.
5. *Scotsman*, 23 January 1841, quoted by Williams, *Portrait of Liszt*, p. 159.
6. For Thomas Hamilton see Colvin, *Dictionary*, pp. 474–7; and *Dictionary of Scottish architects online*, under Thomas Hamilton.
7. For a full description of the Hopetoun Rooms, see Rock, *Thomas Hamilton*, pp. 11–14. See also Colvin, *Dictionary*, p. 475, and *Dictionary of Scottish architects online*, under 'British Hotel and Hopetoun Rooms'. There is an extensive collection of photographs of the Hopetoun Rooms at the RCAHMS, Edinburgh. A new top floor was added in 1873 by David MacGibbon. For Queen Street Gardens, see Byrom, *Edinburgh New Town gardens*, *passim*, particularly p. 167.
8. The *Scotsman*, quoted by Rock, *Thomas Hamilton*, pp. 11–12. Joe Rock gives no date for this description, but on p. 12 he cites the *Scotsman* of 7 July 1824, 4 January 1826, 25 February 1826, 7 May 1831, and 23 August 1834. An undated, anonymous watercolour of the interior of the Hopetoun Rooms is reproduced in Rock, *Thomas Hamilton*, p. 14.
9. Rock, *Thomas Hamilton* p. 12.
10. For the Mary Erskine School, see Skinner, *A family unbroken*, pp. 60, 149. According to Mrs Skinner (p. 149), in the hall where Chopin performed, Alfred Cortot 'played the same pieces again one hundred and one years later'.
11. Reproduced in Rock, *Thomas Hamilton*, p. 13 (plate 5).
12. British Architectural Library / Royal Institute of British Architects, London. Diary of C.R. Cockerell, February 1828 – June 1829 [Monday 17 March 1828], Series 7.9. Coc/10/3 [see Figure 9.4].
13. Niecks, *Chopin*, vol.2, p. 298.
14. Niecks, *Chopin*, vol.2, p. 298.
15. After the concert, writes Niecks, it was 'sold for £30 above the price. Thus, at any rate, runs the legend.' Its sale, in 1849, to 'Wood', is recorded in the Broadwood Archives, Surrey History Centre (Woking), 2185/JB. According to Wainwright, *Broadwood by appointment*, p. 164, at that time a Broadwood grand in rosewood cost 155 guineas.
16. See Weber, *The great transformation of musical taste*, pp. 245–51.
17. The following paragraph is based on Ritterman and Weber, 'Origins of the piano recital in England, 1830–1870', pp. 175–82.
18. Ritterman and Weber, 'Origins of the piano recital in England, 1830–1870', p. 179.
19. Weber, *The great transformation of musical taste*, p. 248, points out that 'Charles Hallé performed more solo recitals than anyone else between 1855 and 1870'.
20. For discussion of Chopin's concert programme, see Niecks, *Chopin*, vol.2, pp. 297–302; Kallberg, *Chopin at the boundaries*, pp. 150–2, 278, nn.37–9; and Brookshaw, 'What did Chopin play in Edinburgh', *Hinrichsen's musical year book*, vols.4–5 (1947–8), pp. 192–3. Hedley, *Chopin*, p. 106, discusses the Hopetoun Rooms concert on pp. 111–12.
21. Niecks, *Chopin*, vol.2, pp. 298–9. The text of the critique from the *Musical World*, 14 October 1848, quoted by Niecks, is given in Atwood, *Pianist from Warsaw*, p. 259. Agresta, 'Chopin in music criticism', p. 498, also provides a text of the article but surprisingly omits the sentence that gives a list of the pieces Chopin played.

22 Hadden, *Chopin*, pp. 149–50.
23 Hadden, *Chopin*, pp. 149–50.
24 Chopin's letter to Grzymała of 1 October from Keir indicates that they were then going back to the Continent. See Niecks, *Chopin*, vol.2, pp. 299–300, and Hedley, *Chopin correspondence*, p. 343.
25 For the texts of these reviews, see Atwood, *Pianist from Warsaw*, pp. 255–9.
26 Hedley, *Chopin correspondence*, editorial note on p. 347.
27 This and the following Chopin quotations in this paragraph are from Hedley, *Chopin correspondence*, pp. 348–50. Chopin to Grzymała, 30 October [1848].
28 Samson, *Chopin*, p. 257.
29 This and the following Chopin quotations in this paragraph are from Hedley, *Chopin correspondence*, pp. 349–50. Chopin to Grzymała, 30 October [1848].
30 See Nowaczyk, 'Chopin mknął Szkocji', in which the author cites and illustrates an advertisement for the Scottish Central Railway from the *Scotsman*, no.2999 (4 October 1848).

10 London

Concert in Guildhall, Thursday 16 November 1848

Once back in London, Chopin stayed first with Henry Fowler Broadwood at No. 46 Bryanston Square and, as his diary shows, moved on 3 November to No. 4 St James's Place, off St James's Street, Piccadilly.[1] He remained there until leaving for Paris on 23 November. Chopin's rooms at St James's Place were found for him by Karol Szulczewski, while Princess Marcelina Czartoryska lived at his former address, No. 48 Dover Street, nearby.[2] Lord Dudley Coutts Stuart resided not far away at No. 34 St James's Place, from 1847 to 1850.[3]

No. 4 St James's Place was one of a terrace of brick-faced houses built in 1685–6, with 'barrel-vaulted cellars beneath the street pavement, three storeys and a garret in front, and five storeys at the back'. Since its original construction, an extra storey has been added, and the street front stuccoed (see Plates 31 and 32). Internally, as late as 1960, the *Survey of London* recorded that No. 4 St James's Place was notable for its staircase and panelled rooms, and in the 1970s a further restoration of the house included refacing of the street front.[4] A blue plaque was erected by the Greater London Council in 1981 (see Plate 33). It bears the inscription:

> From this
> house in 1848
> FREDERIC
> CHOPIN
> 1810–1849
> went to Guildhall to
> give his last public
> performance

The plaque marks the final stage of Chopin's visits to Britain.[5]

At No. 4 St James's Place, Henry Fowler Broadwood provided Chopin with Grand Pianoforte No. 17,047 (London, 1847), now at Hatchlands, which the composer had used for his London recitals at Stafford House, Mrs Sartoris', and Lord Falmouth's, and at the Gentlemen's Concert Hall in Manchester (see Plate 10).[6] On 13 November, Broadwood took this piano away to deliver it to Guildhall for Chopin's performance there, and replaced it at No. 4 St James's Place with Grand

Pianoforte No. 17,284 (London, circa 1847).[7] It was during his stay in St James's Place that Chopin must have signed the Pleyel Grand Pianoforte No. 13,716 (of rosewood, with inlaid veins of copper) with the inscription 'Fr/Chopin, / 15 novembre 1848'. This is now in the Museum of the Collegium Maius, Cracow, and may have been owned by Jane Stirling (see Plate 34).[8]

Before Chopin left Scotland, he had told Gutmann of his reservations about returning to the metropolis. 'The cholera approaches', he complained. 'London is full of fogs and spleen.'[9] Back in London, his health remained poor. On 3 November, Chopin wrote to Dr Lyschiński, in Edinburgh. 'Yesterday I received your kind letter, with a letter from Heidelberg', he noted. 'Here I am as incapable as I was with you, and also have the same affection for you as I had.' After sending his compliments to Lyschiński's wife and neighbours, Chopin comments: 'God bless you! I embrace you heartily.'[10] Chopin added that he had seen Princess Marcelina Czartoryska, who enquired after the doctor 'most affectionately'; living at No. 48 Dover Street, Chopin's former address, the Princess had only to cross Piccadilly, and into St James's Street, to find herself virtually at Chopin's door.[11]

In London, Chopin again turned for medical help to Dr Henry V. Malan, physician to the Marylebone Homeopathic Dispensary, and a friend of Jane Stirling and Mrs Erskine.[12] Letters from Chopin to Grzymała, Mlle de Rozières, and Solange Clésinger describe his last weeks in Britain.[13] 'I have been ill for eighteen days, since the day I reached London', the composer told Grzymała, following his Guildhall recital. 'I have not been out at all, having had such a cold, with headaches, suffocation and all my bad symptoms.' Dr Malan comes to see him every day. 'I have an awful headache in addition to my cough and choking-spasms. The really thick fogs have not yet begun, but in the mornings I already have to have the windows opened to get a breath of fresh air.' Luckily, Chopin has friends who give him every attention. 'I regularly see Szulczewski, good fellow, Broadwood and Mrs Erskine (who is here with Miss Stirling). They followed me here, just as I told you they would.' Most of all, however, Chopin sees Prince Alexander Czartoryski and his wife: 'Princess Marcelina is so kind that she visits me practically every day, just as if I were in hospital.'[14] His neighbour, Lord Dudley Coutts Stuart, also calls. As Chopin told Mlle de Rozières later, he had remained in his bedroom, in his dressing gown, since returning to London from Edinburgh, apart from the one occasion on 16 November when he went out 'to play for our Polish compatriots'.[15]

Chopin's performance in Guildhall on Thursday 16 November was part of the Annual Grand Dress and Fancy Ball and Concert in aid of the funds of the Literary Association of the Friends of Poland. The ball was a regular occurrence on London's social scene, with Lord Dudley Coutts Stuart playing a significant part in it; in this instance, Princess Marcelina Czartoryska, acting as an agent on behalf of the Hôtel Lambert, also helped in its organisation.[16] The *Daily News* of 1 November 1848 carried this advertisement:

> Grand Polish Ball and Concert at Guildhall, under Royal and distinguished patronage, and on a scale of more than usual magnificence, will take place on Thursday, the 16th of November, by permission of the Mayor and Corporation

of the City of London; particulars of which will be shortly announced to the public.

Two weeks later, on 15 November, the *Daily News* duly explained that for the event 'the magnificent decorations used on the Lord Mayor's day' will be preserved, and that 'the concert will comprise the most eminent vocalists'. Tickets (refreshments included) were 21/- for a lady and gentleman, 15/- for a gentleman, and 10/6 for a lady. No mention here, it will be seen, of the names of Chopin or the other performers.[17]

It must be said that the ball was greeted with some opposition, notably from *The Times*, which felt that, in the tumultous year of 1848, Polish aspirations seriously threatened peace in Europe.[18] Parliament that year had cut its subsidy to the Polish refugees, a sign of the anti-Polish sentiment then pervading the country. To many Englishmen, William Atwood writes, 'it seemed that the Poles were deliberately fomenting strife throughout Europe in the hope that a disruption of the current balance of power might allow Poland to reemerge as an independent nation once more.' Lord Dudley Coutts Stuart was given the derisive title of 'King of the Poles', and London papers lambasted the Polish refugees, with the forthcoming ball at Guildhall singled out for special attack: 'Why is it, one of the papers argued, that the "lazy Pole, who eschews employment", gets treated to "the substantial crumbs that fall from the well-decked tables of a civic ball", while an Englishman gets packed off to the workhouse whenever he is down on his luck.' Lord Coutts Stuart, who had been warned that there might be violence at the ball, took the precaution of stationing police both within and outside Guildhall.[19]

Guildhall was begun in the fifteenth century, erected for the government of the City of London (see Figure 10.1).[20] Internally, it features a single-span roof, the second largest structure in the medieval city after St Paul's, and the largest civic hall in England. Surrounding buildings included a chapel and the mayor's court, which (with the hall itself) was refitted after the Great Fire. In 1788–9, George Dance, Junior, completed his entrance porch, with its eclectic mixture of Gothic, classical, and oriental motifs.[21] Although much altered later, and still in existence, this striking feature was still in its early form in Chopin's time, and can be seen in Thomas Hosmer Shepherd's view of 1828.[22] Also designed by George Dance, Junior, but demolished in 1908, was the Common Council Chamber (1777–8), with its spare, top-lit central dome which so influenced Sir John Soane (see Figure 10.2).[23] Here, it seems, Chopin played.

An engraving of 1842 or so, from a study by Shepherd, and published in the part-work *London interiors: a grand national exhibition* (London, 1841–4), illustrates its character. As befits a centre of civic government, the Council Chamber has portraits lining the walls, and a gallery of spectators in attendance, with people waiting to present petitions at the bar. A commentary, published in *London interiors*, explains that 'it is not an infrequent occurrence for individuals to be admitted to the Bar of the Court, in order to address the members in support of petitions presented . . . or, perhaps, Lord Dudley Stuart approaches the Bar, to

218 *London: concert in Guildhall*

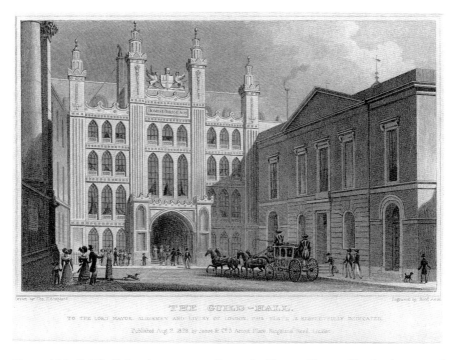

Figure 10.1 Guildhall, London, entrance. Drawn by Thomas Hosmer Shepherd, engraved by Robert Acon, 1828. Private collection

ask for the use of the Guildhall for a ball in favour of the distressed Poles, and to entreat the patronage of the Corporation of London in favour of the object.'[24]

To Frederick Niecks, echoing Fiorentino, Chopin's concert at Guildhall 'may be truly called the swan's song'.[25] The *Illustrated London News* of 18 November observed that 'the elegant decorations with which the hall was fitted up for Lord Mayor's Day were retained for the present occasion: and the vast apartment when brIlliantly lighted, presented a "coup d'oeil" of singular beauty.'[26] The day after it took place, on 17 November, *The Times*' report on the event referred to the dancing, 'Mr Adams' excellent band', the refreshment rooms, 'the gay costumes of some Highlanders and Spaniards', and Lord Dudley Coutts Stuart, 'the great lion of the evening'. The concert, *The Times* noted, 'was much the same as on former anniversaries'. There is not a word about Chopin.[27] Other accounts similarly contain little or no mention of his playing. A sad response, indeed, after he had dutifully roused himself from his sickbed to support his friends and fellow-countrymen.[28]

Music critics reflected this regret. Francis Hueffer, in his book *Musical studies*, quotes 'one present at the occasion' as explaining that 'the people hot from dancing, who went into the room where he played, were but little in the humour

Figure 10.2 Court of Common Council, Guildhall, presentation of a petition. Drawn by Thomas Hosmer Shepherd, engraved by Henry Melville, [1842]. Private collection

to pay attention, and anxious to return to their amusement.' As for Chopin, 'he was in the last stage of exhaustion, and the affair resulted in disappointment. His playing at such a place was a well-intentioned mistake.'[29] This view was endorsed by Henry Fothergill Chorley, in his obituary of Chopin in the *Athenaeum*, on 27 October 1849. The pianist's performance at Guildhall, he wrote, was 'at the instance of ill-judged solicitation . . . At such a miscellaneous gathering the name of so select an artist was hardly an attraction: and the gossip of the indifferent guests drowned his beautiful playing at his last public performance.'[30] 'What a sad conclusion to a noble artistic career!', Niecks adds.[31]

What of the concert itself? The *Illustrated London News* of 18 November records that it was conducted by Julius Benedict and Lindsay Sloper, and that they and the other musicians took no fee. Chopin 'performed some of his beautiful compositions with much applause. The dancing commenced soon after 9 o'clock, and was continued with unabated vigour till an advanced hour in the morning.'[32] Regrettably, we do not know the identity of Chopin's 'beautiful compositions', although Niecks recalls that Sloper 'remembered that Chopin played among other things the *Études* in A flat and F minor' (Op.25, nos 1 and 2).[33] Chopin used the Broadwood Grand Pianoforte No. 17,047 (London, 1847), now at Hatchlands.[34] Poles present included Princess Marcelina Czartoryska who, the next day, told her uncle, Prince Adam Jerzy Czartoryski, about the event. 'The concert went very well', she wrote. 'Chopin played like an angel, much too well for the inhabitants of the City, whose artistic education is a little problematic.'[35]

As a commemoration of the Guildhall recital, and of a memorial concert held on 20 November 1978, the Byron Society, the Anglo-Polish Society, and the Chopin Society presented a plaster bust of Chopin by Jarosław Giercarz Alfer, which is now in the Guildhall Art Gallery.[36] Another version of this bust is held at the Royal Academy of Music, London (see Figure 10.3). On 26 February 1975, a full-length bronze statue of Chopin was unveiled outside the Royal Festival Hall, London; it is by the Polish sculptor Marian Kubica, who won the commission following a competition in Poland. After a period in storage, and restoration, the statue was again unveiled on 18 May 2011. It supplements the casket inside the Royal Festival Hall, containing earth from Chopin's birthplace at Żelowa Wola, which was presented by the Polish government in 1974, on the 125th anniversary of the composer's death.[37]

It was due to Dr Malan's ministrations that Chopin was able to perform at Guildhall. 'But as soon as I had played I came home', he wrote, 'and could not sleep all night. I have an awful headache in addition to my cough and choking-spasms.'

Figure 10.3 Chopin. Plaster bust by Jarosław Giercarz Alfer, 1978. Presented by Her Royal Highness Princess Alice, Duchess of Gloucester, 1979. Royal Academy of Music, London

Lord Coutts Stuart, living nearby at No. 34 St James's Place, was one of the friends who came to see him the day after his concert.[38] In his misery, Chopin's hopes of going back to Paris intensified. Yet, at times, in his gloomier moments, it seemed pointless to do so. 'What's the use of my returning!' 'Why doesn't God finish me off straightaway, instead of killing me by inches with this fever of indecision?', he asked Grzymała.

> Besides, my Scots ladies are getting on my nerves again. Mrs Erskine, who is a very devout Protestant, bless her, would perhaps like to make a Protestant out of me. She brings me her Bible, speaks of my soul and marks psalms for me to read. She is devout and kind, but she is very much concerned about my soul – she's always going on about the next world being better than this one – I know it all by heart, and I answer by quoting from Holy Scripture. I explain that I know and understand it all.

If he had his health, and two lessons a day, Chopin adds, he would have enough to live on decently in London.[39] As it is, he longs to return to Paris: 'One more day here and I shall not die but GO MAD – my Scots ladies are so tiresome! May the hand of God protect them! They have got their grip on me and I cannot tear them off!' The only people who keep him alive are Princess Marcelina, her family, and 'good Szulczewski'.[40]

Chopin never ceases to be sorry for Solange, in her alienation from her mother, George Sand, and writes to her sympathetically about the possibility of her husband, Auguste Clésinger, finding work in England and Russia.[41] But the strongest theme of Chopin's letters in late 1848 is his return to Paris. Luckily, he was able again to rent one of the apartments at No. 9 place d'Orléans, looked after by Mme Etienne.[42] He gives precise instructions to Grzymała about its preparation:

> Please get them to air the bedclothes and pillows. See that they buy plenty of fir-cones – Mme Etienne must not try to economise – so that I can get warmed right through as soon as I arrive . . . Have the carpets laid and the curtains hung. I will pay Perricher, the furnisher, at once, You might even tell Pleyel to send me any kind of piano on Thursday evening – see that he is paid for the transport. On Friday, get them to buy a bunch of violets to scent my drawing-room – let me find a little poetry when I come home, just for a moment as I go through on my way to the bedroom where I know I am going to lie a long, long time.[43]

'I can't wait for the time when I shall be able to breathe more easily, understand what people are saying and see a few friendly faces', he had told Mlle de Rozières.[44] The day before he left London, Chopin admitted to Solange that he was going back to Paris 'scarcely able to crawl, and weaker than you have ever seen me. The London doctors urge me to go. My face is swollen with neuralgia; I can neither breathe nor sleep.' Despite suffering a relapse since his Guildhall concert, Chopin promised to return to London the next year. 'Sir James Clark, the

Queen's physician, has just been to see me and give me his blessing', Chopin told Solange (see Plate 35). 'And so I am going back to lie whimpering at the Place d'Orléans while hoping for better times.'[45]

Chopin's companion on his journey was Leonard Niedźwiedski, at one time honorary librarian in London of the Literary Association of the Friends of Poland, and later librarian of the Polish Library in Paris. Accompanied by Niedźwiedski, Chopin left London on Thursday 23 November, one imagines by one of the South Eastern Railway company trains to Folkestone from London Bridge Station.[46] Princess Marcelina, who had comforted Chopin during the previous few weeks in London, saw him off, accompanied by her husband, Prince Aleksander, and their son Marcel.[47] 'Broadwood had made the same arrangements as for his journey to Scotland', Hedley explains. 'The seat opposite Chopin was reserved, so that he could put his feet up. Niedźwiedski describes in his diary how Chopin had a kind of nervous seizure just as the train moved out. His friend feared he was going to die, but he came round.'[48] When they reached Folkestone (see Figure 10.4), they had a meal of soup, roast beef, and wine at an inn – perhaps the Pavilion Hotel, which the South Eastern Railway Company had opened in 1843 for the benefit of passengers using the New Commercial Steam Packet Company's service to Boulogne.[49] Chopin, who was seasick on the crossing, was only too glad to reach the French port, and they spent the night there.[50] The next day they travelled to Paris, on a journey subsequently celebrated by the photographer Edouard Baldus, in his

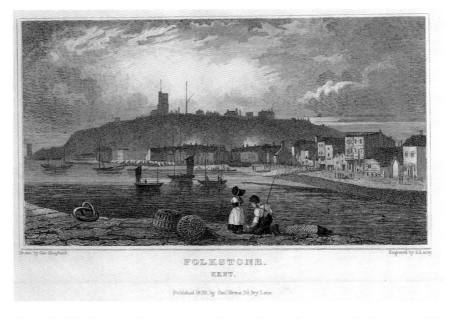

Figure 10.4 Folkestone, Kent. Drawn by George Shepherd, engraved by S. Lacey, 1829. Private collection

album *Chemin de fer du Nord*, published to mark the visit of Queen Victoria to France in 1855.[51] An anecdote, related by Niecks, illustrates Chopin's poor opinion of the English. When they had left Boulogne, and Chopin had been for some time looking at the French landscape through which they were passing, he said to Niedźwiedzki: 'Do you see the cattle in this meadow? 'Ça a plus d'intelligence que les Anglais.'[52]

Chopin and Niedźwiedzki reached Paris about midday on Friday 24 November 1848.[53]

Notes

1 Hedley, *Chopin correspondence*, editorial note on p. 350. The street index in the *Post office directory, London 1851*, lists four occupants of No. 4 St James's Place, one of whom, Miss Margaret Owen, has a 'lodging house'. For St James's Place, see Bradley and Pevsner, *London 6: Westminster*, pp. 620–4; *Survey of London*, vol.30, *The parish of St James Westminster*, part 1, *South of Piccadilly* (1960), pp. 511–13; and Weinreb, Hibbert, and Keay, *London encyclopaedia*, pp. 769–70.

2 Zamoyski, *Chopin*, pp. 269–70, and Zamoyski, *Chopin: prince of the romantics*, p. 280. Princess Marcelina Czartoryska's descriptions of Chopin's time in London in 1848, in French, are contained in letters in BCz (Cracow), 6328 (Ew.841), ff.529–50, dated 18 September, 10 November, 17 November, 18 December 1848, sent from No. 48 Dover Street, Piccadilly, to her uncle, Prince Adam Jerzy Czartoryski. Two letters of 1849, from No. 130 Marine Parade, Brighton (one in French, the other in Polish), are on ff.551–7. I thank Janusz Nowak, at the Biblioteka XX Czartoryskich, Cracow, for showing me these letters, and copying them for me.

3 *Kelly's directory, London 1848*, and *Survey of London*, vol.30 (1960), p. 512.

4 Quotations in this paragraph are from *Survey of London*, vol.30 (1960), p. 512.

5 For Chopin's blue plaque at No. 4 St James's Place, see Cole, *Lived in London*, pp. 474–5, and map 12. For both No. 4 St James's Place, and No. 99 Eaton Place, see Rennison, *London blue plaque guide*, p. 40, and Sumeray, *Discovering London plaques*, p. 44. They are also referred to on p. 147 of the Chopin entry in Sadie, *Calling on the composer*, pp. 140–9. The location of the plaques can be seen in Sumeray, *Track the plaque*, pp. 33, 46.

6 Broadwood Archives, Surrey History Centre (Woking), 2185/JB. For assistance at the Surrey History Centre I am grateful to Robert Simonson.

7 Broadwood Archives, Surrey History Centre (Woking), 2185/JB. Documentation of the movements of Broadwood pianos is contained in the Porters' Books. Probably circa 23 November, Broadwoods took back their Grand Pianoforte No. 17,284. [Add Cobbe material.] Apparently Broadwood reserved Grand Pianoforte No. 17,047 for Chopin, in the hope that he would return to London the next year. It was ultimately sold, and Hipkins had to borrow it for the International Inventions Exhibition of 1885. The subsequent history of the piano, by Alec Cobbe, is given in Macintyre, 'Chopin's true sound', *passim*.

8 Collegium Maius (Cracow), MUJ 6887–30/VIII. The piano is described and illustrated in Ludmiła Bularz-Różycka and Barbara Lewińska, *Krakowskie Chopiniana* (Cracow: Muzeum Uniwersytetu Jagiellońskiego, 1999), pp. 36–7. Could this piano have been in Jane Stirling's London home, in Bentinck Street, and signed by Chopin there? It was bought by Ganche from Mrs Houston at Johnstone Castle.

9 Opieński, *Chopin's letters*, p. 389 (no.266). Chopin to Gutmann, 16 Oct[ober] 1848.

10 Opieński, *Chopin's letters*, p. 398 (no.272). Chopin enclosed a letter to Jane Stirling, 'who doubtless is still at Barnton', asking Lyschiński to forward it to her. An alternative translation appears in Niecks, *Chopin*, vol.2, p. 302. The original letter is in

224 *London: concert in Guildhall*

Edinburgh University Library, Dc.2/82/1 [see Figure 5.12], and is accompanied by a transcript of the Polish text by Mrs Frederick Niecks. Mrs Niecks adds an explanatory note about Chopin's monogram on his seal, which consists of three Cs in the form of horns (with mouthpieces and bells) intertwined. The seal itself is in the Collegium Maius (Cracow). Sydow, *KFC*, vol.2, p. 285, gives a transcript of the Polish text of the letter, and Sydow and Chainaye, *Chopin correspondance*, vol.3, p. 398, offer a French translation. See also the discussion of the letter in Krystyna Kobylańska, 'Odnaleziony list Chopina', *Ruch muzyczny*, vol.34, no.26 (30 December 1990), pp. 1,7, which contains a different version of it.

11 As this letter implies, Princess Marcelina must have met Dr Lyschiński in Edinburgh.
12 Malan held MD degrees from Tübingen (1839) and Aberdeen (1845), and practised in Geneva, Paris, and London. He spent eighteen months at the Hahnemann's homeopathic clinic in Paris. His wife was a distant relative of the Countess of Gainsborough, at whose house Chopin played. A synopsis of Malan's career, including a list of his publications, appears in the *Homeopathic medical directory* for 1853. Bernard Leary kindly alerted me to this reference.
13 In addition, Chopin wrote two letters to Dr Malan, in French, during this period – one inscribed 'Londres, novembre 1848', the other of a similar date. See Sydow and Chainaye, *Chopin correspondance*, vol.3, pp. 402 (no.746), 403 (no.748). From these, one might deduce that Dr Malan declined to charge Chopin any fee for his services.
14 Hedley, *Chopin correspondence*, p. 350. Chopin to Grzymała, 17–18 [November 1848]. According to the index, this is the only reference to Dr Malan (here spelled 'Mallan') in Hedley's volume.
15 Hedley, *Chopin correspondence*, p. 352. Chopin to Mlle de Rozières, 19 [really 20] November [1848].
16 Zamoyski, *Chopin*, p. 270, and Zamoyski, *Chopin: prince of the romantics*, pp. 280–1.
17 These quotations from the *Daily News* are taken from Niecks, *Chopin*, vol.2, p. 304.
18 Zamoyski, *Chopin*, p. 270, and Zamoyski, *Chopin: prince of the romantics*, p. 281.
19 Atwood, *Pianist from Warsaw*, pp. 185–6. The newspaper quoted by Atwood here is *John Bull*, 18 November 1848.
20 For the architecture of Guildhall, see Bradley and Pevsner, *London 1: the City of London*, pp. 298–306, especially p. 298; Colvin, *Dictionary*, pp. 297–8, 711; and Stroud, *George Dance*, pp. 113–23, and plates 35–39b.
21 For George Dance, Junior, see Colvin, *Dictionary*, pp. 295–9, and Stroud, *George Dance, passim*.
22 See Bradley and Pevsner, *London 1: the City of London*, pp. 299–300.
23 See the coverage of Dance and the Common Council Chamber in Stroud, *George Dance*, pp. 113–16, and plates 35, 36; Summerson, *Architecture in Britain*, p. 418, and plate 361 (from Pugin and Rowlandson, *Microcosm of London*, 1808); and Summerson, *Georgian London*, pp. 155–6, and plates 74, 75.
24 *London interiors*, vol.1 (1841), p. 40 (under 'Guildhall').
25 Niecks, *Chopin*, vol.2, p. 304. Niecks describes the Guildhall concert on pp. 304–5. A 'documentary and philatelic exhibition' marking the 150th anniversary of the death of Chopin was held in the Polish Institute and Sikorski Museum, London, in 1999. It was organized by the Chopin Society and the Polish Philatelic Society in Great Britain, and included a display of the description of the concert and ball at Guildhall, taken from the *Annual report of the Literary Association of the Friends of Poland* (1849).
26 Quoted by Atwood, *Pianist from Warsaw*, p. 259. See also Bone, *Jane Stirling*, p. 86.
27 Niecks, *Chopin*, vol.2, p. 305.
28 See Hedley, *Chopin*, p. 112.
29 Hueffer, *Musical studies*, p. 64. This quotation originally appeared on p. 393 in Hueffer's essay, 'Chopin', in the *Fortnightly Review*, new series, vol.22 (1877), pp. 377–94.
30 *Athenaeum*, 27 October 1849 (no.1148), p. 1090.

31 Niecks, *Chopin*, vol.2, p. 305.
32 Quoted in Atwood, *Pianist from Warsaw*, p. 260. On pp. 259–60 are listed the names of ten female and eight male singers who, as well as Benedict and Sloper, 'generously volunteered their gratuitous services' at the concert.
33 Niecks, *Chopin*, vol.2, p. 305.
34 Hipkins, *International inventions exhibition*, p. 12. See also Broadwood Archives, Surrey History Centre (Woking), 2185/JB.
35 Letter, in French, of 17 November 1848, the day after the concert in Guildhall, from 48 Dover Street, Piccadilly, in BCz (Cracow), 6328 (Ew.841), ff.541–4. This letter is almost indecipherable, and the text here is taken from the translation given in Zamoyski, *Chopin*, p. 270, and Zamoyski, *Chopin: prince of the romantics*, p. 281.
36 Catalogue entry in Knight, *Works of art of the corporation of London*, p. 329.
37 For the original unveiling of the statue in 1975, see Mullaly, 'Memorial to Chopin at Festival Hall', *passim*; for the 2011 unveiling, see the website of The Polish Heritage Society (www.polishheritage.co.uk).
38 Hedley, *Chopin correspondence*, pp. 350–1. Chopin to Grzymała, 17–18 [November 1848]. Coutts Stuart's address is in *Kelly's directory, London 1848*.
39 Hedley, *Chopin correspondence*, pp. 351–2. Chopin to Grzymała, 17–18 [November 1848].
40 Hedley, *Chopin correspondence*, p. 353. Chopin to Grzymała, [21 November 1848].
41 Hedley, *Chopin correspondence*, pp. 353–5. Chopin to Solange Clésinger, 22 [November 1848]. 'Not a day has passed when I have not tried to write to you', says Chopin (p. 353).
42 For Chopin's instructions to Grzymała about finding an apartment in Paris see Hedley, *Chopin correspondence*, p. 351. Chopin to Grzymała, 17–18 [November 1848].
43 Hedley, *Chopin correspondence*, p. 353. Chopin to Grzymała, [21 November 1848].
44 Hedley, *Chopin correspondence* p. 352. Chopin to Mlle de Rozières, 19 [really 20] November [1848].
45 Hedley, *Chopin correspondence*, p. 354. Chopin to Solange Clésinger, 22 [November 1848]. For Sir James Clark, 1st Bt, see the entry by R.A.L. Agnew, in *Oxford DNB online*.
46 For the South Eastern Railway Company, see Simmons and Biddle, *Oxford companion to British railway history*, pp. 461–2.
47 For a description of Chopin's departure, see Zamoyski, *Chopin*, p. 271. On p. 318, n.65, Zamoyski quotes his source as Leonard Niedźwiedzki, Private Diary, Library of the Polish Academy of Sciences, Kórnik, MS 2416, p. 278.
48 Hedley, *Chopin correspondence*, editorial comment on p. 355, citing Niedźwiedski's diary. Hedley does not mention a servant, but Niedêwiedzki told Niecks that Chopin was accompanied by one, and that 'during the journey the invalid suffered greatly from frequent attacks of breathlessness.' See Niecks, *Chopin*, vol.2, p. 306. In his letters, Chopin makes allusions to needing accommodation for a servant on his return to Paris.
49 See Carter, *British railway hotels*, pp. 28–9, 123. For the steamers sailing from Folkestone and Dover, see Duckworth and Langmuir, *Railway and other steamers*, pp. 127–32.
50 Hedley, *Chopin correspondence*, editorial comment on p. 355.
51 This consisted of a map of the route, illustrated with large photographs of the towns, monuments, and sites the Queen would see. See Rice, *Parisian views*, pp. 194–207, particularly plate 6.4. More generally, see Daniel, *The photographs of Edouard Baldus*, *passim*. Writing from London on 2 June [1848], Chopin tells Grzymała: 'When I have been jolted up and down in a carriage for three or four hours I feel as though I had travelled from Paris to Boulogne.' Hedley, *Chopin correspondence*, p. 320.
52 Niecks, *Chopin*, vol.2, p. 306, n.39.
53 By midday on Friday I shall be in Paris', Chopin told Grzymała, [21 November 1848]. Hedley, *Chopin correspondence*, p. 353.

Conclusion
Paris 1849: Epilogue

Chopin's death on 17 October 1849 at No. 12 place Vendôme was not unexpected. The oft-told accounts of his final days vary extensively. 'Even if we confine ourselves to those given by eye-witnesses', Niecks wrote, they are 'a mesh of contradictions which it is impossible to wholly disentangle.'[1] On his return to Paris, Chopin resumed his consultations with homeopaths, but found that his trusted Dr Molin had died. It was a severe blow to him. 'Molin had the art of pulling me together', he told Solange Clésinger. 'Since he died I have had Mr Louis, Dr Roth – for two months – and now Mr Simon, who has a great reputation as a homeopathic doctor. But they try their different methods without bringing me relief.'[2] Hardly surprisingly, Chopin was composing little, if anything.[3]

Once back in the place d'Orléans, Chopin enjoyed musical evenings at home, and even went to see Meyerbeer's newest opera, *Le Prophète*, first performed by the Paris Opéra at the Salle Le Peletier on 16 April 1849, with the tenor Roger as Jean de Leyde, and Pauline Viardot as his mother, Fidès. Friends rallied round Chopin, to care for him and to keep him company. Countess Maria Kalergis, Countess Delfina Potocka, and Adolphe Gutmann, all former pupils, appeared, as did Thomas Albrecht, wine merchant and Saxon consul in Paris. Attentive, too, were Chopin's sister Ludwika Jędrzejewicz (with whom Jane Stirling corresponded), Franchomme, and Delacroix, who recorded his impressions of the composer in his *Journal*.[4] Henry Fowler Broadwood was invited to Paris by the composer, but nothing came of it.[5] Writing to Grzymała from No. 4 rue de Chaillot, Chopin tells him that Jenny Lind had been and sung there, and mentions visits from other friends whom he had known in England and Scotland, notably Mme Rothschild, Jane Stirling and Mrs Erskine, and the Czartoryskis.[6]

According to a report by the French writer and diplomat Charles Gavard, quoted by Niecks, the day before he died 'Chopin twice called his friends that were gathered in his apartments around him. "For everyone he had a touching word; I for my part, shall never forget the tender words he spoke to me." Calling to his side the Princess Czartoryska and Mdlle. [Elise] Gavard, he said to them: "You will play together, you will think of me, and I shall listen to you." And calling to his side Franchomme, he said to the Princess: "I recommend Franchomme to you, you will play Mozart together, and I shall listen to you." "And", added Franchomme when he told me this, "the Princess has always been a good friend to me."'[7] Gavard had no doubt about Princess Marcelina's dedication. 'She passed every day a couple of hours with the dying man', Gavard recalled. 'She left him at the last only after having prayed for a long time beside him who had just then fled from this world of illusions and sorrows.'[8]

Jane Stirling and Mrs Erskine continued to express their devotion to Chopin when they were in Paris. Jane visited the city for limited periods, rather than having a permanent home there;[9] at one stage, both she and her friend, Natalia Obrescoff, were living in St Germain-en-Laye, on the Seine.[10] Jane's sister Katherine, wrote Thomas Erskine, of Linlathen, 'was an admirable woman, faithful and diligent in all duties, and unwearied in her efforts to help those who needed her help'.[11] The two sisters expressed their commitment to Chopin in a strange episode, as Arthur Hedley explains:

> Chopin's diary for 1849 shows that his lessons were few in number and could not possibly cover his living expenses. On 8 March (as he noted later) Jane Stirling and her sister decided to make him an anonymous gift of 25,000 francs. Mrs Erskine sent the banknotes in a parcel, which was handed to Mme Etienne, the concierge [at No 9 place d'Orléans]; but Chopin heard nothing of the money until July. His letters give details of this strange affair. In the mean time, on 21 May, he received 1,000 francs from the Rothschilds and also loans from his friends Franchomme and Herbault.[12]

Chopin recounted this story, involving a medium, to Grzymała, and concluded: 'Thank God the money was found. There are many other details which I can't write – the pen is burning my fingers.'[13]

In 1849, the Polish artist Teofil Kwiatowski produced several versions of Chopin's deathbed scene.[14] Featured in them are Aleksander Jelowicki (the priest), Chopin's sister Ludwika, the Princess Marcelina, Wojciech Grzymała, and the painter himself; one of the paintings, showing Ludwika sitting with her brother, may have been commissioned by Jane Stirling.[15] But Stirling herself appears nowhere in these paintings. Considering her relationship with the composer, and her financial and personal generosity towards him, this suggests that she may have been wilfully excluded by Chopin's Parisian friends.

Following Chopin's death on 17 October, Gavard made the arrangements for the funeral in the Church of the Madeleine; owing to the extent of the preparations, it did not take place until 30 October.[16] The funeral, perhaps paid for in part by Jane Stirling and Mrs Erskine, included Mozart's *Requiem*, and special permission was required for women to take part in it. Pauline Viardot and Luigi Lablache were among the singers, and thus able to make their last gesture of devotion to Chopin, though not without some unseemly problems about payment.[17] Kwiatowski completed his sketches, and Auguste Clésinger made death masks, and set to work on his sculptured head to be incorporated in the Chopin monument in the Père Lachaise cemetery in Paris the next year (see Plate 36). Plans were afoot to take Chopin's heart to Warsaw, where it was placed in the Church of the Holy Cross. Writing to Mrs Grote from the United States, after Chopin's death, Jenny Lind reported mournfully of her last visit to Paris: 'Poor dear Chopin, he was not there.'[18]

As expected, the British press reported Chopin's death and funeral. Henry Fothergill Chorley's obituary of Chopin in the *Athenaeum* on 27 October 1849 was long and fulsome.[19] 'On Chopin's pianoforte playing, exquisite and unparagoned after its kind as it was, no school could be founded', Chorley wrote. 'With great elegance of mind, refinement of taste, and nobility of feeling was combined a quiet, quaint, child-like humour, the play of which was as spontaneous as it was original. One of more tender and affectionate nature we have never known.'[20] For his part, J.W. Davison, more than a decade later, published a detailed description of the funeral in the preface to his edition of Chopin's *Mazurkas* (1860).[21] Other reports in the British press of Chopin's funeral appeared in the *Daily News* of 2 November 1849, and the *Musical World* of 10 November 1849.[22] The unveiling of Chopin's monument in the Père Lachaise cemetery in October 1850, on the anniversary of his death, was described in an account in *John Bull* of 26 October 1850.[23]

Jane Stirling's commitment to Chopin continued after his death, as she acquired and distributed his possessions; her preservation of Chopin's memory and his artefacts was extensive and complex.[24] Suffice to say that her dedication continued until her own death. We do not know if Jane was in love with Chopin, but Jane Welsh Carlyle was not alone in finding Jane, as if Chopin's widow, 'pale and dressed in deepest mourning'.[25] Jane Stirling liaised with Fontana over the publication of Chopin's works, and collaborated with Grzymała on a projected biography of the composer.[26] As she assembled and dispersed Chopin's possessions to Cracow, Warsaw, Scotland, and elsewhere, she set in train the assembly and documentation of material which subsequently involved (among many others) Edouard Ganche, in Lyons and Paris, and Mrs Anne Douglas Houston, at Johnstone Castle.[27]

It was Liszt, however, who won the race to publication. Liszt's biography, *Frédéric Chopin*, brought out in Paris in 1852, by Escudier, was the first monograph devoted to the life and work of the composer. Based on a series of articles in the journal *La France musicale* (5 February – 17 August 1851), and partly the work of Princess Carolyne von Sayn-Wittgenstein, it had a controversial reception.[28] Before publication, Liszt had written to Chopin's sister, Ludwika Jędrzejewicz, with twelve questions about her brother; Ludwika, apparently, did not respond, but passed on the questionnaire to Jane Stirling.[29] Her replies, with the questions, were later published by Mieczyław Karłowicz, in French and Polish, in his *Nie wydane dotąd pamiątki po Chopinie* (1904),[30] and in English by Edward N. Waters in his *Frederic Chopin, by Franz Liszt* (1963).[31] All told, Jane Stirling was unhappy with Liszt's book, and felt that Wojciech Grzymała should be the person to write Chopin's biography.

During 1849, Jane Stirling took lessons in Paris from Vera Rubio, a Russian pianist and former pupil of Chopin,[32] and from the Norwegian pianist Thomas Tellefsen, to whom many of Chopin's students transferred their allegiance.[33] Taught by Chopin from 1844 to 1847, Tellefsen, as we have seen, was a Parisian friend of Fanny Erskine, Jane Stirling and Mrs Katherine Erskine, the Schwabes, and the Léos. He also remained close, among others, to Franchomme and Princess Marcelina.[34] In Britain, his activities are obscure, although he seems to have visited Calder House in 1848, and again in 1849,[35] and we have letters written by him from Glenbervie (1848), Gargunnock (1849), Hamilton Palace (1851), and Stirling (1857).[36] In Paris, Tellefsen was highly respected as a teacher, and as a concert pianist in the decade 1850–60, and was also involved in the activities of the Hôtel Lambert.[37] And he composed.[38] Chopin had entrusted Tellefsen with the completion of his pianoforte method, though the book was never published nor even finished. But in 1860, with the publisher Richault, Tellefsen brought out a twelve-volume *Collection des oeuvres pour le piano par Frédéric Chopin*, which, perhaps due to Tellefsen's ill health, proved to be unsatisfactory.[39] According to Tellefsen's family papers, Jane Stirling travelled to Norway on several occasions, where she apparently owned an estate at Natland, near Bergen.[40] It is, however, not mentioned in her will or inventory of 1859.[41]

Jane Stirling died on 6 February 1859, at Calder House, at the age of fifty-four, of a 'disease of the ovary'; her death was certified by Dr Adam Lyschiński, who had attended her the previous day, and she was interred in the 'Burial Ground of Dunblane Cathedral'.[42] On her death, she left behind admiring as well as grieving relatives. Thomas Erskine, of Linlathen, regarded Jane Stirling and the Duchesse de Broglie as 'the most remarkable women he had ever met' (see Figure 11.1).[43] The day after Jane died, Erskine wrote from No. 16 Charlotte Square, Edinburgh, to the Reverend J. McLeod Campbell:

> I cannot express what a loss I feel this to be to myself and to many, above all to Mrs Erskine, who has been a mother as well as a sister to her during the greater part of her life. She clung to life till the very end, feeling that she had things to do which required her life, besides having a particular repugnance to the idea of death both for herself and for others . . . She had two months of great suffering. Her repugnance to death was not connected with any fear of what might follow death, she had a perfect trust in her Father's love, but she regarded death as an enemy and usurper. She desired to be prayed for, and that her life should be prayed for.[44]

A week later, on 14 February 1859, Thomas Erskine wrote similarly to Mrs Julie Schwabe:

> How shall I tell you of the affliction it has pleased God to lay upon us? Jane Stirling has been taken from this world, doubtless to her own great gain, and doubtless for our good, could we understand it aright. In the meantime, however, it is a deep sorrow, a removal of what was the light and joy of many hearts. She was ill for eight weeks, and suffered a great deal . . . I know you will feel this deeply, for you could appreciate the purity and beauty of that stream of love which flowed through her whole life.

Jane's altruism was striking. 'I don't think that I ever knew any one who seemed more entirely to have given up self, and devoted her whole being to the good of others', Erskine added. 'I remember her birth [at Kippenross] like yesterday, and I never saw anything in her but what was lovable from the beginning to the end of her course.'[45]

Figure 11.1 Thomas Erskine of Linlathen (1788–1870), attributed to Charles Baillod. Scottish National Portrait Gallery, Edinburgh

We can do no more than speculate on the location of Jane Stirling's burial. Audrey Bone, biographer of Jane, believed that she was buried at the Kirk of Calder, Mid Calder, not far from Calder House.[46] This church, also known as St John's Parish Church, was begun in the sixteenth century, and 'commissioned, designed and paid for by Magister Peter Sandilands'. It was incomplete on his death, and the nave was never begun. In 1863, the architects Brown and Wardrop added the transepts and belfry.[47] There is also a Sandilands burial vault, where there is a plaque (see Figure 11.2) which reads

DEDICATED
BY
ROBERT 10ᵀᴴ BARON TORPHICHEN
TO THE LOVED MEMORIES
OF HIS MOTHER
MARGARET DOUGLAS 10ᵀᴴ LADY TORPHICHEN
BORN 1784, DIED 1836
AND OF HER SISTER
JANE WILHELMINA STIRLING
BORN 1804, DIED 1859

- - - - - - - - -

> They shall be mine saith the Lord of Hosts
> in that day when I make up my Jewels[48]

Robert Sandilands, 11th Lord Torphichen, was born in 1807 and died in 1869, so the date of the plaque must be circa 1859–69. The tradition was for the Sandilands family members to be buried in the Kirk of Calder, so Jane Stirling may be among them.[49]

At Dunblane, at the time of Jane's death, the cathedral was virtually open to the skies (see Figure 11.3). Dunblane Cathedral, otherwise known as the Cathedral Church of St Blane and St Laurence, Dunblane, with its twelfth-century tower of red sandstone, rises above the town and river.[50] Restorations

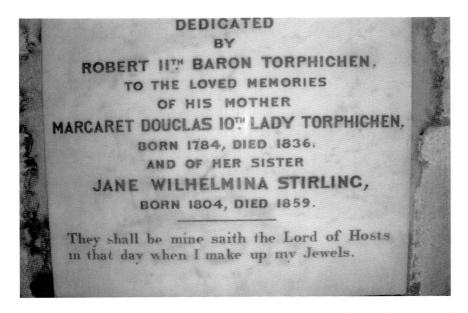

Figure 11.2 Kirk of Calder, Mid Calder. Plaque to Stirling family. Photograph courtesy of Robert Ross, 2014

in the nineteenth century – notably by James Gillespie Graham (1816–19) and Robert Rowand Anderson (1889–93) – brought the ruined nave back into use, and made significant changes.[51] Today, the north aisle of the nave (variously known as the 'Keir' or the 'Stirling' aisle) contains memorials and plaques to the Stirling family (see Figure 11.4).[52] Among the memorials are those to John and Patrick Stirling, of Kippendavie (died 1816), by Peter Turnerelli (1819), and to William Stirling, of Keir (died 1793), by Rowand Anderson (1909). Notable among the plaques, on the north wall of the north aisle, is a brass plate to the Stirlings, of Kippendavie (see Figure 11.5). It bears the following inscription:

> TO THE GLORY OF GOD
> AND IN MEMORY OF
> THOSE MEMBERS OF THE
> HOUSE OF STIRLING
> OF KIPPENDAVIE
> INTERRED IN THIS AISLE
> FROM 1595 TO 1859.
> THIS BRASS IS PLACED
> BY PATRICK STIRLING
> NOW OF KIPPENDAVIE
> 1892.

Figure 11.3 Dunblane Cathedral, Perthshire. Exterior from the south-west. Drawn by Thomas Allom, engraved by W. Radclyffe, circa 1840. Private collection

Figure 11.4 Dunblane Cathedral, Perthshire. North aisle of nave (the 'Keir' or 'Stirling' aisle) with Stirling and other memorials along the north wall. Photograph: Peter Willis, 2008

Figure 11.5 Dunblane Cathedral, Perthshire. North aisle of nave. Brass memorial erected by Patrick Stirling, of Kippendavie, in 1892, to members of the House of Stirling, of Kippendavie, from 1595 to 1859, 'interred in this aisle', which may include Jane Stirling (died 1859). Photograph: Peter Willis, 2008

Colonel Patrick Stirling, of Kippendavie, who erected the plaque, was a leading figure in Rowand Anderson's restoration of the cathedral, and it is notable that the last of the Stirlings referred to was interred in 1859 – the year of the death of Jane Stirling. During the restoration of 1889–93, care was taken not to disturb the remains of persons buried within the cathedral walls, and this suggests that she – and other members of the house of Stirlings, of Kippdendavie – may lie beneath the floor in the north aisle.[53]

On 8 August 1930, on his tour of Scotland, recorded in his book, *Voyages avec Frédéric Chopin*, the French physician and Chopin scholar Edouard Ganche made a pilgrimage to Dunblane, on his way from Calder House, en route to Keir.[54] As the organist played music by Chopin, Ganche and his 'petit cortège' of eight people – among them Mrs Anne D. Houston, of Johnstone Castle – located 'une plaque de bronze, entourée d'un bas-relief, rappelle quelques noms de la famille des Stirling'. Nearby, they laid a floral bouquet which Ganche had brought from Glasgow. The irony was not lost on him: Jane Stirling, who had been involved in the erection of Chopin's tomb in the Père Lachaise cemetery, and placed flowers within it, was buried in an unnamed grave. 'Déjà', Ganche wrote,

> son corps avait disparu dans l'inconnu de l'immense univers de notre amour en éprouvait une blessure. Toutes nos pensées essayaient de se rapprocher de Jane Stirling come si elle pouvait comprendre l'hymne de notre affection et que nous lui apportions avec notre coeur ému l'attestation du sentiment de milliers d'autres coeurs qu'elle a touchés.

Ganche continued to meditate on Jane Stirling's life as he listened to 'une musique lointaine, aux sonorités affaiblies, qui paraissait venir des hautes voûtes'. Chopin's Funeral March, a nocturne, and preludes, played on the cathedral organ, 'disaient pour Frédéric Chopin un langage pathétique et répandaient leurs harmonies avec un enveloppante douceur autour de l'âme, que nous imaginions existante et heureuse, de Jane Stirling'.[55]

Next call, for Ganche and his party, was the Stirling family seat of Kippenross, less than two miles from Dunblane, where Jane Stirling was born: a two-storey classical building, set amidst trees, with lawns descending to a river [see Figure 6.19].[56] As Jane explained in a letter, Chopin, when staying at Keir in 1848, had been prevented by rain from going to Kippenross, so she went alone. As she herself put it: 'J'ai mis une petite feuille de rosier que j'avais cueillie pour lui à Kippenross où je suis née et que j'avais fait sécher dans my bible. Etant à Keir, il voulut aller à Kippenross, mais il plut ce jour-là, et je m'y rendis seule.'[57] Ganche remembers Kippenross as the place where Jane Stirling had prepared 'le contenu de la boîte quelle plaça derrière le médaillon du tombeau de Chopin'. Kippenross, Ganche concludes, 'est the lieu où Jane Stirling revenait méditer sur son premier acheminement vers sa destinée'.[58]

The death in 1868 of Jane Stirling's sister, Katherine Erskine, marked a significant break in the links between Chopin and England and Scotland. Lord Torphichen had died in 1862, and other siblings of the Stirling sisters passed on.[59] The memoirists and memorialists were recording their impressions of the composer. Then, in 1888, there appeared Frederick Niecks' biography, *Frederick Chopin as man and musician*, which benefited substantially from Niecks' friendship and acquaintance with musicians and others who knew Chopin personally. Appropriately, Niecks was Reid Professor of Music at the University of

236 Paris 1849: Epilogue

Edinburgh, and the recipient from Teofil Kwiatowski of one of his portraits of Chopin.

As *Chopin in Britain* has demonstrated, the composer's visits to England and Scotland drew sustenance from his life in Poland and France: they were all of a piece, as he and fellow-musicians crossed the Channel. The Czartoryskis were in frequent touch. The Schwabes appear in both Paris and Manchester. Pauline Viardot and Chopin shared recitals in London and Paris. Chopin's relationship with Jane Stirling and Mrs Erskine, at once both sustaining and problematic, ensured the success of his spells in London, and his visits to Edinburgh, Glasgow, and Scottish country seats. The composer's extensive correspondence shows the frequency with which he wrote to those he loved, and who loved him, and it is impossible in reading his letters not to be aware of the fragility of his health and the desperation of his emotions. He mentions death frequently. Money troubles were always to hand, and Chopin's public performances were tinged with financial concerns; indeed, Chopin's lifestyle was little better than hand-to-mouth. As in Paris and Leipzig, so in Britain, Chopin remained vulnerable to the whims of publishers such as Wessel, and to the demands of the marketplace. Yet, among his well-do-do patrons, Chopin was treated generously and enjoyed a sophisticated lifestyle. In the luxurious ambience of Stafford House, in elegant London town houses, or handsome Scottish country seats, he found equivalent settings to those in Paris, Warsaw, and elsewhere which he knew so well.

Throughout his life, Chopin sought and enjoyed the patronage of the aristocracy, and his letters from England and Scotland reinforce this clearly. But, as Heinrich Heine pointed out, his aspirations were more than social. In his struggles against the misfortunes of life, Chopin is seen by history as a tragic hero. Heine's encomium on the composer is unequivocal. 'Chopin's satisfaction surely does not come from having the dexterity of his hands applauded by other hands', he wrote. Rather,

> he aspires to a higher type of success; his fingers are but the servants of his soul, and his soul is applauded by those who listen not only with their ears but also with their own souls. Hence, he is the favorite of that elite who seek the most elevated intellectual pleasures in music. His success is of an aristocratic sort. His fame, one might say, is perfumed by the praises of polite society; it is elegant, as he himself is.[60]

That said, in more recent times, the Brazilian composer, singer, guitarist, and pianist Antonio Carlos Jobin, has added a more specific claim. 'When a good history of popular twentieth-century music is written', he observed, 'Chopin may appear as a central influence.' It is a challenging idea.[61]

Notes

1 Niecks, *Chopin*, vol.2, p. 316. Niecks' own description of events is on pp. 316–27. For other accounts see, e.g., Samson, *Chopin*, pp. 258–60, and Zamoyski, *Chopin: prince of romantics*, pp. 283–97. More briefly, see Atwood, *Pianist from Warsaw*, pp. 190–2.

2 See Hedley, *Chopin correspondence*, p. 355. Chopin to Solange Clésinger, 30 January 1849. For Chopin's medical treatment on his return to Paris, see Atwood, *Parisian worlds*, pp. 349–55. A wider context is given in Neumayr, *Music and medicine*, vol.3, pp. 105–31, and O'Shea, *Music and medicine*, pp. 146–51.
3 Brown, *Index of Chopin's works*, pp. 173–4 (nos 167, 168), documents Chopin's Mazurkas in G minor (Op.67, no.2) and F minor (Op.68, no.4) as both perhaps written in the summer of 1849, though Chopin's sister Ludwika dates them '1848'.
4 See Delacroix, *Journal, 1822–1863*, notably pp. 214–15, where Delacroix records Chopin's death, and comments on Clésinger's bust for the composer's gravestone.
5 Wainwright, *Broadwood by appointment*, p. 64, writes: '[Henry Fowler] Broadwood received a present in gratitude from Chopin the following February [1849], accompanied by an invitation to visit the composer in Paris. In a cheerfully good-humoured reply, Henry Fowler pleaded that he was too busy making pianos. He sent the good wishes of the Broadwood family "for the restoration of your health". In fact he was arranging for a special grand piano to be made for Chopin as a present – the first of his full iron frame grands. Tragically, Chopin never saw it.'
6 Hedley, *Chopin correspondence*, p. 359. Chopin to Grzymała, 18 June [1849]. In this letter, apart from Lind, Chopin mentions visits from Delphine Potocka, Mme de Beauvau, and Mme Rothschild, as well as referring to the Czartoryskis, Delacroix, Franchomme, Gutmann, and Pleyel.
7 Niecks, *Chopin*, vol.2, p. 317. Niecks indicates (on p. 308, n.3) that he is quoting from a manuscript by Gavard, 'containing reminiscences of the last months of Chopin's life', which was used extensively by Moritz Karasowski. See Karasowski, *Frederic Chopin: his life and letters*, p. 366, for the paragraph here. Elise Gavard, sister of Charles Gavard, was a favourite pupil of Chopin, and the dedicatee of his Berceuse (Op.57). In a note on p. 370, Karasowski records that 'Mlle Gavard cherishes the original manuscript as one of her most precious memorials of the immortal teacher.'
8 Niecks, *Chopin*, vol.2, p. 319.
9 Ritchie, *Chapters from some memoirs*, pp. 23–4. See Willlis, 'Chopin in Britain, vol.1, Chapter 2, pp. 63–8, 83–4, nn.71,72 (etheses.dur.ac.uk/1386/).
10 Wróblewska-Straus, 'Jane Wilhelmina Stirling's letters to Ludwika Jędrzejewicz', p. 62, n.5. A tabulation of Jane's letters from Paris and Barnton House, is on pp. 53–9. Bone, *Jane Stirling*, p. 56, says that, in 1842, Jane was at No. 3 rue de Noailles.
11 Quoted by Niecks, *Chopin*, vol.2, p. 292.
12 Hedley, *Chopin correspondence*, editorial comment on p. 356.
13 Hedley, *Chopin correspondence*, pp. 366–8. Chopin to Grzymała, Saturday 28 July [1849].
14 Kwiatowski spent many years of exile in Paris. His watercolours and drawings of Chopin in his last days brought him considerable fame. See Wróblewska-Straus, 'Jane Wilhelmina Stirling's letters to Ludwika Jędrzejewicz', pp. 73–4, n.10.
15 See Tomaszewski and Weber, *Diary in images*, p. 255, where the painting is reproduced.
16 Descriptions of Chopin's funeral are numerous and varied. See, e.g., Atwood, *Lioness and little one*, pp. 286–91; Niecks, *Chopin*, vol.2, pp. 323–7; and Samson, *Chopin*, p. 282. A poem by Alfred Noyes (1880–1958) entitled 'The death of Chopin', is quoted in Barnett, *Scottish pilgrimage*, pp. 19–20.
17 Bone, *Jane Stirling*, p. 90, is one of the sources which claims that Chopin's funeral was 'paid for by Jane and Mrs. Erskine'. For Viardot's demand for payment of 2,000 francs, see Steen, *Enchantress of nations*, pp. 179–80.
18 Letter quoted in the catalogue of the Sotheby's sale of Continental Manuscripts and Music, London, 26 May 1994, p. 19 (Lot 274). Lots 274–81 consisted of a Jenny Lind Archive. Imaginative references to Chopin's funeral occur in Ganche, *Voyages avec Frédéric Chopin*, pp. 112–15, when the Frenchman meets Mrs Anne D. Houstoun in the garden at Johnstone Castle, and reads the description in the *Daily News* of 2 November 1849. Niecks, *Chopin*, vol.2, p. 324, reproduces part of this article.

19 See Bledsoe, *Chorley*, pp. 178–9. On p. 178 Bledsoe quotes a sympathetic letter to Chorley about Chopin from Turgenev, and on p. 179 gives the text of Chorley's 'memorial sonnet' to Chopin. Chorley also published an article on Chopin in *Bentley's Miscellany*, vol.27 (February 1850), pp. 185–91, and proposed to write others. Note the reference in Cooper, *House of Novello*, p. 140, to the description of Chopin in the *Musical World* on 21 July 1837 as 'the celebrated composer', and the 'different perspective' of the obituary in the *Musical Times* of November 1849, in which Chopin is referred to simply as 'Chopin the Pianist' (see Cooper, *House of Novello*, p. 136). See also the obituary of Chopin in the *Musical World* of 10 November 1849.
20 *Athenaeum*, 27 October 1849 (no.1148), p. 1090.
21 Reprinted in Hipkins, *How Chopin played*, pp. 29–33.
22 Both are quoted *in extenso* in Niecks, *Chopin*, vol.2, pp. 324–5.
23 See Niecks, *Chopin*, vol.2, pp. 326–7. The *Athenaeum* does not seem to have carried a description of the funeral, but brief reference is made to it in the *Athenaeum*, 3 November 1849 (no.1149), p. 1114, in a note announcing that 'a monument is about to be erected in Paris to the memory of Chopin, by his friends and admirers; subscriptions for which will be received by MM. Pleyel, Rue Rochechouart.' Sophie Léo's comments on Chopin, made after his death, appear on pp. 401–3 of her 'Musical life in Paris (1817–1848)'.
24 See the chapter 'Jane Stirling after Chopin's death', in Bone, *Jane Stirling*, pp. 93–107. Key published sources for a study of the dispersal of Chopin's effects include Chopin, *Oeuvres pour piano* (Stirling), pp.VII – XIV, and the documentation in Wróblewska-Straus, 'Jane Wilhelmina Stirling's letters to Ludwika Jędzejewicz'. The bibliographies to catalogues (e.g., Wróblewska-Straus, *Chopin: fame resounding far and wide*, pp. 13–19) provide essential leads.
25 Hedley, *Chopin*, p. 112.
26 See, e.g., Samson, *Chopin*, pp. 283–4.
27 Key sources include Chopin, *Oeuvres pour piano* (Stirling), pp.VII – XLVI. Correspondence between Ganche and Mrs Houston is in the Ganche Papers, BnF (Paris), as are details of the Ganche sale, and the purchases by (notably) the Frederick Chopin Society (TiFC), Warsaw, and the Collegium Maius and the Biblioteka Jagiellońska, Cracow. These last two locations house many Jane Stirling items.
28 See the discussion in Poniatowska, 'The Polish reception of Chopin's biography by Franz Liszt', pp. 262–4.
29 See Poniatowska, 'The Polish reception of Chopin's biography by Franz Liszt', pp. 263–5. See the coverage in Walker, *Liszt: the virtuoso years*, p. 186 (for the questionnaire), and Walker, *Liszt: the Weimar years*, pp. 146, 379–80 (for Liszt's writing of the biography, with Carolyne von Wittgenstein, and its publication). Walker notes on p. 379 here that Ludwika 'refused to cooperate'.
30 Pp. 351–67 (given by Poniatowska, p. 276, n.14). For the French text, see Karłowicz, *Souvenirs*, pp. 200–4.
31 Liszt, *Chopin* (Waters), pp. 18–25.
32 See Eigeldinger, *Chopin vu par ses élèves*, pp. 229–31, and Eigeldinger's entry on Tellefsen in Fauquet, *Dictionnaire de la musique en France au XIXe siècle*, p. 1203. See also the article on Tellefsen by Kari Michelsen in *Grove music online*. In 2014, Ingrid Loe Dalaker published *Thomas Tellefsen: w norweskiej i francuskiej kulturze muzycznej*, based on a Polish translation of her doctoral dissertation of 2005, submitted at the Norwegian University of Science and Technology, Trondheim. I am grateful to Sissel Guttormsen, of the Ringve Museum, Trondheim, for his advice on Tellefsen and other matters.
33 Huldt-Nystrom, 'Tellefsen', p. 198.
34 See the description of Tellefsen in Barlow, 'Encounters with Chopin', p. 246.
35 For instance, see the letter from Chopin to Camille Pleyel of 11 September 1848, sent from Johnstone Castle, in which he recommends Tellefsen to him. An English text is in

Hedley, *Chopin*, p. 110. For the original French text, see Sydow and Chainaye, *Chopin correspondance*, vol.3, p. 386 (letter 736), and for a Polish translation, see Sydow, *KFC*, vol.2, p. 442 (letter 640).
36 Tellefsen, *Thomas Tellefsens familiebreve*, pp. 107–8, 114–15, 128–9, 151.
37 For Tellefsen in Paris, see 'Thomas Tellefsen: "Paris est mon idole" ', in Herresthal and Reznicek, *Rhapsodie norvégienne*, pp. 57–81, and 'Thomas Tellefsen: Paris est mon idole', by Harald Herresthal, in Herresthal et Pistone, *Grieg et Paris*, pp. 18–20. Tellefsen and Princess Marcelina Czartroyska are considered in Diehl, *Musical memories*, pp. 23–9. For Tellefsen in a national context, see Kjeldsberg, *Piano i Norge*, pp. 54, 56–9, 61, 62, 64.
38 'As a composer', Jean-Jacques Eigeldinger remarks, 'Tellefsen left 44 opus numbers, consisting of piano pieces, chamber music and two concertos; about ten of these works are dedicated to students and friends of Chopin.' See Eigeldinger, *Chopin: pianist and teacher*, p. 185.
39 See Eigeldinger, *Chopin vu par ses élèves*, pp. 236–8.
40 Tellefsen, *Thomas Tellefsens familiebreve*, p. 175. See also Bone, *Jane Stirling*, pp. 95–6. Tellefsen's letters to his parents, published in 1923 as *Thomas Tellefsens familiebreve*, give details of his life in Paris and his time in Britain. See Jaeger, 'Quelques nouveaux noms d'élèves de Chopin', p. 88, for a description in French. See also Eigeldinger, 'Présence de Thomas D A Tellefsen', *passim*. For Tellefsen's connection with England, see the two articles by Keith G. Orrell, 'The "Great Sir Thomas" Acland', parts 1 and 2, *passim*.
41 National Archives of Scotland (Edinburgh), SC70/4/63, Edinburgh Sheriff Court Wills, and SC70/1/100, Edinburgh Sheriff Court Inventories, respectively.
42 Details taken from '1859. Deaths in the Parish of Mid Calder in the County of Mid Lothian', p. 2. Lady Torphichen kindly provided me with a copy of this register, which she had been sent by Margaret Kirby, of Edinburgh, in 2003.
43 Niecks, *Chopin*, vol.2, p. 291. See the entry on Thomas Erskine, by Trevor A. Hart, in *Oxford DNB online*. Linlathen House, Angus, was enlarged for Erskine, circa 1820–6, by the builder-architect William Stirling (no relation), and demolished in 1958, and later. See Colvin, *Dictionary*, p. 987, and *Dictionary of Scottish architects online*, under 'Linlathen House'. A letter from Louise de Broglie, Comtesse d'Haussonville, to Chopin about a piano lesson is noted in Karłowicz, *Souvenirs*, p. 137. Her portrait by Scheffer (1837) is now in the Château de Coppet, and by Ingres (1845) in the Frick Collection, New York.
44 Hanna, *Letters of Thomas Erskine of Linlathen (1840–1870)*, p. 129.
45 Hanna, *Letters of Thomas Erskine of Linlathen (1840–1870)*, pp. 129–30. On pp. 130–2 there is a transcript of a letter in French of 15 February 1859, from the Swiss Reformed theologian, Louis Gaussen, in Les Grottes, Geneva, in response to a letter from Erskine giving him the news. Part of Julie Schwabe's letter is quoted in Niecks, *Chopin*, vol.2, p. 291.
46 See Bone, *Jane Stirling*, p. 107.
47 For St John's Parish Church, Mid Calder, see Jaques and McKean, *West Lothian*, p. 100, and McWilliam, *Lothian, except Edinburgh*, pp. 322–4.
48 Malachi, 3:17 (AV).
49 A photograph of the memorial can be found on the website of the Kirk of Calder (www.kirkofcalder.com).
50 For an architectural description of Dunblane Cathedral, by Richard Fawcett, see Gifford and Walker, *Stirling and central Scotland*, pp. 425–40. See also McKean, *Stirling and the Trossachs*, pp. 81–3.
51 For Rowand Anderson's work, see 'The restoration of Dunblane Cathedral, 1889–1893', in Barty, *History of Dunblane*, pp. 286–92.
52 For descriptions of these memorials and plaques, see Mitchell, *Monumental inscriptions in South Perthshire*, p. 115, and the plan of Dunblane Cathedral on p. 97. See also Gifford and Walker, *Stirling and central Scotland*, pp. 439, 440 (graveyard).

53 The proper treatment of the existing graves in the cathedral is examined in Barty, *History of Dunblane*, p. 288.
54 The visits to Dunblane Cathedral and Kippenross are described in Ganche, *Voyages avec Frédéric Chopin*, pp. 102–5.
55 An article on Ganche's visit to Dunblane Cathedral, entitled 'Lady who befriended Chopin', appeared in the *Scotsman*, 9 August 1930. It describes Ganche as 'president of the Société Frédéric Chopin, of France', and 'a man of wide culture and aesthetic tastes'. The writer adds that the Revd Neil T. M'Culloch, assistant minister at the Cathedral, 'offered prayer, and Mr Herd, the Cathedral organist, played several Chopin selections on the organ'. Another newspaper report (its origins untraced) says that 'the wreath was of lilies, gladioli, sweet peas, asters, and red carnations'. Bone, *Jane Stirling*, pp. 106–7, may have been referring to Ganche when she describes 'the visit made by the Chopin Society several years ago' to Dunblane Cathedral. On this occasion, 'Minnie Stirling, an old lady, almost 80 years of age, was asked to lead the way to Jane Stirling's grave.' This she duly did, wryly commenting later that the flagstone she pointed to 'was as good a spot as any'.
56 For Kippenross, see Gifford and Walker, *Stirling and central Scotland*, pp. 564–5, and McKean, *Stirling and the Trossachs*, p. 79. See also above, Chapter 6, note 47.
57 Jane Stirling's letter is quoted in Ganche, *Voyages avec Frédéric Chopin*, p. 105, and is the source of her other comments in this paragraph. However, Ganche's text here differs from the one he published in *Dans le souvenir de Frédéric Chopin*, pp. 120–1, in which Jane Stirling describes the contents of the box which she placed behind the Chopin medallion on his monument in Père Lachaise cemetery. The box included 'un médallion donné par Tellefsen'. On Tuesday 14 January 2003, BBC Radio 4 FM broadcast the imaginative play *A rose for Chopin*, by Lorraine McCann, in which Jane Stirling presents Chopin with a rose from Kippenross when he leaves Edinburgh for London after his concert in the Hopetoun Rooms.
58 Ganche, *Voyages avec Frédéric Chopin*, p. 105. Ganche next moved on to Keir, and thence to Johnstone Castle.
59 For details of the Stirling family, see Willis, 'Chopin in Britain', vol.2, pp. 336–7, 511–14 (http://etheses.dur.ac.uk/1386/).
60 Taken from 'Heinrich Heine: Confidential Letter', published in *Gazette musicale*, 4 February 1838, pp. 41–4, translated by Charles Suttoni, in *Liszt: an artist's journey*, pp. 223–4.
61 Quoted by Brown, 'Chopin came from Ipanema', pp. 20–1.

Bibliography

The following bibliography is limited to sources cited in the endnotes of *Chopin in Britain*, with the omission of minor or passing references. Material from the captions to the plates is also excluded, as are articles from online sources such as the *Dictionary of Scottish Architects online*, *Grove music online* and *Oxford DNB online*, and most entries from biographical dictionaries, encyclopaedias, exhibition catalogues, guides, post office directories, and other reference works.

For a comprehensive survey of Chopin material, including electronic sources, see William Smialek and Maja Trochimczyk, *Frédéric Chopin: a research and information guide*, 2nd ed. (New York and London: Routledge, 2015).

Further documentation of aspects of *Chopin in Britain* can be found in Peter Willis, 'Chopin in Britain: Chopin's visits to England and Scotland in 1837 and 1848; people, places, and activities', PhD dissertation, 3 vols. (University of Durham, 2009) (http://etheses.dur.ac.uk/1386/)

The bibliography of *Chopin in Britain* is divided into the following sections:

Section 1	Unpublished material
Section 2	Books, articles, dissertations, and theses

Section 1: Unpublished material

BCz (Cracow)	Biblioteka XX Czartoryskich, Cracow
	Czartoryski material
BJ (Cracow)	Biblioteka Jagiellońska, Cracow
	Chopin and Jane Stirling material
BK (Kórnik)	Biblioteka Kórnika, Kórnik
	* Chopin MS of song 'Wiosna', inscribed 'Warriston Crescent 1848'
BnF (Paris)	Bibliothèque nationale de France, Paris
	Département de la Musique
	Ganche papers
	Houston letters
	Jane Stirling material
Collegium Maius (Cracow)	Collegium Maius, Cracow
	Chopin and Jane Stirling material

(Continued)

ECA (Edinburgh)	Edinburgh City Archives, Edinburgh Drawings of Hopetoun Rooms, Edinburgh, of 1824 and 1831
EPL (Edinburgh)	Edinburgh Room, Edinburgh Public Library, Edinburgh (Central Library)
EUL (Edinburgh)	Edinburgh University Library, Edinburgh Niecks material
Fitzwilliam Museum (Cambridge)	Fitzwilliam Museum, Cambridge Chopin MS of song 'Wiosna', inscribed 'souvenir de Crumpsal House à Mademoiselle Fanny Erskine', and dated 1 September 1848
MdeFC (Valldemossa)	Musée de Frédéric Chopin et de George Sand, Valldemossa (La Collection d'Anne-Marie Boutroux de Ferrà)
Mitchell Library (Glasgow)	Mitchell Library, Glasgow Records of the Stirling Family of Keir and Cawdor Houston material Prints
Muir Wood Archives	Private collection * Material on John Muir Wood family
NAS (Edinburgh)	National Archives of Scotland, Edinburgh Ogilvy of Inverquharity Papers Unpublished Chopin letter, 12 August 1848 Wills and inventories of Jane Wilhelmina Stirling, Katherine Erskine (née Stirling), Houstons, and John Muir Wood
NLS (Edinburgh)	National Library of Scotland, Edinburgh Carlyle material
NMRS (Edinburgh)	National Monuments Record of Scotland, Edinburgh Architectural material
Norfolk RO (Norwich)	Norfolk Record Office, Norwich * Jenny Lind material
Northumberland Archives (Woodhorn)	Northumberland Museum, Archives and Country Park, Woodhorn, Northumberland Brooks Collection
Private collection	Private collection of the author, including topographical photographs and prints, and signed letters
RCAHMS (Edinburgh)	Royal Commission on the Ancient and Historical Monuments of Scotland, Edinburgh Architectural material
RCM (London)	Royal College of Music (London)
RIBA/BAL (London)	Royal Institute of British Architects/British Architectural Library, London * Diary of C.R. Cockerell, containing drawing of Hopetoun Rooms, Edinburgh, 17 March 184
RNCM (Manchester)	Royal Northern College of Music, Manchester * Susan Fisher Scott material Death mask and hand of Chopin, based on originals by Clésinger, 1849, donated 1910 Bronze statue of Chopin by Ludwika Nitschowa, donated 1973

RPS	Royal Philharmonic Society (London)
RSM (London)	Royal Society of Musicians of Great Britain, London Thyra C. Lange Papers Unpublished Chopin letter, 28 April [1840]
SNPG (Edinburgh)	Scottish National Portrait Gallery, Edinburgh John Muir Wood material
Staffordshire RO (Stafford)	Staffordshire Record Office, Stafford * Sutherland material
Surrey History Centre (Woking)	Surrey History Centre, Woking John Broadwood and Sons, Limited, Piano Manufacturers, London: Business Records, 1719–1981 Unpublished letter from Chopin to Henry Fowler Broadwood, Calder House, 10 August 1848, Broadwood Album Unpublished letter from Princess Marcelina Czartoryska to Henry Fowler Broadwood, undated, Broadwood Album
TiFC (Warsaw)	Towarzystwo imienia Fryderyka Chopina [Frederick Chopin Society, Warsaw] Chopin's pocket diaries for 1848 and *1849 MS Letters and cards of Chopin and his contemporaries Chopin's passport for his visit to London in 1837 Paintings, prints, memorabilia * Photocopies of MS first page, and leather binding, of unpublished Waltz in B major, by Chopin, dated 12 October 1848, 'pour Madame Erskine'

* denotes material not examined personally

Section 2: Books, articles, dissertations, and theses

Publishers' abbreviations

NiFC	Narodowy Instytut Fryderyka Chopina [Fryderyk Chopin Institute, Warsaw]
PiW	Państwowy Instytut Wydawniczy [Polish National Publishing Institute, Warsaw]
PWM	Polskie Wydawnictwo Muzyczne [Polish Musical Editions, Cracow]
TiFC	Towarzystwo imienia Fryderyka Chopina [Fryderyk Chopin Society, Warsaw]

ADAMCZYK-SCHMID, Bożena, 'Katalog Zbiorów Muzeum Fryderyka Chopina i George Sand w celi nr 2 klasztoru kartuzów w Valdemosie', *Rocznik Chopinowski*, vol.18 (1986), pp. 245–55.

AGRESTA, Rosalba, 'Aspect de la réception de Chopin en angleterre pendant les années 1840', in *Chopin's musical worlds: the 1840s*. Conference proceedings, 2007 (Warsaw: NiFC, 2007), pp. 97–114.

AGRESTA, Rosalba, 'Chopin in England', *Revue de la Bibliothèque Nationale de France*, no.34, 'Chopin in Paris: the composer's workshop' (2010/11), pp. 40–5.

AGRESTA, Rosalba, 'Présences de Chopin en Angleterre (1833–1860): la critique musicale, les concerts, les éditeurs'. Thèse de doctorat, histoire de la musique, 2 vols, Paris, EPHE (École pratique des hautes études), 2011.

AGRESTA, Rosalba, 'Chopin in music criticism in nineteenth-century England', in Poniatowska, *Chopin and his critics*, pp. 446–536.

ALBISETTI, James C., 'The "inevitable Schwabes": an introduction', *Transactions of the Lancashire and Cheshire Antiquarian Society*, vol.98 (2002), pp. 91–112.

ALDCROFT, Derek Howard, and Michael FREEMAN, *Atlas of British railway history*, new ed. (London: Routledge, 1988).

ALLIS, Wilfred, 'The Gentlemen's concerts, Manchester, 1777–1920', MPhil. thesis (University of Manchester, 1995).

ALLSOBROOK, David Ian, *Liszt: my travelling circus life* (London and Basingstoke: Macmillan, 1991).

Annual Report of the Literary Association of the Friends of Poland (1849).

ANONYMOUS, 'What did Chopin play in Edinburgh?', *Hinrichsen's musical year book*, vols 4–5 (1947–8), pp. 192–3.

ANONYMOUS, 'Grand historic find: a Chopin discovery, composer's own piano uncovered in Surrey collection', *BBC Music magazine* (May 2007), p. 8.

ANTOINETTI, Guy, *Louis-Philippe* (Paris: Arthème Fayard, 1994).

ARCHER, John H.G., editor, *Art and architecture in Victorian Manchester* (Manchester: Manchester University Press, 1985).

ARONSFELD, C.C., 'A prophetess of liberal education: the life of Julie Salis Schwabe and the founding of the Froebel Institute', *The new era*, vol.38 (May – June 1977), pp. 49–53.

ASHTON, Rosemary, *Little Germany: exile and asylum in Victorian England* (Oxford and New York: Oxford University Press, 1986).

ASHTON, Rosemary, *Thomas and Jane Carlyle: portrait of a marriage* (London: Chatto and Windus, 2001).

ATWOOD, William G[oodson], *Fryderyk Chopin: pianist from Warsaw* (New York: Columbia University Press, 1987).

ATWOOD, William G[oodson], *The lioness and the little one: the liaison of George Sand and Frédéric Chopin* (New York: Columbia University Press, 1980).

ATWOOD, William G[oodson], *The Parisian worlds of Frédéric Chopin* (New Haven and London: Yale University Press, 1999).

AXON, William E[dward] A[rmitage], editor, *The annals of Manchester: a chronological record from the earliest times to the end of 1885* (Manchester and London: John Heywood, 1886).

AZOURY, Pierre, *Chopin through his contemporaries: friends, lovers, and rivals* (Westport, CT, and London: Greenwood Press, 1999).

BAILEY, Peter, and Claude FÉRON, *The story of the cross-channel ferry service, 1847–2001 / L'histoire de la ligne transmanche, 1847–2001* (Luneray: Éditions Bertout, 2001).

BAILEY Rebecca M., *Scottish architects' papers: a source book* (Edinburgh: Rutland Press, 1996).

BALLSTAEDT, Andreas, 'Chopin as "salon composer" in nineteenth-century German criticism', in Rink and Samson, *Chopin Studies 2* (Cambridge), pp. 18–34.

BALZAC, Honoré de, *Ursule Mirouët* [1841], edited by Madeleine Ambrière-Fargeaud (Paris: Gallimard, 1981; paperback 2004).

BALZAC, Honoré de, *Ursula*, translated by Katharine Prescott Wormeley (New York and Berlin: Mondial, 2006).
BAPTIE, David, compiler and editor, *A handbook of musical biography* (London: W. Morley and Co, [1883]; 2nd ed., 1887).
BAPTIE, David, compiler and editor, *Musical Scotland past and present, being a dictionary of Scottish musicians from about 1400 till the present time, to which is added a bibliography of musical publications connected with Scotland from 1611* (Paisley: J. and R. Parlane, 1894; reprinted, Hildesheim and New York: Georg Olms Verlag, 1972).
BARLOW, Jeremy, 'Encounters with Chopin: Fanny Erskine's Paris diary, 1847–1848', in Rink and Samson, *Chopin studies 2* (Cambridge), pp. 245–8.
BARNETT, T[homas] Ratcliffe, *Scottish pilgrimage in the land of lost content* (Edinburgh and London: John Grant, 1942; reprinted 1944, 1949).
BARRY, Nicole, *Pauline Viardot: l'égérie de Sand et de Tourgueniev* (Paris: Flammarion, 1990).
BARTY, Alexander Boyd, *The history of Dunblane* [1944], 2nd ed. (Stirling: Stirling District Libraries, 1994).
BARZUN, Jacques, 'Paris in 1830', in Bloom, *Music in Paris in the eighteen-thirties*, pp. 1–22.
BASHFORD, Christina, 'Learning to listen: audiences for chamber music in early-Victorian London', *Journal of Victorian Culture*, vol.4 (1999), pp. 25–51.
BASHFORD, Christina, 'John Ella and the making of the Musical Union', in Bashford and Langley, *Music and British culture, 1785–1914*, pp. 193–214.
BASHFORD, Christina, *The pursuit of high culture: John Ella and chamber music in Victorian London* (Woodbridge: Boydell, 2007).
BASHFORD, Christina, and Leanne LANGLEY, editors, *Music and British culture, 1785–1914: essays in honour of Cyril Ehrlich* (Oxford: Oxford University Press, 2000).
BEALE, Robert, *Charles Hallé: a musical life* (Basingstoke: Ashgate, 2007).
BEALE, [Thomas] Willert (pseudonym Walter Maynard), *The light of other days seen through the wrong end of an opera glass*, 2 vols (London: Richard Bentley and Son, 1890).
BEAUPAIN, René, *Chronologie des pianos de la Maison Pleyel* (Paris, etc: L'Harmattan, 2000).
BELL, Alan, editor, *Lord Cockburn: selected letters* (Edinburgh: John Donald, 2005).
BELLENGER, Sylvain, and Caroline MATHIEU, *Paris 1837: views of some monuments in Paris completed during the reign of Louis-Philippe I; watercolours by Félix Duban*, translated by Barbara Mellor (Paris: Alain de Gourcuff, 1999).
BELLMAN, Jonathan, 'Chopin and his imitators: notated emulations of the "true style" of performance', *Nineteenth-century Music*, vol.24, no.2 (Fall, 2000) pp. 149–60.
BELOTTI, Gastone, *F. Chopin, l'uomo*, 3 vols (Milan – Rome: Sapere, 1974).
BENNETT, Joseph, *Frederic Chopin*, Novello's Primers of Musical Biography (London: Novello and Company; New York: Novello, Ewer and Co, [1884–5]).
BENNETT, Joseph, *Forty years of music, 1865–1905* (London: Methuen and Co, 1908).
BERGER, Françoise, 'Histoire d'une amitié Pauline Viardot – Frédéric Chopin', in Poniatowska, *Chopin and his work in the context of culture*, vol.1, pp. 130–50.
BIDDLE, Gordon, *Britain's historic railway buildings: an Oxford gazetteer of structures and sites* (Oxford: Oxford University Press, 2003).
BIDDLECOMBE, George, 'The construction of a cultural icon: the case of Jenny Lind', in *Nineteenth-century British music studies*, vol.3, ed. Peter Horton and Bennett Zon (Aldershot: Ashgate, 2003), pp. 45–61.

BIGGS, Maude Ashurst, *The Literary Association of Friends of Poland, 1832–1924: a retrospect* (London: Curwen Press, 1924).
BINENTAL, Léopold, *Chopin: Dukumente und Erinnerungen aus seiner Heimatstadt*, translated from the Polish by A. von Guttry (Leipzig: Breitkopf and Härtel, 1932).
BISHOP, C.H., *Folkestone: the story of a town* (London and Ashford: Printed by Headley Brothers, 1973).
BLAINEY, Ann, *Fanny and Adelaide: the lives of the remarkable Kemble sisters* (Chicago: Ivan R. Dee, 2001).
BLAKEMORE, Colin, and Sheila JENNETT, editors, *The Oxford companion to the body* (Oxford and New York: Oxford University Press, 2001).
BLEDSOE, Robert Terrell, *Henry Fothergill Chorley: Victorian journalist* (Aldershot: Ashgate, 1998).
BLEDSOE, Robert Terrell, 'Mendelssohn's canonical status in England, the revolutions of 1848, and H.F. Chorley's "retrogressive" ideology of artistic genius', *Nineteenth-century British music studies*, vol.2, ed. Jeremy Dibble and Bennett Zon (Aldershot: Ashgate, 2002), pp. 139–53.
BLEW, William C[harles] A[rlington], *Brighton and its coaches: a history of the London and Brighton Road with some account of the provincial coaches that have run from Brighton* (London: John C. Nimmo, 1894).
BLOOM, Peter, editor, *Music in Paris in the eighteen-thirties/La musique à Paris dans les années mil huit cent trente* (Stuyvesant, New York: Pendragon Press, 1987).
BONE, Audrey Evelyn, *Jane Wilhelmina Stirling, 1804–1859: the first study of the life of Chopin's pupil and friend* (Chipstead, Surrey: Starrock Services, 1960).
BORDIER, Cyril, *Louis Le Vau: architecte*, tome 1, *Les immeubles et hôtels particuliers Parisiens* (Paris: Léonce Laget, 1998).
BORY, Robert, *La vie de Frédéric Chopin par l'image*, preface by Alfred Cortot (Paris: Horizons de France, [1951]).
BRADLEY, Simon, and Nikolaus PEVSNER, *London 1: the City of London*, The Buildings of England (London: Penguin Books, 1997; reprinted, New Haven and London: Yale University Press, 2002).
BRADLEY, Simon, and Nikolaus PEVSNER, *London 6: Westminster*, The Buildings of England (New Haven and London: Yale University Press, 2003; reprinted, 2005).
BRANSON, David, *John Field and Chopin* (London: Barrie and Jenkins, [1972]).
BREM, Anne-Marie de, *La maison de George Sand à Nohant* (Paris: Monum, Éditions du Patrimoine, 2005).
BRENDEL, Alfred, *On music: collected essays* [2001], 2nd ed. (London: J.R. Books, 2007).
BRONARSKI, Ludwik, 'Les élèves de Chopin', *Annales Chopin*, vol.6 (1961–4), pp. 7–12.
BROOKSHAW, Susanna, *Concerning Chopin in Manchester* (Manchester: Privately published, 1937; reprinted, with additional information, 1951).
BROOKSHAW, Susanna, 'Concerning Chopin in Manchester', *Hinrichsen's musical year book*, vols 4–5 (1947–8), pp. 189–91.
BROOKSHAW, Susanna, 'Chopin's Jane Stirling', *Musical Opinion* (April 1948), reprinted in Brookshaw, *Concerning Chopin in Manchester*, pp. 38–40.
BROWN, Iain Gordon, *Elegance and entertainment in the new town of Edinburgh: the Harden drawings* (Edinburgh: Rutland Press, 1995).
BROWN, James D[uff], *Biographical dictionary of musicians, with a bibliography of English writings on music* (Paisley and London: Alexander Gardner, 1886; reprinted, Hildesheim and New York: Georg Olms Verlag, 1970).

BROWN, James D[uff], and Stephen S[amuel] STRATTON, *British musical biography: a dictionary of musical artists, authors and composers born in Britain and its colonies* (London: William Reeves, 1897; reprinted, New York: Da Capo Press, 1971).
BROWN, Maurice J[ohn] E[dwin], 'The posthumous publication of Chopin's songs', *The Musical Quarterly*, vol.42, no.1 (January 1956), pp. 51–65.
BROWN, Maurice J[ohn] E[dwin], 'Chopin and his English publisher', *Music and Letters*, vol.39, no.4 (October 1958), pp. 363–71.
BROWN, Maurice J[ohn] E[dwin], *Chopin: an index of his works in chronological order* [1960], 2nd ed. (London: Macmillan; New York: Da Capo Press, 1972).
BROWN, Maurice J[ohn] E[dwin], 'Arthur Hedley', in *The New Grove dictionary of music and musicians*, ed. Stanley Sadie (Macmillan, 1980), vol.8, p. 430.
BROWN, Stephen, 'Chopin came from Ipanema', *Times Literary Supplement* (20 June 2003), pp. 20–1.
BRUBAKER, Bruce, and Jane GOTTLIEB, editors, *Pianist, scholar, connoisseur: essays in honor of Jacob Lateiner* (Stuyvesant, NY: Pendragon Press, 2000).
BUCKNALL, Rixon, *Boat trains and channel packets: the English short sea routes* (London: Vincent Stuart, 1957).
BULARZ – RÓŻYCKA, Ludmiła and Barbara Lewińska, *Krakowskie Chopiniana* (Cracow: Muzeum Uniwersytetu Jagiellońskiego, 1999).
BURCHELL, Jenny, *Polite or commercial concerts? concert management and orchestral repertoire in Edinburgh, Bath, Oxford, Manchester, and Newcastle, 1730–1799* (New York and London: Garland, 1996).
BURGAN, Mary, 'Heroines at the piano: women and music in nineteenth-century fiction', in Temperley, *The lost chord*, pp. 42–67.
BURGER, Ernst, *Frédéric Chopin: eine Lebenschronik in Bildern und Dokumenten* (Munich: Hirmer, 1990).
BURNETT, Richard, *Company of pianos*, with glossary and keyboard chronology by William Dow (Finchcocks, Kent: Finchcocks Press; London: Third Millennium Publishing, 2004).
BURROWS, Donald, 'Victorian England: an age of expansion', in Samson, *The late romantic era*, pp. 266–94.
BYROM, Connie, *The Edinburgh new town gardens: 'blessings as well as beauties'* (Edinburgh: Birlinn, 2005).
CAIRNS, David, trans. and ed., *The memoirs of Hector Berlioz*, Everyman's Library (New York and Toronto: Alfred A. Knopf, 2002).
CANT, Malcolm, *Villages of Edinburgh: an illustrated guide*, 2 vols (Edinburgh: Malcolm Cant, 1997 (vol.1), 1999 (vol.2).
CARLEY, Lionel, *Edvard Grieg in England* (Woodbridge: Boydell, 2006).
CARLYLE, Thomas, *The life of John Sterling* (London: Chapman and Hall, 1851).
CARTER, Oliver, *An illustrated history of British railway hotels, 1838–1983* (St Michael's, Lancashire: Silver Link Publishing, 1990).
CHAPPLE, J[ohn] A[lfred] V[ictor], and Arthur POLLARD, editors, *The letters of Mrs Gaskell* [1966], 2nd ed. (Manchester: Mandolin, [1997]).
CHARLTON, David, 'The nineteenth century: France', in Parker, *Oxford illustrated history of opera*, pp. 122–68.
CHARLTON, H[enry] B[uckley], *Portrait of a university (1851–1951): to commemorate the centenary of Manchester University* [1951], 2nd ed. (Manchester: Manchester University Press, 1952).

CHARTON, Bernard, and Jacqueline BARBANCEY, *Personnes et personnages: profils homéopathiques* (Paris: Similia, 1994).
CHERRY, Bridget, and Nikolaus PEVSNER, *London 3: north west*, The Buildings of England (London: Penguin Books, 1991; reprinted, New Haven and London: Yale University Press, 2001).
CHERRY, Bridget, and Nikolaus PEVSNER, *London 4: north*, The Buildings of England (London: Penguin Books, 1998; reprinted, New Haven and London: Yale University Press, 2002).
CHILVERS, Ian, *The Oxford dictionary of art and artists*, 4th ed. (Oxford: Oxford University Press, 2009).
CHITI, Patricia Adkins, editor, with phonetic transcriptions by John Glenn PATON, *Songs and duets by Garcia, Malibran and Viardot: rediscovered songs by legendary singers* (Van Nuys, California: Alfred Publishing Company, 1997).
CHOMIŃSKI, Józef Michał, and Teresa Dalila TURŁO, *(KDFC) Katalog dzieł Fryderyka Chopina/A catalogue of the works of Frederick Chopin* (Cracow: PWM; Warsaw: TiFC, 1990).
CHOPIN, Frédéric, *Oeuvres pour piano: facsimilé de l'exemplaire de Jane W. Stirling avec annotations et corrections de l'auteur (Ancienne collection Édouard Ganche)*, introduction by Jean – Jacques Eigeldinger, preface by Jean-Michel Nectoux (Paris: Bibliothèque nationale, 1982).
CHOPIN, Frédéric, *Frédéric Chopin: esquisses pour une méthode de piano*, texts assembled and presented by Jean-Jacques Eigeldinger (Paris: Flammarion, 1993).
CHORLEY, Henry Fothergill, *Thirty years' musical recollections*, 2 vols (London: Hurst and Blackett, 1862; reprinted, New York: Da Capo Press, 1984).
CHRISTIANSEN, Rupert, *The visitors: culture shock in nineteenth-century Britain* (London: Chatto and Windus, 2000).
CLARKE, M[artin] L[owther], *George Grote: a biography* (London: Athlone Press, 1962).
CLINKSCALE, Martha Novak, *Makers of the piano*, vol.1, 1700–1820 (Oxford: Oxford University Press, 1993; reprinted, 1995); vol.2, 1820–1860 (Oxford: Oxford University Press, 1999).
COBBE, Alec, *A century of keyboard instruments, 1760–1860* (Cambridge: Fitzwilliam Museum, 1983).
COBBE, Alec, *Composer instruments: a catalogue of the Cobbe collection of keyboard instruments with composer associations*, technical data compiled by David Hunt (Hatchlands, Surrey: The Cobbe Collection Trust, in association with The National Trust, 2000).
COBBE, Alec, *Chopin's swansong: the Paris and London pianos of his last performances in the Cobbe collection* (London: The Chopin Society, in association with The Cobbe Collection Trust, 2010).
COBBE, Alec, and NOBBS, Christopher, technical particulars compiled by David Hunt and Christopher Nobbs, *Three hundred years of composers' instruments: the Cobbe Collection* (Hatchlands, Surrey: The Cobbe Collection Trust, in association with The National Trust, 2014)
COLE, Emily, editor, *Lived in London: blue plaques and the stories behind them* (New Haven and London: Yale University Press, 2009).
COLT, C.F., with Anthony MIALL, *The early piano* (London: Stainer and Bell, 1981).
COLVIN, Howard [Montagu], *A biographical dictionary of British architects, 1600–1840*, 4th ed. (New Haven and London: Yale University Press, 2008).
COMRIE, John D[ixon], *History of Scottish medicine*, 2nd ed., 2 vols (London: Ballière, Tindall and Cox (for the Wellcome Historical Medical Museum), 1932).

CONNELY, Willard, *Count D'Orsay: the dandy of dandies* (London: Cassell, 1952).
CONRAD, Doda, 'Chopin the song-writer', in Mizwa, *Chopin*, pp. 41–6.
COOK, Susan C., and Judy S. TSOU, introduction, *Anthology of songs: Pauline Duchambge, Loïsa Puget, Pauline Viardot, Jane Vieu* (New York: Da Capo Press, 1988).
COOPER, Victoria L., *The house of Novello: practice and policy of a Victorian music publisher, 1829–1866* (Aldershot: Ashgate, 2003).
COOTER, Roger, editor, *Studies in the history of alternative medicine* (New York: St Martin's Press, 1988).
CRANMER, John Leonard, 'Concert life and the music trade in Edinburgh, circa 1780 – circa 1830', PhD dissertation (University of Edinburgh, 1991).
CRANMER, John Leonard, 'Music retailing in late 18th- and early 19th-century Edinburgh', *The Consort: Journal of the Dolmetsch Foundation*, no.55 (1999), pp. 46–65.
DALAKER, Ingrid Loe, *Thomas Tellefsen: w norweskiej i francuskiej kulturze muzycznej* (Warsaw: NiFC, 2014).
DANIEL, Malcolm R., *The photographs of Édouard Baldus*, introduced by Barry Bergdoll (New York: Metropolitan Museum of Art; Montreal: Canadian Centre for Architecture. 1994).
DARCY, C.P., *The encouragement of the fine arts in Lancashire, 1760–1860* (Manchester: Manchester University Press, for the Chetham Society, 1976).
DASENT, Arthur Irwin, *The history of St James's Square, and the foundation of the west end of London, with a glimpse of Whitehall in the reign of Charles the Second* (London and New York: Macmillan, 1895).
DASENT, Arthur Irwin, *Piccadilly in three centuries, with some account of Berkeley Square and the Haymarket* (London: Macmillan 1920).
DAVISON, Alan, 'The musician in iconography from the 1830s and 1840s: the formation of new visual types', *Music in Art*, vol.28, nos 1–2 (2003), pp. 147–62.
DAVISON, Henry, compiler, *From Mendelssohn to Wagner, being the memoirs of J.W. Davison, forty years music critic of 'The Times'* (London: William Reeves, 1912).
DAVISON, James William, *An essay on the works of Frederic Chopin* (London: Wessel and Stapleton, [1843]).
DAYAN, Peter, *Music writing literature, from Sand via Debussy to Derrida* (Aldershot: Ashgate, 2006).
DELACROIX, Eugène, *Journal, 1822–1863*, preface by Hubert Damisch, introduction and notes by André Joubin, revised by Régis Labourdette (Paris: Plon, 1996).
DELAGE, Roger, 'Delacroix et la musique', in *Delacroix: la naissance d'un nouveau romantisme*, exhibition catalogue (Rouen: Musée des Beaux-Arts, 1998; Paris: Réunion des musées nationaux, 1998), pp. 129–40.
DELAIGUE-MOINS, Sylvie, *Chopin chez George Sand: sept étés à Nohant* (Saint-Cyr-sur-Loire: Christian Pirot, 2005).
DELAIGUE-MOINS, Sylvie, *Les hôtes de George Sand à Nohant* (Saint-Cyr-sur-Loire: Christian Pirot, 2009).
DELAPIERRE, André, with Thomas CHLUNKE, *Chopin à Paris* (Paris: L'Harmattan, 2004).
DENT, Alan, *Nocturnes and rhapsodies* (London: Hamish Hamilton, 1950).
DENT, Alan, 'Chopin – and the lang Scots miles', in Dent, *Nocturnes and rhapsodies*, pp. 184–8.
DE REDÉ, Baron, *Collection du Baron De Redé provenant de l'Hôtel Lambert*, sale catalogue, 2 vols (Paris: Sotheby's, 16–17 March 2005).
DIEHL, A.M. (pseudonym Alice Mangold), *Musical memories* (London: Richard Bentley and Son, 1897).

250 Bibliography

DINGES, Martin, editor, *Patients in the history of homoeopathy* (Sheffield: European Association for the History of Medicine and Health Publications, 2002).

DOD, Charles R[oger], *Electoral facts from 1832 to 1853 impartially stated, constituting a complete political gazetteer*, 2nd ed. (London: Whittaker, 1853), facsimile reprint, edited by H.J. Hanham (Brighton: Harvester Press, 1972).

DUCKWORTH, Christian Leslie Dyce, and Graham Easton LANGMUIR, *Railway and other steamers*, 2nd ed. (Prescot, Lancashire: T. Stephenson and Sons, 1968).

DURIE, Alastair J., *Scotland for the holidays: a history of tourism in Scotland, 1780–1939* (Phantassie, East Linton: Tuckwell, 2003).

DURIE, Alastair J., 'Tourism and the railways in Scotland: the Victorian and Edwardian experience', in Evans and Gough, *The impact of the railway on society in Britain*, pp. 199–209.

EASTLAKE, Elizabeth [Lady, formerly Rigby], *Mrs Grote: a sketch* (London: John Murray, 1880).

EDDIE, William Alexander, *Charles Valentin Alkan: his life and his music* (Aldershot: Ashgate, 2007).

EHRLICH, Cyril, *The piano: a history*, rev. ed. (Oxford: Clarendon Press, 1990).

EHRLICH, Cyril, *First Philharmonic: a history of the Royal Philharmonic Society* (Oxford: Clarendon Press, 1995).

EHRLICH, Cyril, and Simon McVEIGH, 'Music', in McCalman, *An Oxford companion to the romantic age of British culture*, pp. 242–50.

EHRLICH, Cyril, and Dave RUSSELL, 'Victorian music: a perspective', *Journal of Victorian Culture*, vol.3 (1998), pp. 111–22.

EICHNER, Barbara, 'Singing the songs of Scotland: the German musician Johann Rupprecht Dürrner and musical life in nineteenth-century Edinburgh', in *Nineteenth-century British music studies*, vol.3, ed. Peter Horton and Bennett Zon (Aldershot: Ashgate, 2003), pp. 171–91.

EIGELDINGER, Jean-Jacques, *Chopin: pianist and teacher, as seen by his pupils*, translated by Naomi Shohet, with Krysia Osostowicz and Roy Howat, ed. Roy Howat (Cambridge: Cambridge University Press, 1986).

EIGELDINGER, Jean-Jacques, 'Présence de Thomas D.A. Tellefsen dans le corpus annoté des oeuvres de Chopin (exemplaire Stirling)', *Revue de musicologie*, vol.83, no.2 (1997), pp. 247–61.

EIGELDINGER, Jean-Jacques, *L'univers musical de Chopin* (Paris: Arthème Fayard, 2000).

EIGELDINGER, Jean-Jacques, 'Chopin and Pleyel', *Early Music*, vol.29, no.3 (August 2001), pp. 388–96.

EIGELDINGER, Jean-Jacques, *Frédéric Chopin* (Paris: Arthème Fayard, 2003).

EIGELDINGER, Jean-Jacques, 'Chopin et la manufacture Pleyel', in Eigeldinger and Waeber, *Frédéric Chopin: interprétations*, pp. 89–106.

EIGELDINGER, Jean-Jacques, *Chopin vu par ses élèves*, 4th ed. (Paris: Arthème Fayard, 2006).

EIGELDINGER, Jean-Jacques, *Chopin et Pleyel* (Paris: Arthème Fayard, 2010).

EIGELDINGER, Jean-Jacques, and Jacqueline WAEBER, editors, *Frédéric Chopin: interprétations*. Symposium international, Université de Genève (Geneva: Librairie Droz, 2005).

ELLSWORTH, Therese, 'The piano concerto in London concert life between 1801 and 1850', PhD dissertation (University of Cincinnati, 1991).

ELLSWORTH, Therese, and Susan WOLLENBERG, editors, *The piano in nineteenth-century British culture: instruments, performers and repertoire* (Aldershot: Ashgate, 2007).

EVANS, A.K.B, and J.V. GOUGH, editors *The impact of the railway on society in Britain: essays in honour of Jack Simmons* (Aldershot: Ashgate 2003).
EWALS, Leonardus Joseph Ignatius, 'Ary Scheffer: sa vie et son oeuvre', Doctor of Letters thesis (Catholic University of Nijmegen, 1987).
EWALS, Leo, *Ary Scheffer (1795–1858): gevierd romanticus*, Dordrechts Museum, Dordrecht (Zwolle: Waanders, 1995).
EWALS, Leo, *Ary Scheffer (1795–1858)*, Musée de la Vie romantique (Paris: Éditions des Musées de la Ville de Paris, 1996).
FARMER, Henry George, *A history of music in Scotland* (London: Hinrichsen, [1947]; reprinted, New York: Da Capo Press, 1970).
[FARMER, Henry George] COWL, Carl, and Sheila M. CRAIK, *Henry George Farmer: a bibliography* (Glasgow: Glasgow University Library, 1999).
FAUQUET, Joël-Marie, 'La musique de chambre à Paris dans les années 1830', in Bloom, *Music in Paris in the eighteen-thirties*, pp. 299–326.
FAUQUET, Joël-Marie, editor, *Dictionnaire de la musique en France au XIXe siècle* (Paris: Arthème Fayard, 2003).
FELDMANN, Dietrich, 'Maison Lambert, Maison Hesselin und andere Bauten von Louis Le Vau (1612/13–1670) auf der Île Saint-Louis in Paris', Doctoral thesis, University of Hamburg, 1973 (Hamburg, 1976).
FERGUSON, Niall, *The world's banker: the history of the House of Rothschild* (London: Weidenfeld and Nicolson, 1998).
FIDDES, Edward, *Chapters in the history of Owens College and of Manchester University, 1851–1914* (Manchester: Manchester University Press, 1937).
FIELDEN, Jay, 'Backstage notes', *The New Yorker*, 23 November 1998, p. 32.
FIORENTINO, Pier Angelo, 'Chopin', in *Dictionnaire de la conversation et de la lecture: supplément*, tome 10 (Paris: Librairie de Firmin Didot Frères, 1868), pp. 427–8.
FISKE, Roger, *Scotland in music: a European enthusiasm* (Cambridge: Cambridge University Press, 1983).
FITZLYON, April, *The price of genius: a life of Pauline Viardot* (London: John Calder, 1964).
FLANDERS, Judith, *Consuming passions: leisure and pleasure in Victorian Britain* (London: Harper Press, 2006).
FORBES, Elizabeth, *Mario and Grisi: a biography* (London: Victor Gollancz, 1985).
FORBES, R.J., 'The death-mask of Chopin', *Manchester Guardian*, Wednesday 22 February 1933.
FOREMAN, Lewis, editor, *Information sources in music* (Munich: K.G. Saur, 2003).
FOREMAN, Lewis, and Susan FOREMAN, *London: a musical gazetteer* (New Haven and London: Yale University Press, 2005).
FORREST, Denys, *St James's Square: people, houses, happenings*, 2nd ed. (London: Quiller Press, 2001).
FOULKES, Nick, *Last of the dandies: the scandalous life and escapades of Count D'Orsay* (London: Little, Brown, 2003).
FRANÇOIS-SAPPEY, Brigitte, editor, *Charles Valentin Alkan* (Paris: Arthème Fayard, 1991).
FRASER, William, *The Stirlings of Keir and their family papers* (Edinburgh: Privately printed, 1858).
Frederic Chopin and his publishers, exhibition catalogue (Chicago: Department of Special Collections, University of Chicago Library, 1998).
FREEMAN, Michael, *Railways and the Victorian imagination* (New Haven and London: Yale University Press, 1999).

FREEMAN, Michael, and Derek ALDCROFT, *The atlas of British railway history* (London, Sydney, and Dover, New Hampshire: Croom Helm, 1985).
[GALIGNANI, A., and W. GALIGNANI], *Galignani's new Paris guide* (Paris: Galignani, various editions from 1841).
GANCHE, Édouard, *Frédéric Chopin: sa vie et ses oeuvres, 1810–1849*, 3rd ed. (Paris: Mercure de France, 1913).
GANCHE, Édouard, *Dans le souvenir de Frédéric Chopin*, 9th ed. (Paris: Mercure de France, 1925).
GANCHE, Édouard, *Voyages avec Frédéric Chopin* (Paris: Mercure de France, 1934).
GANCHE, Édouard, *Souffrances de Frédéric Chopin: essai de médecine et de psychologie*, 6th ed. (Paris: Mercure de France, 1935).
GARNIER-PELLE, Nicole, *Chantilly, Musée Condé: peintures des XIXe et XXe siècles*, (Paris: Éditions de la Réunion des musées nationaux; Chantilly: Musée Condé, 1997).
GAVOTY, Bernard, *Frédéric Chopin* (Paris: Bernard Grasset, 1974; new impression, 1986). (In French)
GAVOTY, Bernard, *Frederic Chopin*, translated by Martin Sokolinsky (New York: Charles Scribner's Sons, 1977). (In English)
GÉRIN, Winifred, *Elizabeth Gaskell: a biography* (Oxford: Clarendon Press, 1976).
GÉRIN, Winifred, *Anne Thackeray Ritchie: a biography* (Oxford: Oxford University Press, 1981; paperback, 1983).
GÉTREAU, Florence, 'Romantic pianists in Paris: musical images and musical literature', *Music in Art*, vol.29, nos 1–2 (2004), pp. 188–202.
GIBBS, Christopher H., and Dana GOOLEY, editors, *Franz Liszt and his world* (Princeton, NJ, and Oxford: Princeton University Press, 2006).
GICK, Rachel, 'The emergence of the chamber music concert in Manchester during the period 1838–1844: context, repertoire, institutions and performers', MusM thesis (University of Manchester, 1999).
GICK, Rachel, 'Chamber music concerts in Manchester, 1838–1844', *Manchester Sounds*, vol.2 (2001), pp. 59–87.
GICK, Rachel, 'Concert life in Manchester, 1800–1848', PhD dissertation (University of Manchester, 2003).
GIFFORD, John, Colin McWILLIAM, and David WALKER (Medieval buildings by Christopher WILSON), *Edinburgh*, The Buildings of Scotland (Harmondsworth: Penguin Books, 1984; reprinted with corrections, New Haven and London: Yale University Press, 2003).
GIFFORD, John, and Frank Arneil WALKER, *Stirling and central Scotland*, The Buildings of Scotland (New Haven and London: Yale University Press, 2002).
GOLD, John R., and Margaret M. GOLD, *Imagining Scotland: tradition, representation and promotion in Scottish tourism since 1750* (Aldershot: Scolar Press, 1995).
GOLDBERG, Halina, 'Chopin in literary salons and Warsaw's romantic awakening, *The Polish Review*, vol.45, no.1 (January 2000), pp. 53–64.
GOLDBERG, Halina, editor, *The age of Chopin: interdisciplinary enquiries* (Bloomington and Indianapolis: Indiana University Press, 2004).
GOLDBERG, Halina, ' "Remembering that tale of grief": the prophetic voice of Chopin's music', in Goldberg, *The age of Chopin*, pp. 54–92.
GOLDBERG, Halina, *Music in Chopin's Warsaw* (New York: Oxford University Press, 2008).
GOSSETT, Philip, 'Music at the Théâtre-Italien', in Bloom, *Music in Paris in the eighteen-thirties*, pp. 327–64.

GOTCH, Rosamund Brunel, *Mendelssohn and his friends in Kensington: letters from Fanny and Sophie Horsley, written 1833–1836* (London: Oxford University Press, 1934).
GOTTSCHALK, Louis Moreau, *Notes of a pianist*, edited by Jeanne Behrend, new foreword by S. Frederick Starr (Princeton, NJ, and Oxford: Princeton University Press, 2006).
GOW, Ian, 'Fit for an empress: imperial staircase in Edinburgh', *Country Life*, 13 September 1990, pp. 216, 218.
GOW, Ian, *Scottish houses and gardens, from the archives of 'Country Life'* (London: Aurum, 1997).
GOW, Ian, *Scotland's lost houses* (London: Aurum, 2006).
GOWER, Lord Ronald, *My reminiscences*, vol.1 (London: Kegan Paul, Trench and Co, 1883).
GRABOWSKI, Christophe, 'Wessel's *Complete collection of the compositions of Frederic Chopin*: the history of a title-page', *Early Music*, vol.29, no.3 (August 2001), pp. 424–33.
GRABOWSKI, Christophe, 'Publication des valses, Op.64, dans un contexte historique et documentaire', in Eigeldinger and Waeber, *Frédéric Chopin: interprétations*, pp. 53–68.
GRAMIT, David, editor, *Beyond 'the art of finger dexterity': reassessing Carl Czerny* (Rochester: University of Rochester Press; Woodbridge: Boydell and Brewer, 2008).
GRAY, Adrian, *South Eastern Railway* (Midhurst, West Sussex: Middleton Press, 1990).
GRENIER, Katherine Haldane, *Tourism and identity in Scotland, 1770–1914: creating Caledonia* (Aldershot: Ashgate, 2005).
GROTE, Mrs [Harriet], *Memoir of the life of Ary Scheffer* (London: John Murray, 1860).
GROTE, Mrs [Harriet], *The personal life of George Grote, compiled from family documents, private memoranda, and original letters to and from various friends*, 2nd ed. (London: John Murray, 1873; reprinted, Bristol: Thoemmes Press, 2002).
GUILLOT, Pierre, 'De Coquette (ca 1848) à tristesse (1939): une interprétation (très large . . .) des oeuvres de Chopin en France', in Pistone, *L'interprétation de Chopin en France*, pp. 45–61.
GUIZOT, François, *Lettres à sa fille Henriette (1836–1874)*, edited by Laurent Theis, with a biographical essay by Catherine Coste ([Paris]: Perrin, 2002).
GUT, Serge, 'Frédéric Chopin et Franz Liszt: une amitié à sens unique', in Pistone, *Sur les traces de Frédéric Chopin*, pp. 53–68.
HADDEN, J[ames] Cuthbert, *Chopin* [1903], (London: J.M. Dent and Sons, Ltd; New York, E.P. Dutton and Co, 1926 printing; many subsequent reprints).
HAEHL, Richard, *Samuel Hahnemann: his life and work* . . . translated from the German by Marie L. Wheeler and W.H.R. Grundy, edited by J.H. Clarke and F.J. Wheeler, 2 vols (London: Homoeopathic Publishing Company, [1931]).
HAIR, John, *Regent Square: eighty years of a London congregation* (London: James Nisbet and Co, 1898).
HALL-WITT, Jennifer L[ee], 'Representing the audience in the age of reform: critics and the elite of Italian opera in London', in Bashford and Langley, *Music and British culture, 1785–1914*, pp. 121–44.
HALL-WITT, Jennifer L[ee], *Fashionable acts: opera and elite culture in London, 1780–1880* (Durham, NH: University of New Hampshire Press; Hanover, NH, and London: University Press of New England, 2007).
[HALLÉ, Sir Charles], *The autobiography of Sir Charles Hallé, with correspondence and diaries*, edited, with an introduction, by Michael Kennedy (London: Paul Elek Books, 1972).

HALLÉ, C[harles] E[mile], and Marie HALLÉ, editors, *Life and letters of Sir Charles Hallé, being an autobiography (1819–1860) with correspondence and diaries* (London: Smith, Elder and Co, 1896).

HAMILTON, David, *The healers: a history of medicine in Scotland*, 2nd ed. (Edinburgh: Mercat Press, 1981; repr. 2003).

HANDLEY, Rima, *A homeopathic love story: the story of Samuel and Melanie Hahnemann* (Berkeley, California: North Atlantic Books, and Homeopathic Educational Services, 1990).

HANDLEY, Rima, *In search of the later Hahnemann* (Beaconsfield, Buckinghamshire: Beaconsfield Publishers, 1997).

HANNA, William, editor, *Letters of Thomas Erskine of Linlathen (1800–1840)* (Edinburgh: David Douglas, 1877).

HANNA, William, editor, *Letters of Thomas Erskine of Linlathen (1840–1870)* (Edinburgh: David Douglas, 1877).

HARASOWSKI, Adam, 'Arthur Hedley, 1905–1969', *Music and Musicians*, vol.18, no.7 (1970), pp. 25–7, 70–1.

HARASOWSKI, Adam, *The skein of legends around Chopin* (Glasgow: William MacLellan, 1967; reprinted, New York: Da Capo Press, 1980).

HARDING, Rosamond E.M., *The piano-forte: its history traced to the Great Exhibition of 1851* [1933], 2nd ed. (London: Heckscher, 1978; reprinted, 1989).

HARLAND, John, compiler, arranger, and editor, *Collectanea relating to Manchester and its neighbourhood, at various periods*, 2 vols (Manchester: The Chetham Society, 1866, 1867).

HARLEY, Maria, *see* TROCHIMCZYK, Maja.

HARRIS, David Fraser, *Saint Cecilia's Hall in the Niddry Wynd: a chapter in the history of the music of the past in Edinburgh* (Edinburgh and London: Oliphant Anderson and Ferrier, 1899).

HARTWELL, Clare, 'Manchester and the golden age of Pericles: Richard Lane, architect', in Hartwell and Wyke, *Making Manchester*, pp. 18–35.

HARTWELL, Clare, with contributions by John H.G. Archer and Julian Holder, *Manchester*, Pevsner Architectural Guides (New Haven and London: Yale University Press, 2001; reprinted with corrections, 2002).

HARTWELL, Clare, Matthew HYDE, and Nikolaus PEVSNER, *Lancashire: Manchester and the south-east*, The Buildings of England (New Haven and London: Yale University Press, 2004).

HARTWELL, Clare, and Terry WYKE, editors, *Making Manchester: aspects of the history of architecture in the city and region since 1800; essays in honour of John H.G. Archer* (Manchester: Lancashire and Cheshire Antiquarian Society, 2007).

HEDDERWICK, James, *Backward glances, or some personal recollections* (Edinburgh and London: William Blackwood and Sons, 1891).

HEDLEY, Arthur, *Chopin* [1947, 1963], revised by Maurice J[ohn] E[dwin] Brown (London: J.M. Dent, 1974).

HEDLEY, Arthur, translator and editor, *Selected correspondence of Fryderyk Chopin* (London: Heinemann, 1962; New York, Toronto and London: McGraw-Hill, 1963; reprinted, New York: Da Capo Press, 1979). [*In English*, abridged from Sydow, *KFC*, with additional material.]

HERRESTHAL, Harald, and Ladislav REZNICEK, *Rhapsodie norvégienne: les musiciens norvégiens en France au temps de Grieg*, translated from Norwegian into French by Chantal de Batz (Caen: Presses Universitaires de Caen, 1994).

HERRESTHAL, Harald, and Danièle PISTONE, editors, *Grieg et Paris: romantisme, symbolisme et modernisme franco-norvégiens* (Caen: Presses Universitaires de Caen, 1996).

HEUBERGER, Georg, editor, *The Rothschilds: a European family*, exhibition guide, Jüdisches Museum, Frankfurt (Frankfurt am Main: Thorbecke; Woodbridge: Boydell, 1994).

HEWLETT, Henry Gay, compiler, *Henry Fothergill Chorley: autobiography, memoir, and letters*, 2 vols (London: Richard Bentley and Son, 1873).

HILLER, Ferdinand, *Felix Mendelssohn Bartholdy: Briefe und Erinnerungen* (Cologne: M. Du Mont-Schauberg, 1874), translated by M.E. von Glehn, as *Mendelssohn: letters and recollections* (London: Macmillan, 1874; reprinted, New York: Vienna House, 1972).

[HIPKINS, Alfred James], *International inventions exhibition: division – Music; John Broadwood & Sons . . .* (London: Fargues & Co, Printers, 1885) [includes a section entitled 'Chopin's pianoforte', pp. 12–13].

HIPKINS, Alfred James, *A description and history of the pianoforte, and of the older keyboard stringed instruments* (London and New York: Novello, Ewer and Co, 1896), 3rd ed. (London: Novello, 1929), reprinted, with an introduction by Edwin M. Ripin (Detroit: Information Coordinators, 1975).

HIPKINS, Edith J., *How Chopin played, from contemporary impressions collected from the diaries and note-books of the late A.J. Hipkins, FSA* (London: J.M. Dent, 1937).

HOBHOUSE, Hermione, *Lost London: a century of demolition and decay* (London and Basingstoke: Macmillan, 1971).

HOBHOUSE, Hermione, *Thomas Cubitt: master builder*, 2nd ed. (Didcot: Management Books 2000, 1995).

HOESICK, Ferdynand, *Chopin: zycie i twórczosc*, 4 vols (Cracow: PWM, 1904–11; reprinted, 1962–6).

HOLLAND, Henry Scott, and W.S. ROCKSTRO, *Jenny Lind the artist (1820–1851): a memoir of Madame Jenny Lind Goldschmidt, her art-life and dramatic career; from original documents, letters, MS diaries, &c., collected by Mr Otto Goldschmidt*, new and abridged edition (London: John Murray, 1893).

HOLLAND, Jeanne, 'Chopin's teaching and his students', PhD dissertation (University of North Carolina, Chapel Hill, 1973).

HOLLAND, Jeanne, 'Chopin the teacher', *Journal of the American Liszt Society*, vol.17 (1985), pp. 39–48.

HOLLAND, Jeanne, 'Chopin's piano method', *Piano Quarterly*, vol.33, no.129 (1985), pp. 32–43.

HOWARTH, David, *The invention of Spain: cultural relations between Britain and Spain, 1770–1870* (Manchester and New York: Manchester University Press, 2007).

HUEFFER, Francis, 'Chopin', *Fortnightly Review*, new series, vol.22 (1877), pp. 377–94.

HUEFFER, Francis, *Musical studies: a series of contributions* (Edinburgh: Adam and Charles Black, 1880).

HULDT NYSTROM, Hampus, 'Thomas Dyke Acland Tellefsen', *Norsk Musikkgranskning, Arbok 1956–1958* (Oslo: Johan Grundt Tanum, 1959), pp. 80–198.

HUMPHRIES, Charles, and William C. SMITH, *Music publishing in the British Isles, from the beginning until the middle of the nineteenth century: a dictionary of engravers, printers, publishers and music sellers, with a historical introduction*, 2nd ed., with supplement (New York: Barnes & Noble, 1970).

HUNEKER, James, *Chopin: the man and his music* (London: William Reeves, 1913).

HUNT, Tristram, and Victoria WHITFIELD, *Art treasures in Manchester: 150 years on* (Manchester: Manchester Art Gallery; London: Philip Wilson Publishers, 2007).

HUNT, Una, 'George Alexander Osborne, a nineteenth-century Irish pianist-composer', PhD dissertation (National University of Ireland, Maynooth, 2006).

HURD, Douglas, *Robert Peel: a biography* (London: Weidenfeld and Nicolson, 2007).

IRELAND, George, *Plutocrats: a Rothschild inheritance* (London: John Murray, 2007)

JACKSON, Peter, introduction and biographical essay, *John Tallis's London street views, 1838–1840, together with the revised and enlarged views of 1847* (with indexes on CD-ROM) (London: Topographical Society, 2002).

JACOBSON, Bernard, 'The Songs', in Walker, *Chopin: profiles*, pp. 187–211.

JAEGER, Bertrand, 'Quelques nouveaux noms d'élèves de Chopin', *Revue de musicologie*, vol.64, no.1 (1978), pp. 76–108.

JAGODIŃSKI, Zdzisław, *Anglia wobec sprawy polskiej w okresie Wiosny Ludów, 1848–1849* (Warsaw: Institut Historii Pan/Wydawnictwo Neriton, 1997).

JAQUES, Richard, and Charles McKEAN, *West Lothian: an illustrated architectural guide* (Edinburgh: Rutland Press, 1994).

John Broadwood and Sons, Limited, Piano Manufacturers (London: Business Records, 1719–1981).

JOHNSON, Douglas W., *Guizot: aspects of French history, 1787–1874* (London: Routledge and Kegan Paul; Toronto: University of Toronto Press, 1963).

JOHNSON, James H., *Listening in Paris: a cultural history* (Berkeley, Los Angeles, and London: University of California Press, 1995).

JONES, J. Barrie, 'Nationalism', in Rowland, *Cambridge companion to the piano*, pp. 176–91.

JONSON, G[eorge] C[harles] Ashton, *A handbook to Chopin's works*, 2nd ed., revised (London: William Reeves, [1908]).

JORGENSEN, Cecilia and Jens, *Chopin and the Swedish nightingale: the life and times of Chopin and a romance unveiled 154 years later* (Brussels: Icons of Europe, 2003).

JOURDAN, Paul, 'The hidden pathways of assimilation: Mendelssohn's first visit to London', in Bashford and Langley, *Music and British culture, 1785–1914*, pp. 100–19.

JUÁREZ, Marita Albán, and Ewa SŁAWIŃSKA-DAHLIG, *Chopin's Poland: a guidebook to places associated with the composer*, translated and edited by John Comber (Warsaw: NiFC, 2008).

KALLBERG, Jeffrey, 'The Chopin sources: variants and versions in later manuscript and printed editions', PhD dissertation (University of Chicago, 1982).

KALLBERG, Jeffrey, *Chopin at the boundaries: sex, history, and musical genre* (Cambridge, Massachusetts, and London: Harvard University Press, 1996).

KALLBERG, Jeffrey, 'Chopin's march, Chopin's death', *Nineteenth-century Music*, vol.25, no.1 (2001), pp. 3–26.

KALLBERG, Jeffrey, '"Voice" and the nocturne', in Brubaker and Gottlieb, *Pianist, scholar, connoisseur*, pp. 1–46.

KALLBERG, Jeffrey, 'Hearing Poland: Chopin and nationalism', in Todd, *Nineteenth-century piano music*, pp. 221–57.

KALLBERG, Jeffrey, 'La Marche de Chopin', in Eigeldinger and Waeber, *Frédéric Chopin: interprétations*, pp. 11–42.

KAŁUŻA, Zofia, 'Chopin i Marcelina Czartoryska', *Ruch Muzyczny*, vol.18, no.17 (18 August 1974), pp. 13–14.

KARASOWSKI, Moritz, *Frederic Chopin: his life and letters*, translated by Emily Hill, 3rd ed. (London: William Reeves, 1938).

KARŁOWICZ, Mieczysław, editor and collector, *Nie wydane dotąd parmiątki po Chopinie* (Warsaw: Fiszer, 1904).

KARŁOWICZ, Mieczysław, editor and collector, *Souvenirs inédits de Frédéric Chopin*, translated by Laure Disière (Paris and Leipzig: Welter, 1904).

KELLY, Thomas Forrest, *First nights: five musical premières* (New Haven and London: Yale University Press, 2000).
Kelly's Directory, London 1848 (Cinderford, Gloucestershire: Archive CD Books, 2001).
KEMBLE, Frances Anne [Fanny], *Records of a later life*. 3 vols, 2nd ed. (London: Richard Bentley, 1882).
KENDALL-DAVIES, Barbara, *The life and work of Pauline Viardot Garcia*, vol.1, *The years of fame, 1836–1863* (Amersham, Buckinghamshire: Cambridge Scholars Press, 2003).
KENNEDY, Michael, 'Manchester before Hallé', *Manchester Sounds*, vol.1 (2000), pp. 5–11.
KING, David, *The complete works of Robert and James Adam* and *Unbuilt Adam* 2 vols in 1, reprinted, with corrections and additions (Oxford: Architectural Press, 2001).
KITSON, Richard, 'James William Davison, critic, crank and chronicler: a re-evaluation', in *Nineteenth-century British music studies*, vol.1, edited by Bennett Zon (Aldershot: Ashgate, 1999), pp. 303–10.
KJELDSBERG, Peter Andreas, *Piano i Norge: 'Et uundvaerligt instrument'* (Oslo: C. Huitfeldt Forlag AS, 1985).
KNIGHT, Vivien, compiler, *The works of art of the Corporation of London: a catalogue of paintings, watercolours, drawings, prints and sculpture* (Cambridge: Woodhead-Faulkner, 1986).
KOBYLAŃSKA, Krystyna, editor and collector, *Chopin in his own land: documents and souvenirs* (Cracow: PWM, 1955).
KOBYLAŃSKA, Krystyna, editor and collector, *Korespondencja Fryderyka Chopina z rodziną* (Warsaw: PIW, 1972). [In Polish, with (in appendices) letters in French to Chopin from his father.]
KOBYLAŃSKA, Krystyna, *(RUC) Rękopisy utworów Chopina. Katalog/Manuscripts of Chopin's works. Catalogue*, 2 vols (Cracow: PWM, 1977).
KOBYLAŃSKA, Krystyna, *(TB-W) Frédéric Chopin: thematisch-bibliographisches Werkverzeichnis* (Munich: Henle, 1979).
KOBYLAŃSKA, Krystyna, editor and collector, with French text by Julia Hartwig, *Korespondencja Fryderyka Chopina z George Sand i z jej dziećmi*, 2 vols (Warsaw: PIW, 1981). [In French and Polish, with Polish translations into French.]
KOBYLAŃSKA, Krystyna, 'Odnaleziony list Chopina', *Ruch Muzyczny*, vol.34, no.26 (30 December 1990'), pp. 1, 7.
KOLB, Marthe, *Ary Scheffer et son temps, 1795–1858* (Paris: Boivin, 1937).
KOROPECKYJ, Roman, *Adam Mickiewicz: the life of a romantic* (Ithaca and London: Cornell University Press, 2008).
KOŹMIAN, Stanisław, *Anglia i Polska*, 2 vols (Poznań: J[an Konstanty] Ż[upański], 1862).
KRAMER, Lloyd S., *Threshold of a new world: intellectuals and the exile experience in Paris, 1830–1848* (Ithaca and London: Cornell University Press, 1988).
KUBBA, Adam K., and Madeleine YOUNG, 'The long suffering of Frederic Chopin', *Chest*, vol.113, no.1 (January 1998), pp. 210–16; and 'Communications to the editor', *Chest*, vol.114, no.2 (August 1998), pp. 654–6.
KUHE, Wilhelm, *My musical recollections* (London: Richard Bentley and Son, 1896).
KUKIEL, Marian, *Czartoryski and European unity, 1770–1861* (Princeton, NJ: Princeton University Press, 1955).
KUZEMKO, J.A., 'Chopin's illnesses', *Journal of the Royal Society of Medicine*, vol.87 (December 1994), pp. 769–72.
LACH-SZYRMA, Krystyn, *Letters, literary and political, on Poland, comprising observations on Russia and other Sclavonian nations and tribes* (Edinburgh: Printed by G. Ramsay for Archibald Constable and Co, 1823).

LACH-SZYRMA, Krystyn, *Anglia i Szkocya: przypomnienia y podróży roku 1823–1824 odbytey*. 3 vols (Warszawa: W Druk Gałęzowskiego, 1828–9).

LACOME, Hervé, *The keys to French opera in the nineteenth century*, translated from the French by Edward Schneider (Berkeley, Los Angeles, and London: University of California Press, 2001).

LAMBERT, Anthony J., *Nineteenth-century railway history through 'The Illustrated London News'* (Newton Abbot, London, and North Pomfret, VT: David & Charles, 1984).

LANGLEY, Leanne, 'The English musical journal in the early nineteenth century', PhD dissertation, 2 vols (University of North Carolina at Chapel Hill, 1983).

LANGLEY, Leanne, 'Italian opera and the English press, 1836–1856', *Periodica Musica*, vol.6 (1988), pp. 3–10.

LANGLEY, Leanne, 'The musical press in 19th-century England', *Notes: Quarterly Journal of the Music Library Association*, vol.46, no.1 (September 1989), pp. 583–92.

LANGLEY, Leanne, 'Music', in Vann and VanArsdel, *Victorian periodicals and Victorian society*, pp. 99–126.

LASDUN, Susan, *Victorians at home* (London: Weidenfeld and Nicolson, 1981).

LAWSON, Julie, 'Photographs by John Muir Wood', *Antiques Collector*, vol.59 (1988), pp. 98–105.

LENZ, Wilhelm von, *The great piano virtuosos of our time from personal acquaintance: Liszt, Chopin, Tausig, Henselt*, translated from the German by Madeleine R. Baker (New York: Schirmer, 1899; reprinted, New York: Da Capo Press, 1973).

LENZ, Wilhelm von, *Les grands virtuoses du piano: Liszt, Chopin, Tausig, Henselt; souvenirs personnels*, translated, edited and introduced by Jean-Jacques Eigeldinger (Paris: Flammarion, 1995).

[LÉO, Sophie], 'Musical life in Paris (1817–1848): a chapter from the memoirs of Sophie Augustine Léo', annotated translation by W[illiam] Oliver Strunk, *The Musical Quarterly*, vol.17, nos 2–3 (1931), pp. 259–71, 389–403.

LEONTYEVA, Galina, introduction, *Karl Briullov: the painter of Russian romanticism* (Bournemouth: Parkstone Publishers; St Petersburg: Aurora Art Publishers, 1996).

LEWIN, Thomas Herbert, collector and editor, *The Lewin letters: a selection from the correspondence and diaries of an English family, 1756–1884*, 2 vols (London: Privately printed, 1909).

LIEBERMAN, Richard K., *Steinway and sons* (New Haven and London: Yale University Press, 1995).

List of the graduates in medicine in the University of Edinburgh, from 1705 to 1866 (Edinburgh: Printed by Neill and Company, 1867).

[LISZT, Franz], *Frederic Chopin, by Franz Liszt*, translated, with an introduction, by Edward N. Waters (New York and London: The Free Press of Glencoe [Macmillan], 1963).

LISZT, Franz, *An artist's journey: lettres d'un bachelier ès musique, 1835–1841*, translated and annotated by Charles Suttoni (Chicago and London: University of Chicago Press, 1989).

LOCKE, Ralph P, 'Paris: centre of intellectual ferment', in Ringer, *Early romantic era*, pp. 32–83.

LOCKSPEISER, Edward, *Music and painting: a study in comparative ideas from Turner to Schoenberg* (London: Cassell, 1973).

LONG, Esmond Ray, *A history of the therapy of tuberculosis, and the case of Frederic Chopin* (Lawrence, KS: University of Kansas Press, 1956).

LOVE, Benjamin, *The hand-book of Manchester*, 2nd ed. (Manchester: Love and Barton, 1842).

[LOVE and BARTON], *Manchester as it is: or, notices of the institutions, manufactures, commerce, railways, etc* (Manchester: Love and Barton; London: W.S. Orr and Co, and Ball, Arnold and Co, 1839; reprinted, Manchester: E.J. Morten, 1971).

LUMLEY, Benjamin, *Reminiscences of the opera* (London: Hurst and Blackett, 1864; reprinted, New York: Da Capo Press, 1976).

M'CALL, Hardy Bertram, *The history and antiquities of the parish of Mid-Calder with some account of the religious house of Torphichen founded upon record* (Edinburgh: Richard Cameron, 1894).

MACARTNEY, Hilary, 'Sir William Stirling Maxwell as historian of Spanish art', PhD dissertation (Courtauld Institute of Art, University of London, 2003).

MACDONALD, Hugh, *Beethoven's century: essays on composers and themes* (Woodbridge: Boydell Press, 2008).

MACDONALD, Hugh, 'Paganini, Mendelssohn and Turner in Scotland', in Macdonald, *Beethoven's century*, pp. 28–41.

MACDONALD, Hugh, *Music in 1853: the biography of a year* (Woodbridge: Boydell Press, 2012).

MACINTYRE, Ben, 'Chopin's true sound can be heard at last after discovery of his piano', *The Times*, Saturday 17 March 2007, pp. 26–7.

MACMILLAN, Duncan, ' "Born like Minerva": D.O. Hill and the origins of photography', in Weaver, *British photography in the nineteenth century*, pp. 25–36.

MARCHAND, Leslie Alexis, *The Athenaeum: a mirror of Victorian culture* (Chapel Hill: University of North Carolina Press, 1941; reprinted, New York: Octagon Books, 1971).

MAREK, George R., and Maria GORDON-SMITH, *Chopin* (London: Weidenfeld and Nicolson, 1979).

MARION, Arnaud, *Pleyel: une histoire tournée vers l'avenir* (Paris: Éditions de La Martinière, 2005).

MARSHALL, C.F. Dendy, *A history of the Southern Railway*, 2nd ed., revised by R.W. Kidner, 2 vols (London: Ian Allan, 1963).

[MASON, Lowell], *A Yankee musician in Europe: the 1837 journals of Lowell Mason*, ed. Michael Broyles (Ann Arbor, Michigan, and London: UMI Research Press, 1990).

MAVER, Irene, *Glasgow* (Edinburgh: Edinburgh University Press, 2000).

McCALMAN, Iain, general editor, *An Oxford companion to the romantic age of British culture, 1776–1832* (Oxford and New York: Oxford University Press, 1999; paperback, 2001).

McKEAN, Charles, *Stirling and the Trossachs: an illustrated architectural guide* (Edinburgh: Rutland Press, 1994).

McKEAN, Charles, David WALKER, and Frank WALKER, *Central Glasgow: an illustrated architectural guide* (Edinburgh: Rutland Press, 1994).

McKERRACHER, Archie, *The street and place names of Dunblane and district* (Stirling: Stirling District Libraries, 1992).

McLEOD, Mona Kedslie, *Agents of change: Scots in Poland, 1800–1918* (Phantassie, East Lothian: Tuckwell, 2000).

McLEOD, Mona Kedslie, editor, based on translation by Helena Brochowska, *From Charlotte Square to Fingal's Cave: reminiscences of a journey through Scotland, 1820–1824, by Krystyn Lach-Szyrma* (Phantassie, East Lothian: Tuckwell, 2004).

McWILLIAM, Colin, *Lothian, except Edinburgh*, The Buildings of Scotland (Harmondsworth: Penguin Books, 1978; reprinted with corrections, New Haven and London: Yale University Press, 2003).

MESSINGER, Gary S., *Manchester in the Victorian age: the half-known city* (Manchester: Manchester University Press, 1985).

METHUEN-CAMPBELL, James, *Chopin playing: from the composer to the present day* (London: Victor Gollancz, 1981).

METHUEN-CAMPBELL, James, 'Currents in the approach to the interpretation of Chopin's music, as exemplified by the rise and fall of the pianist as a Chopin specialist', in Poniatowska, *Chopin and his work in the context of culture*, vol.2, pp. 27–34.

MICHAŁOWSKI, Kornel, *Bibliografia chopinowska (Chopin bibliography), 1849–1969* (Cracow: PWM, 1970; updated in subsequent issues of the journal *Rocznik Chopinowski*).

MICHAŁOWSKI, Kornel, compiler, *Polish music literature (1515–1990): selected annotated bibliography*, revised, with additions, by Gillian Olechno-Huszcza (Los Angeles: Friends of Polish Music, University of Southern California, School of Music, 1991).

MILEWSKI, Barbara, 'Chopin's mazurkas and the myth of the folk', *Nineteenth-century Music*, vol.23, no.2 (1999), pp. 113–35.

MILLAR, A.H., *The castles and mansions of Renfrewshire and Buteshire, illustrated in sixty-five views, with historical and descriptive accounts* (Glasgow: T. & R. Annan and Sons, 1889).

MIRSKA, Maria, and Władysław HORDYŃSKI, *Chopin na obczyźnie: dokumenty i pamiàtki* (Cracow: PWM, 1965).

MITCHELL, John Fowler, and Sheila MACBETH or MITCHELL, *An index of monumental inscriptions (pre-1855) in south Perthshire*, revised by Alison Mitchell (Edinburgh: Scottish Genealogy Society, 2000–2001).

MIZWA, Stephen P., editor, *Frederic Chopin, 1810–1849*, The Kosciuszko Foundation (New York: Macmillan, 1949).

MORRIS, Edward, 'Ary Scheffer and his English circle', *Oud Holland*, vol.99, part 4 (1985), pp. 294–323.

MORRIS, Edward, 'Provincial internationalism: contemporary foreign art in nineteenth-century Liverpool and Manchester', *Transactions of the Historic Society of Lancashire and Cheshire*, vol.147 (1997), pp. 81–113.

MORRIS, Edward, *French art in nineteenth-century Britain* (New Haven and London: Yale University Press, 2005).

[MOSCHELES, Ignatz], *Recent music and musicians, as described in the diaries and correspondence of Ignatz Moscheles, edited by his wife, Charlotte Moscheles, adapted from the original German by A.D. Coleridge* (New York: Henry Holt, 1873; reprinted, New York: Da Capo Press, 1970).

MULLALY, Terence, 'Memorial to Chopin at Festival Hall', *The Times*, Thursday 27 February 1975.

MURDOCH, William, *Chopin: his life* (London: John Murray, 1934; New York: Macmillan, 1935; reprinted, Westport, Connecticut: Greenwood Press, 1971).

Musée de la musique: guide (Paris: Musée de la musique (Cité de la musique), 1997).

NALBACH, Daniel, *The King's Theatre, 1704–1867: London's first Italian opera house* (London: The Society for Theatre Research, 1972).

NEAD, Lynda, *Victorian Babylon: people, streets and images in nineteenth-century London* (New Haven and London: Yale University Press, 2000).

NECTOUX, Jean-Michel, and Jean-Jacques EIGELDINGER, 'Édouard Ganche et sa collection Chopin', *Revue de la Bibliothèque nationale*, vol.3, no.7 (March 1983), pp. 11–26.

NEUMAYR, Anton, *Music and medicine*, vol.3, *Chopin, Smetana, Tchaikovsky, Mahler: notes on their lives, works, and medical histories*, translated by David J. Parent (Bloomington, IL: Medi-Ed Press, 1997).

NEWELL, J. Philip, 'A.J. Scott and his circle', PhD dissertation (University of Edinburgh, 1981).
NEWELL, J. Philip, *Listening for the heartbeat of God: a Celtic spirituality* (London: SPCK, 1997; reissued, 2008).
NICHOLLS, Phillip A., *Homoeopathy and the medical profession* (London, New York and Sydney: Croom Helm, 1988).
NICHOLLS, Phillip A., 'Class, status and gender: toward a sociology of the homoeopathic patient in nineteenth-century Britain', in Dinges, *Patients in the history of homoeopathy*, pp. 141–56.
NIECKS, Frederick, *Frederick Chopin as man and musician* [1888], 3rd ed., 2 vols (London: Novello, [1902]).
NIECKS, Frederick, *Programme music in the last four centuries: a contribution to the history of musical expression* (London: Novello and Co; New York: H.W. Gray Co, [1906]).
NOWACZYK, Henryk F., 'Chopin mnkął do Szkocji z prędkością 80 km/godz.', *Ruch Muzyczny* (2008), no.6 (16 March 2008), pp. 31–5.
NOWACZYK, Henryk F, ' "The Scotsman" o recitalu Chopina', *Ruch Muzyczny* (2008), no.7 (30 March 2008), pp. 34–8.
OLIFERKO, Magdalena, *Fontana and Chopin in letters*, translated by John Comber (Warsaw: NiFC, 2013).
OPIEŃSKI, Henryk (collector), translated, with preface and editorial notes, by E[thel] L[illian] Voynich, *Chopin's letters* (New York: Alfred A Knopf, 1931; reprinted, New York: Vienna House, 1973; reprinted, with corrections, New York: Dover, 1988). [In English]
ORRELL, Keith G., 'The "Great Sir Thomas" Acland and his Norwegian namesake. Part 1: The establishment of the Acland – Tellefsen connection', *The Devon Historian*, vol.71 (2005), pp. 25–34.
ORRELL, Keith G., 'The "Great Sir Thomas" Acland and his Norwegian namesake. Part 2: Sir Thomas meets his namesake', *The Devon Historian*, vol.72 (2006), pp. 15–23.
OSBORNE, George Alexander, 'Berlioz', *Proceedings of the Musical Association*, vol.5 (1878–9), pp. 60–75.
OSBORNE, George Alexander, 'Reminiscences of Fredrick [sic] Chopin', *Proceedings of the Musical Association*, vol.6 (1879–80), pp. 91–105.
OSBORNE, George Alexander, 'Musical coincidences and reminiscences', *Proceedings of the Musical Association*, vol.9 (1882–3), pp. 95–113.
O'SHEA, John, *Music and medicine: medical profiles of great composers* (Oxford: Oxford University Press, 1994).
OSTROWSKA, Teresa, 'Cultural relations between England and Poland, with special focus on medicine', *Arhiwum historii i folozofii medycyny*, vol.57 (1994), pp. 289–96.
PAPWORTH, John B., *Select views of London*, (1816), p. 54.
PARAKILAS, James, and Others, *Piano roles: three hundred years of life with the piano* (New Haven and London: Yale University Press, 1999).
PARKER, Roger, editor, *The Oxford illustrated history of opera* (Oxford: Oxford University Press, 1994; paperback 2001).
PARKINSON, John A., *Victorian music publishers: an annotated list* (Warren, Michigan: Harmonie Park Press, 1990).
PEKACZ, Jolanta T., 'Deconstructing a "national composer": Chopin and Polish exiles in Paris, 1831–1849', *Nineteenth-century Music*, vol.24, no.2 (Fall, 2000), pp. 161–72.
PEKACZ, Jolanta T., 'Memory, history and meaning: musical biography and its discontents', *Journal of Musicological Research*, vol.23 (2004), pp. 39–80.

PEKACZ, Jolanta T., editor, *Musical biography: towards new paradigms* (Aldershot: Ashgate, 2006).
PEKACZ, Jolanta T., 'The nation's property: Chopin's biography as a cultural discourse', in Pekacz, *Musical biography*, pp. 43–68.
PERONE, James E., *Louis Moreau Gottschalk: a bio-bibliography* (Westport, CT, and London: Greenwood Press, 2002).
PIGGOTT, Patrick, *The life and music of John Field (1782–1837): creator of the nocturne* (London: Faber and Faber, 1973).
PISARENKO, Olgierd, 'Chopin and his contemporaries, Paris, 1832–1860', in Żebrowski, *Studies in Chopin*, pp. 30–48.
PISTONE, Danièle, editor, *Sur les traces de Frédéric Chopin* (Paris: Honoré Champion, 1984).
PISTONE, Danièle, collector and editor, *L'interprétation de Chopin en France* (Paris: Honoré Champion, 1990).
PISTONE, Danièle, *Nineteenth-century Italian opera from Rossini to Puccini*, trans. E. Thomas Glasow (Portland, OR: Amadeus Press, 1995).
PISTONE, Danièle, 'Pianistes et concerts parisiens au temps de Frédéric Chopin', in *Chopin w kręgu przyjaciół/Chopin parmi ses amis*, vol.5 (Warsaw: Wydawnictwo Neriton, 1999), pp. 40–53.
PLATZMAN, George W, *A catalogue of early printed editions of the works of Frédéric Chopin in the University of Chicago Library* (Chicago: University of Chicago Library, 1997).
PLATZMAN, George W, *A descriptive catalogue of early editions of the works of Frédéric Chopin in the University of Chicago Library*, 2nd edition, revised and enlarged (Chicago: University of Chicago Library, 2003).
Pleyel au temps de Frédéric Chopin (Museo del Pianoforte Antico, Ala (Trento, Italy): Edizioni del Museo, 1999).
POCKNELL, Pauline, 'A temporary fellowship: Franz Liszt's and Adelaide Kemble's symbiotic relations, socio-critical aspects and aftermath of their concerts in London, Liège and the Rhineland in 1841', *Journal of the American Liszt Society*, vol.25 (2000), pp. 61–90.
PONIATOWSKA, Irena, studies editor, *Chopin and his work in the context of culture*, 2 vols (Cracow: Polska Akademia Chopinowska, NiFC, Musica Iagellonica, 2003).
PONIATOWSKA, Irena, 'The Polish reception of Chopin's biography by Franz Liszt', in Goldberg, *The age of Chopin*, pp. 259–77.
PONIATOWSKA, Irena, editor. *Chopin and his critics: an anthology (up to World War I)*. (Warsaw: The Frederick Chopin Institute, 2011).
POURTALES, Guy de, *Polonaise: the life of Chopin*, translated by Charles Bayly, Jr (New York: Henry Holt, circa 1927).
POWELL, David A., *While the music lasts: the representation of music in the works of George Sand* (Lewisburg, PA: Bucknell University Press; London: Associated University Presses, [2001]).
PRIDEAUX, Tom, and the editors of Time-Life Books, *The world of Delacroix: 1798–1863* (New York: Time-Life Books, 1966).
The Princes Czartoryski Museum: a history of the collections, English text by Adam Zamoyski (Cracow: The National Museum in Cracow, 2001).
PURSER, John, *Scotland's music: a history of the traditional and classical music of Scotland from the earliest times to the present day* (Edinburgh and London: Mainstream, 1992).

RAMBEAU, Marie-Paule,'Chopin et son poète, Stefan Witwicki', in Eigeldinger, *Chopin interprétations*, pp. 107–26.
RAMSAY, Philip A., *Views in Renfrewshire, with historical and descriptive notices* (Edinburgh: William H Lizars; Paisley: Murray and Stewart; and Glasgow: Thomas Murray, 1839).
RANKIN, Glynis, 'Professional organisation and the development of medical knowledge: two interpretations of homoeopathy', in Cooter, *Studies in the history of alternative medicine*, pp. 46–62.
READ, Benedict, and Joanna BARNES, editors, *Pre-Raphaelite sculpture: nature and imagination in British sculpture, 1848–1914* (London: The Henry Moore Foundation, in association with Lund Humphries, 1991).
REID, Martine, and Bertrand TILLIER, *L'ABCdaire de George Sand* (Paris: Flammarion, 1999; paperback, 2002).
RENNISON, Nick, *The London blue plaque guide*, 2nd ed. (Stroud, Gloucestershire: Sutton, 2003).
RICE, Shelley, *Parisian views* (Cambridge, MA, and London: MIT Press, 1997).
RICHARDSON, Robert D., *Emerson: the mind on fire; a biography* (Berkeley, Los Angeles and London: University of California Press, 1995).
RIGBY, Charles, *Sir Charles Hallé: a portrait for today* (Manchester: Dolphin Press, 1952).
RINGER, Alexander L, editor, *The early romantic era: between revolutions, 1789 and 1848*, Music and Society (Basingstoke: Macmillan; Englewood Cliffs, NJ: Prentice-Hall, 1990).
RINK, John, 'The profession of music', in Samson, *Cambridge history of nineteenth-century music*, pp. 55–86.
RINK, John, and Jim SAMSON, editors, *Chopin studies 2* (Cambridge: Cambridge University Press, 1994).
RIPOLL, Luis, *Chopin's winter in Majorca, 1838–1839*, translated by Alan Sillitoe, foreword by Robert Graves (Palma da Mallorca: Collección Siurell, 1955).
RITCHIE, Anne Thackeray, *Chapters from some memoirs* (London and New York: Macmillan, 1894; London and New York: Macmillan (Macmillan Colonial Library),1895; Leipzig: Bernhard Tauchnitz, 1895).
RITCHIE, Anne Thackeray, *Journals and letters*, biographical commentary and notes by Lillian F. Shankman, edited by Abigail Burnham Bloom and John Maynard (Columbus, Ohio: Ohio State University Press, 1994).
RITTERMAN, Janet, 'Piano music and the public concert, 1800–1850', in Samson, *Cambridge companion to Chopin*, pp. 11–31.
RITTERMAN, Janet, and William WEBER, 'Origins of the piano recital in England, 1830–1870', in Ellsworth and Wollenberg, *The piano in nineteenth-century British culture*, pp. 171–91.
ROCK, Joe, *Thomas Hamilton, architect (1784–1858)*. Exhibition catalogue (Talbot Rice Art Centre, University of Edinburgh, 1984).
ROHR, Deborah, *The careers of English musicians, 1750–1850* (Cambridge: Cambridge University Press, 2001).
ROSE, Jerome, editor, *Chopin – Viardot: twelve mazurkas for voice and piano* (New York: International Music Company, [1988]).
ROSENTHAL, Harold, *Two centuries of opera at Covent Garden* (London: Putnam, 1958).
ROSS, Raymond [Raszkowski], 'My hallucinatory sojourn in Chopin's Caledonia', *The Sunday Times*, 24 August 2003, Edinburgh Festival section, p. 6.

ROUDIER, Alain, Bruno di LENNA, and Others, *Rifiorir d'antichi suoni: Trois siècles de pianos: Three centuries of pianos* (Rovereto (Tn): Edizioni Osiride, 2003).

ROWAN, Alistair, 'Keir, Perthshire', *Country Life*, vol.158 (7, 14 August 1975), pp. 326–9, 390–3.

ROWLAND, David, editor, *The Cambridge companion to the piano* (Cambridge: Cambridge University Press, 1998).

RUHLMANN, Sophie, 'Chopin – Franchomme', in *Chopin w kręgu przyjaciół*, vol.2 (Warsaw: Wydawnictwo Neriton, 1996).

SACHS, Joel, 'London: the professionalization of music', in Ringer, *Early romantic era*, pp. 201–35.

SADIE, Julie Anne, and Stanley SADIE, *Calling on the composer: a guide to European composer houses and museums* (New Haven and London: Yale University Press, 2005).

SADLEIR, Michael, *Blessington – D'Orsay: a masquerade* (London: Constable, 1933; London: The Folio Society, 1983).

SADLEIR, Michael, *The strange life of Lady Blessington*, revised American edition (New York: Farrar, Straus and Co, 1947).

SALAMAN, Charles [Kensington], 'Pianists of the past: personal recollections by the late Charles Salaman', *Blackwood's Edinburgh Magazine*, vol.170 (September 1901), pp. 307–30.

SAMSON, Jim, *The music of Chopin* (London: Routledge and Kegan Paul, 1985; Oxford: Clarendon Press, 1994).

SAMSON, Jim, editor, *The late romantic era: from the mid-nineteenth century to World War I* (Basingstoke: Macmillan; Englewood Cliffs, NJ: Prentice-Hall, 1991).

SAMSON, Jim, editor, *The Cambridge companion to Chopin* (Cambridge: Cambridge University Press, 1992, 1994, 1996).

SAMSON, Jim, 'Myth and reality: a biographical introduction', in Samson, *Cambridge companion to Chopin*, pp. 1–8.

SAMSON, Jim, *Chopin* (Oxford: Oxford University Press, 1996).

SAMSON, Jim, editor, *The Cambridge history of nineteenth-century music* (Cambridge: Cambridge University Press, 2002).

SAND, George, *Story of my life: the autobiography of George Sand*, group translation, edited by Thelma Jurgrau, with critical introduction by Thelma Jurgrau, and historical introduction by Walter D. Gray (Albany, NY: State University of New York Press, 1991).

SCHARLITT, Bernard, *Friedrich Chopins gesammelte Briefe, zum erstenmal herausgegeben und getreu ins Deutsche übertragen* (Leipzig: Breitkopf & Härtel, 1911).

[SCHEFFER, Ary], *Museum Ary Scheffer: catalogue der kuntwerken en andere voorwerpen* (Dordrecht: Dordrecht Museum, 1934).

SCHERER, F.M., *Quarter notes and bank notes: the economics of music composition in the eighteenth and nineteenth centuries* (Princeton, NJ, and Oxford: Princeton University Press, 2004).

SENKOW, Anne, 'Les musiciens polonais de Paris à l'époque de Chopin', in Pistone, *Sur les traces de Frédéric Chopin*, pp. 29–52.

SERVAT, Henry-Jean, 'Guy de Rothschild: le premier départ', *Paris Match*, no.3031 (21–7 June, 2007), pp. 84–9.

SHAEN, Margaret Josephine, editor, *Memorials of two sisters: Susanna and Catherine Winkworth* (London: Longmans Green and Co, 1908).

SHANKMAN, Lillian, Abigail Burnham BLOOM, and John MAYNARD, editors, *Anne Thackeray Ritchie: journals and letters* (Columbus, OH: Ohio State University Press, 1994).

SHATTOCK, Joanne, *The Oxford guide to British women writers* (New York and Oxford: Oxford University Press, 1993; paperback 1994).
SHAW, William Arthur, *Manchester old and new . . . with illustrations after original drawings by H.E. Tidmarsh*, 3 vols (London: Cassell, [1896]).
SHUSTER, Carolyn [Jean], 'Six mazurkas de Frédéric Chopin transcrites pour chant et piano par Pauline Viardot', *Revue de musicologie*, vol.75, no.2 (1989), pp. 265–83.
SIELUŻYCKI, Czesław, *Chopin: geniusz cierpiący* (Podkowa Leśna: Wydawnictwo Aula, 1999).
SIELUŻYCKI, Czesław, 'On the health of Chopin: truth, suppositions, legends', *Chopin Studies* (Warsaw), vol.6 (1999), pp. 99–156.
SIEPMANN, Jeremy, *Chopin: the reluctant romantic* (London: Victor Gollancz, 1995).
SIMEONE, Nigel, *Paris: a musical gazetteer* (New Haven and London: Yale University Press, 2000).
SIMMONS, Jack, *The express train and other railway studies* (Nairn: David St John Thomas, 1994).
SIMMONS, Jack, *The Victorian railway* (London: Thames and Hudson, 1991; paperback, 1995).
SIMMONS, Jack, and Gordon BIDDLE, editors, *The Oxford companion to British railway history, from 1603 to the 1990s* (Oxford and New York: Oxford University Press, 1997).
SKINNER, Lydia, *A family unbroken, 1694–1994: the Mary Erskine School tercentenary history* (Edinburgh: The Mary Erskine School, 1994).
SKOWRON, Zbigniev, 'Creating a legend or reporting the facts? Chopin as a performer in the biographical accounts of F. Liszt, M.A. Szulc, and F. Niecks', in Artur Szklener, ed, *Chopin in performance: history, theory, practice* (Warsaw: NiFC, 2005), 9–24.
SMALL, John, *Castles and mansions of the Lothians, illustrated in one hundred and three views, with historical and descriptive accounts*, 2 vols (Edinburgh: William Paterson, 1883).
SMIALEK, William, and Maja TROCHIMCZYK, *Frédéric Chopin: a research and information guide*, 2nd ed. (New York and London: Routledge, 2015).
SMITH, Ronald, *Alkan: the man, the music* (London: Kahn and Averill, 2000).
SORENSEN, David R., and Roger L. TARR, editors, *The Carlyles at home and abroad* (Aldershot: Ashgate, 2004).
STARR, S. Frederick, *Bamboula!: the life and times of Louis Moreau Gottschalk* (Oxford and New York: Oxford University Press, 1995; paperback edition, entitled *Louis Moreau Gottschalk*, Urbana and Chicago: University of Illinois Press, 2000).
STEEN, Michael, *The lives and times of the great composers* (Cambridge: Icon Books, 2003; paperback, 2010).
STEEN, Michael, *Enchantress of nations: Pauline Viardot, soprano, muse and lover* (Cambridge: Icon Books, 2007).
STEVENSON, Sara, *David Octavius Hill and Robert Adamson: catalogue of their calotypes taken between 1843 and 1847 in the collection of the Scottish National Portrait Gallery* (Edinburgh: National Galleries of Scotland, 1981).
STEVENSON, Sara, 'David Octavius Hill and Robert Adamson', in Weaver, *British photography in the nineteenth century*, pp. 37–53.
STEVENSON, Sara, *Facing the light: the photography of Hill & Adamson* (Edinburgh: Scottish National Portrait Gallery, 2002).
STEVENSON, Sara, *The personal art of David Octavius Hill* (New Haven and London: Yale University Press, 2002).

STEVENSON, Sara, and others, *Light from the dark room: a celebration of Scottish photography; a Scottish – Canadian collaboration* (Edinburgh: National Galleries of Scotland, 1995).

STEVENSON, Sara, and Duncan FORBES, *A companion guide to photography in the National Galleries of Scotland* (Edinburgh: National Galleries of Scotland, 2001).

STEVENSON, Sara, Julie LAWSON, and Michael GRAY, *The photography of John Muir Wood (1805–1892): an accomplished amateur* (Edinburgh: Scottish National Portrait Gallery (The National Galleries of Scotland); London: Dirk Nishen Publishing, 1988).

STEVENSON, Sara, and A.D. MORRISON-LOW, *Scottish photography: the first thirty years* (Edinburgh: National Museums Scotland, 2015).

STROUD, Dorothy, *George Dance, architect (1741–1825)* (London: Faber and Faber, 1971).

SUCHOWIEJKO, Renata, 'Les pianistes polonais dans la presse musicale parisienne à l'époque de Chopin: contexte sociopolitique', in Poniatowska, *Chopin and his work in the context of culture*, vol.1, pp. 184–92.

SUMERAY, Derek, *Discovering London plaques* (Princes Risborough, Buckinghamshire: Shire Publications, 1999).

SUMERAY, Derek, *Track the plaque: thirty-two walks around London's commemorative plaques* (Derby: Breedon Books, 2003).

SUMMERSON, John (Newenham), *Architecture in Britain: 1530–1830*, 9th ed. (New Haven and London: Yale University Press, 1993).

SUMMERSON, John [Newenham], *Georgian London*, ed. Howard Colvin (New Haven and London: Yale University Press, 2003).

Survey of London, Royal Commission on the Historical Monuments of England (RCHME) (London, 1900 onwards: various publishers).

SWINDELLS, Thomas, *Manchester streets and Manchester men*, 5 vols (Manchester: Cornish, 1906–8).

SYDOW, Bronisław Edward, editor, *Korespondencja Fryderyka Chopina (KFC)*, 2 vols (Warsaw: PIW, 1955). [In Polish and French]

SYDOW, Bronislas Édouard, collected, revised, annotated and translated, in collaboration with Suzanne and Denise CHAINAYE, *Correspondance de Frédéric Chopin*, 3 vols (Paris: Richard-Masse, 1981). [In French]

SZULC, Tad, *Chopin in Paris: the life and times of the romantic composer* (New York: Scribner, 1998).

TAIT, A.A., 'The Duke of Hamilton's Palace', *Burlington Magazine*, vol.125 (July 1983), pp. 394–402.

TALMA-DAVOUS, Ewa, 'Georges Mathias (1826–1910), ou la chrysalide musicienne', in Poniatowska, *Chopin and his work in the context of culture*, vol.2, pp. 114–33.

TAYLOR, Derek, and David BUSH, *The golden age of British hotels* (London: Northwood, 1974).

TAYLOR, S.K., editor, *The musician's piano atlas (and supplement)* (Macclesfield, Cheshire: Omicron, 1981).

TELLEFSEN, Thomas, editor, *Thomas Tellefsens familiebreve*, foreword by Gerhard Schjelderup (Kristiania: Steenske Forlag, 1923).

TEMPERLEY, Nicholas, 'Domestic music in England, 1800–1860', *Journal of the Royal Musical Association*, vol.85 (1958), pp. 31–48.

TEMPERLEY, Nicholas, editor, *The lost chord: essays on Victorian music* (Bloomington and Indianapolis: Indiana University Press, 1989).

TEMPERLEY, Nicholas, editor, with the assistance of Yunchung YANG, *Lectures on musical life: William Sterndale Bennett* (Woodbridge: Boydell, 2006).

THEIS, Laurent, *François Guizot* (Paris: Arthème Fayard, 2008).
THOMAS, John, *Scotland: the Lowlands and the Borders; a regional history of the railways of Great Britain*, vol.6, revised and enlarged by Alan J.S. Paterson (Newton Abbot: David St John Thomas, and David and Charles, 1984).
THOMPSON, Joseph, *The Owens College: its foundation and growth; and its connection with the Victoria University, Manchester* (Manchester: J E Cornish, 1886).
TODD, R. Larry, editor, *Mendelssohn and his world* (Princeton, NJ: Princeton University Press, 1991).
TODD, R. Larry, editor, *Mendelssohn studies* (Cambridge: Cambridge University Press, 1992).
TODD, R. Larry, *Mendelssohn: a life in music* (Oxford and New York: Oxford University Press, 2003).
TODD, R. Larry, editor, *Nineteenth-century piano music*, 2nd ed. (New York and London: Routledge, 2004).
TOMASZEWSKI, Mieczysław, 'The presence of Chopin's music in the works of his contemporaries and successors', *Chopin Studies* (Warsaw), vol.7 (2000), pp. 128–208.
TOMASZEWSKI, Miecysław, *Chopin: człowiek, dzieło, rezonans* (Cracow: PWM, 2005).
TOMASZEWSKI, Mieczysław, and Bożena WEBER, *Fryderyk Chopin: a diary in images*, translated by Rosemary Hunt (Arkady: PWM, 1990).
TOMASZEWSKI, Wiktor, editor, *The University of Edinburgh and Poland: an historical review* (Edinburgh: Graduates of the Polish School of Medicine, 1968).
TROCHIMCZYK, Maja (i.e., Maria HARLEY), 'From art to kitsch and back again?: thoughts on Chopin's reception by women composers', in Poniatowska, *Chopin and his work in the context of culture*, vol.2, pp. 336–53.
TROCHIMCZYK, Maja (i.e., Maria HARLEY), 'Chopin and the "Polish race": on national ideologies and the Chopin reception', in Goldberg, *The age of Chopin*, pp. 278–313.
TUNLEY, David, *Salons, singers and songs: a background to romantic French song, 1830–1870* (Aldershot: Ashgate, 2002).
VANN, J[erry] Don, and Rosemary T. VANARSDEL, editors, *Victorian periodicals and Victorian society* (Toronto and Buffalo: University of Toronto Press; Aldershot: Scolar Press, 1994; paperback, University of Toronto Press, 1995).
WAAGEN, Gustav Friedrich, *Galleries and cabinets of art in Great Britain* (London: John Murray, 1857). [Supplementary volume to Waagen, *Treasures of art in Great Britain*, 3 vols (London: John Murray, 1854).]
WACH, Howard Michael, 'The condition of the middle classes: culture and society in Manchester, 1815–1850', PhD dissertation (Brandeis University, 1987).
WACH, Howard M[ichael], 'Culture and the middle classes: popular knowledge in industrial Manchester', *The Journal of British Studies*, vol.27, no.4 (October 1988), pp. 375–404.
WACH, Howard M[ichael], 'A "still, small voice" from the pulpit: religion and the creation of social morality in Manchester, 1820–1850', *The Journal of Modern History*, vol.63, no.3 (September 1991), pp. 425–56.
WADDINGTON, Patrick, 'Henry Chorley, Pauline Viardot, and Turgenev: a musical and literary friendship', *Musical Quarterly*, vol.67, no.2 (April 1981), pp. 165–92.
WADDINGTON, Patrick, compiler, *The musical works of Pauline Viardot-Garcia (1821–1910): a chronological catalogue with an index of titles and a list of writers set and composers arranged*, 2nd ed. (Pinehaven, New Zealand: Whirinaki Press, 2004).
WAEBER, Jacqueline, editor, *La note bleue: mélanges offerts au Professor Jean-Jacques Eigeldinger* (Berne: Peter Lang, 2006).

WAINWRIGHT, David, *Broadwood by appointment: a history* (London: Quiller Press, 1982).
WALKER, Alan, editor, *Frédéric Chopin: profiles of the man and the musician*, 2nd ed. (London: Barrie and Jenkins, 1979).
WALKER, Alan, *Franz Liszt: the virtuoso years, 1811–1847*, vol.1, 2nd ed. (Ithaca, NY, and London: Cornell University Press, 1988; London: Faber and Faber, 1989 [paperback]).
WALKER, Alan, *Franz Liszt: the Weimar years, 1848–1861*, vol.2 (London: Faber and Faber, 1989).
WALKER, David, 'The Stirlings of Dunblane and Falkirk: fragments of five architectural biographies', *Bulletin of the Scottish Georgian Society*, vol.1 (1972), pp. 40–59.
WALKER, Frank Arneil, *Argyll and the islands: an illustrated architectural guide* (Edinburgh: Rutland Press, 2001).
WALKER, Frank Arneil, *Argyll and Bute*, The Buildings of Scotland (London: Penguin Books, 2000; reprinted, New Haven and London: Yale University Press, 2002).
WALSH, Basil F, *Catherine Hayes: the Hibernian prima donna* (Dublin and Portland, OR: Irish Academic Press, 2000).
WARD, Laurence, *The London County Council bomb damage maps, 1939–1945* (London: Thames and Hudson, 2015).
WARD JONES, Peter, 'Mendelssohn and his publishers', in Todd, *Mendelssohn studies*, pp. 240–55.
WAUGH (later HOBHOUSE), Rosa, *The life of Christian Samuel Hahnemann, founder of homoeopathy* (London: C.W. Daniel, 1933).
WEAVER, Mike, editor, *British photography in the nineteenth century: the fine art tradition* (Cambridge: Cambridge University Press, 1989).
WEBER, Bożena Zofia, *Chopin: the women in his life/Chopin: die Frauen in seinem Leben* (Paris: Opus 111, 1999).
WEBER, William, *Music and the middle class: the social structure of concert life in London, Paris and Vienna between 1830 and 1848*, 2nd ed. (Aldershot: Ashgate, 2004).
WEBER, William, *The great transformation of musical taste: concert programming from Haydn to Brahms* (Cambridge: Cambridge University Press, 2008).
WEINREB, Ben, Christopher HIBBERT, John KEAY, and Julia KEAY, editors, Matthew WEINREB, photographer, *The London encyclopaedia*, 3rd ed. (Basingstoke and Oxford: Macmillan, 2008).
WEINTRAUB, Stanley, *Charlotte and Lionel: a Rothschild love story* (New York: The Free Press, 2003).
WELLISZ, Léopold, *Les amis romantiques: Ary Scheffer et ses amis polonais* (Paris: Éditions Trianon, 1933).
WESTON, Peter, *The Froebel Educational Institute: the origins and history of the college* (Roehampton: University of Roehampton, 2002).
WHITE, Eric Walter, *A history of English opera* (London: Faber and Faber, 1983).
WHITE, Jerry, *London in the nineteenth century: 'a human awful wonder of God'* (London: Jonathan Cape, 2007).
WIERZYŃSKI, Casimir, *The life and death of Chopin*, translated by Norbert Guterman, foreword by Artur Rubinstein (London: Cassell, 1951).
WILKINSON, Alan, *Christian socialism: Scott Holland to Tony Blair* (London: SCM Press, 1998).
WILLIAMS, Adrian, translator and editor, *Franz Liszt: selected letters* (Oxford: Clarendon Press, 1998).
WILLIAMS, Adrian, *Portrait of Liszt, by himself and his contemporaries* (Oxford: Clarendon Press, 1990).

WILLIAMSON, Elizabeth, Anne RICHES, and Malcolm HIGGS, *Glasgow*, The Buildings of Scotland (London: Penguin Books, 1990; reprinted, New Haven and London: Yale University Press, 2002).
WILLIS, Peter, 'Chopin in Britain: Chopin's visits to England and Scotland in 1837 and 1848; people, places, and activities', PhD dissertation, 3 vols. (University of Durham, 1999).
WILLIS, Peter, 'Chopin's recital in the Gentlemen's Concert Hall, Monday 28 August 1848', *Manchester Sounds*, vol.8 (2009–10), pp. 84–119.
WILLIS, Peter, *Chopin in Manchester* (Newcastle upon Tyne: Elysium Press, 2011).
WILSON, Alison, editor, *An index of monumental inscriptions (pre-1855) in south Perthshire*, rev. ed., vol.2 (Edinburgh: Scottish Genealogy Society, 2001).
WIRTEMBERSKA, Maria, *Malvina, or the heart's intuition*, translated, with an introduction, by Ursula Phillips (London: Polish Cultural Foundation, 2001).
WITTEN, David, 'Ballads and ballades', *The Piano Quarterly*, Special Chopin edition, no.113 (Spring 1981), 33–7.
WOLFF, W, 'Recollections of Chopin's stay in England', *Musical Opinion and Music Trade Review*, vol.18 (1894), pp. 506, 575–6.
WOLMAR, Christian, *Fire and steam: a new history of the railways in Britain* (London: Atlantic Books, 2007).
WOOD, Herbert Kemlo, 'Chopin in Britain, I', *The Voice of Poland*, vol.2, no.20 (301) (3 October 1943), pp. 10–12.
WOOD, Herbert Kemlo, 'Chopin in Britain, II', *The Voice of Poland*, vol.2, no.21 (302) (17 October 1943), pp. 6, 10.
WOOD, Herbert Kemlo, 'When Chopin was in Glasgow: today's centenary of recital', *Glasgow Herald*, 27 September 1948.
WOOD, James L., *Building railways: Scotland's past in action* (Edinburgh: National Museums of Scotland, 1996).
WOOD, J. Muir and Co, *A descriptive account of Glasgow, illustrated* (Brighton: W.T. Pike and Co, [1894]).
WRIGHT, Beth S., editor, *The Cambridge companion to Delacroix* (Cambridge: Cambridge University Press, 2001).
WRIGHT, William, 'Liszt in Manchester', *Journal of the American Liszt Society*, vol.41 (January – June, 1997), pp. 1–20.
WRIGHT, William, 'Master Liszt in England', *Journal of the American Liszt Society*, vols 54, 55, and 56 (2003–5), pp. 22–44. [Festschrift in honor of Fernando Laires upon his 80th birthday, edited by David Butler Cannata.]
WRIGHT, William, *Liszt and England*, Franz Liszt Studies Series No. 16 (Hillsdale, NY: Pendragon Press, 2016).
WRÓBLEWSKA-STRAUS, Hanna, 'Jane Wilhelmina Stirling's letters to Ludwika Jędrzejewicz', *Chopin Studies (Warsaw)*, vol.1 (1985), pp. 45–152.
WRÓBLEWSKA-STRAUS, Hanna, 'Nieznany list Juliana Fontany: jeszcze o pobycie Chopina w Anglii w 1837 r., *Ruch Muzyczny*, no.24 (1997) pp. 34–5.
WRÓBLEWSKA-STRAUS, Hanna, *Chopin: Daleko rozsławił swe imię; wystawa zorganizowana w sto pięćdziesiątą rocznicę śmierci kompozytora/Chopin: fame resounding far and wide* (Warsaw: TiFC, 1999).
WYKE, Terry, with Harry COCKS, *Public sculpture of Greater Manchester*, Public sculpture of Britain, vol.8 (Liverpool: Liverpool University Press, 2004).
Year of photography at the National Galleries of Scotland (Edinburgh: National Galleries of Scotland, 2002).

YORKE, James [Alexander], *Lancaster House: London's greatest town house* (London: Merrell, 2001).

YOUNG, Percy M[arshall], *The concert tradition, from the middle ages to the twentieth century* (London: Routledge and Kegan Paul, 1965; New York: Roy Publishers, 1969).

YULE, Bill, *Matrons, medics and maladies: Inside Edinburgh Royal Infirmary in the 1840s* (Phantassie, East Lothian: Tuckwell, 1999).

ZAŁUSKI, Iwo and Pamela, *The Scottish autumn of Frederick Chopin* (Edinburgh: John Donald, 1993).

ZAMOYSKI, Adam, *Chopin: a biography* (London: Collins, 1979).

ZAMOYSKI, Adam, 'Paris', in *The Princes Czartoryski Museum: a history of the collections* (Cracow: The National Museum in Cracow, 2001), pp. 89–101.

ZAMOYSKI, Adam, *Chopin: prince of the romantics* (London: Harper Press, 2010).

ŻEBROWSKI, Dariusz, editor, *Studies in Chopin* (Warsaw: TiFC, 1973).

Index

Note: Page numbers in italic indicate a figure on the corresponding page.

Adam Jerzy, Prince Czartoryski 2–3, *3*, 20
Adamson, Robert 128, *131*
Alary, Giulio 102, 104, 106–9
Aleksander, Prince Czartoryski 37, 41, 195, 216
Alexander, George Russell 200
Alfer, Jarosław Giercarz 220
Alkan, Charles-Valentin 9
Anglia i Polska (Koźmian) 19
Anglo-Polish Society 220
Anna, Princess Czartoryski 2
Annals of the artists of Spain (Stirling Maxwell) 154, *155*
Annan, Thomas 158–9, *159*
Annual Grand Dress and Fancy Ball (1848) 21, 216–17
antiquities of Athens, The (Stuart and Revett) 180
Antrobus, Lady Anne 93
Apponyi, Antoine, Count 9–10
Arc de Triomphe 2
Art Union: Monthly Journal of the Fine Arts (later *Art Journal*) 58
Arundel, England 24
Ashbee, C.R. 92
Ashton, Rosemary 92
Athenaeum 10–11, 25, 41, 42, 75, 100
Atwood, William 11, 217

Backward glances, or some personal recollections (Hedderwick) 200–3
Baldus, Edouard 222–3
Balfe, Michael William 195
Bally, William 178
Balzac, Honoré de 60
Baring, Henry Bingham 59

Barlow, Jeremy 49
Barnton House (Edinburgh) 140–2, *142*
Barry, E.M. 79
Barry, Sir Charles 94
Bashford, Christina 109
Beale, Thomas Willert 183, 184
Beatrice di Tenda (Bellini) 7
Beaumont, Thomas Wentworth 20
Beazley, Samuel 61
Beckford, William 166
Beethoven, Ludwig van 25, 26
Beethoven Quartett Society 109
Belhaven, Lady 162–3
Bellini, Vincenzo 7–8
Benedict, Julius 94, 96, *97*, 99
Bennett, Joseph 72
Bentinck, William (2nd Duke of Portland) 62
Bentinck Street, London 62, *65*
Bentley's Miscellany (magazine) 42
Blackburn, Jemima 109
Blainey, Ann 109
Blessington, Countess of (Marguerite Gardiner) (Lady Blessington) 68, 112–16, *113*
Bohemian Girl, The (Balfe) 195
Bone, Audrey 230
Boscawen, George Henry *see* Falmouth, 2nd Earl of
Bösendorfer (piano firm) 26
Boulogne, England 61
Bovy, Jean Francois Antoine 17
British Homeopathic Society (Faculty of Homeopathy) 133
British Hotel 206, *208*
British Journal of Homeopathy (*Homeopathy*) 133

Index

Broadwood (piano firm) 10, 18, 26, 27; *see also* pianos
Broadwood, Henry Fowler (son of James) 26, 27, 70–2, *71*
Broadwood, James Shudi (son of John) 10, 25–8, *27*, 70
Broadwood, John 26
Broadwood, Thomas (son of John) 26
Brookshaw, Susanna 189, 211
Bruce, Frances Ann (Fanny) *45*, 129
Brunnow, Philip Graf von, Baron 59
Byron Society 220

Cadogan, Lady Mary 68
Calais, England 18, 61
Calder House (Scotland) 5, 147, *150*
Caledonian Mercury 212
Campbell, Thomas 19, 20
Carlyle, Jane Welsh *92*, 92–3, 112
Carlyle, Thomas *92*, 92–3
Carolyne, Princess von Sayn-Wittgenstein 228
carriage accident, Johnstone Castle 160–1
Castles and manors of Renfrewshire and Buteshire (Millar) 158–9, *160*
Castles and mansions of the Lothians (Small) 140, *142*
Catherine, Princess de Souzzo 59
Chambers, William 135
Champs Élysées 2
Chapters from some memoirs (Thackeray) 47
Chemin de fer du Nord (Baldus) 222–3
Chopin (Hadden) 44, 46–7, 196
Chopin, Frédéric: autograph letter to Lyschiński *141*; bronze head and statue of 207, 220; bronze portrait medallion of *17*; care from family and friends 216, 226–7; death and funeral 226–7; desire for royal patronage 96–7, 98; friendship with C. Pleyel 8–9, 18; friendship with J. Stirling and K. Erskine 44–6, 63–4, 149–51, 157–8, 212–13, 221, 227, 228; friendship with Princess Marcelina 195, 216, 220, 226–7; health and illness 11–12, 81–2, 91, 147, 157, 189, 199–200, 212, 216, 220–1; income concerns 67, 69–70, 116; opinion of the English 167, 223; Parisian aristocracy influence on 9–10; physical attributes 18; as piano teacher 9, 44, 46–7, 68–70, 151–2, *152*; plaster casts and bust of 191, 220, *220*; tour of Scottish aristocratic country-houses 147, 149–51, 162–9
Chopin, Frederick, Society of Poland 191, 207
Chopin monument, Père Lachaise cemetery 227, 228
'Chopin playing' (Sterling) 112
Chopin Society (Warsaw) 139, 220
Chorley, Henry Fothergill: admiration of Chopin 41–2, 58, 94; Chopin obituary 219, 228; on Countess Blessington 115–16; essay on Chopin 75–7; music reviews 74–7, 99–100, 102, 109, 111–12, 219; portrait *43*; reputation at *Athenaeum* 10–11
Christus consolator (Scheffer) 5
church of the Madeleine (Paris) 227
City Hall (Glasgow opera venue) 195
Claremont (London country house) 65
Clark, William Donaldson 128, *130*
Clarke, M.L. 80
Clerk, Sir John 109
Clésinger, Auguste 39, 191, 227
Clésinger, Solange 37, 39, 159–60, 191, 221
Cobbe Collection Trust 46, 68, 74, 98
Cockerell, C.R. 207
Collection des oeuvres pour le piano par Frédéric Chopin 229
Collegium Maius, Museum of 216
Common Council Chamber (Guildhall) 217, *219*
Complete collection of the compositions of Frederic Chopin (Wessel) 29
Concerning Chopin in Manchester (Brookshaw) 189
Concert Hall (Gentlemen's Concert Hall) 180–2, *181–2*
Concerts of Ancient Music 24
Consuelo (Sand) 39
Conversations of Lord Byron with the Countess of Blessington (Blessington) 114
Cooper, Victoria, on domestic presence of pianos 60–1
Costa, Michael 24, 78
Coutts Stuart, Lord Dudley 20, *21*, 24, 212, 216, 217
Covent Garden (formally Theatre Royal) 25, 77–80, *78*
Craig, James 134–6
Cramer, Beale & Co 60, 73, 81, *82*, 100
Crumpsall House (England) 176, *177*, 189
Cubitt, Thomas 100
Czartoryski, Marcel 195
Czartroyski family and Polish aristocratic community 2–3, 37, 40–1, 195
Czerny, Carl 117

Index 273

Daily News (London) 216–17, 228
Dance, George, Junior 217
Daniel (Chopin's servant) 119, 137, 157
Davison, J.W. 27, 59–60, 74, *75*, 98, 228
Delacroix, Eugène 38, 40
description and history of the pianoforte, A (Hipkins) 72
Devéria, Achille 129
Dictionary of music and musicians (Grove) 72
Dictionnaire de la conversation et de la lecture, supplément (Fiorentino) 91
Dieppe, England 61
Dilke, Charles Wentworth 41
Dordrechts Museum (Netherlands) 4
D'Orsay, Count (Alfred Gabriel) 113–14
Dorus-Gras, Julie 91
Douglas Hotel (Edinburgh) 134, 136–7, *140*
Douglas Russell, Marion (Mrs. William Houston) 130, *134*
Dover, England 18, *19*, 61, *61*
Drechsler, Louis 69
Dudevant-Sand, Solange *see* Clésinger, Solange
Dunblane Cathedral (Scotland) 231–5, *232–4*

Eastlake, Lady Elizabeth 6, 80
Eaton Place (London) 100
Edinburgh: Chopin's time in 137–9, 206; geographical description of 128, *129*, *138*, *140*; musical life in 133–4
Edinburgh Advertiser 212
Edinburgh Evening Courant 211–12
Edinburgh Homeopathic Dispensary 133
Edinburgh Musical Association 133
Eigeldinger, Jean-Jacques 9, 44–6, 51, 131
Ella, John 10, 80, 109
Elliot, Andrew 136–7
Encyclopaedia Britannica, 9th ed. 72
England, Chopin's musical reputation in 58–61, 211
English Channel, travelling through 18, 61
Érard (piano firm) 10, 26–7, 72; *see also* pianos
Érard, Sébastien 67
Erinnerungen aus Paris (1817–1848) (memoirs of Sophie Léo) 52
Erskine, Fanny ('lady now resident in Bedford') 46–7, 49–51, 179, 195–6, 199–200
Erskine, Katherine (Mrs. Erskine) 68, 128–9, *133–4*, 227, 235
Erskine, Thomas 129, 190, 229, *230*

Euphemia, Susan (Duchess of Hamilton) *166*, 166–7
Examiner (London) 106

Falmouth, 2nd Earl of (George Henry Boscawen) 40, 109–10
Fantasia in F minor, Op.49 (Chopin) 59
Farmer, H.G., on Edinburgh musical life 133
February Revolution (1848) 52, 53, 70
Ferguson, Niall 42–4
Field, John 182
Filtsch, Karl 42
Fiorentino, Pier Angelo 91
Fisher Scott, Susan 191
Folkestone, England 61, 222, *222*
Fontana, Julian 3, 10, 21–3, *22*
France 1, 2, 52, 53, 70
Francesco da Rimini (Scheffer) 4
Franchomme, Auguste 39, 51, 53
Fraser, William 156
Frederic Chopin (Bennett) 72
Frédéric Chopin (Gavoty) 189–90
Frederic Chopin, by Franz Liszt (Waters) 228
Frederick Chopin as man and musician (Niecks) 235–6
Frederick Chopin Society of Poland 191, 207
French Second Republic 1

Galleries and cabinets of art in Great Britain (Waagen) 154
Ganche, Edouard 147, 203, 235
García, Manuel 39, 49, 51
Gardiner, Marguerite *see* Blessington, Countess of
Gare de l'Est 2
Gare de Lyon 2
Gare du Nord 2
Gare Saint-Lazare 2
Gargunnock House (Scotland) 164, *165*
Gavard, Charles 58–9, 226–7
Gavoty, Bernard 189–90
Gentlemen's Concert Hall (Concert Hall) 180–2, *181–2*
Gentlemen's Concert Society 175, 180
Gibson, Milner 91
Gillespie Graham, James 137, 158, 162, 232
Glasgow, Scotland 195, 196, *196–7*
Glasgow Citizen 200
Glasgow Courier 197, 198
Glasgow Evening Citizen 200

274   Index

Glasgow Herald 197, 198
Glyn Garth House (England) 176, *177*
Godoy, Manuel de 26
Goldberg, Halina 3–4, 10
Gore House (Kensington) 112–15, *114*, *115*
Grand architectural panorama of London, Regent Street to Westminster Abbey 30
Great Exhibition (1851) 72
Grisi, Giulia 24, 78
Grote, George 5–6
Grote, Harriet 5–6, *6*, 80–1, 191
Grzymała, Wojciech 3, 38, *63*
Guildhall (London) 217, *218*
Guildhall Art Gallery 220
Guizot, François 70
Gutmann, Adolphe 44, 169

Hadden, J. Cuthbert 44, 46–7, 196, 200, 211
Hahnemann, Melanie (née the Marquise d'Hervilly) 11, 46
Hahnemann, Samuel 11–12, *12*, 46
Hall, Samuel Carter 58–9
Hallé, Charles 5, 52, 75, *76*, 77, 102, 189
Hamilton, 10th Duke of (Alexander) 164–6
Hamilton, David 140, 155–6, 164
Hamilton, Duchess of (Susan Euphemia) *166*, 166–7
Hamilton, Thomas 206
Hamilton Palace 164–6, *165*
hand-book of Manchester, The (Love) 180–2
Handel, George Frideric 195
Handley, Rima 46
Harasowski, Adam 70
Harden, John 61, *137*
Hardwick, Philip 118
Hartwell, Clare 180
Hedderwick, James 200–3, *201*
Hedley, Arthur 7, 58, 222, 227
Henry Fothergill Chorley: autobiography, memoir, and letters (Hewlett) 10, 41–2, 116
Herbault, Édouard 10
Her Majesty's Theatre (formally King's Theatre) 24, *25*, 77–80
Hermann, Friedrich 58
Hewlett, Henry 10, 41–2, 116
Hill, David Octavius 128, *131*
Hiller, Ferdinand 28
Hipkins, A. J. 10, 67–8, 72–4, *73*, 139
Hipkins, Edith J. 72
history and antiquity of the parish of Mid Calder, The (McCall) 147

History of Greece (Grote) 6
homeopathy 11, 81
Hopetoun Rooms (Edinburgh) 206–7, *207–9*
Hôtel de Ville 2
Hôtel Lambert 1, 37, 40–1, *41*, 66, 216
Houston, Ludovic 158
Houston, Mrs. William (Marion Douglas Russell) 130, *134*
How Chopin played (Hipkins) 72
Hueffer, Francis 218–19
Hungarian National Museum 26

idler in France, The (Blessington) 114
idler in Italy, The (Blessington) 114
Ignace Pleyel et fils aine *see* Pleyel (piano firm)
Illustrated London News 96, 111, 218, 219
Ingres, Jean-Auguste-Dominique 5
International Exhibition in South Kensington (1862) 72
International Inventions Exhibition (1885) 67, 72
Italian Opera House (Salle Ventadour) 7, *7*
Italian Opera House, Covent Garden (formally Theatre Royal) *see* Covent Garden

Jędrzejewicz, Ludwika 140, 228
Jermyn, Henry 65
Jewsbury, Geraldine 179–80
Joachim, Joseph 44
Jobin, Antonio Carlos 236
John Broadwood and Sons *see* Broadwood (piano firm)
John Bull (publication) 111, 228
Johnstone Castle (Scotland) 158–9, *159–61*, 203
Jullien, Louis 24
July Monarchy 1, 2

Kalkbrenner, Frédéric 9, 18, 58
Kallberg, Jeffrey 29, 199
Kapliński, Leon 4, 40
Karasowski, Moritz 70
Karłowicz, Mieczyław 228
Keir House (Scotland) 154–6, *156–7*
Kemble, Adelaide *see* Sartoris, Adelaide
Kemble, Charles 98
Kemble, Fanny 98
Kemp, George Meikle 128
King's Theatre *see* Her Majesty's Theatre
Kippenross House (Scotland) 164, *164*, 235
Kirk of Calder (church) 230–1, *231*
Koźmian, Andrzej Edward 10

Koźmian, Jan (John) 19
Koźmian, Stanisław Egbert 19, 21–5, 67
Kubica, Marian 220
Kuhe, Wilhelm 104–5, *105*
Kwiatowski, Teofil 4, 41, 227, 236

Lablache, Luigi 24, 78, 96, 227
'lady now resident in Bedford' *see* Erskine, Fanny
La France musicale 228
La Musée de la Vie romantique (formerly L'Hôtel Scheffer-Renan) 5
Lancashire General Advertiser 186
Lancaster House (formallly Stafford House) 94
Lane, Richard 180
Laporte, Pierre François 24
La sonnambula (Bellini) 7, 24, 176
Le Brun, Charles 40
Le Christ consolateur (Shepherd) 129
Lennoxlove House (Scotland) 166–7
Lenz, Wilhelm von 9, 44
Léo, Auguste 10, 51–2
Léo, Hermann 51–2
Léo, Sophie Augustine (née Dellevie) 51, 52
Le Péletier 8
Les amis romantiques (Wellisz) 4
'Le secret' ('Un secret') (Musset) 107, *107*
Les Salons de MM. Pleyel et Cie *see* Chopin, Frédéric, performances
Le Sueur, Eustache 40
Lever, William 94
Leveson-Gower, Alexandrina 94
Leveson-Gower, Constance 68, 98
L'Hôtel Scheffer-Renan (later La Musée de la Vie romantique) 5
Life and Letters of Sir Charles Halle: Being an Autobiography (Hallé) 5
Lind, Jenny 58, 78, 80, 176–7
Lipiński, Karol 118
Liszt, Franz 26, 58, 98–9, 134, 182, 228
Literary Association of the Friends of Poland 19–21, 66, 94, 216
livre d'or (Rothschild) 44, 93
London: architectural expansion in 18–19, *20*, 61–2, *64–5*; Chopin's impression of 23–5; Chopin's musical reputation in 58–61, 211; musical life in 18, 24, 77; operatic scene 77–9, 134; Polish aristocratic community in 20–1
London & Birmingham Railway 118, *119*
London Daily News 111
London Interiors (Shepherd) 217–18
London & Paris Hotel 61

London Philharmonic Society (Royal Philharmonic Society) 18, 24
London street views (Tallis) 62, *66*
Lord Warden Hotel 61, *61*
Louis-Philippe, King (formerly Louis-Philippe Duc d'Orléans) 1, 4, 65
Love, Benjamin 180–2
Lumley, Benjamin 24, 78
Lyschińska, Mrs. (wife of Adam Lyschiński) 139
Lyschiński, Adam 128, 133, 137–40, *141*, 229

Maberly, Catherine 46, 68
Maddox, Willes 166
Madeleine, church of the 2
Malan, Henry V. 11–12, 81–2, 216, 220
Malibran, Maria 39
Manchester, England 176, *176*
Manchester Courier 186
Manchester Examiner 186–7
Manchester Guardian 182–6
Marcelina, Princess Czartoryska: friendship with Chopin 195, 216, 220, 226–7; involvement with Polish aristocratic community 37, 40–1; portrait *42*
Margueritters, Adelasio de 197–8
Mario, Giovanni 78, 96, 102, 103–7, *106*
Markiewicz, Józef 139, 207
Marylebone Homeopathic Dispensary 81, 216
Matuszyński, Jan 3, 24
McCall, Melanie 147
Memoir of the life of Ary Scheffer (Grote) 6
Mendelssohn, Felix 10, 27, 28, 50, 80
Mendi, Antonia de 53, 109, 110, 111–12
Merchant City (Glasgow) 196, *196*
Merchants' Hall (Glasgow) 196, *197*
Messiah (Handel) 195
Metropolitan improvements (Shepherd) 18
Meyerbeer, Giacomo 8
Mickiewicz, Adam 3, 4, 40
Milliken House (Scotland) 162, *162–3*
Modern Athens (Shepherd) 128
Moke, Marie 9, 29
Molin, Jean Jacques 11, 81, 226
Morning Post (London) 96
Morris, Edward 180
Moscheles, Ignaz 9, 25, 28, 51–2, 100, 211
Mrs. Grote: a sketch (Eastlake) 6
Muir, John (partner of Andrew Wood) 116
Muir, Wood & Co (later Wood & Co) 116
Muir Wood, John *see* Wood, John Muir
Murray, George 195
Murray, Mary (née Rigby) 69, 167–8

276 Index

Murray, Sir John Archibald 69, 168, *168*
Museum of the Collegium Maius 216
Musical Association in London 187
Musical studies (Hueffer) 218–19
Musical Times 4, 28
Musical Union 80, 109
Musical World 28, 102, 186, 228
Musset, Alfred de 107, *107*
My musical recollections (Kuhe) 104–5

Napier, William 162
Napoléon III, Emperor 1
Nash, John 24
National Museum of Hungary, Budapest *see* Hungarian National Museum
National Portrait Gallery (London) 72
National Trust (London) 92
Neale, John Preston 162, *163*
Nectoux, Jean-Michel 131
Neukomm, Sigismond 179, 180
Newhaven, England 61
Nicholas I, Czar of Russia 20
Niecks, Frederick: artistic life in England 77; Chopin and Broadwood meeting 28; Chopin and Lyschińskis 139; Chopin and opera 77; Chopin biography 235–6; Chopin's concerts 91, 96, 199, 200, 207–8, 218, 219–20; Chopin's musical reputation 58, 59; death of Chopin 226; Hipkins and 72
Niedźwiedski, Leonard 222–3
Niemcewicz, Julian 3, 20
Nie wydane dotąd pamiątki po Chopinie (Karłowicz) 228
Nitschowa, Ludwika 191
No. 13 of The Album Mario 107, *108*
Nohant (Sand's country estate) 1, 37–8, *39*, 40
Norma (Bellini) 24, 99

Obrescoff, Dimitri de 59
Obrescoff, Natalia de 59, 227
opera 7–8, 24–5, 77–9
Opéra, Paris *see* Paris Opéra
Osborne, George 9, 44, 58, 184, 187, *188*
Ostrowska, Teresa 20–1

Paganini, Niccolò 134
Palais du Quai d'Orsay 2
Paris: artistic community 4–6; Chopin longs to return to 221–3; cultural life 1, 39; July Monarchy renovation of 2; as a magnet for pianists 9; operatic scene in 7–8; Polish aristocratic community in 1, 2–4, 37; travel between London and 18, 61

Paris Conservatoire 49
Paris Exhibition (1867) 72
Paris Opéra (Académie Royale de la Musique) 1, 2, 7
Pasta, Giuditta 7, 24
Pavilion Hotel 61, *62*, 222
Pekacz, Jolanta 9–10
Pembroke, 12th Earl of (Robert Henry Herbert) 59
Père Lachaise cemetery 191, 227, 228
performances: domestic recitals 91–3; Earl of Falmouth's matinée musicale 109, 110–12, *112*; Eaton Place (Mrs. Sartoris') matinée musicale 100, *101*, 102–4, *103*; Guildhall concert (London) 216–20; Hopetoun Rooms concert (Edinburgh) *210*, 210–12; Manchester concert (Concert Hall) 175, 180, 182–9, *184–5*; Merchants' Hall concert (Glasgow) 175, 196–203, *198*; Salons Pleyel *(Soirée de M. Chopin)* 39–40, 52–3; Stafford House concert 94, 96–8; Tuileries Palace concert 65
Persiani, Fanny 24, 78
Persiani, Giuseppe 78
Perthuis, A. de, Count 65
Perthuis, Emilie de, Countess 65
Philharmonic Society, London (Royal Philharmonic Society) 18, 24, 98
pianos: Broadwood 67, 74, 98, 104, 111, 183, 198, 210, 215–16, 220; domestic popularity of 60–1; Érard 46, 67, 158; favoured by Chopin 68, 74, 152; manufacturing of 26; pianist endorsements of 10, 26; Pleyel 68, 152, 160, 216; *see also* Broadwood (piano firm); Érard (piano firm); Pleyel (piano firm)
Piccadilly Street, London *64*, 65
Pixis, Johann Peter 9, 117
place de la Concorde, Paris 2
Pleyel (piano firm) 9, 10, 25, 27; *see also* pianos
Pleyel, Camille *8*, 8–9, 18–19, 25–6
Pleyel, Ignace 9, 18
Polish aristocratic community: anti-Polish sentiment 217; Chopin and 3–4, 37, 41; Czartroyski family and 2–3, 37, 40–1; in London 20–1; in Paris 1, 2–4, 37; supporters of 94
Polish Literary and Historical Society (Polish Literary Society) 3, 40
Portland, 2nd Duke of (William Bentinck) 62
'professionalisation of music,' in London 24

Professional Society of Musicians (Edinburgh) 133
Programme music (Niecks) 29

Queen's Rooms (opera venue) 195
Quinn, Frederick Hervey Foster 81, 133

Rambuteau, Comte de 2
Ramsay, Mary 140
Ramsay, Philip A. 158, *159*
Ramsay, William 140
Rapkin, John 134–5, *138*
recital, musical introduction of 210–11
Regent Street, London *20*
Repton, G.S. 24
Revett, Nicholas 180
Revue et gazette musicale 53
Rich, Mary 47, 49, 50, 176
Richards, Brinley 91
Richmond, George 51
Robert, Edouard 109
Robert le diable (Meyerbeer) 8
Rock, Joe 206–7
Roger, Gustave-Hippolyte 53
Rothschild, Betty de, Baroness 42–4
Rothschild, Charlotte de 44, 93
Rothschild, Hannah de 69
Rothschild, James de, Baron 42–4
Rothschild, Lionel de 93
Rothschild family salon 42–4
Rowand Anderson, Robert 232, 234
Royal Academy of Music (London) 49, 74, 220
Royal Bank of Scotland 135–7
Royal Festival Hall (London) 220
Royal Institution (Royal Scottish Academy) 128, *129*, *130*
Royal Italian Opera House, Covent Garden *see* Covent Garden
Royal Northern College of Music (Royal Manchester College of Music) 191
Royal Philharmonic Society (London Philharmonic Society) 18, 24, 98
Rozières, Marie de 158, *158*
Rubini, Giovanni 24
Rubio, Vera 77, 228

Sablonière Hotel 23
Salaman, Charles 102–3
Salle Ventadour (Italian Opera House) 7, *7*
Salvi, Lorenzo 183
Samson, Jim 212
Sand, George 1, 5, 17, 33, 37–9, *38*, 221
Sand, Maurice 37, 39
Sandilands, James *see* Torphichen, 10th Baron of
Sandilands, Peter 230
Sandilands, Robert 231
Saponieri, Francesco 166
Sartoris, Adelaide (née Kemble) 98–102, *99*, 109
Sartoris, Edward John 98, 109
Scheffer, Ary 4–7, 129, 149
Schlesinger, Maurice 29
Schröder-Devrient, Wilhelmine 25
Schwabe, Julie 49, 176, 178–80, 191
Schwabe, Salis 49, 176, *178*, 178–80, 191
Scotland 147, *148*–*9*
Scotsman 206, 210, 211
Scott, Sandy (Alexander John) *190*, 190–1
Scott Monument, Edinburgh 128, *131*
Seligmann, Julius 198–200
Seymour, Charles Alexander 183
Shepherd, Thomas H. 18, 128, 217
Shudi, Burkat 26
Singverein (male choir) 69
Sloper, Lindsay 44
Słowacki, Juliusz 3, 4
Small, George 116
Small, John 140, *142*
Smirke, Robert 78, 94
Sobociński, Robert 191
Sontag, Henriette 24
South Eastern Railway Company 62
Stafford House (later Lancaster House) 94, *96*, 97–8
Stapleton, Frederic 29, 60
St Augustine and St Monica (Scheffer) 4
Steinway, Henry 26
Stephenson, Robert 118
Sterling, Anthony Coningham 112
Sterndale Bennett, William 27, 211
Stevenson, Sara 118
Stirling, Jane: Ary Scheffer and 5, 130; beauty of 129–30; death 229–31; devotion to Chopin after his death 227, 228; family history 128–9; friendship with Chopin 44–6, 48–9, 53, 62–4, 130–1, 212; interest in homeopathy 46; portraits of *45*, *132–5*; solicits pupils for Chopin 46–7, 51
Stirling, John 128, *132*
Stirling, Margaret Douglas 148
Stirling, May 129–30
Stirling, Patrick 234
Stirling family, memorials and plaques of 232–5, *233–4*
Stirling Maxwell, Sir William, 9th Baronet 154, *155*
Stirlings of Keir (Fraser) 156
St James's Place No.4, London 215–16
St James's Square, London *110*, *111*

Stodart, William 29
St Paul (Mendelssohn) 10, 27
Strachur House 167–8
Stuart, Dudley *see* Coutts Stuart, Dudley
Stuart, James 180
Survey of London 215
Sutherland, 2nd Duke of (George Leveson-Gower) 94
Sutherland, Duchess of (Harriet Leveson-Gower) 94–6, *95*
Szulczewski, Karol 66–7

Tallis, John 62, *66*
Tamburini, Antonio 78, 96
Tellefsen, Thomas 9, 49–50, *50*, 51, 228–9
Thackeray, Anne Isabella "Anny" (later Lady Ritchie) 47–9
Thackeray, William Makepeace 47
Théâtre-Italien (Paris) 1, 7, 8
Theatre Royal *see* Covent Garden
Thompson Parkinson, James 27–8
Thun-Hohenstein family 101–2
Times (London) 98, 100, 110, 216, 218
Tomkison, Thomas 18
Torphichen, 10th Baron of (James Sandilands) 148–9, 151, *151*

Ursule Mirouët (Balzac) 60
Usher Hall (Edinburgh) 139, 207

Valldemossa, Majorca 37
Viardot, Louis 6–7, 38
Viardot, Pauline: Chopin's admiration of 80; Chopin's funeral 227; performances with Chopin 39–40, 110, 111–12; singing voice 6–7
Victoria, Queen 65, 94–6
Victorian literature, as example of domestic popularity of pianos 61
Views in Renfrewshire (Ramsay) 158, *159*
views of noblemen's and gentlemen's seats in Scotland (Neale) 162, *163*
Voice of Poland 175
Voyages avec Frédéric Chopin (Ganche) 147

Waagen, Gustav Friedrich 154, 166
Wainwright, David 28
Walenty, Prince Radziwiłł 10
Waters, Edward N. 228
Wellisz, Léopold 4
Wessel, Christian Rudolph 29–30, 58
Wessel & Co 30, 81
Wessel & Stapleton (later Wessel & Co) 29–30, 59
Wessel & Stodart (later Wessel & Stapleton) 29, *32*
'What did Chopin play in Edinburgh?' (Brookshaw) 211
Wiadomsci Polskie (newspaper) 40
Wieck, Clara 51
Wielobycki, Dionysus 133
Wilson, Charles 195
Wilson, William 147, *150*
Winterhalter, Franz Xaver 94, 130
Wishaw House (Scotland) 162–4, *163*
Witwicki, Stefan 4, 38, 40
Wodzińska, Maria 17, 30–3
Wodzińska, Teresa 30–3
Wood, Andrew (father of John Muir & George) 116
Wood, George (son of Andrew) 116, 118, 195
Wood, Herbert Kelmo (son of John) 117–18, 175
Wood, John Muir (son of Andrew) 116–19, *117*, 175, 196–9, 200
works: ballades 29, 44; boleros 102; contracts for manuscripts of works 29–30, *30*; etudes 44, 111, 220; impromptus 29; lost manuscript from Calder House 153, *153*–4; mazurkas 29, 44, 46, 65; nocturnes 29, *32*, 44, 46, 130–1, *136*; piano concertos 9, 44; polonaises 52, 102; preludes 37; scherzos 111; sonatas 33, 53, 65; waltzes 29, 44, 73, 75–6, 81, 104; Wiosna (17 Polish songs), autograph score 139, 179, *179*
Wyatt, Benjamin Dean 94
Wyatt, Philip 94
Wyatt, Sir Matthew 92